FIELD & STREAM
The Complete Hunter

Printed in Canada

10 9 8 7 6 5 4 3 2 1

Library of Congress Cataloging-in-Publication Data is available

FIELD & STREAM
The Complete Hunter

Doug Painter, Phil Bourjaily,

William Tarrant, Bob Robb,

Thomas McIntyre, Jerome B. Robinson,

and the Editors of *Field & Stream*

THE LYONS PRESS

Contents

Contents

Contents

FIELD & STREAM

The Complete Hunter

Book One

Firearms Safety

Doug Painter

Illustrations by George DeCrosta

Willy Yocam and the Monster Buck

The work had gone quickly on Saturday, and by late in the after-noon they were nailing the last of the plywood panels onto the rafters. It was then that it had happened. Willy couldn't remember why he had stopped nailing all of a sudden, or why he had looked up, his gaze landing just over the peak of the roof. But when he did, standing not 80 yards away at the edge of the clear cut where the power line had gone through was the largest buck he had ever seen. His rack was awesome: massive symmetrical beams that curved backward, then out and forward. Willy was sure that he counted twelve points.

The buck didn't seem to notice him at all. He stood at the edge of the clearing for a few moments, then trotted across the open ground to the woods beyond. Willy almost fell off the roof.

When Willy finally got down, he could hardly get his words out straight.

"You wouldn't believe it; you just wouldn't believe it."

"Believe what? You came down from the roof like you'd seen a ghost."

"Biggest buck I've ever seen. Biggest damn deer anyone's seen around here. Just standing up there in the power line cut like he was king of the world."

Sitting there on the tailgate of Mickey's pickup, they made plans for opening day. The land around the ski house was owned by the ski resort, and Mickey was one of only a handful of men who had permission to hunt the property. They both knew that was a big advantage. On opening day there wouldn't be an army out

there pushing deer all over the place, especially into the really thick stuff. No, they figured, if luck was on their side, that buck just might stick to his daily pattern. "That old orchard," Mickey had said, "it can't be more than 50 yards beyond the power line. I'd bet anything that's exactly where the ol' rascal is heading every night. Never knew a deer that could get his fill of apples."

It never crossed Willy's mind that Mickey might try to shoot the monster buck. Mickey just wasn't like that. Hell, Mickey rarely shot bucks at all. Most every season, he ended up taking a nice fat doe on his antlerless permit. "The meat's a whole lot better," he would say, "and, anyway, I'm usually back home watching the ball game while the rest of you guys are still out here freezing your tails off."

Willy made Mickey swear that he'd tell no one about the buck. "I'm not even going to tell my wife," Willy told him.

Even though it was still pitch black outside, Willy didn't need his alarm to wake up on this morning. The day had finally arrived. He'd been dozing on and off since three, listening to the steady drum of the rain during the times he was awake. The rain, unusual for this late in the year, had tapered off to a drizzle by the time he left the house to meet Mickey. A good omen, Willy thought. The woods would be quiet. Lousy weather for the skiers, but great for us.

Mickey was waiting when he pulled up in front of the Judd Mountain ski house. Over coffee in the cab of Mickey's truck, they went over their strategy one last time: Mickey would follow the logging road around to the north side of the mountain. From there, he would crest the ridge and start working his way down the south slope. Once at the base, he would start a slow zig-zag pattern, working his way west back toward the ski house.

Even if the buck had changed his pattern, Mickey believed the deer was still bedding down in the thick brush at the base of the mountain and, with a little luck, he could push him toward the power line cut.

Willy's job was easier. He had selected a stand at the base of an old red oak on a small knoll about 50 yards down from the house. From there, he had a clear view of the cut, especially the spot where the buck had appeared a few days ago.

"Well, Mickey," Willy said as he got out of the truck, "I sure hope this works."

"Relax, this one's in the bag. Just you be ready when that buck steps out under the wires."

"Don't worry about that. I'll have my eyes glued to that spot all day."

Even in the darkness it didn't take Willy long to find the oak he'd chosen for his stand. He was confident that nothing would happen till later in the day, but just in case, it didn't hurt to be ready at first light. Actually, Willy never did mind the hours of waiting on a deer stand. By the time the sun came up, he always had the feeling that he'd somehow become a fixture of his chosen corner of the woods. Even on this damp and chilly morning, it was a snug, secure feeling. Of course, Willy realized that just standing there, trying to move around as little as possible, was about as close as you could come to doing nothing. But it was doing nothing with a purpose.

Looking down, he could see that it was a good year for acorns. His father would have liked that. Dad had never been much of a deer hunter, but had dearly loved to go after squirrel. When Willy was twelve, his father had bought him a single-shot, bolt-action .22. It had a knob on the end of the bolt that you had to pull back before the gun would fire. Anyone can pump the woods full of lead, he remembered his father saying. Waiting and watching, son, that's what real hunting is all about. You sit there just as still as you can be, and sooner or later curiosity will get the best of most any bushytail. He'll eventually poke his head out and then come sneaking around to your side of the tree. And when he does, one shot is all you need.

It took Mickey three hours to come over the mountain and work his way down the south slope. The land leveled out at the base of the ridge, but here, the hardwoods gave way to dense thickets interspersed with stands of short pine. Whitetail heaven, Mickey thought. There could be a hundred deer in this stuff, and I'd never see a one. They'll be sneaking past me like I was wearing a blindfold.

Once he was sure of his bearings, Mickey began to head west, stopping occasionally to break the pattern of a steady walk and always angling back and forth to cover as much ground as possible.

Around three-thirty, the rain picked up again, a steady, cold drizzle. Willy had stuffed a poncho in his pack but didn't dare make a move to put it on. There was only an hour of daylight left. Time was running out. "Come on, come on," he whispered to himself. "Where the hell are you?"

Willy was cold, he was tired, and he was getting edgy. Just standing there, trying not to move a muscle, had become an ordeal. Now, it was all he could do to concentrate, to keep his eyes focused on the power line. Had that buck somehow got wind of him? Was he just standing back in the edge of the woods waiting till dark to come out?

No, Willy reassured himself. That's a crazy thought. But right now I'd give anything to know for sure. "Damn," he said softly, "if only something would happen."

Mickey was sure he was somewhere close to the ski house. Not much farther he thought, and I'll be out of this mess. During the past hour he had heard several deer and caught a glimpse of two does as they disappeared into the pines. But whether Willy's buck was still in front of him, had circled back around, or, for that matter, was in the area at all, he had no idea. Nor did he really care anymore. At this point, he could only think of how good a few beers and a thick steak at Pat's would taste.

Another squirrel? No, the noise seemed too loud and too steady. Without trying to move his head, Willy scanned the power line. Where was that sound coming from? Yes, there it was, just below the big clump of brambles about halfway up the cut. For a moment, he was sure that he saw something move through the tightly packed gray birch. That ol' rascal, Willy thought; he's waiting till the very last minute. Willy's grip tightened around his rifle, and he carefully eased the safety off. For Willy, time seemed to stop.

"You wouldn't have believed it," he could hear himself say to the guys later that night at Pat's. "Only a few minutes of light left and, all of a sudden, there he was. A grand, last-minute appearance. But you guys know how it is with these monster bucks. They don't get that way by being dumb."

"They sure don't," Bob would say. "And, I'll say right now that's the biggest buck taken in this country in more than a few years. He'll top 250 pounds easy."

For a few seconds, Willy could see only a dark mess, but then the deer began to take shape. He was hardly moving, walking with his head down, likely on the trail of a doe. Willy didn't remember bringing his rifle up, but he could feel the damp stock pressed to his cheek. His sights centered just behind the big buck's shoulder. He could hardly breathe. "Squeeze the trigger," he said under his breath, "pull it off nice and easy."

The bullet from Willy's 30-06 struck Mickey on his left side just below his fourth rib. Mickey Ringold was pronounced dead on arrival in the emergency room of the Dorville Memorial Hospital at 6:38 p.m.

Hunting Accidents:
Causes and Types

UNTIL THE DAY Willy shot his best friend, he had every reason to believe he was a safe hunter. After all, like most of his friends, Willy had grown up with guns. He had hunted since he was 10, first with a .22 for squirrels and rabbits and, when he turned 14, had started going after deer. During the past nine seasons, he had taken six nice bucks. Where Willy lived, handling a rifle, like driving a tractor, was something you just naturally grew into at an early age. Not that he had now become careless: Willy had a healthy respect for his 30–06 and knew exactly what it could do. Guns were simply not something you fooled around with, no different really than the big 10-inch cut-off saw Willy often used on site. You had to watch what you were doing every minute of the way.

Accidents? Well, they always happened to someone else.

Indeed, most veteran hunters view hunting accidents with a similar sense of skepticism. The classic reaction, for example, to any mistaken-for-game accident goes something like this: "I just can't understand how anything like that happens. I mean, how could any hunter who isn't half-blind actually mistake a man for a deer in the woods?" The implication is, of course, clear. We assume that it takes a true incompetent, a real idiot, to make that kind of awful error—someone who has likely spent little or no time in the woods and is the kind of "hunter" who might also shoot a cow or goat thinking it was a whitetail.

While this attitude is understandable, it is far from correct. In large measure, the opposite is true: Most mistaken-for-game incidents actually involve experienced hunters, typically mature men with more than five years of hunting experience. Indeed, veteran hunters are

9

more likely to be involved in all accident types in which there is an intentional discharge. And as often as not, the victim in a hunting accident is a close friend or family member. As much as hunting accidents are personal tragedies for all involved, they also become statistics such as these, facts and figures that can provide a better understanding of what causes accidents in the field, which, in turn, can help us all become safer hunters.

To begin with, most hunting accidents aren't really accidents at all, at least not in the sense of being chance misfortunes. Unavoidable circumstances or just plain bad luck are rarely, if ever, contributing factors. What, then, is involved? An analysis of yearly hunting accident reports from throughout the country underscores a distinct and familiar pattern to hunting accidents from one season to the next. The same mistakes are repeated each year, with almost all accident cases falling into relatively few categories both as to cause and type.

Indeed, four categories account for close to 50 percent of all hunting accidents each year, including about 45 percent of all accidents that result in a fatality. Each accident in these categories involves an intentional discharge.

1. Victim was out of sight of the shooter.
2. Victim was mistaken for game.
3. Victim was covered by a shooter swinging on game.
4. Victim moved into line of fire.

A common thread runs through all these categories: Accidents in each involved a critical judgment error in a "shoot/don't shoot" situation. The abundance of these accidents underscores the impact of attitudes and emotions as major contributing factors to hunting accidents. Hunters who place a tremendous importance on success in terms of game bagged, who are highly competitive in the field, who are easily frustrated, or who may become overly anxious and excited are far more likely to make snap judgments, to pull the trigger before giving sufficient consideration as to whether or not a shot is safe.

Accident reports also reveal that some 33 percent of all accidents are self-inflicted. However, when those accident categories in which the possibility of a self-inflicted injury is impossible or unlikely are eliminated, the percentage soars to over 60 percent. The risk of a self-inflicted injury—or fatality—is extremely high in the following categories:

1. The shooter stumbled and fell.
2. Someone carelessly handled a firearm.
3. The trigger caught on an object.
4. Someone removed a firearm or placed a firearm in a vehicle.
5. A firearm fell from an insecure rest.
6. A firearm discharged in a vehicle.
7. Someone crossed an obstacle improperly.

The common denominator among these accident types should be obvious to every hunter. In each case, an accident occurred either because a fundamental safety rule or safety law was violated, or a proper gun-handling procedure was not followed. There is nothing complicated here, but these statistics reinforce the concept that accidents almost always are caused by some hunter's mistake, whether through carelessness, ignorance, or lack of skill in handling a gun.

Accident statistics confirm that the safety record of hunting continues to improve, even though hunter density in many areas has increased. In the early 1980s, for example, total accidents averaged more than 1,600 a year. Almost 20 years later, annual accidents had dropped to an average of 1,100. Similarly, in this time frame the average number of annual hunting fatalities has decreased from 222 to 99.

One big reason for this decline has been the tremendous growth of hunter-education programs throughout North America. Today, some three quarters of a million young hunters receive instruction in the safe and responsible use of firearms each year. Courses are sponsored by various wildlife agencies in all 50 states and all Canadian provinces. Most programs include a minimum of 12 hours of instruction, and many states and provinces offer advanced programs of study. Every hunter in North America owes a vote of thanks to the International Hunter Education Association and the some 60,000 volunteers involved in hunter-safety education. Thanks largely to their efforts, many serious injuries have been avoided, and many lives have been saved.

The widespread use of fluorescent orange clothing is another major reason for the decline of hunting accidents, especially line-of-sight incidents. States with mandatory fluorescent (hunter) orange laws have typically been able to reduce these types of accidents by half, sometimes by as much as three-quarters. Today, the use of hunter orange is mandatory in 40 states.

Though significant progress has been made in reducing hunting accidents throughout the country, there can be no room for complacency. Too many accidents still occur. They almost always result in a serious injury, and some 10 percent of all accidents are fatal. Whether we are novice or veteran hunters, there are still lessons to be learned, new perspectives on the subject to be gained.

To be sure, hunting and firearms safety is not a subject of choice. As hunters, we'd much rather read about misty mornings in the duck blind; great dogs and fine double guns; perhaps share in the experience of a Yukon sheep hunt or maybe pick up a few tips on how to find more grouse and keep our dogs working in close. Yet as hunters, we can never forget that safety must always be our foremost concern.

How Does This Gun Work?

On a narrow shelf about three-quarters of the way up from the floor and running the full length of each wall in the L-shaped bar sat some three dozen decoys, mostly divers, but with a sprinkling of blacks and mallards, each an old working block now retired from active duty. Beneath the shelves, hung in a haphazard array, were mostly old waterfowling photographs: hunters, with well-worn doubles or Winchester 97s, standing next to Model A Fords, both draped with countless ducks and geese; Labs and the occasional Chessie lined up in formal pose; even a few grainy stills of the long-outlawed punt guns, their cannonlike barrels jutting past the bows of narrow, shallow draft skiffs.

A martini? No, Cal Lockhart thought: bourbon, with just a splash of water. This place was exactly as it was supposed to be—not some New York designer's interpretation of sporting ambiance.

"So, you think the birds will be flying tomorrow morning?" the man sitting next to Cal asked without introducing himself.

"Sure hope so," Cal replied. "It's my first time here."

"I've heard all the theories," the man continued. "Rain, fog, snow, sleet . . . storm front moving in, or just going out. Phase of the moon, you name it. To tell you the truth, all those guides can say what they want. I think it's just a matter of luck. The geese either come in, or they don't. You do much hunting?"

"Oh, when I was a kid," Cal said. "A few rabbits, a squirrel or two. That sort of thing. It's been a lot of years, though. Don't really have much time for it anymore."

"No need to worry," the man said as he got up to leave. "It's a lot like riding a bike. Once you get back on, it all comes right back."

The skid blind had been pulled to the middle of a large field, some 25 acres of now-harvested corn and 20 more in soybeans still drying on the stalk. More than 100 decoys, a combination of goose silhouettes and shells, had been set out around the blind the night before. Cal and his hunting partner, Ken Trombley, arrived at six-thirty in the morning.

"Well, you think they'll be flying today?" Ken asked just after they had settled into the blind.

"From what I heard in the bar last night," Cal came back, "no one really knows for sure."

"I see you're learning fast," Ken said. "How about a cup of coffee?"

Ken Trombley had leased the farm for the entire season, an expensive proposition, but one he hoped would pay good dividends. Cal Lockhart was his biggest client.

By eight o'clock, it was obvious that it was not going to be a classic waterfowling day. Though the temperature remained in the high 30s, there was no wind and just a few high, wispy clouds: real bluebird weather. Over the next few hours, the men did see a flight or two, but the geese were off in the distance and flying high. By eleven, not even the blackbirds were flying.

Ken was upset that they hadn't even come close to getting a shot that morning. "Listen, nothing will be up and moving till late afternoon," he said. "Why don't we go back to the inn for a bowl of snapper soup and maybe a few crab cakes?"

"Sounds good," Cal replied, "but don't worry about me. I'm having a great time just sitting right here."

"No phone, no messages, no meetings. I know what you mean," Ken replied, feeling relieved. "I'll tell you what: let's have some lunch and then we'll come right back out."

Cal's shotgun was in front of him, standing upright, the barrel resting in a notch cut into the 2 by 4 that braced the blind. It was a 12-gauge pump he had borrowed from Ken for the weekend. Cal picked up the gun, ready to unload before leaving the blind.

"You all set?" Ken asked, opening the plywood board that served as a door to the blind.

"I will be as soon as I get the slide to go back. Seems to be stuck."

"No, you have to first pull back on that metal catch on the trigger guard. Then you can pump the shells out."

Cal tried to get a good grip on the serrated edge of the catch with his gloved hand, but, as he pulled, his finger slipped. The blast inside the blind was deafening. The load of high brass No. 2 shot blew a jagged hole in the side of the blind and then struck one of the shell-bodied decoys, sending it cartwheeling through the corn stubble.

After a moment of stunned silence, Ken said, "Good lord, Cal, I didn't know you wanted a goose that badly."

Cal Lockhart just sat where he was and didn't say a thing. On top of everything else, he realized he'd never put the safety on. Or perhaps he'd pushed it off when he had mounted the gun to get the feel of it that morning? Of one thing he was sure: There was nothing, absolutely nothing, funny about what he had just done.

Firearms and Ammunition

COMMON SENSE and early experience had led Cal Lockhart to do the right thing: unload before he left the blind. But it had been a long time since he'd had any practice. In fact, Cal hadn't touched a gun in over 20 years. To be sure, that's not an everyday example, but it's not unusual for many hunters to handle their equipment only a few times each year.

Being familiar with your gun—and knowing what it's capable of doing—is the first and most basic step in becoming a safe hunter. That point seems obvious, but it's surprising how often it's overlooked. Each season, more than several hundred accidents occur when guns are simply being loaded or unloaded.

First of all, if you lend a gun to a friend, always take a few minutes to explain and demonstrate the key features of that particular firearm. For example, be sure that the person who'll be using your gun knows:

- How the action works.
- How to properly load and unload the gun.
- How to operate the safety switch.
- What ammunition should be used.

The same advice holds true for any gun that you own. Whenever you buy a new gun, for instance, don't neglect to go over the instruction manual that comes with it. (If you bought a used gun or did not receive an instruction booklet with your new gun, write to the manufacturer for the appropriate manual. They'll be happy to send you one.) Getting acquainted with a new gun the morning of opening day can be not only frustrating, but can also be dangerous. So, before you shoot that new gun:

- Be sure you have followed all instructions for assembly, if required. Conversely, do not disassemble the gun beyond the point the manufacturer recommends.
- Be sure you understand how the action works and how to properly load and unload the gun.
- Be sure you know where the safety switch is and how it works.
- Be sure you understand the steps involved in cleaning your gun. Before loading the gun, make absolutely sure that the inside of the barrel is free of dirt or other objects. Even a small obstruction can result in a serious injury. Never try to remove an object from the barrel by loading another cartridge or shell and firing.
- Be sure you know what is the proper ammunition for your new gun. **Ammunition must be in the same caliber or gauge as that marked on the firearm by the manufacturer.** It's a good idea to carry only the proper ammunition for the gun you are shooting. A 20-gauge shot-shell, for example, will pass through the chamber of a 12-gauge and lodge in the barrel. So, whenever you head out, check the pockets of your hunting coat or vest to be sure you are carrying only the ammunition specifically intended for the gun you're using.

If you lend a gun to a friend, always take a few minutes to explain and to demonstrate the key features of that particular firearm: how the action works, how to properly load and unload, how to operate the safety, and what ammunition should be used.

Whenever you buy a new gun, don't neglect to go over the instruction manual that comes with it.

Before you shoot any gun, be sure you know the location of the safety and how it works.

When it comes to matching ammunition with a firearm, "close" is never good enough. The Sporting Arms and Ammunition Manufacturers' Institute (SAAMI) reminds us that "The firing of a cartridge or shell other than that for which the firearm is chambered can result in the cartridge or shell rupturing and releasing high pressure gas that can damage or destroy the firearm and kill or seriously injure the shooter and persons nearby."

Certain dangerous ammunition and firearm combinations are easily recognizable, but many also have similar chamber and cartridge dimensions. There are countless dangerous combinations; however, SAAMI has developed an extensive list of specific unsafe arms and ammunition combinations.

Rimfire rifle

IN FIREARMS CHAMBERED FOR	DO NOT USE THESE CARTRIDGES
.22 WRF	.22 BB, .22 CB
	.22 Short
	.22 Long
	.22 LR
	.22 LR Shot
.22 WMRF	.22 BB, .22 CB
	.22 Short
	.22 Long
	.22 LR
	.22 LR Shot
.22 Win Auto	.22 BB, .22 CB
	.22 Short
	.22 Long
	.22 LR
	.22 LR Shot
5-mm Rem RF Magnum	.22 BB, .22 CB
	.22 Short
	.22 Long
	.22 LR
	.22 LR Shot
	.22 Win Auto
.25 Stevens Long	5-mm Rem RF Magnum

Shotgun

IN SHOTGUNS CHAMBERED FOR	DO NOT USE THESE SHELLS
10 Gauge	12 Gauge
12 Gauge	16 Gauge
12 Gauge	20 Gauge
16 Gauge	20 Gauge
20 Gauge	28 Gauge

IN SHOTGUN CHAMBERED FOR	DO NOT USE THESE CENTERFIRE METALLIC CARTRIDGES
410 Bore	Any

With any gauge, shot shells of a given nominal length should not be fired in a gun the chamber length of which is shorter than the fired shell length; for example, a 3-inch (75-mm) shell fired in a 2 ¾-inch (70-mm) chamber.

Centerfire Pistol and Revolver

IN FIREARMS CHAMBERED FOR	DO NOT USE THESE CARTRIDGES
9-mm Luger (Parabellum)	9-mm NATO (Military) .40 S&W 9 × 18 Makarov
9-mm Win Mag	9 × 18 Makarov
9 × 18 Makarov	9-mm Luger .38 Auto .38 Super Auto .380 Auto
.32 H & R Mag	.32 Long Colt
.32 S&W	.32 Auto .32 Long Colt .32 Short Colt
.32-20 Win	.32-20 High Velocity
.38 Auto	.38 Super Auto +P* 9-mm Luger
.38 Super Auto +P	9-mm Luger 9 × 18 Makarov
.38 S&W	.38 Auto .38 Long Colt .38 Short Colt .38 Special 9 × 18 Makarov
.38 Special	.357 Magnum .380 Auto
.38-40 Win	.38-40 High Velocity
.40 S&W	9-mm Luger
.44-40 Win	.44-40 High Velocity
.45 Auto	.38-40 Win

*+P ammunition is loaded to a higher pressure, as indicated by the +P marking on the cartridge case headstamp, for use only in firearms especially designed for this cartridge and so recommended by the manufacturer.

Centerfire Pistol and Revolver (continued)

IN FIREARMS CHAMBERED FOR	DO NOT USE THESE CARTRIDGES
	.44 Rem Magnum
	.44 Special
	.44–40 Win
.45 Colt	.38–40 Win
	.44 Rem Magnum
	.44 S&W Special
	.44–40 Win
	.454 Casull
.45 Win Mag	.45 Auto
	.454 Casull

Centerfire Rifle

IN FIREARMS CHAMBERED FOR	DO NOT USE THESE CARTRIDGES
6-mm Remington (244 Rem)	.250 Savage
	7.62 × 39
6.5-mm Remington Magnum	.300 Savage
6.5 × 55 Swedish	7-mm BR Remington
	7.62 × 39
	.300 Savage
7-mm Express Remington	7-mm Mauser (7 × 57)
	.270 Winchester
	.30 Remington
	.30–30 Winchester
	.300 Savage
	.308 Winchester
	.32 Remington
	.375 Winchester
	.38–55 Winchester
7-mm Mauser (7 × 57)	7.62 × 39
	.300 Savage
	.30–30 Win
7-mm Remington Magnum	7-mm Express Remington
	7-mm Mauser (7 × 57)

Centerfire Rifle (continued)

In firearms chambered for	Do not use these cartridges
	7-mm Weatherby Magnum
	8-mm Mauser
	.270 Winchester
	.280 Remington
	.303 British
	.308 Winchester
	.35 Remington
	.350 Remington Magnum
	.375 Winchester
	.38–55 Winchester
7-mm Weatherby Magnum	7-mm Express Remington
	7-mm Mauser (7 × 57)
	7-mm Remington Magnum
	8-mm Mauser
	.270 Winchester
	.280 Remington
	.303 British
	.308 Winchester
	.35 Remington
	.350 Remington Magnum
	.375 Winchester
	.38–55 Winchester
7-mm-08 Remington	7.62 × 39
8-mm Mauser (8 × 57)	7-mm Mauser (7 × 57)
	.35 Remington
8-mm Remington Magnum	.338 Winchester Magnum
	.350 Remington Magnum
	.358 Norma Magnum
	.375 Winchester
	.38–55 Winchester
.17 Remington	.221 Remington Fireball
	.30 Carbine
.17–223	.17 Remington
	.221 Remington Fireball
	.30 Carbine

Centerfire Rifle (continued)

IN FIREARMS CHAMBERED FOR	DO NOT USE THESE CARTRIDGES
.220 Swift	7.62 × 39
.223 Remington	5.56-mm Military .222 Remington .30 Carbine
.240 Weatherby Magnum	.220 Swift .225 Winchester
.243 Winchester	7.62 × 39 .225 Winchester .250 Savage .300 Savage
.25–06 Remington	7-mm BR Remington 7.62 × 39 .308 Winchester
.257 Roberts	7.62 × 39 .250 Savage
.257 Weatherby Magnum	.25–06 Remington .25–35 Winchester 6.5-mm Remington Magnum .284 Winchester 7-mm-08 Remington 7-mm Mauser 7.62 × 39 .308 Winchester .300 Savage .303 Savage .307 Winchester .30–30 Winchester .32 Winchester .32–40 Winchester .35 Remington .350 Remington Magnum .356 Winchester .358 Winchester .375 Winchester .38–55 Winchester

Centerfire Rifle (continued)

In firearms chambered for	Do not use these cartridges
.264 Winchester Magnum	.270 Winchester
	.284 Winchester
	.303 British
	.308 Winchester
	.350 Remington
	.375 Winchester
	.38–55 Winchester
.270 Weatherby Magnum	.25–06 Remington
	.270 Winchester
	.284 Winchester
	7-mm-08 Remington
	7–30 Waters
	.30 Remington
	.30–30 Winchester
	.308 Winchester
	.300 Savage
	.303 Savage
	.307 Winchester
	.32 Winchester
	.32 Winchester Special
	.32–40 Winchester
	.35 Remington
	.35 Remington Magnum
	.356 Winchester
	.358 Winchester
	.375 Winchester
	.38–55 Winchester
.270 Winchester	7-mm Mauser (7 × 57)
	7.62 × 39
	.30 Remington
	.30–30 Winchester
	.300 Savage
	.308 Winchester
	.32 Remington
	.375 Winchester
	.38–55 Winchester
.280 Remington	7-mm Mauser (7 × 57)
	7.62 × 39

Centerfire Rifle (continued)

IN FIREARMS CHAMBERED FOR	DO NOT USE THESE CARTRIDGES
	.270 Winchester
	.30 Remington
	.30–30 Winchester
	.300 Savage
	.308 Winchester
	.32 Remington
	.375 Winchester
	.38–55 Winchester
.284 Winchester	7-mm Mauser (7 × 57)
	.300 Savage
.30–06 Springfield	7.62 × 39
	8-mm Mauser (8 × 57)
	.32 Remington
	.35 Remington
	.375 Winchester
	.38–55 Winchester
.30–40 Krag (30 Govt)	.303 British
	.303 Savage
	.32 Winchester Special
.300 Holland & Holland Magnum	8-mm Mauser (8 × 57)
	.30–06 Springfield
	.30–40 Krag
	.375 Winchester
	.38–55 Winchester
.300 Savage	7.62 × 39
.300 Weatherby Magnum	.338 Winchester Magnum
.300 Winchester Magnum	8-mm Mauser Rd. Nose Bullet
	.303 British
	.350 Remington Magnum
	.375 Winchester
	.38–55 Winchester
.303 British	.30–30 Winchester

Centerfire Rifle (continued)

In firearms chambered for	Do not use these cartridges
	.32 Winchester Special
.303 Savage	.30-30 Winchester
	.32 Winchester Special
	.32-40 Winchester
.308 Winchester	7.62 × 39
	.300 Savage
.338 Winchester Magnum	.375 Winchester
	.38-55 Winchester
.340 Weatherby Magnum	.350 Remington Magnum
	.375 Winchester
	.38-55 Winchester
	.444 Marlin
.348 Winchester	.35 Remington
.375 Winchester	.38-55 Winchester
	.41 Long Colt
.378 Weatherby Magnum	.444 Marlin
	.45-70 Government
.375 H&H Magnum	.375 Winchester
	.38-55 Winchester
.38-55 Winchester	.375 Winchester
	.41 Long Colt
.416 Rigby	.416 Remington
.416 Weatherby Magnum	.416 Remington
	.416 Rigby
	.45-70 Government
.460 Weatherby Magnum	.458 Winchester

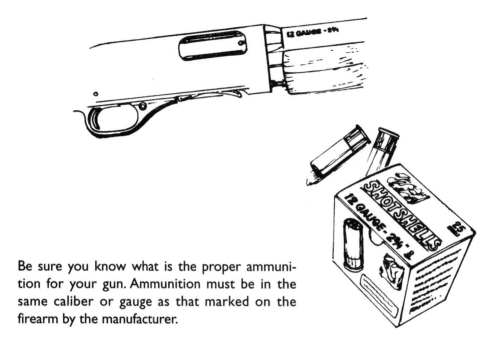

Be sure you know what is the proper ammunition for your gun. Ammunition must be in the same caliber or gauge as that marked on the firearm by the manufacturer.

GUNSMITHING

Working on guns is very much like working with electricity. In either case there is no room for guesswork. If you're still at the "let's give it a try" stage, you'll most likely get yourself into trouble. At best, you might end up with a gun that doesn't work. At worst, your handiwork can turn a gun into a truly hazardous piece of equipment. Sure, go ahead and reshape and refinish a stock, touch up the blueing, or add a recoil pad or swivels and a sling, but stay clear of modifying or in any way altering the basic firearm, *especially* any work that involves adjusting the trigger or changing the shape or size of the sear, sear notch, or any other parts in the trigger assembly. It's also a point to keep in mind when buying a used gun. Was the former owner an amateur gunsmith? Have any of the critical parts of the gun been altered? If you're not sure, don't take a chance. Have the gun looked over by a qualified gunsmith. It's cheap insurance.

The same advice holds true for any gun—whether it's an old double-barreled shotgun from your grandfather or a deer rifle you picked up for a bargain price—that you have the slightest doubt is in

If you have the slightest doubt that a gun is in good working condition, have it looked over by a qualified gunsmith.

good working condition or is safe to shoot. Outward appearances can be deceiving: the proper engagement of key internal parts, such as sears and hammers, may have been affected by old oil and grease that's turned to varnish or simply by many years of wear and tear.

HOW FAR WILL YOUR GUN SHOOT?

Shotguns

How many times have you watched a flight of geese come over just a bit too high for a clean shot or sat helplessly by as the ducks came in 25 yards beyond the outer edge of your rig? The fact is, situations such as these keep reminding all of us who hunt with shotguns that they are effective at only relatively short range.

There is, remember, another kind of range that you must be familiar with: *the maximum range your shot load will carry.* From a safety standpoint, this knowledge is equally important.

Indeed, whether you're a duck and goose hunter or a grouse and woodcock hunter, *you should never forget that the maximum effective range of your load is always substantially less than the maximum distance the shot charge will travel.*

The following are the approximate maximum horizontal distances for the leading pellets of shotstrings fired from a 12-gauge shotgun.

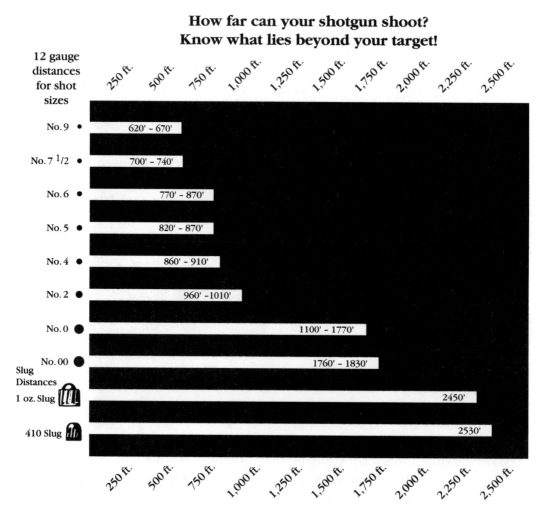

**How far can your shotgun shoot?
Know what lies beyond your target!**

Many countries in the more populous and built-up areas of the East and the South require deer hunters to use shotguns, either with buckshot or rifled slugs, instead of centerfire rifles. The reasoning behind this requirement involves a basic safety consideration: the maximum distance a 12 gauge, 1-ounce rifled slug will travel is about one-fifth the maximum distance of a popular deer caliber such as a

30–30. A load of 12-gauge buckshot has an approximate maximum distance about 200 yards less than the rifled slug.

While these shotgun loads will travel significantly shorter distances than centerfire bullets, the point to always remember is that they can travel far beyond your target. The effective range, for example, of a 12-gauge slug is in the vicinity of 100 yards—yet that slug can travel over 800 yards.

So whenever you're in the field, whether you're hunting waterfowl, upland game, deer, or are just out for an afternoon of informal clay target shooting, *always think along the lines of a "safety zone" in all directions of fire.*

- Where, and how far away, is your hunting partner? In which direction, if any, would a shot at a low-flying bird be safe?
- If you're practicing with clay targets, do you have a safe background of at least 300 yards?
- Are you familiar with the area where you hunt?
- Is there a new vacation home just beyond your favorite grouse covert?
- How about farm buildings, livestock or roads in the vicinity of your deer stand?

It's your responsibility to know the answers to questions such as these whenever you head out. And, if you're even in doubt—*don't shoot.*

Rifles

Exactly the same logic applies to rifles, even more so. Indeed, instead of thinking in terms of feet, with rifles it's a matter of miles. The bullet from a 30–06, for example, one of the most popular and time-tested of all big-game calibers, can travel almost 4 miles, even farther at high elevations. By any standard, that's a long, long way. Even a .22, minuscule by comparison to a 30–06, should never be underestimated. A high velocity .22 long rifle pushes a 40-grain solid-point bullet out of the barrel at 1,255 feet per second and develops 140 foot pounds of energy at the muzzle. It will travel its first 100 yards in 0.26097 seconds. Velocity at 100 yards will still be at 1,016 feet per second, and at 200 yards the bullet will still be traveling at 893 feet per second. And a .22 has a maximum range of over a mile and a half. That's over 2,200 yards—22 football fields laid end to end.

The following chart provides the maximum range of a variety of popular rimfire and centerfire cartridges.

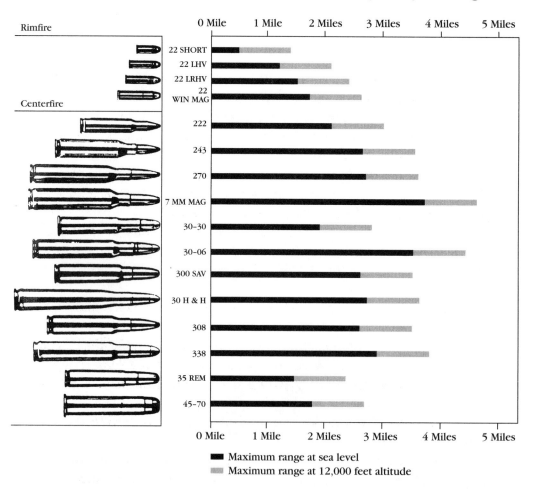

How far can your rifle shoot? Know what lies beyond your target!

■ Maximum range at sea level
▨ Maximum range at 12,000 feet altitude

Again, the underlying safety point is that you must be fully aware that the bullet from your rifle, whether a .22 or a 30-06, can travel a very substantial distance beyond your target. Never take a shot unless you have a safe backstop or you are absolutely sure of what lies in the area beyond your target.

5

One Careless Moment

To Art Sorensen, the true measure of seasons past was not in the years, but in his dogs. Each dog, beginning with Czar in '47, had for him become a distinct and separate block of time, a well-defined cycle of seasons and memories—some short, others long—every one an era unto itself.

Now in his 68th year, he was once again starting a new era: his ninth dog, 'Maggie,' a young springer spaniel, a gift from his long-time hunting partner and neighbor, Tyler Metcalf.

With each new dog there was always a wonderful sense of anticipation. What would this one be like? Yet for the first time his joy was tempered by the thought that she just might be the end of the line, his last hurrah.

"I sure hope she's a good one," he said when Tyler had first brought her over to the house that summer.

"Don't you start thinking like that," Tyler had kidded him. "That's exactly why I gave 'Maggie' to you. I figure the only way for an old-timer like you to stay young is to spend your time chasing after a flushing dog."

"Tyler, what I really like about you is the way you're always looking out for me."

Art and Tyler had been members of the same pheasant club for the past 20 years. Nothing fancy, just an old clapboard clubhouse with some kennels out back and about 150 acres of land, mostly in old pasture that was cut back every few years, and a few fields planted in short sorghum. It was a perfect place to work the dogs. Plenty of good cover and an unlimited supply of birds. "I don't care about a dog's so-called potential," Art had often told Tyler. "If you

don't shoot a whole lot of birds over him, he'll never amount to much."

Art let down the tailgate of his old Wagoneer. "Okay, young lady, show Tyler here what you can do." "Maggie" was out before he had finished, running tight circles around him, nose to the ground. It was warm for late September, so Art had planted only half a dozen birds. A quick morning's workout, he told Tyler, just something to get our hearts started.

Not 50 yards out, "Maggie" ran by her first bird, wheeled around when she picked up the scent, and came crashing back through the sorghum. The cock bird got up, pumping hard for altitude. Art was still some 30 yards back. He saw tailfeathers with his second shot, but the bird didn't go down.

"He's hit, but not hard. I've got him marked. Glided down the hill toward the swamp."

"Where'd the dog go?"

"Where do you think, Art? She took off after that bird the moment you shot. She's got to be at the bottom of the hill by now."

"Thanks for the backup, Tyler."

"Old buddy, since when did you need me to do your shooting?"

"Yeah, I know. Should have stayed up closer to her. Thought she was just working off a little steam. I didn't plant our birds in this field."

"Well, Art, maybe when she gets older, she'll know which birds are ours."

"Okay, wise guy. I'll go on down and see what she's up to."

It was a steep and slippery climb down the hill and even tougher going down below. It had been many years since he and Tyler had pushed the swamp for holdover birds. Now, he remembered why. You either slogged your way through the muck or jumped from one grass hummock to another.

Art fell twice before he finally crossed the swamp and reached drier ground. He hadn't yet spotted "Maggie," but he knew the going would be easier along the edge. He was upset that she'd taken off after the bird but, then, what young dog wouldn't have? About 40 yards down, he spotted her. She was sitting at the base of a long-dead hickory, her eyes fixed on the pheasant that was perched high on one of the bare branches. He knew there was only one thing he could do. The shot from his 20 gauge dropped the cock pheasant instantly, and "Maggie" was on the bird in a flash. "Good girl, good girl," he said, as "Maggie" came over and dropped the bird by his feet.

Art realized he'd been gone almost half an hour, and he pushed himself to get back. By the time he reached the top of the hill, he was breathing hard and his light canvas shirt was blotched with perspiration. Tyler was where he had left him, seated on an old stone wall, smoking his pipe.

"Well, 'Maggie,' from the looks of him, you'd think he was the one doing all the work."

Art was too tired to say a thing. His back hurt, and he could feel the chill in his legs from his wet pants. He sank down next to the wall and propped his shotgun up alongside him.

"Okay, young lady," Tyler said, "let's take a look at your first bird."

Art struggled to pull the pheasant from his game pocket and then flipped it over to Tyler. "Maggie" lunged for the bird.

The shot was deafening.

In the next few weeks, neither Art nor Tyler could remember whether it was the dog or one of them that had knocked the gun over, not that it really made any difference.

In any case, Art considered himself lucky. He lost only three toes from his left foot.

Playing by the Rules

SOME HUNTERS simply don't know any better; others think the rules were written for someone else. A few are just downright reckless. Art Sorensen certainly knew better than to lean a loaded gun against a wall. As a rule, he was a careful and conscientious gun handler and had hunted without incident for over 30 years. What happened? In Art's case, the real culprit was fatigue. He had become tired to the point of being exhausted, and for one brief moment he had stopped thinking. The result? A careless and very dangerous mistake.

Accident statistics show that accidents classified as "gun handling" or "safety rule violations" are most likely to occur among very young hunters, and those who are older, typically 55 and up. Among the former, lack of skill and lack of familiarity with guns is often a major contributing factor. Among the latter, fatigue typically plays a major role. In each and every case, however, the accident happened because a fundamental rule of safe hunting or safe gun handling was ignored.

Take a moment and read through the following accident reports selected at random from a variety of state accident summaries. Each is presented as written by investigating authorities.

- Victim decided to cross fence. He threw gun over his back; gun discharged and went into his back and buttocks.
- Shooter asked victim if gun was loaded. Victim answered no. Shooter picked up gun with his finger in the trigger guard. The shotgun discharged, and the blast hit the victim in the stomach.
- Victim was running through the forest when gun went off and hit him in the leg. He did not know the gun was loaded.

- Victim was running toward a wild hog when gun leaning against a tree fell from its resting place and gun discharged— hitting victim in the back.
- Victim stated that he had leaned the shotgun against the left side of the Bronco and sat in the driver's seat. He saw shotgun slide down the side of the Bronco and hit the door jamb and the gun went off.
- Victim was a passenger in an airboat which had stopped. While stopped, victim was feeding dog, lost his balance and fell onto loaded gun he was holding. Rifle discharged striking victim in the forearm and left side of stomach.
- Shooter was walking toward victim when he tripped and his rifle fired. The 6mm soft core bullet struck victim in the right bicep. He bled to death before reaching a hospital.
- Shooter was walking behind victim. Uncocked his 410 shotgun and hammer slipped. Gun discharged, striking victim in the back of his leg at the knee.
- Subject hunting rabbits, put muzzle of his rifle on foot and unintentionally pulled trigger.
- Subject hunting rabbits in heavy brush and firearm got hung up in bush, trigger caught on branch, firearm discharged into victim's stomach.
- Subject hunting partridge. In process of turning around, he accidentally pulled trigger and shot himself in right foot.
- Victim hunting rabbits. Walking 30 feet ahead of shooter. Victim crouched down, looking for tracks. Shooter stumbled and fell at same time and gun accidentally discharged, striking victim on left side of stomach. Shooter charged under Criminal Code.
- Victim was about to shoot at ducks on a pond when he changed his mind and started to put his gun down. The gun went off, striking him in the leg.
- Shooter struck tree with butt of his gun in an attempt to scare a squirrel. His gun discharged: the shot struck the victim in the shoulder.
- Victim was climbing a tree with his shotgun. He fell, the gun discharged and the shot struck the victim in the chest.
- Victim was riding in an All Terrain Vehicle with his shotgun resting between his legs. He hit a bump and the gun discharged. The shot struck him above the right knee.

- Victim was using the butt of his loaded shotgun to clear limbs from a tree. The gun fired on impact; the shot entered his upper body.
- Shooter was jumping on a brush pile . . . the gun went off, striking him in the left foot.

Bizarre circumstances? A once in a million sequence of events? A freak accident? Pure chance, or plain misfortune? Hardly: Accidents such as these didn't just happen. Each was caused by some hunter's mistake. All, and many others like them, could have been avoided. It's a point that can't be emphasized enough.

Whenever you pick up a gun, no matter what the circumstances—whether you're excited or relaxed, tired or anxious to get going, whether you're cold, wet, frustrated, feeling disappointed, or just wishing you were back home in front of the fire—you can never forget . . . not even for a moment . . . that handling your gun in a safe and responsible manner should be your first and foremost concern.

Whenever you pick up a gun, no matter what the situation—whether you're hot on the trail of a big buck or admiring your first grouse of the season, whether you're breaking for lunch in the field or packing up at the end of the day—you can never forget . . . not even for a moment . . . that handling your gun in a safe and responsible manner should be your first and foremost concern.

This may all sound redundant, but safety never is.

7

Safe Gun Handling, Step by Step

ALL TOO MANY ACCIDENTS occur in and around vehicles, the place where most hunts start and finish.

So to begin with, be absolutely sure your gun is unloaded before you put it in your trunk or the back of your wagon or truck. There's never a good reason to carry a loaded firearm in your vehicle, even if you're just driving a short distance to a new hunting location. You should be aware that having a loaded gun in a vehicle is a game-law violation in most areas; indeed, it's surprising just how many so-called accidents also involve a violation of the law.

Once you arrive at your destination, leave your gun in the vehicle while you get the rest of your gear organized. Some hunters are always in a big rush to get their guns out, and then end up leaning them against the side of the car or truck or other insecure rest such as a fencepost or tree—invariably where a gun could easily be knocked over or slip. It's a bad habit to get into. Uncase your gun only when you're ready to go, and when you do, keep it unloaded with the action open as you head out. **The only time your gun should be loaded is when you're in the field and actually hunting.**

When you do load, make sure that your next step is to place the safety in the "on" position—and don't take it "off" until just before you shoot. If your target flares or gets out of range before you can get a shot off, don't forget to put the safety back on. While you should never neglect to properly use the safety, neither should you rely on it as foolproof. As with any other mechanical device, it cannot guarantee safety.

Even when your hands are full, you must pay strict attention to where the muzzle of your gun is pointing.

In some circumstances, if a loaded gun is dropped, the safety may not be sufficient to prevent the firing pin from striking the cartridge or shell and firing the gun. Careless handling can never be excused with the phrase, "Don't worry, the safety is on." One more point about safeties: Keep your fingers away from the trigger while moving the safety, and never pull on the trigger when the safety is engaged.

A very large number of accidents could be avoided each season if all hunters **treated their guns as if they were loaded at all times.** In large measure, this means keeping the muzzle always pointed in a safe direction. **Never point your gun at anything you do not intend to shoot.**

Never assume that any gun is unloaded. Always check yourself to make sure.

Always handle your gun by the stock, whether you're placing it in, or taking it out of, a car, truck, or boat—wherever it might be. Never grab onto a gun by the barrel and pull it toward you or anyone else. Whether you're standing around waiting for your partner to catch up or passing a gun over to a friend—whatever the situation—the moment you pick up a gun, you should start thinking, "Where is the muzzle pointing?" And don't stop thinking about it until the gun is safely put away. This is a cardinal rule of safe gun handling, and it applies to any gun, whether it's loaded or not. **Never assume that any gun is unloaded. Always check yourself to make sure.**

In the field, there's not only the question of muzzle awareness but also the matter of muzzle control. Whenever a gun is in your hands, it's essential that you maintain the ability to control the direction in which the muzzle is pointing. There is more than one way to do this safely and still have your gun ready for quick use. It's largely a matter of choosing the right carry for the right situation.

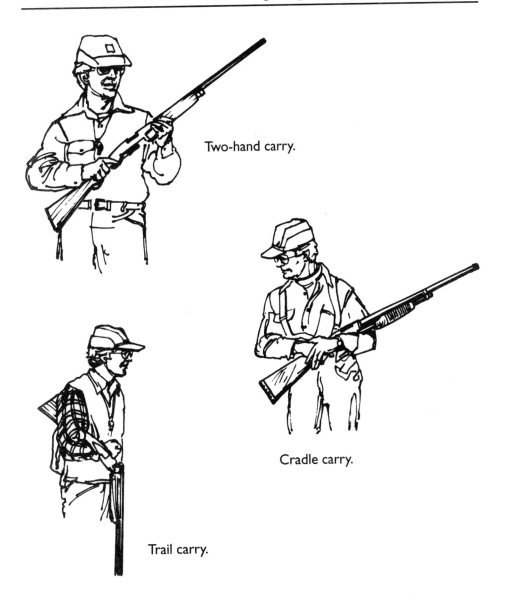

Two-hand carry.

Cradle carry.

Trail carry.

Hunter safety instructors suggest the following:

- The *two-handed* or *ready carry* gives excellent control of the gun and the muzzle. It's safe and, at the same time, allows you to raise your gun for a quick shot.
- The *cradle carry* is safe to use but has one drawback: Since the muzzle is pointed to one side, it should not be used when a person is walking beside you.

Side carry.

Sling carry.

Shoulder carry.

- The *trail carry* is safe to use when walking abreast of several people. It can also be used when you are the leader in single file. However, do not use this carry when following others.
- The *elbow* or *side carry* is safe when walking in open terrain. In brushy areas, however, it's easy for a twig or branch to catch onto the barrel and push it downward. This carry should not be used when hunters are ahead of you.
- The *sling carry* is used by many rifle hunters when walking long distances. This carry has the advantage of leaving both hands free, but should be avoided when moving through thick brush or low overhangs. The muzzle could get caught, causing the rifle to fall off your shoulder.
- The *shoulder carry* is a good choice when walking beside or behind other hunters. A word of caution with this carry: Since the muzzle is out of sight, you must be careful to keep the barrel pointed upward. In any case, this carry should not be used when others are behind you.

In any situation where you might slip or fall, be sure to carry your gun unloaded, with the action open.

Of course, no matter which way you carry your gun, your finger should always be outside the trigger guard and the safety should be "on." A special note when using handguns: Carry a loaded revolver with empty chamber under the hammer. Carry loaded pistols with the magazine inserted but with an empty chamber.

Muzzle control involves knowing when to unload your gun. In the field, there are countless situations in which the risk of losing your balance, of slipping and falling, is simply too great to justify carrying a loaded gun. It might be going down a muddy ditch, making your way up a rocky embankment, or crossing a swampy area or stream or it might be going over an obstacle, such as a fence or fallen tree. In every case, unload your gun—and leave the action open—before you proceed. If you do fall or stumble, be sure to check that your barrel is completely clear of any mud, dirt, or snow.

The same logic applies when moving through dense cover: You don't want to be caught pushing branches out of the way or pulling brambles off your pants with a loaded gun in the other hand.

Obviously, there can't be a rule to cover every potentially danger-

Whenever you encounter an obstacle, such as a fence or fallen tree, unload your gun—and leave the action open—before you proceed. If you should fall or stumble, check that your barrel is completely clear of any mud, dirt, or snow.

ous situation when handling a gun. That's where common sense comes in. When you have a gun in your hands, avoid any action that might cause you to lose control and subsequently point the muzzle in an unsafe direction. Don't run with a gun or jump up and down on a brushpile, for example. And never lean a gun against any part of your body. A gun isn't a walking stick or a support of any kind, and it should never be used as a tool to probe or clear away twigs or branches. These points may seem to be an elaboration of the obvious. Unfortunately that's not the case with all hunters. The proof is in the accident reports written up each year.

Muzzle control applies to all shooting situations in terms of safe zones of fire. Simple in concept, your safe zone of fire is defined by the horizontal and vertical arcs in which you may fire a shot without endangering others. Though we usually think of zones of fire in relation to our hunting partner(s), they also may apply when hunting in areas in which buildings, roads, livestock, or other human activity make shooting in certain directions unsafe. You should be aware of

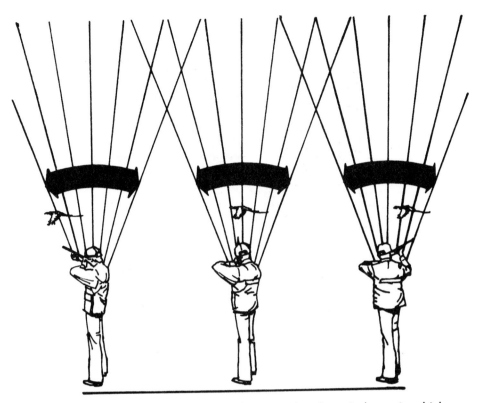

Your safe zone of fire is defined by the horizontal and vertical arcs in which you may fire a shot without endangering others.

any "off-limits" shooting areas where you hunt, and you should be sure to point them out to everyone in your group before you head out. And if you're getting permission to hunt on someone else's land for the first time, be sure to inquire about any "off-limits" shooting areas.

Good planning is the critical ingredient to establishing safe zones of fire. **Never set up a situation in which anyone in your hunting party could inadvertently end up in the line of fire of another. Remember: The vast majority of line-of-sight accidents involve members of the same hunting party.**

The larger the hunting party, the more difficult it is to maintain prearranged positions and movements when in the field. In almost all hunting situations, try to limit your group to no more than three hunters.

If you're walking, start out—and always stay—abreast of each other. With three in a party, the center hunter has all the going-away shots at targets on their respective sides. Never swing "down the line."

If you're walking, start out—and always stay—abreast of one another. Whether there are two or three of you, this straight-line deployment gives each hunter a clear and well-defined zone of fire. With three in a party, for example, the center hunter has all the going-away shots, whereas the hunters on each end have safe shots at targets on their respective sides. In no case should anyone swing "down the line."

Staying "on line" is especially critical when moving through heavy cover or hilly country—any terrain where it's easy to get out of alignment or lose sight of your partner(s). If an obstacle forces you to change your course, let your partner(s) know right away. **You can't know your safe zone of fire unless you know the location of your hunting partner(s) at all times.** If you do lose sight of one another, don't hesitate to whistle or call out to re-establish contact. When visibility is a problem, wearing hunter (fluorescent) orange provides an enormous safety advantage. It's amazing to what degree this high-visibility color can help you spot your partner in the brush and in low-light conditions.

Establishing well-defined zones of fire is equally important when hunting from fixed positions, often the case when hunting dove, pass shooting at ducks or geese, or deer hunting from stands. When selecting sites, each hunter should know in advance his or her safe zone of fire, and if the group is large, one member of the party should coordinate the placement of the entire group. Each hunter should be familiar with his or her assigned spot and the location of everyone else.

When a bird flushes or a rabbit bursts out of a brush pile, for example, you'll often have only a brief second to decide whether it's a safe shot or not. So always keep a clear mental picture of just what

You can't know your safe zone of fire unless you know where your partner is at all times. If you do lose sight of one another, don't hesitate to whistle or call out to reestablish contact.

Establishing well-defined zones of fire is equally important when hunting from fixed positions, often the case when hunting doves, pass shooting at ducks or geese, or deer hunting from stands.

is your safe zone of fire. By constantly thinking ahead and anticipating the kind of shot you might be presented with, you'll know in advance which shots will be safe and which will not be.

During any hunt, there are times when you'll take a break, whether it's just for a few minutes to catch your breath or to sit down for lunch in the field. Whenever you do, be sure that your first move is to unload your gun and leave the action open. Unloaded or not, never prop your gun up or rest it where it might easily be knocked down or slip over.

It's doubtful that many hunters are insomniacs. A day spent crouched in a duck blind or a day spent slogging through the brush in search of grouse takes a lot out of you. Come sundown, the walk back to the car always seems twice as long, and your gun feels as if it's gained a pound or two. It's a potentially dangerous time for every

Whenever you take a break, be sure that your first move is to unload your gun and leave the action open. Never prop your gun up or rest it in a way where it might easily be knocked down or slip over.

hunter. Even if you're in good shape, your coordination and concentration aren't what they were when you started off in the morning. And when you're tired, whether just pleasantly so or downright exhausted, it's easy to become a little sloppy in the way you handle your gun. It's time for extra and deliberate caution. So be sure to double-check your gun to make sure there are no shells in the chamber or the magazine. The hunt isn't over until your gun is cased and safely put away.

If you're a young hunter, you're probably at an age when you're also starting to drive. Getting behind the wheel and handling a gun have much in common. The rules of the road and the rules of gun safety are not complicated. And driving a car or shooting a gun are not especially difficult. Sure, both are something you have to learn and practice. Yet the real key to safe driving and safe gun handling is a matter of concentration. The moment you start thinking about the term paper you haven't finished, the pass you dropped in the end zone, or whether you should ask Mary out for Saturday night, instead of paying attention to the road, is just when you'll drive right past a stop sign or right through a red light. Exactly the same logic holds true when handling a gun. The moment you stop thinking about what you're doing is the moment you realize that your muzzle is pointing right at your partner's back.

When driving or handling a gun, you simply can't allow your mind to wander. Even a small lapse in concentration can have tragic results. And in either case, the responsibility for safety rests entirely on your shoulders.

Once You Pull the Trigger . . .

Phil Westhoff wasn't sure if the intermittent kee-kee *sounds came from a hen or from a tom, but he was certain that, for the first time in his life, he was listening to a wild turkey. For a few minutes, he thought the calls might be getting closer, but half an hour later they seemed neither louder nor fainter than before.*

Phil had heard how hard it was to sneak up on a turkey, but it was after 10 A.M. and he'd been in the woods since before daylight. Why not give it a shot? He was bored sitting in one spot, and, in any case, this was the only bird he'd heard all day. Trying to make as little noise as possible, he got up and began to head in the direction of the calls. Every few steps, he stopped to listen. The bird, it seemed, was staying put. Another 30 yards or so, and Phil thought he might be within range.

Phil was so startled by the next series of calls that he almost jumped backward. The bird must be just ahead. His first impulse was to make a dash for it. Maybe he could get close enough for a quick shot. No, he knew he didn't really stand much of a chance. But he couldn't just stand there in the open. Getting down on all fours, he inched his way to a fallen tree and, careful not to snap a twig or branch, crouched behind the blowdown.

For a full minute he didn't dare move. Then the turkey called again and, from the sound of it, was now straight ahead and maybe a little to the right. Phil peered over the edge of the log. At first, he could make nothing out; but as his eyes focused farther out, he picked up a flash of red from the turkey's neck. The bird was deep in the undergrowth at the base of a red oak, about 25 yards away.

Phil suppressed the urge to stand up and shoot. Instead, he slowly pushed the barrel of his shotgun across the log and pivoted the gun until the front bead centered on the turkey's neck. His index finger found the safety and pushed it off. The bird seemed to jump straight up in the air. Had the soft click spooked him? Phil froze but kept staring at the spot where the turkey had been.

A flash of gold . . . a hand? What was going on? Had he dozed off for a minute? Was he dreaming? Nothing made any sense. Yet something was there. His eyes raced to complete the puzzle, trying to fit the pieces together. The curve of a man's shoulder . . . legs pulled tightly to his chest . . . a head covered by camo netting. All of a sudden, everything came into focus. It was now all clear as day. There at the base of the oak sat another turkey hunter. Phil watched him wipe his forehead with a red bandana and then tuck it back into his hip pocket.

Phil could feel the air push out of his lungs. His right hand wouldn't stop shaking. My God, he thought, I almost shot you.

Phil couldn't resist looking back toward the tree. He was positive that there had been a turkey right there. But now, he could only see the man. There was no turkey, after all. Only the high-pitched kee-kee *sounds as the other hunter started calling again.*

The Illusion of
Early Blur

PERCEPTION, like beauty, is often in the eye of the beholder.

In our mind's eye we can easily build an image of what we want to see, especially if it's something we expect to come into view. That's precisely what happened to Phil Westhoff. He was out hunting turkey, and his every sense was attuned to that expectation. Whatever he saw or heard in the woods, he was likely going to translate into turkey.

It's surprising just how little information we sometimes need to construct an entirely lifelike mental picture. The initial visual clues may be rudimentary and few in number—a red bandana, a brown hunting coat, an oddly shaped branch, or just the play of light and shadows among the rustling leaves—but all of a sudden, standing there in front of us is a wild turkey or a white-tailed deer. All hunters, no matter how many years they've spent in the field, are susceptible. Indeed, the more we know what to look for, the easier we can be fooled.

As hunters, we are predisposed to see and to hear the game we're hunting. Typically, we've scouted an area and have chosen a location in which game sign is abundant. As a result, we often don't need much coaxing to convince ourselves that game is nearby. The crude form that first catches our eye, perhaps supplemented by a sound or movement, is enough to trigger a mental process wherein our mind's eye rapidly fills in the missing parts of what we anticipated seeing. A patch of brown moving in the brush blossoms into a full-fledged 10-

Researchers recognized that some brilliant color was needed to help hunters stand out instead of blending into their surroundings.

point buck. A red bandana becomes a big tom. The illusion is hardly subtle. Hunters involved in mistaken-for-game accidents often insist that they actually shot at an animal and that the victim somehow appeared and stepped into the line of fire.

The nature of this type of hallucination—the phenomenon of "seeing" what we want to see—was not understood by the hunting community until the late 1950s, when a series of tests were undertaken to determine which color was the most visible against a woodland scene and could help hunters "stand out" instead of blend into their surroundings. The tests, conducted with the cooperation of the U.S. Army, conclusively demonstrated that fluorescent (hunter) orange was by far the most easily seen and recognized bright, unnatural color against a natural background.

During the testing, the researchers became aware of a study on human perception being conducted at Harvard University. In one experiment, the researchers began by showing subjects hopelessly blurred side transparencies on a screen. The images were slowly brought into focus, and the subjects were asked to identify the picture as soon as they could. Although the subjects could eventually identify the image, it was obvious that their perception came well after the point when anyone just walking into the room would have immediately recognized what was on the screen. Apparently, there was something about the early blur of the image that hampered recognition.

To confirm their suspicions, the researchers conducted further tests, this time with two groups of subjects who were shown identical pictures. The first group was exposed to slides that changed slowly from a hopeless blur to a middling point of focus. After the projector was turned off, only 25 percent of the subjects were able to correctly identify the picture. The second group was exposed to the pictures in reverse order, starting from a medium blur and then going farther back out of focus. In this group, 75 percent of the subjects—unhampered by the effects of early blur—were able to shortly recognize the picture.

Perhaps the most revealing by-product of this research involved the significant number of subjects who identified a picture while it was still blurred and then continued to believe their original hypothesis—to still "see" what they had initially only guessed at—even after the picture had been brought into sharp focus.

This study helped prove that hunters were prime candidates for the effects of "early blur." In 1965, one researcher noted that, "Might not the sportsman, his mind attuned to the hunt, his every sense groping for a deer, suffer a like illusion? More than any other individual, the big game hunter often works in the world of early blur. His is the first, pale hour of dawn in the wilderness, and the last blue wash of gathering twilight. He stalks his quarry in the gloom of black growth and in the big cedar swamps where, even at midday, broken shadows and splotchy patches of sunlight confuse vision."

As any veteran hunter of the backwoods whether he's ever seen a deer, only to find, after careful stalking, that the "deer" was a curiously shaped stump or the silhouette of a bush against the sky? Invariably, the answer is "yes."

Over the past 40 years, hunter orange has proved to be an enormously effective deterrent to mistaken-for-game accidents. The color is so bright and so effectively shouts "human-made," that it shatters the illusions influenced by early blur. The color overrides and dispels the visual clues that initially activated our imagination. "One spot of hunter orange," a researcher notes, "and the human mind instantly rejects the formation of a mental deer or game image."

Massachusetts was the first to pass a mandatory hunter orange regulation, requiring Bay State deer hunters to wear no less than 500 square inches of hunter orange clothing. Consequently, dramatic results were achieved in Massachusetts and in other states requiring hunter orange. Indeed, nationwide, few if any mistaken-for-game victims have been shot while wearing hunter orange.

Every hunter should understand that hunter orange is by far the easiest color to see and least likely to be confused with anything in nature. Yellow, for instance, can be seen as white at certain hours of the day, and the once traditional hunter's red can appear as a dull hue to those with color-vision deficiencies. Hunter orange is the only satisfactory color to wear under all weather and light conditions and, in fact, its fluorescence is accentuated during the poor light at dawn or dusk or when the shadows are heavy. Keep in mind that hunter orange clothing will fade and, when it does, it loses a large measure of its effectiveness. So, be sure to replace your vest, jacket, and cap as soon as they've lost their original brilliance.

As important as it is to wear hunter orange (where it is appropriate for the game you're hunting), it is equally important *not* to wear or carry anything that might make you resemble a game animal. When deer hunting, avoid the colors brown and white. When turkey hunting, avoid red, white, or blue.

Evidence to date indicates that deer see in black, gray, and white. We may never know for sure, but it's a fact that hunter success has not declined in those areas where hunter orange is mandatory. When state game officials in Maine first tested the effectiveness of hunter orange, they required its use in only one county. At the end of the season, hunter success in that county had increased, but stayed the same in the rest of the state.

More than 80 percent of the states now have some type of mandatory hunter-orange requirement, and all states strongly recommend its use. You should be knowledgeable about the specific requirements in your state and in any other state where you plan to hunt.

U.S. States and Canadian Provinces Mandating Hunter Orange (as of 1995)*

UNITED STATES

ALABAMA All hunters during gun deer season must wear a vest or cap with at least 144 square inches of **solid** hunter orange, visible from all sides. Deer hunters in tree stands elevated more than 12 feet from the ground need not wear hunter orange, except when traveling to and from tree stands. Only hunter orange, blaze orange, or ten mile cloth is legal. (Exception: waterfowl, turkey, and dove hunters and those hunting legally designated species during legal right time hours.)

ALASKA Upland and big-game hunters are strongly recommended to wear hunter orange.

ARIZONA Upland and big-game hunters are strongly recommended to wear hunter orange.

ARKANSAS It shall be unlawful to hunt any wildlife, or to accompany or assist anyone in hunting wildlife, during a gun or muzzle-loading deer season without wearing an outer garment above the waistline, of daylight fluorescent blaze orange (hunter orange) within the color range of 595 nm–color range of 555–565 nm (hunter safety green) totaling at least 400 square inches, and a fluorescent blaze orange or fluorescent chartreuse head garment must be visibly worn on the head. **EXCEPTIONS:** (1) While migratory bird hunting. (2) While hunting in areas in which hunting of deer with guns is prohibited. **PENALTY:** $50 to $1,000.

CALIFORNIA Upland and big-game hunters are strongly recommended to wear hunter orange.

COLORADO It is unlawful to not wear at least 500 square inches of **solid** (camouflage orange is not legal; mesh garments are legal, but not recommended) daylight fluorescent orange material in an outer garment above the waist, part of which must be a hat or head covering visible from all directions while hunting deer, elk, or antelope during any muzzle-loading rifle or rifle seasons. Bow hunters are not required to wear orange during the archery only seasons.

*Source: Highland Industries.

CONNECTICUT No person shall hunt any wildlife from September 1 through the last day of February without wearing at least a total of 400 square inches of fluorescent orange clothing above the waist visible from all sides. This color requirement shall not apply to archery deer hunting during the separate archery season (except on private lands during the muzzle-loader deer season); to archery and firearms turkey hunting; to waterfowl hunters hunting from blinds or a stationary position; to raccoon and opossum hunting from one-half hour after sunset to one-half hour before sunrise; or to deer hunting by a landowner on his own property.

DELAWARE During a time when it is lawful to take deer with a firearm, any person hunting deer in this state shall display on his head, chest and back a total of not less than 400 square inches of hunter orange material.

FLORIDA All deer hunters, and those accompanying them, on public lands during open deer season must wear at least 500 square inches of hunter orange on an outer garment above the waist. (Exception: bow hunters during bow season.)

GEORGIA All deer, bear, and feral hog hunters, and those accompanying them, during firearm deer seasons must wear at least 500 square inches of hunter orange on outer garments above the waist.

HAWAII All persons in any hunting area where firearms are permitted must wear a hunter orange outer garment above the waist, or a piece of hunter orange material of at least 144 square inches on both their front and back, above the waist. A **solid** hunter orange hat is recommended.

IDAHO Upland and big-game hunters are strongly recommended to wear hunter orange.

ILLINOIS It is unlawful to hunt or trap any species, except migratory waterfowl, during the gun deer season in counties open to gun deer hunting when not wearing 400 square inches of solid blaze orange plus a hat. It is unlawful to hunt upland game (pheasant, rabbit, quail, or partridge) when not wearing a hat of solid blaze orange.

INDIANA Deer (bow and gun), rabbit, squirrel, grouse, pheasant, and quail hunters must wear at least one of the following **solid** hunter orange garments: vest, coat, jacket, coveralls, hat, or cap. (Exception: bow hunters for deer during first archery deer season.)

IOWA All firearm deer hunters must wear at least one or more of the following articles of visible **external** apparel: A vest, coat, jacket, sweatshirt, sweater, shirt, or coveralls, the color of which shall be **solid** hunter orange.

KANSAS Big-game clothing requirements: (a) Each individual hunting deer or elk, and each individual assisting an individual hunting deer or elk, shall wear hunter orange clothing having a predominant lightwave length of 595–605 nm; (b) The bright orange color shall be worn as follows: (1) a hat with the exterior of not less than 50 percent of the bright orange color, an equal portion of which is visible from all directions; (2) a minimum of 100 square inches of the bright orange color on the front of the torso; and (3) a minimum of 100 square inches of the bright orange color on the back of the torso.

KENTUCKY Hunter orange garments shall be worn by all deer hunters while hunting on any location on property where any deer gun season is permitted by regulations. Garments shall be worn as outer coverings on at least the head, chest and back. They shall be of a solid, unbroken pattern. Any mesh weave opening shall not exceed ¼ inch by measurement. Garments may display a small section of another color. Camouflage pattern hunter orange garments do not meet these requirements.

LOUISIANA Any person hunting deer shall display on his head, chest, and/or back a total of not less than 400 square inches of material of a daylight fluorescent orange color known as hunter orange during the open gun deer hunting season. Persons hunting on privately owned, legally posted land may wear a cap or a hat that is completely covered with hunter orange material in lieu of the foregoing requirements to display 400 square inches of hunter orange. These provisions shall not apply to persons hunting deer from elevated stands on property which is privately owned and legally posted, or to archery deer hunters hunting on legally posted land where firearm hunting is not permitted by agreement of the owner or lessee.

MAINE Anyone who hunts with a firearm during any open firearm season on deer is required to wear two thirds of **solid-colored** hunter orange clothing (fluorescent orange) which is in good and serviceable condition and which is visible from all sides. One article must be a hat. The other must cover a major portion of the torso, such as a jacket, vest, coat, or poncho. Regulations require that anyone who hunts in the moose-hunting district during the moose season must wear one article of **solid** hunter orange clothing.

MARYLAND All hunters and those accompanying them must wear either (1) a cap of **solid** daylight fluorescent orange color; (2) a vest or jacket containing back and front panels of at least 250 square inches of **solid** daylight fluorescent orange color. Maryland requires 50 percent of camouflage hunter orange garment to be **daylight fluorescent orange color;** or (3) an outer garment of camouflage fluorescent orange worn above the waist which contains at least 50 percent daylight fluorescent orange color. (Exception: Hunters of wetland game birds, fur-bearing mammals, doves, crows, wild turkeys, bow hunters during archery season only, falconers, and unlicensed hunters on their own property.

MASSACHUSETTS All hunters during shotgun deer season and deer hunters during primitive firearm season must wear at least 500 square inches of hunter orange on their chest, back, and head. (Exception: waterfowl hunters in a blind or boat.) All hunters on wildlife management areas during pheasant and quail season must wear a hunter orange hat or cap. (Exception: waterfowl hunters in a blind or boat and raccoon hunters at night.)

MICHIGAN All firearm hunters on any land during daylight hunting hours must wear a hat, cap, vest, jacket, rainwear, or other outer garment of hunter orange visible from all sides. All hunters, including archers, must comply during gun season. Camouflage hunter orange is legal provided 50 percent of the surface area is **solid** hunter orange. (Exception: Waterfowl, crow, and wild turkey hunters, and bow hunters for deer during open archery season.)

MINNESOTA A person may not hunt or trap during the open season in a zone or area where deer may be taken by firearms, unless the visible portion of the person's cap or outer clothing above the waist, excluding sleeves and gloves, is blaze orange within each square foot. Blaze orange includes a camouflage pattern of at least 50 percent blaze orange with each square foot. The commissioner may, by rule, prescribe an alternative color in cases where blaze orange would violate the Religious Freedom Restoration Act of 1993, public law number 103-141.

MISSISSIPPI All deer hunters during any gun season must wear in full view at least 500 square inches of **solid,** unbroken hunter orange visible from all sides.

MISSOURI During firearm deer season, all hunters must wear a cap or hat and a shirt, vest, or coat having the outermost color be hunter orange and must be plainly visible from all sides while being worn. Camouflage orange garments do not meet this requirement. (Exception: Department of Conservation areas where deer hunting is restricted to archery methods.)

MONTANA All big-game hunters and those accompanying them must wear at least 400 square inches of hunter orange above the waist. A hat or cap alone is not sufficient. (Exception: bow hunters during special archery season.)

NEBRASKA All deer, antelope, or elk hunters with firearms must wear at least 400 square inches of hunter orange on the head, back, and chest. Upland game hunters are strongly recommended to wear hunter orange.

NEVADA Upland and big-game hunters are strongly recommended to wear hunter orange.

NEW HAMPSHIRE Upland and big-game hunters are strongly recommended to wear hunter orange.

NEW JERSEY All hunters with firearms for deer, rabbit, hare, squirrel, fox, or game birds must wear a cap of **solid** hunter orange or other outer garment with at least 200 square inches of hunter orange visible from all sides. (Exception: waterfowl, wild turkey, and bow hunters.)

NEW MEXICO Upland and big-game hunters are strongly recommended to wear hunter orange.

NEW YORK Upland and big-game hunters are strongly recommended to wear hunter orange.

NORTH CAROLINA Any person hunting game animals other than foxes, bobcats, raccoons, and opossums, or hunting upland game birds other than wild turkeys, with the use of firearms, must wear a cap or hat on his head made of hunter orange materials or an outer garment of hunter orange, visible from all sides. (Exception: landowners hunting on their own land.)

NORTH DAKOTA Every person, while hunting big game, shall wear a head covering and an outer garment above the waistline, both of daylight fluorescent orange color, totaling 400 square inches or more and both to be worn conspicuously on the person. This section does not apply to any person hunting big game with bow and arrow during special bow hunting seasons. Additionally, while the muzzle-loader and the deer gun seasons are in progress in an area, all big-game hunters, including bow hunters, are required to wear a head covering and an outer garment above the waistline of **solid** daylight fluorescent orange color, totaling at least 400 square inches.

OHIO All deer hunters during gun deer seasons must wear a visible hunter orange hat, cap, vest, or coat.

OKLAHOMA All firearm deer hunters must wear a head covering and outer garment above the waist with at least 500 square inches of clothing of which 400 square inches must be hunter orange. All other hunters must wear either a head covering or outer garment of hunter orange during open gun deer season. (Exception: waterfowl, crow, or crane hunters, and those hunting fur-bearing animals at night.)

OREGON Upland and big-game hunters are strongly recommended to wear hunter orange.

PENNSYLVANIA All fall small game, turkey, bear and deer hunters during the regular firearm deer season, and special archery deer season hunters during any portion of the archery season that coincides with the general small game or turkey seasons, must wear at least 250 square inches of hunter orange material on the head, chest and back combined. Spring turkey hunters must wear a minimum of 100 square inches of hunter orange on the head or back and chest while moving from one location to another. Groundhog hunters must wear 100 square inches of hunter orange on the head. *All* required hunter orange must be visible in a 360 degree arc. (Exceptions: waterfowl, mourning dove, crow, flintlock deer season, and archery season hunters except as specified.)

RHODE ISLAND Statewide, October 17–February 28 all hunters, unless bow hunting, hunting raccoon or fox at night, and waterfowl hunting as provided, must wear an outer garment consisting of a minimum of 200 square inches of **solid** daylight fluorescent hunter orange material worn above the waist, and visible in all directions. This may be a hat and/or vest. Statewide, during shotgun season for deer, all hunters, except waterfowl hunters as provided, must wear an outer garment containing a minimum of 500 square inches of

solid daylight fluorescent hunter orange material, worn above the waist visible from all directions and must include a head covering. (Exceptions: during muzzle-loading season all hunters must wear 200 square inches as stated above.) State management areas: October 17–February 28 all users, except as otherwise provided and except users of boat launching sites, must wear at least 200 square inches of **solid** daylight fluorescent hunter orange material as defined above.

SOUTH CAROLINA On all WMA lands and lands within the Central Piedmont, Western Piedmont, and Mountain Hunt units during the gun hunting season for deer, all hunters must wear either a hat, coat, or vest of **solid** visible international orange. Hunters are exempt from this requirement while hunting for dove, duck, and turkey. Small-game hunters while hunting at night or on privately owned lands within the hunt unit are also exempt.

SOUTH DAKOTA All big-game hunters with firearms must wear one or more exterior hunter orange garments above the waist. (Exception: turkey hunters.)

TENNESSEE All big-game hunters with firearms must wear at least 500 square inches of hunter orange on a head covering and an outer garment above the waist, visible front and back. (Exception: turkey hunters during gun hunts proclaimed by the commission and those hunting on their own property.)

TEXAS All hunters and persons accompanying a hunter on national forests and grasslands must wear a minimum of 144 square inches of hunter orange visible on both the chest and back plus a hunter orange cap or hat. Call the U.S. Forest Service and the U.S. Army Corps of Engineers for more information.

UTAH A person shall wear a minimum of 400 square inches of hunter orange material while hunting any species of big game. Hunter orange material must be worn on the head, chest, and back. A camouflage pattern in hunter orange does not meet the requirements of Subsection (1)(a). A person is not required to wear hunter orange material during an archery, muzzle-loader, or big horn sheep hunt unless a centerfire rifle hunt is in progress in the same area.

VERMONT Upland and big-game hunters are strongly recommended to wear hunter orange.

VIRGINIA Hunters during firearm deer season and those accompanying them must wear hunter orange on the upper body, visible from all sides, or a hunter orange hat, or display 100 square inches of hunter orange within body reach, at shoulder level, or higher, visible from all sides.

WASHINGTON All hunters must wear fluorescent hunter orange clothing with a minimum of 400 square inches of fluorescent hunter orange exterior, worn above the waist and visible from all sides. (Exception: Persons who are hunting upland game birds during an upland game bird season with a muzzle-loading firearm, bow and arrow, or falconry.)

WEST VIRGINIA All deer hunters during deer gun season must wear at least 400 square inches of hunter orange on an outer garment.

WISCONSIN All hunters during gun deer season must have 50 percent of their outer garments above the waist, including any head covering, colored hunter orange. (Exception: waterfowl hunters.)

WYOMING All big-game hunters must wear one or more exterior garments (i.e., hat, shirt, jacket, coat, vest, or sweater) of hunter orange. (Exception: bow hunters during special archery season.)

Canada

ALBERTA No garment color requirements or recommendations.

BRITISH COLUMBIA No garment color requirements or recommendations.

MANITOBA A solid blaze orange hat and an additional 2,580 square centimeters of blaze orange above the waist and visible from all sides must be worn by big-game hunters. Bow hunters are exempt during bow hunting seasons or in bow hunting areas only. Wolf hunters are exempt when hunting in game hunting areas while no other big game season is on. Black bear and wolf hunters are exempt during the spring season.

NEW BRUNSWICK Every person, while hunting or being a licensed guide accompanying any person engaged in hunting, shall wear a hat and upon his or her back, chest, and shoulders an exterior garment of which not less than 2,580 square centimeters in aggregate shall be exposed to view in such a manner as to be plainly visible from all directions, and the color of the hat and the exterior garment shall be solid hunter orange.

NEWFOUNDLAND AND LABRADOR Upland and big-game hunters are strongly recommended to wear a minimum of 2,580 square centimeters of hunter orange (400 square inches).

NORTHWEST TERRITORIES Upland and big-game hunters are strongly recommended to wear hunter orange.

NOVA SCOTIA All hunters and those accompanying them must wear a cap or hat and a vest, coat, or shirt of solid hunter orange visible from all sides. Camouflage hunter orange is permitted during bow hunter season for deer as long as there are at least 400 square inches visible from all sides.

ONTARIO Upland and big-game hunters are strongly recommended to wear a minimum of 2,580 square centimeters of hunter orange (400 square inches).

PRINCE EDWARD ISLAND All upland game hunters are encouraged to wear hunter orange.

QUEBEC All hunters, guides, and companions must wear at least 2,580 square centimeters (400 square inches) of hunter orange on their back, shoulders, and chest, visible from any angle. During hunting season through December 1, coyote, fox, and wolf hunters and guides are required to wear the same as other hunters. (Exceptions: crow or migratory bird hunters and those hunting deer or moose during special archery seasons.)

SASKATCHEWAN All big-game hunters must wear a complete outer suit of scarlet, bright yellow, hunter orange or white, and a head covering of any of these colors except white. (Exception: bow hunters and black powder hunters during special archery muzzle-loading seasons.)

YUKON No garment color requirements or recommendations.

Note: **Maryland, Michigan, Minnesota**, and **Wisconsin** require 50 percent of a camouflage hunter orange garment be open hunter orange.

Maryland requires 50 percent of camouflage hunter orange garment to be daylight fluorescent orange color.

Nova Scotia refuses to recognize camouflage hunter orange as a legal fabric except during archery deer season.

Wisconsin accepts camouflage orange, though solid hunter orange is recommended.

The IHEA recommends the description of hunter orange as "having a dominant wavelength between 595 and 605 nanometers, a luminance factor of not less than 40 percent, and an excitation purity of not less than 85 percent." Highland guarantees that Ten Mile Cloth, Camo Ten, Easy Ten, and TenAcious meet these specifications.

With the now widespread use of hunter orange, some hunters may be tempted to assume that anything that is not orange is not human. Nothing could be more dangerous. Not everyone in the woods is a hunter, and not every hunter is going to be wearing hunter orange.

Every hunter wants to be successful, to get a deer, elk or antelope, to come home with a nice brace of pheasant or grouse. In good measure, that's what hunting is all about. The younger and less experienced we are, the more emphasis we place on being "successful," and that's natural. As the seasons go by, for most of us, this aspect of hunting becomes less important; but when we're in the field, it's still easy to become excited and more than a little bit anxious when we sense that game is nearby. Is that a buck? a doe? just a noisy squirrel? We hold our breath. All our senses come alive, and the seconds of waiting seem to turn into minutes. Will we get a shot or not?

Novice or veteran, it's during moments such as these—the sometimes split second when we must decide to pull the trigger or hold up—that **we must consciously make sure our emotions don't override our good judgment.**

Not all mistaken-for-game accidents are caused by "early blur." All too often, the prime contributing factor is the overeager and overanxious attitude on the part of some hunter. They are typically the kinds who enter the woods determined not to come home empty-handed. Already primed, they need but a small catalyst—a sound or movement in the brush, a spot of color—to shoulder the gun and fire.

Hunting is not a competitive sport. At the end of the day, there are no winners or losers. Sure, there are moments of high excitement and anticipation; what would hunting be without them? And that's exactly why emotional control and mental discipline are essential to safe hunting. Whatever the situation, your decision to shoot must be deliberate and thoughtful. In hunting, there's simply no room for snap judgments. Once you pull the trigger, you can never call that shot back.

In any circumstances where there might be a possibility of mistaking a human being for a game animal, you should take care to:

- Always assume that any movement or sound is another person—not a game animal. **Never shoot at a sound or movement.**
- Never hurry a shot. If you have even the slightest doubt about the identity of your target, hold up. Glance away and then look back. Try to get a view from a different angle. If you have to move, do so. It is far better to spook an animal than to risk an unsafe shot.
- Be doubly cautious during the poor light conditions of dawn and dusk or when the weather has restricted visibility. Such times and conditions are especially conducive to "early blur."
- Take into account that your emotions may be running in high gear. Don't allow your imagination to take over, and don't anticipate a shot. Keep reminding yourself that all you should be concentrating on is to clearly identify your target.
- No matter how tempting, never risk a shot when you can identify only a part of the animal. **The only time you should shoot is when your target is fully and clearly visible.**

Line-of-Fire Accidents

GOOD JUDGMENT—knowing whether it's safe to shoot or not—is the critical issue not only in mistaken-for-game accidents but also in those cases where the victim was out of sight of the shooter, was covered by a shooter swinging on game, or moved into the line of fire. These are among the most common types of accidents that occur each season throughout the country.

Not every accident can be wholly attributed to a single cause. Often, several contributing factors are involved. Careless positioning or careless movement in the field together with poor shooting judgment are a particularly dangerous combination. Time and again, they literally set the stage for a tragic incident. Here again are some verbatim accident summaries:

- Victim struck in head when party members shot at a deer crossing a road; all were on the gravel road.
- Victim and shooter on stands during a deer drive. Shooter fired at a deer between them. Hit victim 310 feet away.
- Victim struck by a bullet fired down a roadway at a deer crossing the road; victim was over 370 yards away.
- Victim struck by a slug fired at a deer by a party member 545 feet from victim; victim out of sight.
- Victim was hunting with a group of friends. A group of doves came in low, and the party opened fire at the birds. Victim was struck over the right eye by a single birdshot-size pellet.
- Shooter swinging on bird shot victim standing in brush.
- Neither subject could see each other when hunter A fired at a rabbit. Hunter B suffered gunshot wounds to the right leg.

- Hunters were in thick cover and underbrush. Shooter fired at a deer not knowing for sure where his partner was. Victim received gunshot wound to the right hip.
- Shooter shot at rabbit and killed same that was running on top of a little hill. Victim was standing on opposite side of hill completely obscured from shooter's view. BBs went through grass and hit victim in head.
- Victim and shooter were hunting along a state road approximately 300 yards apart. Shooter saw deer and fired three shots. One pellet from the last shot struck the victim in the head.
- Shooter shot at deer. He did not notice his father standing beyond the deer and the father was shot.
- Victim and shooter were riding in a Jeep with two other people. Shooter was shooting at a rabbit, victim jumped out of Jeep as shot was fired. Victim was shot in the back of the head.
- Shooter shot deer down; deer got up and started to run. Shooter shot again, hitting victim (his father) beyond the target.
- Dogs jumped a deer; someone yelled, "It's a buck!" The shooter fired, went over to his target and found victim lying face down in the water at the edge of a lake.

There is a distressing similarity to practically all of these accidents. In the vast majority of cases, the incident could have been avoided if only those involved had better organized and planned their hunt. Whatever hunting technique you and your partner(s) use—whether it involves stationary positions or some kind of drive—it is absolutely essential that you **develop a safe strategy before you head out, and stay with that strategy throughout the hunt.** The larger your party, the more important this becomes.

Of course, part of every effective hunting strategy involves positioning hunters in a way that will maximize their chances of getting a shot at game. Yet the primary objective of every hunting plan must be safety: Establishing clear and well-defined zones of fire is critical. Remember, most line-of-fire accidents involve members of the same hunting party. It bears repeating again: **You can't know what is your safe zone of fire unless you know the location of all your hunting partners.** So, never change your location or line of travel without letting your partners know. Hunter orange clothing not only helps in avoiding the risk of being mistaken for

Always plan your hunt with safety as your primary objective. Develop a safe strategy before you head out, and stay with that strategy throughout the hunt.

game but is also a great aid in helping you keep track of everyone in your group.

In many hunting situations, the direction of fire is predictable and should be taken into account when positioning yourself and your partners. Extreme caution should be taken when placement puts all of you in a likely line of fire. For example, you and your partners hope to get a shot at deer as they cross over a power line cut or abandoned logging road. Everyone wants the opportunity for a clear shot and selects stands along the edge of the road or cut. Even though your positions may be many yards apart, keep in mind that any deer that passes through the line will present a shot that places one—or all of you—in the direct line of fire. The same logic applies when driving deer to standers. Drives require careful planning and execution. There should never be any confusion about the line of travel or the location of both drivers and standers. Accidents in which the victim was out of sight happen all too often during drives for deer.

Any time that you and your hunting partners are walking, make every possible effort to stay in your agreed-upon position, especially when game is nearby. Hunters who move around too much, who

Never take a shot unless you know what lies in the area beyond your target. What's behind this pronghorn antelope? Who knows?

"break formation," can easily lose track of one another. If at any moment you're not sure where your partner is, don't hesitate to call out. Extra caution should be taken when moving through heavy cover. When you and your partner(s) can't see one another, stay in verbal contact.

In any hunting situation, you not only must be sure that your target is fully and clearly visible but you must also know what lies in the area beyond your target. **Never shoot unless you're positive that you have a safe background.** Whether you're using a rifle or shotgun, never forget that the bullet or shot charge can travel well beyond your target. And be especially careful when taking a second or third shot at flying or running game. In a moment of excitement, it's easy to get carried away and swing beyond your safe zone of fire.

Accidents that involve a hunter's judgment, whether mistaken-for-game or line-of-fire, account for almost half of all accidents that occur each year. Accidents of this type also account for a disproportionately large number of fatalities. Whether you're a novice or a veteran of many seasons, you should:

Never hurry or anticipate a shot. If you have the slightest doubt, hold up.

- Always wear hunter orange outerwear, if appropriate for your kind of hunting.
- Never assume that if something is not orange it's not human.
- Never wear or carry anything that resembles a game animal.
- Always assume that any unidentified sound or movement is another human being—not a game animal.
- Always try to maintain the right attitude toward hunting. Never overemphasize the importance of being "successful."
- Never allow your emotions to override your good judgment. Mental discipline is critical to safe hunting.
- Never hurry or anticipate a shot. If you have the *slightest* doubt, hold up. Never use your rifle scope as a pair of binoculars.
- Always be doubly cautious about taking a shot during the poor light conditions of dawn or dusk or when the weather has restricted visibility.

- Never risk a shot when you can identify only part of an animal. The only time you should shoot is when your target is fully and clearly visible.
- Always plan your hunt with safety as your primary objective.
- Always be sure you know your safe zone of fire, and never take a shot outside your zone.
- Always know the location of your hunting partners—at all times.
- Always stay in your agreed-upon position when hunting with partners, especially when moving through heavy cover.
- Never take a shot unless you know what lies beyond your target.
- Drag, never carry, your deer out of the woods.

11

Special Considerations: Turkey and Waterfowl Hunting

TURKEY-HUNTING SAFETY

A true native species, the wild turkey originally ranged throughout most all regions of the North American continent. However, by the 1930s encroaching civilization and subsistence hunting had reduced populations to a point where the future of the species was in doubt. Only small and scattered flocks, mostly in the Deep South, remained.

Efforts by wildlife managers to restore the turkey have been nothing short of spectacular. In just some 50 years, restocking programs have brought wild turkey back to 44 states, including some places where the bird was not found in the days of the Indians. Today, 49 states offer spring turkey hunting, and 39 states have a full turkey season. Since turkey hunting is still new to many hunters, it's well worth looking at the specific safety issues that apply when hunting this challenging bird.

At first glance, the very nature of turkey hunting may appear to encourage mistaken-for-game accidents. Consider: When hunting turkey you are (1) typically wearing camouflage clothing; (2) in a well-concealed position; (3) using a call to imitate "turkey talk."

Actually, turkey hunting should be among the safest types of hunting. Knowledgeable turkey hunters, those who hunt in a sporting and ethical fashion by calling birds in to a point where a clean kill is assured, are rarely, if ever, the cause of turkey-hunting accidents. Ironically, however, they are most often the victims.

An analysis of turkey-hunting accidents reveals that in the vast majority of cases the shooter stalked his victim, and the shooter thought he was shooting at a calling turkey.

Ethical standards and knowledge of game can play an important role in hunting safety. Hunters, for example, who try to stalk a bird often lack not only a basic understanding of turkey hunting but of turkeys as well. New York state game officials point out that the only legal turkeys in the spring are those with beards. During the spring season, a caller is imitating the call of a hen—not a tom. There is no resemblance between the yelp of a hen and the gobbling of a male. Why, then, would anyone try to sneak up to a calling hen? Some hunters simply don't know any better. Others may choose to ignore the fact. In either case, an accident can easily result.

What about the use of hunter orange for turkey hunters? Frankly, the issue is still being debated. Accident statistics indicate that this safety color may not be the answer. Victims in most accidents were wearing some sort of contrasting colors—usually red, white, or blue; and in one reported case hunter orange gloves. Apparently, such colors are easily mistaken for the tom turkey's colorful head. Hunters in full camouflage gear—the standard for most turkey hunters—were involved in far fewer accidents.

All hunters have an obligation to become familiar with the hunting methods that are appropriate for the game they hunt and to become knowledgeable about the species' habits and characteristics. Every turkey hunter should also be aware of the safety rules that specifically apply to turkey hunting developed by the National Wild Turkey Federation:

1. Don't ever attempt to approach closer than 100 yards to a hen or a gobbler.
2. Never select a calling site with your back to a tree that is smaller than the width of your shoulders.
3. Never jump and turn suddenly because you hear a turkey close behind you.
4. Never select a calling site where you can't see at least 40 yards in all directions.
5. Never stalk a turkey.

Never presume that what you hear or what answers you is a turkey.

6. Don't use a gobbler call unless it's one of those rare situations where circumstances really warrant trying something different.
7. Don't think because you're fully camouflaged that you're totally invisible.
8. Never wear red, white or blue clothing, not even undergarments of these colors.
9. Never presume that what you hear or what answers you is a turkey.
10. Don't try to hide so well that you can't see what's happening.

WATERFOWL AND BOATING SAFETY

Waterfowlers are a different breed of hunter. At a time when most upland gunners have called it a season, the duck and goose hunter is in full swing, waiting for winter's worst and the chance to break skim ice at 5 A.M. on a day when the clouds are low and the wind is up. But more than just weather or the time of year, waterfowling involves some special safety considerations.

First, in most waterfowling situations you will be shooting within a few feet of your partners. So, whether you're hunting from a boat, pit, or blind, **the need for precisely defined and religiously adhered to zones of fire is of paramount importance.** Establishing zones of fire should always be the first thing you and your partners decide on, even before loading up.

In some situations, it's best if only one gunner fires at a time.

A boat is no place for a loaded gun. Guns should be unloaded, with the action open, when getting in or out of a boat.

Some boats and blinds, for example, are simply too small and cramped to allow two, or more, gunners to shoot at once. If that's the case, **be sure that everybody knows the shooting order— and sticks with it.** As a reminder, each shot should be called in advance, "It's your shot, Joe." A classic waterfowling accident involves two hunters getting up simultaneously, each thinking the shot is "his." All too often, one hunter ends up in the direct line of fire of the other.

Since boats, pits, and blinds are confined and often crowded, it's essential that you and your partners know exactly when and in which direction it's safe to shoot.

One of the cardinal rules of safe gun handling is to have control of your gun at all times. When duck and goose hunting, this typically involves having your shotgun in a secure rest with the muzzle pointing in a safe direction. For instance, never simply prop your gun up with the barrel resting against the side of the blind or pit. Left this way, it could easily slip or be knocked over by an anxious retriever. If there's no secure rest, hold your gun firmly with the muzzle pointing up and away from the boat, blind, and companions.

In the close quarters often experienced when duck and goose hunting, extra caution should also be taken when loading and unloading. In either case, stand up and point the muzzle outside the blind in a safe direction. **Under no circumstance should you try to get in or out of a blind, pit, or boat with a loaded gun.**

Maneuvering inside a blind or pit—and especially in a small boat—is tricky, so be sure to always pay strict attention to where the muzzle of your gun is pointing. Never reach over and pull a shotgun toward you, muzzle first. And when the time comes to pull your boat ashore, be sure your gun is not still in the boat, its muzzle pointing at your back.

While many waterfowlers use boats, not enough waterfowlers think of themselves as "boaters." Instead, boats are often seen as just another piece of gear, something to be hauled out and put into the water a few times each season.

As with any other type of equipment, you should be thoroughly familiar with your boat and know how to handle it in a safe manner. And that's not just pro forma advice: Each season, more hunters die from boating accidents than they do from shooting mishaps. Indeed, sportsmen such as duck and goose hunters are far more likely to be involved in boating accidents than the traditional summer boaters.

Boating accident statistics show that most accidents occur "out of season," during the spring and fall months, and typically involve a small boat equipped with either no motor or one of 10 horsepower or less.

Maintaining the stability of a small boat is critical—and doubly so when out in cold waters. No boat should ever be overloaded or overpowered. Check the capacity plate on your boat, and never exceed the craft's maximum ratings for weight or horsepower. And remember, a small boat is no place to stand up. If you do have to change positions, keep a low profile, and keep your weight centered toward the middle of the craft.

Falling out of a boat into cold water is extremely dangerous. Cold water conducts heat from your body some 30 times faster than cold air. Your survival time in near-freezing water is literally a matter of minutes. In fact, hypothermia, the rapid and drastic chilling of the body core, is more often than not the cause of death in victims who fall into cold water.

What should you try to do in case you fall overboard? Try not to panic. The more you thrash around, the faster your body heat will escape. And don't worry about your heavy duck-hunting clothes dragging you under. Actually, by trapping air, they will help you stay afloat and also help preserve body heat. Your number one priority is to get out of the water as fast as you possibly can.

Your chances of making it are greatly increased if you are wearing a personal flotation device (pfd). Just having a pfd in the boat is not enough. Even in mild temperatures, getting into a pfd once you're in the water is tricky. In cold water, the task is next to impossible. Today, there are a wide variety of flotation jackets and vests specifically designed for the waterfowler. If your duck and goose hunting takes you out in a boat, buy one—and wear it. More than any other piece of equipment, it could save your life.

Remember that during the waterfowl season you'll likely be the only "boaters" out on the water. Should something happen, you can't expect help to come quickly, if at all. So being well prepared for an emergency is especially important.

Should you fall overboard when out in cold water, your chances of survival are greatly increased if you are wearing a personal flotation device (pfd). More than any other piece of equipment, a pfd could save your life.

A few other points to be *sure* of:

- Be sure to dress properly. Several layers of light clothing offer better protection than a single heavy layer. And wool retains its insulating properties even when wet.
- Be sure to check the weather forecast before planning your trip, and tell someone where you're going and when you expect to return. When out on the water, be conscious of weather patterns and changes. Don't push your luck. If the wind really picks up and the skies darken, head back in—even though the ducks may be piling into your rig.
- Be sure your boat and motor are in good condition and are adequate for the water conditions you might encounter. On board, be sure to have a bailing device, oars or paddles, a signaling device, and a class B1 fire extinguisher if the boat has an inboard engine or built-in gas tanks.
- Be sure never to overload your boat. An overloaded boat can easily capsize, even in calm conditions.
- Be sure to **always wear a personal flotation device.**

12

Alcohol Abuse

NO SANE INDIVIDUALS drive when they have had a few drinks. Nor do sane individuals handle guns after they have had a couple of drinks. Even the normally safety-conscious hunter or shooter becomes an accident just waiting to happen when under the influence of alcohol. Safe gun handling requires coordination, balance, and an alert mind. And every shooting situation involves a judgment call, a decision, often made in a brief second, whether to shoot or hold up. Alcohol depresses brain functions. As a result, it takes us longer to process information, and still more time to react. What's more, alcohol affects focus and depth perception and makes it difficult to judge speed correctly or track moving objects. And finally, alcohol reduces inhibitions, causing normally cautious individuals to try stunts they would avoid when sober. This is especially true of inexperienced drinkers.

To be sure, alcohol affects everyone differently, depending on factors such as body size, drinking experience, and the amount of food in the stomach. But whether you're an experienced drinker or not, the point to remember is that alcohol can seriously jeopardize the safety of everyone in your hunting party.

Consider these facts:

- Beer or wine is not less intoxicating than hard liquor. One 12-ounce can of beer contains the same amount of alcohol as 4 ounces of wine or 1½ ounces of 86 proof liquor.
- Alcohol enters the bloodstream immediately. It takes 1½ hours for a 12-ounce beer to leave the body of an average-size adult. A cold shower, coffee, or fresh air will not help you sober up.
- Alcohol does not warm you up. In small amounts, it does dilate

the small blood vessels close to the skin and give a deceptive "glow" of warmth. However, dilated blood vessels reduce your body's ability to guard against heat loss.

If you use a boat when hunting, you should also be aware that alcohol is by far the number one killer on the water. Alcohol is the major contributing factor in as many as 70 percent of all boating deaths.

Most boating fatalities are caused by an accidental fall out of the boat. Balance and coordination are among the first things affected by drinking. Once in the water, even an able swimmer can easily drown. And with alcohol in the blood, the numbing effects of cold water occur much faster than when you're sober.

Drinking when handling a gun, or a boat or an automobile, for that matter, is not only an invitation to disaster but also against the law. If you do drink, save the cocktail hour for the fireside stories when you get home in the evening.

CHAPTER 13

Muzzle-Loading Safety

EVEN THOUGH OBSOLETE for more than three-quarters of a century, the use of muzzle-loading rifles, shotguns, and handguns is currently enjoying an enormous revival. Today, there are more than 3 million muzzle-loading enthusiasts throughout the country, both hunters and target shooters. In fact, most states now have a muzzle-loading-only big-game season.

The National Muzzle Loading Rifle Association, Box 67, Friendship, Indiana 47201, provides shooting news, safety and handling hints, and a wealth of technical information for black-powder shooters. The following safety information is provided courtesy of the NMLRA.

Powder

Use only black powder or the proper grade of pyrodex in all muzzle-loading firearms. Pyrodex is unsuitable for flintlocks. The term *black powder* refers to a type of gunpowder, not a color. If in doubt, don't use it. **Never use smokeless powder in a muzzle-loading firearm.**

Black Powder Types

Fg—The coarsest. Use in big-bore (70-caliber and up) arms, scale-model cannons, and shotguns.

FFg—Use in smooth-bore muskets, in rifles over 45 caliber, and in shotguns.

FFFg—Most common. Use in rifles up to .45 caliber and in all pistols and revolvers.

FFFFg—Finest granulation. Use only for priming flintlocks.

Patches

Use only linen or 100 percent cotton for shooting patches. Fabric should have a hard finish and be tightly woven, between .007 inches and .020 inches thick.

Recommended precut patch sizes

Caliber	Patch diameter (inches)
.45	1
.50	1⅛
.54	1¼
.58	1⅜

All patches should be lubricated before loading. Use a clean-burning grease or commercial patch lube (such as Hoppes #9, Hodgdon's Spit Patch) or saliva.

Ball or Bullet

The patched round ball is thought to be the most accurate bullet for use in rifled, single-shot muzzle-loading firearms.

Use pure lead only in casting any type of bullets for use in muzzle loaders. Plumber's lead is good. Wheel weights are too hard.

Always use a lubricated cloth patch when using a round ball. And always load a round ball with the sprue up (the sprue is the flat place on the cast round ball).

Ignition Systems

The two most common forms of ignition in contemporary muzzle-loaders are flintlock and percussion. In the flintlock system, a piece of flint strikes a hardened piece of steel (the frizzen), causing a shower of sparks, which in turn ignites a small quantity of powder in the lock pan. This ignites the main charge in the barrel and fires the gun.

In the percussion system, the priming charge is replaced by the percussion cap. This cap is placed on the nipple, or cone. When struck by the hammer, it produces a small, hot flame that ignites the main powder charge. Of the two systems, the caplock is the less complicated and the less susceptible to dampness.

Be sure to check periodically the action of your locks, especially with muzzle-loading shotguns. If performance is doubtful, take them to a gunsmith who is familiar with muzzle-loading firearms. Poor locks are a menace to shooters and spectators alike.

Determining Powder Charges

Since there are many variances among muzzle-loading firearms available in today's market, it is essential that you follow the manufacturer's powder-charge recommendations. If you seek the advice of a reputable dealer or muzzle-loading expert, be sure to bring your firearm with you. He or she will want to see the gun before advising you. Remember, in any muzzle-loading firearm, moderate loads are more accurate.

Loading Procedure for Rifle and Single-Shot Pistol

1. Check that your firearm is empty and unprimed.
2. Put the hammer at half-cock.
3. Run a dry patch through the barrel to remove any remaining oil.
4. When the line is clear to handle firearms, snap a cap or strike a pan of powder to dry the breech.

Never fire a muzzle loader unless the ball or shot charge is firmly seated against the powder charge.

5. Put the butt on the ground between your feet when loading a rifle, with the muzzle away from you.
6. Measure a charge of powder—level full without jarring the measure.
7. Pour the measured charge into the barrel. Tap the side of your barrel with your hand to settle the powder in the breech.
8. Center a lubricated patch on the muzzle.
9. Place a round ball on the patch, sprue up.
10. Drive the patch/ball into the barrel using a short starter (bullet starter).
11. Using the ramrod, press the ball and patch all the way down against the powder charge. Seat them firmly with even pressure.
12. Remove the ramrod.
13. Cap or prime with powder.
14. Aim and fire.

Loading Procedure for Shotgun

1. Check that the shotgun is empty and unprimed.
2. Put the hammer at half cock.
3. Run a dry patch through the barrels to remove any remaining oil.
4. When the line is clear to handle firearms, snap a cap or strike a pan of powder to dry the breech.

5. Put the butt on the ground between your feet with the muzzle away from you.
6. Measure a charge of powder—level full without jarring the measure.
7. Pour the measured charge into the barrel. Tap the side of the barrel with your hand to settle the powder in the breech.
8. Place Nitro card wad over the powder, followed by a wet fiber wad. Seat each wad firmly.
9. Pour the measured shot into the barrel. Equal powder and shot charges by volume work best.
10. Finally, add the overshot card wad. Seat firmly—don't pound down.
11. Remove the ramrod.
12. Cap or prime with powder.
13. Bring the hammer to full cock.
14. Aim and fire.

After firing both barrels, make it a fixed habit always to put hammers at half-cock position to lessen the chance of an accidental discharge. If reloading one barrel while the other barrel is still loaded, **always remove cap** from the nipple of the loaded barrel to prevent accidental discharge of that barrel.

Loading Procedure for Revolver

1. Make sure the revolver is empty and unprimed.
2. Run a dry patch through the barrel and cylinder to remove any remaining oil.
3. When the line is clear to handle firearms, cap each chamber and snap it to make sure every nipple is clear of oil or powder fouling.
4. Pour the measured powder into the chamber.
5. Seat the ball (0.001–0.002 over the cylinder bore diameter) firmly down on the powder. Try to apply the same pressure in loading each chamber.
6. When all are loaded, grease the chambers on top of each ball. Use commercial lubes, Crisco, or a similar substance.
7. Cap the revolver nipples with tight-fitting caps. Choose caps with care. Make sure that they fit well (almost too tight) and

that they break up uniformly and completely when fired rather than merely enlarging.
8. Carefully aim and fire.

As an alternative to grease over the end of each cylinder chamber, you may wish to use a greased or waxed felt wad approximately ⅛-inch thick. This will go on top of the powder charge, under the ball.

Muzzle-Loading Safety Rules

1. Muzzle-loading firearms are not toys. Treat them with the same respect due any firearm.
2. Use only black powder of the proper granulations in your muzzle-loading firearms. Such guns are not designed to withstand the higher pressures developed by modern smokeless powders.
3. Never fire a muzzle loader unless the ball or shot charge is firmly seated against the powder charge. And always make sure that the ball or shot charge is seated against the powder. An air space between the powder and the projectile will cause the barrel to be ringed or bulged and in some cases may cause the barrel to rupture.
4. Do not exceed the manufacturer's recommended maximum loads or attempt to load multiple projectile loads. When in doubt, secure information concerning proper loads from an authoritative source.
5. When loading, do not expose your body to the muzzle. Grasp the ramrod only a short distance above where it protrudes from the barrel, pushing it down in short strokes, rather than grasping it near the outer end, where, in the event the rod breaks, serious injury can be rendered by the shooter's arm coming into contact with the splintered end of the broken rod.
6. Always make sure that your down-range area is a safe impact area for your projectiles. Round balls may carry as far as 800 yards and elongated projectiles well beyond this distance.
7. Never smoke while loading, shooting, or handling black powder.

When shooting a muzzle loader, keep in mind that round balls may carry as far as 800 yards and elongated projectiles well beyond this distance.

8. Do not load directly from a powder horn or flask. Always use a separate measure. A lingering spark in the barrel can ignite the incoming charge, causing the horn or flask to explode in your hand.

9. The half-cock notch is the safety notch on a muzzle loader. Always be sure it is functioning properly. If your lock or triggers seem to be improperly functioning, take your firearm to a competent muzzle-loading gunsmith.

10. Never use 4F black powder as a main charge. It burns too fast and could burst a barrel.

11. When you prime your pan, fill it only one-quarter or one-third full. More powder gives an excessive flash.

12. Never snap a percussion lock. It will often break the tumbler. If you snap a flintlock to adjust or test the flint, never do so with the rifle loaded. Even though the pan is not primed, many rifles will fire from the sparks alone.

13. Always wear eye and ear protection.

14. Treat a misfire or failure to fire as though the gun can fire at any second. Wait at least one minute with gun pointed at the target.

15. Do not use a plastic patch. The ball-to-plastic patch fit is critical. If an improper fit or a sharp jolt occurs, the ball will roll down the barrel, leaving an air gap between the ball and the plastic patch. The ball will then act as an obstruction and will cause serious injury to the firearm and possibly the shooter.

16. The nature of a muzzle-loading firearm requires that you, the shooter, exercise caution and skill in the care, loading, and use of such a firearm. Make certain that you are informed as to the proper steps in such care and use.

CHAPTER 14

Clay-Target Safety, Plinking Safety, and Range Commands

Sporting Clays

Introduced to American shooters in the early 1980s, sporting clays has rapidly become one of America's favorite clay-target sports. Today, more than 3½ million shooters enjoy the sport at some 1,500 sporting-clays courses around the country.

With target presentations at each station that simulate the flight of popular game birds, sporting clays is an ideal "hunter's game" providing not only excellent wingshooting practice but a realistic environment for the new hunter to practice safe gun-handling skills such as a safe carry as squad members walk from station to station through woods or fields.

Not surprisingly, the safety rules that apply to other clay-target games, such as trap and skeet, are also applicable to sporting clays. Always carry your shotgun unloaded with the action open as you walk from station to station, and when arriving at a new station, place your shotgun in the gun rack provided. The only time you should load is when you're in the shooting cage and ready to shoot.

Keep in mind that most sporting-clays targets involve doubles—targets thrown simultaneously or one right after the other. On some doubles, when the pair fly close together, it's possible to break both with one shot. In your excitement, don't forget that you still have an unfired round in your shotgun. When finished at a station, always double check to be absolutely sure that your shotgun is unloaded and that the action is open before you leave the shooting cage.

Trap and Skeet

Accidents at trap and skeet clubs are almost unheard of. A key reason is that gun-club safety has become a practiced ritual, a step-by-step pattern that knowledgeable shooters are always careful to follow.

If you're a new shooter, you'll find that the correct approach to safety on the trap and skeet field has a lot in common with developing good shooting skills. In both cases, the vital ingredient is consistency.

Among top shooters, there is a deliberate effort to break targets at each station in the same way. The manner in which the shotgun is mounted, the angle of the muzzle in relation to the house, foot position, and the like, are all part of a style the shooter attempts to duplicate from one round to the next.

Experienced shooters also coordinate the necessary safety procedures into their movements and actions while on the field. The result is a safe, consistent style that soon becomes second nature to the shooter.

If you are new to clay-target shooting, you may find it helpful to think of safety as a specific series of actions that are duplicated from station to station, from round to round.

When at the club, keep these points in mind:

1. Always be sure the trap boy is safely inside the house before you shoot.
2. Should a delay occur while you are in a shooting position, open your gun, extract the shell, and do not reload until you are ready to resume shooting.
3. Never place your hand over the muzzle or lean a gun against your body. Watch the direction of the muzzle at all times.
4. Always carry your gun unloaded with the action open when you are not in firing position. The only time your gun should be loaded is when you're on station and ready to shoot.
5. Never load more than one shell unless you are shooting doubles.

6. Before you head out to the field, check your vest or shell pouch to be sure you're not carrying shells of a different gauge than the gun you're using.

7. Safeties are not used because your gun should never be loaded until you're ready to fire.

8. In skeet, you should not move to the next station until all squad members have finished shooting. Carry guns open from one station to the next.

9. When shooting trap, your gun should be unloaded and open when changing stations, and when moving from station 5 to 1, you should be sure to walk behind other squad members.

10. When you leave your field, double check to make sure your gun is unloaded and be sure to leave the action open.

11. Always wear eye and ear protection!

When plinking or target shooting, be sure you have a safe backstop. The best backstop is a high dirt bank free of rocks and stones.

Plinking

While plinking may be described as informal target shooting, there's never an excuse for a casual approach to gun safety.

To begin with, always select a site with a safe backstop and a safe background. If shooting clay targets thrown from a hand or portable trap, you'll need a safety zone of at least 300 yards. For handgun and rifle shooting, the best backstop is a high dirt bank free of rocks and stones. Such a backstop provides adequate stopping power and eliminates the danger of ricochets. And remember never to shoot at a hard, flat surface or the surface of water.

Second, it's always a good idea to establish a firing line. When shooting, spectators must be behind the firing line. And when you go down range to change targets, all guns should be unloaded, with the actions open, and placed in a secure rest.

Plinking can provide hours of enjoyment in a relaxed atmosphere; but, as in any situation where firearms are involved, there can be no letdown when it comes adhering to all the rules of safe gun handling.

Range Commands

If you have the opportunity to shoot at a formal range, it will be helpful to be familiar with the standard range officer commands:

"Relay No. ( ) and Match No. ( ) on the firing line. The preparation periods starts now."
"With (No. of rounds you'll be using), load."
"Is the line ready?" (If you're not, notify the range officer.)
"Ready on the left. Ready on the right. Ready on the firing line."
"Commence firing."
"Cease firing."
"Unload—actions open, magazines out—guns on the table."

15

Eye and Ear Protection

IF YOU'VE EVER HEARD ringing in your ears after shooting, it's a clear signal that you've subjected yourself to potentially damaging sound levels. Numerous sound-level tests have shown conclusively that combined exposure to gunfire can cause gradual hearing damage. While the ringing in your ears may go away, any damage to your hearing is permanent.

The faintest sound most of us can hear is around 1 decibel, a very soft whisper. Normal conversation is 50–70 decibels, and hearing loss will result from continuous exposure to sound levels around 130 decibels. *Most gunfire is louder than this 130-decibel level.*

Peak sound-pressure levels produced, for example, by the firing of various rifles (at the U.S. Army Proving Grounds in Aberdeen, Maryland) were measured at 160 to 172.5 decibels. Industry tests have measured the report of a 12-gauge shotgun at 140 decibels. Handguns and other short-barreled firearms, even those of small caliber, produce an unexpectedly loud and sharp report. While the peak sound-pressure level from a .22 rifle measured out at 130 decibels (the measurement was taken 2 feet to one side of the muzzle), a .22 pistol delivered 153 decibels.

Clearly, the repetitious firing on skeet, trap, and target ranges produces the most damage to your hearing. When at the club or range, there's simply no excuse not to wear some type of effective hearing protection. There is a wide variety of hearing protectors available today, from foam plugs and custom molded inserts, to ear-muff devices. Choose the type you find most comfortable—and always use them.

Hearing loss caused by exposure to loud noise is typically a gradual process. As nerve endings in the inner ear are destroyed, certain

Your eyes and ears are irreplaceable. Always wear eye and ear protection when at the range.

sounds can no longer be heard. At first, you may not notice any impairment. But when you do, it's too late. Any hearing damage that's been caused is permanent. No medical or surgical treatment can restore it.

Your eyes, like your ears, are irreplaceable, and there's not a shooting situation in which a pair of high-quality, impact-resistant shooting glasses won't offer an important measure of safety. Most critically, perhaps, shooting glasses can protect you from injury in the unlikely event of a ruptured case or firearm malfunction. In the field, shooting glasses will protect your eyes should you accidentally walk into a sharp twig or get hit in the face by a swinging branch. In such cases, your glasses can prevent what might have been a serious injury or head off the discomfort of an irritated eye that could bring an early end to your hunt. When there are a number of shooters afield, such as during a dove hunt, glasses will also protect your eyes from falling shot. And shooting glasses are an absolute must at the trap and skeet range, where flying clay-target chips and shards can pose a serious hazard to your eyes.

CHAPTER

16

Reloading Safety

THE OLD SAYING that one person's trash is another's treasure certainly rings true when it comes to a shotshell hull. Left scattered about a trap or skeet field by some shooters, it is—for the reloader—a valued component of a rewarding and money-saving hobby. Beyond the economics, there's an undeniable satisfaction in breaking clay targets or downing game with your "own" loads.

For the rifle and pistol shooter, reloading not only offers savings but also the ability to custom "tune" ammunition to a particular gun and to a specific purpose, whether for target or hunting use.

There's nothing complicated or difficult about reloading, yet it is not something you should attempt until you're familiar with the basic rules of reloading safety.

1. To begin with, reload only when you can give your undivided attention. It's best to develop a reloading routine, and to always load at an unhurried pace.
2. Always wear safety glasses when reloading.
3. If you're new to reloading, take the time to carefully review the introduction section of your loading manual or guide.
4. Again, if you're just starting out, do not reload without an instruction manual for the machine you're using. Take your time and follow the step-by-step instructions. Use your reloading equipment only as the manufacturer recommends.
5. Observe good housekeeping rules in your reloading area. Clean up spilled powder and primers promptly and completely.
6. Store powder and primers beyond the reach of children and away from heat and open flames. Keep no more powder than needed in an open container. Immediately return unused powder to its original factory container. This will preserve its identity and shelf life. Do not store primers in bulk. Primers in bulk can explode spontaneously. Storage areas containing only primers are recommended. These cabinets should be ruggedly constructed of lumber at least 1 inch (nominal) thick to delay or minimize the transmission of heat in the event of fire. Do not store primers with propellant powders or other highly combustible materials. Store primers only in their original factory containers. The use of glass bottles, fruit jars, and plastic and metal containers is extremely hazardous. Take care in filling and handling auto-primer feed tubes.
7. Reload only according to data published in recognized reloading manuals. Never exceed recommended loads, and never use the heaviest recommended powder charge until lighter charges of the same powder have been tried and found safe in each individual gun. Before you start loading, take a second look at the manufacturer's reloading data, which instructs you to use a particular set of components.
8. Do not use any powder unless its identity is positively known. Scrap all mixed powders and those of uncertain or unknown identity.
9. Do not smoke while reloading, and keep a fire extinguisher within reach of your reloading bench.

10. Use priming tools and accessories precisely as the manufacturer recommends. Do not make alterations, substitutions, or changes to priming tools, systems, or accessories.

11. Keep accurate and complete records of your reloads, and be sure to label each box of shells and cartridges.

CHAPTER 17

Firearms Safety in the Home

SOME HUNTERS may think of safety as largely a matter of proper gun handling in the field, but safety in the home is equally important. Indeed, National Safety Council figures reveal that about twice as many firearms accidents occur in the home as outdoors.

There's nothing complicated about gun safety in the home, but beyond the basic safety precautions is the equally important need to maintain a serious attitude when handling firearms. Guns are not toys and should never be treated as such by anyone in your household.

As a first step in home firearms safety, double check to make absolutely sure that all your guns are unloaded. More than one veteran shooter has experienced the disturbing sensation of discovering a shell in the chamber of a gun he thought was unloaded.

Even if you're positive a gun is unloaded, you should not handle it, or show it to a friend, without first opening the action and checking again. Among experienced gunners, this is a kind of ritual that is expected whenever a firearm is examined. It's a good habit to get into.

Your next step should be to review your firearms storage facilities. In a nutshell, all guns—rifles, shotguns, handguns—should be kept in secure, locked racks, cabinets, or safes. Locking storage is doubly important if there are children in the household.

Standing a shotgun in the corner behind the kitchen door or keeping a handgun in the desk drawer is not suitable. If secure storage is not available, trigger locks that open with a key or similar add-on safety devices that prevent the action from being operated should

Firearms in the home should be kept in locked racks or cabinets.

be used. Again, if there are children in the household, such locking devices are essential.

For complete safety, all ammunition should be kept under lock and key and in a location separate from your firearms. An extra safety measure, particularly with children present, can be realized by storing ammunition in another room or on a different floor. The objective is to create a situation in which a conscious effort is required to bring firearms and ammunition together.

Most fatal home firearms accidents occur when youngsters—often children who do not live in the home—discover firearms that adults thought were safely hidden or physically inaccessible. As a gun owner, your most important responsibility is ensuring that children cannot encounter firearms in your home. The precautions you take must be completely effective. Anything less invites tragedy.

Along the lines of occasionally checking the batteries in your smoke detectors, it's a good idea to also periodically go through a home firearms safety review, a checklist that all firearms and ammunition are properly stored and secured. Accidents have occurred, for example, when a firearm was lent to a friend and returned to storage while it was still loaded.

Education is important as well. If you have young children in the home, they should clearly understand the following safety advice: (1) Don't go looking for guns, in your house or a friend's house; (2) if you find a gun in your house—or anywhere else—leave it alone. Don't touch it. Don't let anyone else touch it. Tell an adult immediately; (3) even if a gun looks like a toy, don't touch it. Some real guns look like toy guns, so don't take a chance. Tell an adult.

Air guns and BB guns should also never be treated as toys. All shooting should be under adult supervision in a safe location with an appropriate backstop. Indeed, all the rules of safe gun handling are equally applicable when shooting air or BB guns.

FIELD & STREAM

The Complete Hunter

Book Two

Turkey Hunting

Phil Bourjaily

About Turkeys

IF YOU PICKED this book up, you're a turkey hunter or you're thinking of becoming one. You might live anywhere from Maine to Hawaii; yet chances are you can hear turkeys gobble a short drive from your home.

Five subspecies of our largest upland gamebird live in every state but Alaska, thriving in habitats as diverse as Florida's near-tropical swamps to Minnesota's farms. Today, there are around 4 million wild turkeys in America. Only 70 years ago turkeys roosted on the brink of extinction. The comeback of the wild turkey stands as a tribute to the dedication of sportspeople and wildlife professionals and as a testament to the adaptability of this fascinating bird.

SUBSPECIES

The turkey, of course, is not from Turkey at all but is indigenous to North America. Europeans looked at the big, bareheaded birds and assumed they were giant guineafowl, which in those days were called "turkey cocks." The name stuck.

Four main subspecies of wild turkeys inhabit the United States, although there's considerable overlap and interbreeding among them in some places. When turkey hunters speak of the "Grand Slam" they're talking about bagging an eastern wild turkey, a Rio Grande turkey, a Merriam's turkey, and an Osceola, or Florida, turkey. A fifth subspecies, the Gould's turkey, lives primarily in Mexico, although a few birds range north of the border into New Mexico and Arizona. Here's a short guide to the four subspecies of the Grand Slam:

Wild Turkey Distribution

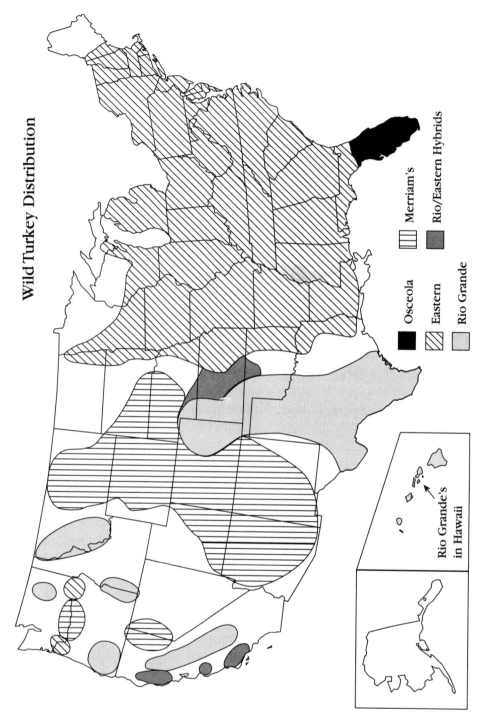

Osceola

Eastern

Rio Grande

Merriam's

Rio/Eastern Hybrids

Rio Grande's in Hawaii

The five subspecies of wild turkeys and their hybrids may be found in every state but Alaska.

The Eastern Wild Turkey

This subspecies is the most widespread and abundant, found in 38 states and Ontario. Three million easterns range from the East Coast to Texas, Missouri, parts of Kansas, Oklahoma and Nebraska, Iowa and Minnesota. Transplanted easterns thrive outside their original range—in Oregon, Washington, and California as well. Their scientific name, *Meleagris gallopavo silvestris,* means "forest turkey," and the eastern is indeed a bird of hardwood timbers, although it also adapts readily to swamps and farm country. The biggest of the four main subspecies, easterns can weigh as much as 30 pounds in the northern part of their range, although 20-plus pounds is more common for gobblers, 8 to 12 pounds for hens. Eastern wild hens and gobblers both may be identified by the chocolate-colored tips of their tailfeathers.

Rio Grande Turkey

Rio Grande turkeys inhabit the wide-open arid spaces of Texas, Oklahoma, and Kansas. Second only to the eastern in population, Rios number over 600,000 birds and have been transplanted far beyond their home range to the Pacific Northwest. The tips of a Rio's tailfeathers are tan, darker than a Merriam's tail but lighter than an eastern's, hence the scientific name—*Meleagris gallopavo intermedia*—because Rios are halfway in between eastern and western turkeys in appearance. In Kansas especially, where easterns and Rios' ranges overlap, there is a large population of Rio/eastern hybrids. Gobblers weigh 20 pounds, hens 8 to 12 pounds.

The Merriam's Turkey

Named for C. Hart Merriam, the first chief of the U.S. Biological Survey, *Meleagris gallopavo merriami* inhabit the ponderosa pines of the mountain west. Like elk and mule deer, Merriam's turkeys will migrate from high country to low with the onset of winter, returning

Writer L. P. Brezny and calling champion Eddie Salter teamed up on this Osceola gobbler. Note the dark-barred primary feathers. *Photo by Julia C. McClellan.*

to higher elevations in the spring. Nearly as big as eastern wild turkeys, Merriam's are easily distinguished from *silvestris* by their white-edged fans and rump feathers. Historically found in Colorado, New Mexico, and Arizona, the Merriam's has adapted to the northern mountain states as well as the prairies of South Dakota and Nebraska and parts of the Pacific northwest. In all, the Merriam's population totals around 200,000.

The Osceola or Florida Turkey

Meleagris gallopavo Osceola, named for the famous Seminole chief, may be found only in the pine woods and cypress swamps of the Florida peninsula. With a population of around 80,000, the Osceola is the least numerous of the four main subspecies. Smaller but similar in appearance to easterns, Osceolas can best be identified by

Eastern wild turkeys can live in a variety of habitats, from midwestern farmland to this South Carolina swamp.

their darker-barred primary feathers. Gobblers weigh less than 20 pounds.

HABITAT REQUIREMENTS

All turkeys must roost off the ground out of reach of nocturnal predators. Most eastern turkeys roost in hardwoods; Merriam's use ponderosa pines, and Osceolas often choose cypress trees. Rio Grande turkeys may prefer a tall cottonwood, but in the absence of suitable trees Rios will roost on power lines and windmill towers.

Newly hatched turkeys need the protein they get from a diet of insects. At one month of age they switch over to plant matter. For the rest of their lives, they will feed primarily on nuts, seeds, leaves, and berries. Adult turkeys sometimes eat ants, bees, grasshoppers, caterpillars, crickets, even fish and an occasional salamander. Birds in the northern states will supplement their diet with corn as a source of high energy during winter.

Turkeys usually feed twice a day, although gobblers hardly eat at all during the spring breeding season. Instead, they rely on the fat stored over the winter in their "breast sponge" to see them through the courtship battles of spring.

Turkeys are gregarious flocking birds with a well-developed social pecking order. They're vocal and for the most part seek out other turkeys. Whereas eastern and Osceola turkeys occupy a fairly small home range, Rios and Merriams may travel miles in a day in search of food and water.

In the spring, the winter flocks break up and gobblers fight to establish dominance. Displaying and gobbling to attract hens, the dominant or "boss" gobbler does most of the breeding. Hens nest by making a depression in the ground, then lay an egg a day until they have a clutch of around 12. After a 28-day incubation period, the poults hatch and quickly grow feathers. At 10 to 12 days of age, young turkeys can fly. By the next spring, the birds of the year are sexually mature. One-year-old males, known as jakes, usually aren't as big as full-grown toms. Jakes sport short, ½-inch to 2½-inch beards, and their central tail feathers are longer than the rest. Turkeys reach full adult size in two years. One way to age a tom is by the spurs. Jakes have no more than a nub on the back of their legs, whereas two-year-old birds' spurs measure up to an inch. Three-year and older toms grow sharp "hooks" over an inch long. Although turkeys have been known to live up to 10 years in captivity, they rarely last longer than 5 years in the wild.

Bobcats, coyotes, foxes, great horned owls, and golden eagles all prevent turkeys from attaining ripe old age. An adult wild turkey, however, is no easy prey even for the fiercest predator. Turkeys can run 12 m.p.h. and fly at 35 m.p.h. for short distances, and if need be they can fight back with their wings and spurs.

Turkeys have remarkably sharp eyesight, with excellent daylight vision and keen color perception. A turkey's peripheral vision extends an impressive 300 degrees. He can periscope his long neck until his eyes are nearly 4 feet off the ground, which enables him to spot danger even when facing the other direction. Turkeys also rely on sharp hearing to detect predators. The turkey's sense of smell,

L-R: 1 YR., 2 YRS., 3+ YRS.

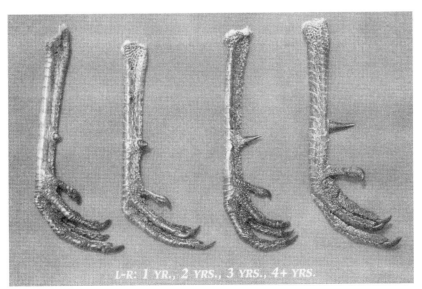

L-R: 1 YR., 2 YRS., 3 YRS., 4+ YRS.

Spur and beard length are two indications of a gobbler's age. *Photos by Gene Smith. Courtesy of NWTF.*

however, is not well developed. Hunters like to say if turkeys could smell as well as they see and hear, we'd never kill them at all.

History of the Turkey in America

Turkeys possessed all the same acute senses 400 years ago they have now. What they hadn't yet learned was the profound distrust of people that keeps them alive today. The Pilgrims and other early settlers in North America found a promised land rich with food and game, including flocks of gullible turkeys. Thomas Morton, wrote in his 1637 book, *New English Canaan:* "Turkies there are, which divers times in great flocks have sallied by our doores; and then a gunne, being commonly in redinesse, salutes them with such a courtesie, as makes them take a turne in the Cooke roome. They daunce by the doore so well."

Although the Pilgrims ate lots of turkey and owed the birds a debt of gratitude for being dumb, plentiful, and good to eat, the turkey didn't become the traditional main course at Thanksgiving until the 1800s. Ben Franklin, incidentally, never nominated the turkey as our national symbol, either. He did, however, write a letter to his daughter, Sarah Bache, comparing turkeys favorably to eagles two years after the eagle was chosen.

Year round, unregulated hunting fed a growing, westward-moving population throughout the seventeenth, eighteenth, and nineteenth centuries. Overshooting and widespread clearing of the eastern primeval forest wiped turkeys out of New England. As settlement moved west, turkeys disappeared. The last turkey was seen in Massachusetts in 1851; in Ohio in 1878; in Iowa in 1907.

Turkeys in the West fared little better than eastern birds. In his book *A Trip to Indian Territory with General P. H. Sheridan,* General William E. Strong tells of a nighttime roost shoot in Kansas shortly after the Civil War. The hunters stole under a huge flock of roosted turkeys in the darkness and opened fire with shotguns and rifles. Strong wrote: "The firing began in earnest after my first shot, and grew into such a cannonade as I never heard before or since on a hunting field. We killed and brought to bag nineteen fine turkeys, I judge as many more were brought down from the trees badly wounded or killed outright, but which we failed to find, owing to the darkness...."

By 1900, fewer than 100,000 turkeys survived in the United States, most of them in inaccessible swamps and forests of Pennsylvania and

Wild-turkey release in Washington state. Trap-and-transfer programs have restored turkeys to 49 states. *Photo by Julia C. McClellan.*

the Southeast. Laws banning the sale of game were passed early in the twentieth century. With the birds gone and much of their habitat cleared, however, it seemed unlikely the turkey would ever return.

RESTORATION

Turkey populations hit all-time lows between 1900 and 1930. Abandoned farms began to revert to forest. The Pittman–Robertson excise tax of 1937 on sporting goods and ammunition generated funds for wildlife restoration. Early attempts to trap and transfer turkeys began in the thirties and forties.

Meanwhile, the Commonwealth of Pennsylvania experimented with releasing game farm turkeys. Blessed with remnant flocks of wild birds and huge expanses of inaccessible mountainous habitat, the Game Department established a state turkey hatchery in 1929. Pennsylvania game protectors collected wild eggs and brought them to the hatchery. Without wild hens to raise them in the woods, however, game farm turkeys had low survival rates in the wild.

The first shot in the successful war to restore the wild turkey was fired in South Carolina's Francis Marion National Forest in 1951 when a battery of blackpowder cannons launched a net over a flock of turkeys pecking at a pile of bait. The cannon net finally gave wildlife managers the ability to trap large numbers of turkeys at once.

Since 1951, trap and transfer efforts have succeeded beyond anyone's wildest imaginings: By 1999, there were 4 million turkeys nationwide.

The turkey's recent successes in proliferating are due in part to the nonprofit National Wild Turkey Federation (NWTF) founded in 1973. One hundred eighty thousand members strong, the NWTF (770 Augusta Rd., Edgefield, S.C. 29824) provides turkeys and turkey hunters with a strong voice. The NWTF has raised and spent over $90 million on restoration, research, and habitat projects over the last 25 years.

Target 2000, a cooperative initiative between the NWTF and state and federal wildlife agencies aims to restore birds to all 60 million remaining acres of turkey-suitable habitat by the century's end. Currently, 49 states hold hunting seasons. We have only ourselves to blame for the near eradication of this wonderful and very American bird. Happily, we also have ourselves to congratulate for its return. With the strict regulation of sport hunting, and the turkey's ability to give us hunters the slip on a leveled playing field, we won't run out of turkeys again.

CHAPTER **2**

Turkey Calls

THE TURKEY that would be the first gobbler I ever tagged sat roosted in a short mulberry tree on the bank of the Iowa River, gobbling, on average, at least three times a minute. Sitting in the mud 100 yards from his tree, I worked the diaphragm call up to the roof of my suddenly dry mouth and called timidly. *"Cluck ... cluck ... cluck?"* I ventured.

Deafening silence followed. There was no response from the mulberry tree. Even the cardinals, geese, and wood ducks seemed to stop calling and stare at me. After an interminable few seconds, the turkey gobbled. The woods came back to life. I let out the breath I was holding.

Fifteen minutes later, I worked up the nerve to call again. This time the turkey answered right back. Not long after, he jumped off the branch and, to my amazement, came to me. "What ever did I say to him?" I wondered as he closed the distance between us.

Good scouting kills probably more turkeys than good calling, but talking to the animals à la Dr. Dolittle is, nonetheless, the essence of turkey hunting. The only way you will ever learn to call turkeys is to go hunting and make some noise. Like me, you may get lucky long before you have any idea what you're doing.

(If you're a complete beginner in need of step-by-step calling instructions, put this book down and buy a video on turkey calling. You'll be able to see and hear for yourself how calls work much better than I could ever tell you in print. Then come back and read the rest of this chapter.)

The more types of callers you know how to use, the more versatile and more successful you'll be in your hunting. All calls work some of the time, none of them work all of the time, and no one knows which one will fire up a certain gobbler on a particular day.

Popular turkey calls include the slate, made of either slate or glass; the box call; and the pushbutton box. *Photo Courtesy of Outlaw Decoys.*

Case in point: a roosted creek-bottom gobbler I set upon a few years ago. I had my favorite call with me, a Lynch World Champion box, as well as a triple-reeded diaphragm call in my mouth. To any discerning ear, one sounded exactly like a turkey, the other sounded, well, like me blowing a mouth call. Guess which call the gobbler liked? The sweetest, most lifelike yelps on the Lynch box provoked the stoniest silence from the roosted bird. The slightest squeak on the mouth call, however, and he'd go berserk. It took 10 or 15 minutes to reel him in after flydown, and he ignored the box and gobbled to the diaphragm every step of the way. Go figure.

Turkey calls are inexpensive, they're fun to fool with, and you really never can have too many. Here's a rundown of the various types, with commentary provided by Matt Morrett of Hunter's Specialties and Brad Harris of Lohman Game Calls, two well-known experts.

DIAPHRAGM CALLS

The original diaphragm calls, made from jasmine leaves or dogwoods, were used both by the Indians and early settlers. With the

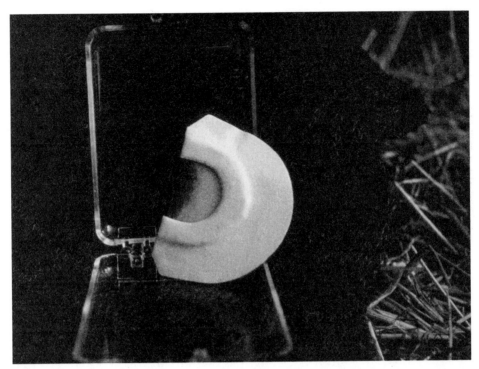

The diaphragm call takes practice to master, but it allows the hunter to make all the calls of the wild turkey without moving his hands. *Photo by Julia C. McClellan.*

invention of latex in the middle of the last century, the mouth call as we know it became possible. Today, diaphragms made from stretched latex are tremendously popular—the diaphragm being to turkey calling what the plastic worm is to bass fishing. Beginning hunters soon learn, however, that the mouth call is difficult to master.

"If you're learning the diaphragm, don't rush," advises Morrett. "Too many people try to make turkey sounds right away and develop bad habits they never unlearn. At first, just concentrate on getting comfortable with the call in your mouth. Then, work on making a single clear note. When you can do that, you've got it made."

Pick a single-reed or thin double-reeded call to start with if you've never blown a mouth call before. It's much easier to get that all-important first clear sound out of a call with only one or two thin reeds. Trust me: After a few days' practice, you won't even be aware of the ticklish, buzzing sensation you feel in the roof of your mouth when you first blow a call. Learn to carry the diaphragm between cheek and gum. That way, it won't lodge in your throat when you trip and fall in the woods. With a little practice you can flip it with your tongue from your cheek to the roof of your mouth.

With practice, you can make every vocalization of the wild turkey with a diaphragm. More important, you can do it while remaining motionless. "Also," says Harris, "if you hold your cupped hand by your mouth and turn your head, you can throw your sound effectively. I've had turkeys walk right by me toward the spot I've thrown my calls."

Morrett agrees: "I never call right at a turkey. If he hears the sound coming from one spot, it's easy for him to pinpoint your position and see you. I'll move the sound around and keep the bird guessing where the call is coming from."

While thick-reeded, extra-raspy, old-hen-type calls are popular with many hunters, both Morrett and Harris prefer high-pitched calls.

"I think turkeys hear high pitches better and respond to them more readily," says Morrett. "I used to keep wild turkeys in a pen. We lived near a firehouse, and that high-pitched whistle would really get the toms going in the spring."

Harris says he often uses single-reed calls in the woods: "They're easy to blow and they produce high-pitched calls that make birds respond. I always carry two or three others, though, because I want to be able to give the turkey the sound he wants to hear."

You can prolong the life of your mouth calls by storing them in a cool, dark place—refrigerators are perfect—in the off-season. Some hunters stick flat toothpicks between the reeds to prevent them from sticking together.

BOX CALLS

Although Harris is skillful enough with a diaphragm to have won Missouri state calling titles, he uses a box call 85 percent of the time.

"I started calling in 1970 with a box my grandpa made for me, and I've used boxes ever since," he says. "Now, in the video age, I can watch turkeys on tape and really study the way birds react to calling. From what I've seen, it's easier to fire a bird up to a high level of intensity with a box call."

The box is a versatile instrument that can be played several ways. "I don't turn it upside down like so many callers do; that creates too

Even calling experts like Brad Harris rely on the easy-to-use box call. *Photo courtesy of Outland Sports.*

much movement," says Harris. "Instead I use the thumb of the hand I hold the call in as a bumper on the lid when I cutt. I also take off the rubberbands. They restrict you too much."

"Don't squeeze the box, cradle it lightly. That gives you the high-pitched, ringing sound birds respond to."

Morrett, on the other hand, feels he has better control when he turns his box upside down, and he likes to slide his thumb along the sides to dampen the sound as birds get closer.

"I like to tone down the box, because calling too loud makes a lot of turkeys hang up," he says, "and boxes can be very loud."

Slate calls make excellent clucks and purrs. *Photo by Julia C. McClellan.*

The volume of the box call does make it a great locator call, and there's another advantage to it as well: "You lose too much of your hearing when you use a mouth call," Morrett explains. "You can hold a friction call away from your ears and hear gobbles better."

The biggest weakness of a box call is that it simply won't work when it's wet, although a few new composite and aluminum boxes will run in the rain. Morrett's solution for wooden calls is to store the box inside a Ziploc bag. "On rainy days, you can use the call right inside the bag," he notes.

Besides keeping your box call dry, you have to keep it properly chalked. Don't use white blackboard chalk; it's often mixed with wax, which, rather than increasing friction, reduces it, deadening the call's sound. If your call starts to sound tired and muffled, take a green scouring pad (never use sandpaper) and clean the chalk off the lid and lips or rails of the call, then lightly rechalk it.

You can also tune a call by tightening or loosening the screw that holds the lid on the box, thereby moving the point at which the lid touches the curved sides of the call; fool around with it and you'll find the call has a sweet spot.

SLATE CALLS

Morrett switched to a slate call in the crowded woods of his home state of Pennsylvania because he thought turkeys were getting educated to the sound of mouth calls. Today, with five World Friction Calling Championships to his credit (as well as being the first ever to win the Grand Nationals with a friction call, in 1990) he's the acknowledged master of the slate.

"I like the slate call for everything; you can call loud and tone it down, it's a very versatile call, and it will make every sound of the wild turkey but the gobble. The tone and quality is built into a friction call, so all you need to learn is the rhythm," he says.

"Most people don't know you can throw your sound with a slate call. The sound comes out the bottom, so you hold the call up and aim it in different directions. Trouble is, you can't do it when the turkey's in close."

Like many hunters, Harris reserves the slate call for soft, close-in calling. "I like the slate call for quiet clucks, purrs, and soft yelps. Late in the season, when visibility is low because of the foliage and the turkeys have been hammered with calling, I'll get in close and call sparingly, one or two quiet yelps and clucks. It's a boring way to hunt, but it's extremely effective, and the slate is the best for soft calling."

Traditional slate calls and wooden strikers don't work well in wet weather unless you take precautions. "To use a slate when it's wet," says Morrett, "really rough the call up before you head to the woods, and be sure to carry a Plexiglas striker." Use sandpaper to rough-up a glass call, a scouring pad for slate. New carbon and aluminum slates are virtually waterproof and will keep on squawking in a downpour. They also produce the high-frequency sounds that are currently popular among hunters.

Morrett ordinarily carries three strikers with him into the woods so he can vary his sound as needed.

"I like to try to mimic the sound of the hens in a particular area. Sometimes I'll even try to imitate one specific hen I've heard while scouting. I think a tom recognizes the voice of a hen he's been meeting. If you can imitate her tone and rhythm, you can call that tom."

PUSHBUTTON BOXES

The pushbutton call is the easiest of all turkey calls to use. A raw beginner can make turkey sounds on one with a few minutes' practice.

"We [at Lohman Manufacturing] sell a gun mount pushbutton that works great for close-in calling," says Harris. "It fits under the gun barrel and you work it with a string. You can have your gun shouldered and call the bird all the way in with very little motion."

"We were all taught to shut up and make the bird look for us when he gets close," continues Harris, "but there are so many turkeys in the woods today that I believe you have to keep calling or you'll lose the bird to another hen."

"Pushbuttons are good confidence builders for beginning callers," says Morrett, "but I think people worry too much about sounding perfect. Real hens don't always sound very good." He adds, "I don't carry a pushbutton call in the woods because it's too difficult to control the volume; you only have two choices: Go loud or muffle the call against your leg."

TUBES AND WINGBONES

The tube call is a mouth call utilizing a latex reed, but it doesn't go inside the hunter's mouth, as a diaphragm does. Originally, tube calls were made from snuff cans or pill bottles with part of the top cut away and a piece of latex stretched halfway across. Tubes are good calls for people who want to use a mouth call but have gag reflexes that prevent them from using a diaphragm," says Morrett.

The tube is a great call to gobble with, although gobbling is not a safe practice in many parts of the country. Tube calls are great loca-

Alex Rutledge cutts on a tube call to locate turkeys.

tors and absolutely wonderful for cutting; once you've got the hang of the tube, all it takes is a light *"tut-tut-tut-tut . . ."* and you can cutt all day.

Wingbones were known to turkey hunters in America long before the arrival of Columbus, and they're traditionally made from three bones of a hen's wing. You suck on a wingbone to make a yelp. Experienced wingbone users—and there aren't very many of them—can make turkeys gobble at long range. The wingbone is difficult to master, but Morrett says he's seen wingbones make turkeys answer when no other call would.

Add to the calls that imitate the vocalizations of the turkey two calls that imitate the sound of birds moving through the woods. Simply raking leaves with your hand makes the sound of a turkey looking for acorns. Done at the right time, raking can drive a gobbler crazy, because he knows there's a hen nearby but she won't answer his calls.

Another old trick is to use an actual dried turkey wing, flapped to sound like a bird flying down from the roost or across a creek. Even brushing the wingtip lightly against the bark of a tree can make a roosted turkey gobble early in the morning. Two manufacturers now sell wing calls, so you no longer need to shoot a fall hen to make your own.

LOCATOR CALLS

Locating a turkey by making him gobble increases your chances and boosts your confidence. Turkeys gobble at provocative sounds, and most successful hunters carry a number of locator calls.

"I've found the crow call to be my best all-around locator," says Harris. "Coyote howlers are great for western birds, and good for eastern turkeys, too."

"Don't categorize your calls by time of day," Harris advises, noting that some hunters hoot only in the morning and evening and crow-call only at midday. "Use what works no matter what time of day, and be ready to try all three [categories of calls]."

"Stick with a short, distinct series. Call too much and you'll drown out the answer."

Morrett also uses crow calls and owl hooters. "I use crow calls at midday after I've made a bird gobble with a cutt; crow calls work best when a bird's already fired up. I'll crow-call as I'm moving in on the bird so I know where he is. I don't like to use hen calls when I'm on my way to a tom; I like to get in as close as I'm going to get, then call like a hen."

Pileated-woodpecker and peacock calls work too, even in areas where there aren't any pileated woodpeckers, much less peacocks. Bear in mind that turkeys gobble to all sorts of loud noises—sirens, gunshots, foghorns, thunder—and you should always pause and listen after any loud noise in the woods to see if it's startled a bird into gobbling.

Both Morrett and Harris carry a box, a slate with multiple strikers, several mouth calls, and two or three locators with them when they go hunting. Although an arsenal of calls increases the hunter's odds, both men have spent enough time in the woods to know that some days none of them work. Says Morrett: "If there were such a thing as a foolproof turkey call, most call makers would be out of business and turkey hunting wouldn't be any fun."

To which Harris adds philosophically: "There are some turkeys I just can't call if the time isn't right, no matter what I do. The real secret of game calling is to call them when they're ready to be called."

A Dictionary of Turkey Sounds

Turkeys communicate with a wide variety of noises, most sounding like a rusty gate squeaking shut. Hunters only need to know how to yelp and perhaps cluck to succeed in the woods, but if you visit a place, it's always good to learn the language. Here's a Turkey-to-English guide of the most common sounds, and their uses by both turkeys and hunters:

Cackle (15 or 20 yelps, starts very fast, then slows): Hens often cackle loudly as they fly up and down to the roost. Some hunters imitate the cackle early in the morning while beating their hat against their leg to simulate wingbeats.

Cackling at dusk can help you locate birds by making them gobble in response. A cackle at that time also sets the stage for the next morning, since the gobbler has heard a new hen (you) close by.

Cluck (like a chicken's cluck, usually with long pauses between each cluck): Turkeys cluck when they're happy, feeding, or just walking around. It's a soft, distracted sound, as if they were humming tunelessly. Clucks let other turkeys know where they are, in a low-key way. For hunters, clucks are good calls to use when birds have been pressured with a lot of aggressive calling.

The sound is a little popping noise. When gobblers cluck, it sounds as if they've got peanut butter stuck to the roof of their mouths. You'll often hear jakes gobbler-clucking when they come to a hen call.

Cutt (Cutts are a series of fast, syncopated *puck* sounds): Cutts are a series of sharp, syncopated clucks made by excited hens. You'll hear as many as 10 or 15 fast clucks when a hen cutts. Gobblers often respond to cutting by gobbling, making the cutt an excellent locator call and a call used by "run and gun"–style hunters.

Drumming (a *ffft* sound, then a low hum): Drumming is a humming sound made by the gobbler as he struts. It's a low-frequency hum, or so I'm told. Some people, myself included, can't hear drumming turkeys at all, no matter how close by they may be. Others can hear toms drum 100 yards away and, since turkeys will often strut without gobbling, it's a real advantage to learn to recognize the sound.

Gobbling (sounds like a high-pitched *Gil-obble-obble-obble;* hard to mistake for anything else): Turkeys actually gobble year round. Male turkeys gobble to assert dominance over one another, to stake out territories, to attract hens, and as a reflex, or "shock gobble."

Most gobbling occurs on the roost, especially in the morning but sometimes in the evening as well. Merriam's and Rio Grandes gobble all day long and generally more often than do easterns.

Some hunters will gobble at dominant gobblers to challenge them during the hunt or to locate them on the roost either in the morning or the evening. For safety's sake, always remember that the gobble call makes you sound exactly like the bird other hunters are trying to shoot; then decide if you really think it's a good idea to gobble at that time and place.

Kee Kee (three to five shrill whistles, sounds like *hurry, hurry, hurry*): Known as the whistle, it's a poult's attempt at a yelp. The high-pitched series of whistles, sometimes followed by a few yelps, is a very important call in the fall after you've broken up a flock.

Purr (a trilled *trrrrr* sound; turkeys often make several short purrs): Purrs, like clucks, are primarily contentment noises. Turkeys will cluck and purr about happily as they feed. Turkeys also purr loudly when they're angry, and gobblers will purr as they posture before and during a fight. Quiet clucking and purring works well on pressured birds.

So-called "fighting purrs" can bring gobblers in exactly the same way rattling horns attract whitetails.

Putt (sounds like *Putt!* or *pert!;* a short and explosive sound; turkeys usually make just one or two): Turkeys putt when they're nervous. A bird that's spotted danger—say, you, with a gun—will become quite agitated and putt. Beginning hunters live in terror of accidentally making the alarm putt, which differs only from the cluck in intensity. Don't worry about it; if you make a sound you think is a putt, just throw in some quiet clucks or purrs.

Some hunters will putt loudly on purpose to make a turkey come out of strut and stick his head up for a clear shot.

Yelps: (*yawk, yawk, yawk,* often a series of five to eight yelps): Along with the cluck, the yelp is the basic turkey noise. Hunters used to call hen yelps "love yelps" because they are the primary sound hens make to gobblers in the spring. Hens also yelp to gather their young. Gobblers yelp, too. Gobbler yelps are lower-pitched, coarser, and slower than hen yelps. If a gobbler yelps back to your calls, he may have mistaken you for a gobbler that wants to fight.

If you learn no other call, you can end up killing plenty of turkeys simply by yelping at them first.

3

Turkey Guns

"SHOOT HIM when you can," the guide whispered into my ear. No better time than the present: The gobbler stood just 25 yards away, his white head nearly glowing in the pale morning light.

The gun boomed. The turkey flew.

I had always wondered how people managed to miss wild turkeys. Now I know. Aim too high, jerk the trigger, raise your head, he's gone. A standing turkey should be a sitting duck, yet hunters miss gobblers much more often than you'd think.

Shooting turkeys into their bodies with big pellets cripples birds, and many states have banned the use of shot larger than No. 4 for safety reasons. Instead, you need to swarm a turkey's head and neck with a cloud of small pellets, relying on three or more of them to strike the brain or vertebrae.

TURKEY GUN CHOICES

Countless turkeys have fallen to long-barreled, full-choked duck guns over the years; however, most serious hunters shoot specialized turkey guns. Some like the simplicity of pumps, others prefer the recoil reduction of an autoloader. Since rate of fire doesn't matter in turkey hunting, a few hunters choose bolt actions or even single shots. What sets these guns apart? Three or three-and-a-half-inch 12-gauge chambers; short barrels for easier handling; supertight turkey-gun choke tubes; matte or camo finishes; and sling swivels. Most come with iron sights or are drilled and tapped for scope mounts. All the major manufacturers now make a turkey model of almost any pump or auto in their line.

This Remington 11-87 has all the features of a modern turkey gun: short barrel, extra-full choke, magnum chamber, front and middle beads, camo finish and a sling. *Photo courtesy of Remington.*

SIGHTS

At 20 yards, some turkey chokes jam almost 100 percent of the pellets into a clump so small you can cover it with both hands. Placing tight patterns effectively requires sights more sophisticated than a single plain bead. Not only will sights let you aim your pattern accurately, they can compensate for a barrel that doesn't shoot straight. I once owned an Auto-5 that shot so high I had to aim at a gobbler's toes to hit him in the head. A set of adjustable Williams "Slugger" sights on the rib made that gun into a fine turkey shooter.

If your gun has a front and middle bead, you at least have the benefit of two sights to align. However, iron sights, peeps, red dots, and even scopes work much better.

The newest aftermarket sights, by Tru-Glo, Hi-Viz, and others, feature fiber-optic beads that show up extremely well in low light. As of this writing, some Remington and Winchester guns were available with factory-equipped fiber-optic sights. The venerable Williams peep sight affords an even better view of the target than do iron sights. Just unscrew the rear disk and aim through the threaded aperture for quicker target acquisition early in the morning.

Battery-operated red-dot sights such as the Aimpoint appear on more turkey guns every year. Instead of crosshairs, these no-power scopes feature a bright red aiming dot. They're great early in the morning and extremely quick any time of day. If you choose a red-dot model, pick one with a large aiming dot. Dots are measured in minutes of angle (MOA). A 5 MOA dot, for instance, covers 5 inches at

A low-power scope can help you accurately place the tight patterns of modern turkey chokes. *Photo by Julia C. McClellan.*

100 yards. For turkey hunting, look for a dot in the 10 to 15 MOA size; it will show up much better than the smaller 1 to 5 MOA dots popular with handgun shooters.

When shopping for scopes, consider something in the 1 to 2.5x range. Several specialty turkey scopes have "circle-plexes" to help you estimate range. These are regular crosshairs with a circle the size of a shot pattern at 40 yards, superimposed.

There are a number of aftermarket, no-gunsmithing mounts available from B-Square and other manufacturers for most pumps and autos if you want to mount a scope or red-dot sight to your gun. Sev-

Modern turkey loads pack as much shot into a 12-gauge hull as old-time market hunters loaded into their 8-bores. *Photo by Julia C. McClellan.*

eral varieties of aftermarket iron sights and fiber-optic beads either clamp onto the rib of the gun or stick to it with powerful magnets.

TURKEY LOADS

The more pellets you sling at a turkey's head, the better your chances of putting two or three into his brain. In recent years, manufacturers have learned to cram up to 2¼ ounces of shot into 12-gauge hulls. In truth, the old 2¾-inch 1½-ounce magnums kill turkeys extremely well. The new stuff kills them deader (if that's possible), albeit at a hefty price in increased recoil. Nos. 4, 5, and 6 shot remain the most popular sizes. They have adequate energy to penetrate skulls and vertebrae, yet their pellet counts are high enough to ensure good pattern density.

Regardless of what load you choose, you need to pattern your

Turkey loads and chokes can swarm a gobbler's head and neck with multiple hits for clean kills. *Photo courtesy of Winchester.*

gun. Look for a shell that at your maximum range prints at least 16 hits above the feather line on your paper turkey-head target. Sixteen hits should ensure at least three hits in the skull and neck vertebrae. Briley Manufacturing's Chuck Webb says his company arrived at the 16:3 formula after shooting thousands of rounds at turkey-head targets while developing their turkey chokes.

Even the same box of 10 shells can produce surprising variation from one shot pattern to the next. Don't shoot one pattern and assume that's how your gun prints a particular load. Instead shoot, 3-, 5-, or even 10-shot strings to get a real idea of how your gun and choke perform.

PRACTICE

Outside of shooting a couple of test patterns, few hunters actually practice with their turkey guns. It pays to run a couple of boxes of shells through your gun, shooting paper turkey-head targets from various distances. Take a few shots while you're twisting around a tree. If you're right-handed, try some left-handed shots. It's very difficult for a right-hander to twist and shoot to his or her right side. You'll find it's much easier to switch shoulders without spooking a bird than it is to scoot all the way around the tree to get a bead on a turkey that sneaks in from your right.

Concentrate on keeping your cheek on the stock. When you aim at a turkey target, don't hold on the head. Instead, pick a point halfway down the neck. The center of your pattern will strike the neck while the top half hits the head. If you shoot high, there's a good chance you'll drop the bird with a head shot anyway. Also, with a midneck hold, you're less likely to miss if the turkey suddenly moves his head.

Do your shoulder and wallet a favor and practice with light trap loads. Just be sure to try a few magnums before the season to make absolutely certain they shoot to the same point of impact.

ESTIMATING RANGE

You can rely on most standard full chokes to kill turkeys cleanly at 30 yards and a step or two more. Superfull turkey chokes add 8 to 10 yards to your effective range.

Regardless of your choke choice, accurate range estimation is critical to good turkey shooting. Even the dense patterns of the superfull chokes loosen up quickly after a certain point. At long range, a few yards can make the difference between a sure-kill cluster and a patchy, marginal spread.

Since turkeys are big birds, lots of hunters underestimate range. To many people, a gobbler always looks closer than it really is. More than one southerner, accustomed to hunting 18-pound gobblers at home, has come up to the Midwest and seriously miscalculated the range on our waddling 25-pounders, shooting far too soon.

A West Virginia hunter told me last spring about watching through his new 4x scope as a bird came in. He waited until it looked as big as a Holstein in the crosshairs, then shot, only to find that in real-life 1x vision the bird was still 75 yards away.

Rather than judging range by the size of the turkey, you're better off picking range markers—trees, rocks, bushes—in a circle 30 yards away from your setup. Practice your range-estimating skills by picking objects in your backyard or on the sidewalk, guessing the range, then pacing off the distance. If you can't learn to estimate yardage fairly accurately, take a bowhunter's rangefinder into the woods. Choose a model like the Ranging R-60 Sureshot that accurately measures short distances, say, from 10 to 60 yards.

Finally, although closer is usually better, optimum shooting range at turkeys lies between 20 and 30 yards, where your pattern has an opportunity to open up a little. Let turkeys come into range, but don't let them sit in your lap.

MAKING THE SHOT

If you're right-handed, sit with your back to a tree, facing slightly to the right of where you expect the turkey to appear. Draw both knees up, rest the receiver of your gun on your knees, and tuck the butt lightly under your arm. (A padded sling, incidentally, can double as a gun rest to keep the sharp steel edges of the receiver from digging into your knee.) Ideally, you'll have to do nothing more than ease the gun forward and lower your face onto the stock when you're ready to shoot. With the gun balanced on your knee, you'll have a good solid shooting position, and one you can easily hold while waiting for the right moment to shoot. Try to move only when the turkey is behind a tree trunk or brush pile and can't spot you. Just before the shot, some hunters make a single alarm putt to make the bird stop and raise his head.

After you shoot, run to the bird quickly, and stand on his neck until he's done thrashing. Pick up a dead turkey while he's still kicking and you risk a nasty spurring. Every once in a while, your pattern may miss the brain and vertebrae but sever an artery instead. In that case, a fatally hit bird may run or fly off. Always assume you've hit any turkey you've shot at, and make a careful search for the body.

BLACKPOWDER SHOTGUNS, RIFLES, AND BOWS

Although most hunters carry pump or autoloading shotguns into the woods, you might someday choose to hunt with a rifle (where legal), a bow, or a blackpowder shotgun.

Rifles

Despite the heritage of Colonial turkey shoots and Sergeant York, rifles are fading from modern turkey hunting and today are legal in only a few states. If you do hunt turkeys with a rifle, choose one of the smaller .22s, such as the .22 rimfire magnum, .22 Hornet, .218 Bee, .222 or .223. Stay away from rapidly expanding varmint bullets, which ruin meat. Shoot a bullet that expands more moderately, or, if you're an absolute dead-eye, shoot solids and place them very carefully.

Try to shoot your bird at the base of the neck, which should result in a clean kill and little meat damage. It's an easy shot if the bird is facing right at you, trickier if he's sideways and you have to figure out where the feathers end and the turkey begins.

Bows

Luring a turkey into bow range and drawing on him without getting busted is one of toughest feats in all of hunting. That challenge motivates hunters like Will Walker of Primos Game Calls, who's hunted turkeys exclusively with a bow for 10 years.

Walker reduces his draw weight from 70 pounds down to 50 to 55 pounds when he switches from deer to turkeys. "It's easier for me to hold the bow at full draw," he says. "When you turkey-hunt, your muscles stiffen from long periods of sitting still."

Lately, Walker has changed over to expandable broadheads that stay in the turkey's body when the arrow strikes. Accuracy, he believes, should be the bowhunter's number one concern. "Shoot the broadhead you shoot most accurately," he advises.

Walker's favorite shot is broadside, at the butt of the wing. He also likes the rear-end shot when the bird is turned straight away from him. He cautions against shooting birds facing straight ahead. There's too much chance of the arrow glancing off the sternum and tearing through the breast, leaving only a deep flesh wound.

Will Walker with a Florida gobbler. Walker reduces the draw on his compound from 70 pounds to 55 for turkey hunting. *Photo courtesy Primos, Inc.*

Blackpowder Shotguns

Turkey hunting being a sport in which quick reloads don't matter, many hunters find that blackpowder shotguns add the perfect touch of nostalgia and extra challenge to the hunt. In truth, blackpowder guns can be loaded to deliver such excellent patterns that they hardly handicap the hunter at all. My Knight muzzleloading shotgun has a screw-in extra-full tube and shoots tighter patterns than any of my modern guns. To get the best performance from a blackpowder gun, you'll need a plastic shotcup that will protect the pellets from deformation as they travel down the bore.

I've found a shotcup designed for modern 3½-inch 12-gauge

Author took this 22-pound Missouri gobbler with a Modern Muzzleloading 12-gauge.

steel reloads that fits perfectly in my gun and holds nearly 2 ounces of shot. I load my powder, ram the shotcup into place, add shot, then push a plastic-foam overshot wad snugly on top of the whole load.

Consult your gun's manufacturer for maximum recommended loads. If you shoot an antique gun, talk to a good gunsmith before experimenting with different loads. Blackpowder is a much more forgiving propellant than modern smokeless powders. Part of the fun of shooting blackpowder guns lies in the freedom you have to mix and match various components while searching for the ideal load.

Although some new muzzleloading guns can be loaded to near-modern ballistics, you'll shoot your best patterns with fairly light powder charges, which translate into lower velocities and less energy retained downrange. Knowing I have only one chance, I try to limit my shots at turkeys with blackpowder to well under 35 yards.

You pick your perfect turkey gun, learn what it can and can't do, practice, and take your chances in the woods. Realize that if you chase turkeys long enough you'll whiff some birds. Think of it as part of the fun, or, at least, cultivate a philosophical attitude. One vastly experienced and well-adjusted turkey hunter tells me he's missed 1 out of every 10 turkeys over the years. He says: "When I stop getting so excited that I never miss anymore, it'll be time to quit."

Number of pellets in selected turkey loads

SHOT SIZE:	4	5	6
1¼ ounces	169	212	281
1½ ounces	202	255	337
1⅝ ounces	219	276	366
2 ounces	270	340	450
2¼ ounces	304	382	506

Scouting

S HROUDED BY the early morning darkness, I eased into a hollow in the trunk of an old locust tree that seemed to have been shaped with a turkey hunter's back in mind. Propping the shotgun on my knees, I waited and watched the sun rise, the gobbler 100 yards to my front sounding off so regularly as to almost become monotonous. Two hundred yards behind me, I heard the hen wake up and begin to yelp softly. The gobbler answered her. I clucked, he gobbled. Short story made even shorter: He hopped off the branch and strutted right in, gobbling to every call I made.

Even world champions will admit that the best way to be a good caller is to sit where the turkey wants to go. Put in your time scouting before the season, and you greatly increase the odds that your hunt will be a quick and happy one. I'd begun scouting that particular gobbler long before opening day. I knew where he roosted, and I knew where he went to meet his hens in the morning. I'd learned to find my way quickly into the woods in the dark, and I even had a comfortable tree picked out to sit against.

Turkey scouting often begins months before the spring season opens and lasts right up until the night before a hunt.

FALL AND WINTER: WHERE THE BIRDS ARE

You can start looking for places to hunt spring gobblers during deer season, with the following caveat: Good spring turkey habitat may hold no turkeys in the fall. Occasionally, you'll see turkeys in the fall

Steve Puppe glasses the Black Hills for Merriam's turkeys. A high vantage point like this one makes a good place to listen for gobbling, too. *Photo by Julia C. McClellan.*

in places where you won't find them come spring. Although eastern wild turkey don't migrate like Merriam's, they may move up to 2 or 3 miles from their winter to their spring range. Merriam's turkeys may travel 30 or 40 miles in the spring as they migrate from low to high elevations.

So, rather than looking for turkeys, look for good habitat. Turkeys were once thought to be birds of the big woods, but in fact ideal habitat for easterns includes a mix of mast-bearing hardwoods and clearings. Turkeys love pastures and hayfields; gobblers like to strut where they can be seen, while poults rely on the ready supply of insects they find in the grassy fields.

Late Winter, Early Spring: Setting the Stage

The more familiar you are with the terrain you hunt, the better your chances of calling toms into range. I've wasted plenty of time trying to call up turkeys that were, unbeknownst to me, on the far side of impassable obstacles, including, once, a golf course.

Buy a U.S. Geological Survey quadrangle map of your hunting area (write to: USGS Map Sales, Box 25286, Denver, CO 80225, or call 1–800-USA-MAPS). These topographic maps show elevations, water sources, and timbered areas. Carry a pocket notebook on scouting trips to record features of interest, then copy your notes onto your topo map at home. Mark creeks, sloughs, steep draws, brush piles, fences, and anything else that may prevent a turkey from coming to your call. A GPS unit is ideal for this type of scouting, as you can record the location of features of interest on the GPS, then transfer them to your map later. By studying the map before and after trips to your hunting grounds, you'll build a detailed picture of the area in your mind.

Now is also the time to learn your way around the woods so you won't get lost in the dark. Look for landmarks you can recognize before dawn, and memorize the location of that old strand of barb-wire that stretches across the trail.

Spring: Finding and Patterning Turkeys

As the season approaches, the hens will gravitate toward nesting spots, and the toms will begin to stake out their territories and gobble. You'll probably hear more gobbling in the weeks before the season begins than at any other time of the spring; birds will sound off all day as they challenge one another and fight. Now, with the birds easy to locate, you can begin looking and listening for actual turkeys to hunt.

Scouting is really pretty simple; just keep your eyes and ears open. As Hunter's Specialties Pro Ray Eye told me once: "Six weeks before the season comes in, you'll hear a bird start to gobble, then another one will answer a quarter-mile away. The gobbles get louder and louder as the birds get closer together. You'll hear a terrible fight, and the squirrels and jays and crows will all go nuts. Then the woods go quiet, and you'll hear one bird gobbling back to where he started. I make a note, *Here's where I'm going to hunt.*"

A gobbler's primary feathers can measure up to 18 inches.

Gobblers are big birds, and they leave big sign: 18-inch primaries, 4½-inch footprints, long, J-shaped droppings. Scratches in the leaves near mast trees tell you where turkeys have been feeding. Look for drag marks left by the wingtips of strutting gobblers; in dirt or sand they look like a mark you might make by spreading your fingertips and dragging them on the ground. Mark areas where you find plenty of sign on your topo map.

Piles of droppings beneath the branches of a tree indicate a roost. Although turkeys do not always roost in exactly the same tree, they often use the same general area. Turkeys prefer a hardwood with sturdy, horizontal branches as a roost, but I've seen them spend the night in all kinds of trees, including near-saplings no more than 10 feet tall.

Once you've determined where the turkeys are, you can start to pattern a few birds. Get out in the woods at dawn and listen for gob-

Turkeys leave big sign. A gobbler's footprints measure 4 to 4½ inches long.

bling. Note the direction a tom travels after flying down; he's probably on his way to meet his hens in a particular spot. Glass open fields later on in the morning, and you may see him strutting and gobbling at the same time and place every day, too. Learn his routine, and you can be waiting for him.

THE NIGHT BEFORE: ROOSTING A TOM

The final step in preseason scouting is to roost a bird the night before a hunt. At dusk, listen for gobblers gobbling on the roost, hens cackling as they fly up, and the unforgettable sound of huge wings lifting 20-pound bodies into the air.

Crow, coyote, owl and gobble calls will make roosting toms gobble, as will a gobble call. Some hunters like to imitate the fly-up cackle of a hen, both to provoke a gobble and on the theory that the turkey will come looking for the "hen" the next morning. If turkeys roost close to your position, wait until full darkness before leaving the area. The next day, arrive well before first light, and set up near the roost in the direction you believe the bird will travel. Roosting a bird is far from a sure thing if you don't have an idea which way he plans to go in the morning. If you have to guess, try to set up between the roost and the nearest open area where the turkey may go to strut. Although conventional wisdom says you should try to call a bird downhill, I've seen turkeys fly down from hillsides and head straight for the creek bottoms to strut in the flats.

Although many successful hunters are happy only if they have several turkeys patterned before the season begins (so they have backups in case someone else shoots "their" bird), any scouting you can do is better than no scouting at all. One year I didn't bother visiting my favorite river-bottom timber until opening morning, only to find my prime hunting spot under 3 feet of fast-moving water.

At the very least, you should know if you need to build an ark.

CHAPTER 5

The Dawn Patrol

LEANING BACK against the tree trunk, I've got the best seat in the house this morning. All around me crows caw, owls hoot, geese honk, cardinals call "fierce, fierce." A raccoon scuttles past on his way home to bed after a night's foraging. Cock pheasants sound off so close by I can hear their wingbeats as they stretch and crow like barnyard roosters. Every few minutes, the electric gobble of the turkey slices through the din in the busy timber: He's right where I left him last night, in the branches of a maple tree 100 yards up the creek bottom.

Straining my ears for the *woofing* of huge wings, I yelp quietly on the slate as soon as the turkey flies down. The tom gobbles back immediately. I answer, and he gobbles again 10 seconds later, the sound telling me he's closing the distance between us rapidly.

The tom first rolls into view atop a bank 45 yards away. He's blown himself up like a beachball and tilted his fan to catch the soft dawn light. He manages to look both majestic and faintly ridiculous at the same time, as only a strutting turkey can. The bird follows a deer trail down the bank, stepping daintily as if trying to negotiate stairs in heels and a hoopskirt. Once inside gun range, he obligingly stops, deflates, and looks around. The crash of the 12-gauge silences the morning woods, save for the thrashing of the bird in the leaves.

And that is how classic early-morning turkey hunting is supposed to go. You slip into the predawn woods and sit up against a tree 100 to 200 yards from a roosted gobbler. On the limb the turkey gobbles to owls, crows, other turkeys, the sunrise. He answers your calls, then flies down from his roost about the time the sun cracks the horizon. He struts into gun range, interrupting your every yelp with an eager gobble. When you put your tag on his leg, it's still at least an hour too early to call all your friends and tell them you've got a turkey.

While I've shot most of my gobblers before 6:30 in the morning, the magic hour at dawn isn't always the easiest time to bag a bird. Toms gobble hard early in the morning, so you know where they are. On the other hand, that gobbler often knows right where he's going first thing in the morning, and you're also faced with competition from real hens.

FINDING A TURKEY

If you haven't roosted a turkey the night before the hunt, you need to be up on a ridgetop or in an open field listening for turkeys to crank up in the morning.

The old advice was, that first gobble may be the only one you hear all morning, so get to it immediately. Hunters crashed through the darkened woods after the faintest gobble, ran up and down steep ridges, and forded icy streams to reach distant toms. Having grown up spoiled in an era of many turkeys, I wait until I think all the turkeys are awake and gobbling, then take my pick.

Although turkeys will gobble to crow calls, coyote calls, and owl hoots in the morning, it's often better to stay quiet and let them start on their own if possible so you don't alert them to your presence. Just because a bird gobbles—which he does out of reflex— doesn't mean he thinks a sound is natural. You could probably locate turkeys by yelling "Hey!" but you wouldn't kill very many of them.

Once you've started on your way to the bird, however, hoot- or crow-call as you move through the woods, both to pinpoint the location of the bird and to make sure there aren't other, closer turkeys around. One of my fondest turkey-hunting memories is of standing in the dark at the edge of a woodlot with Ray Eye, preparing to move in on a bird we'd heard gobble once. We held the following whispered conversation:

RAY (gesturing to a spot 50 yards away): Do you think we need to get over to that next ridge?

Many hunters try to set up above gobblers and call them uphill.

ME: I don't know Ray, he sounded pretty close to me.

RAY: I'll just hoot once. (Hoots softly.)

FIVE TURKEYS: (all within 50 to 75 yards): *Gobble, Gobble, Gobble, Gobble, Gobble, Gobble, Gobble, Gobble, Gobble, Gobble.*

RAY: (pauses, as if carefully pondering our next move): I think we should sit right here.

ME: (trying hard not to laugh out loud): You're the guide, Ray.

Twenty minutes later I put my tag on a 23-pound bird.

How close you set up to a tom in the morning can make the difference between success and sitting in the woods. M.A.D. Calls's Mark Drury likes to roost turkeys the night before a hunt, then sneak in well before dawn to sit within 60 yards of the bird.

"Once I started roosting birds and getting in tight on them the next morning, my success rate jumped way up," he says. "If you can get close and set up on the uphill side, when he flies down he'll

Flapping a wing in the morning to simulate a flying hen is an effective call.

almost be in gun range. All you have to do is convince him to walk a few yards in your direction."

Drury's approach has its risks; if you get too close to a bird, he might spot you, ending the hunt before it begins. I try to find a spot between 100 and 200 yards from a roosted turkey. Early in the season, when the branches are bare, a turkey in a tree can see a long way at first light. As the trees leaf out, however, you often can sneak to within 100 yards fairly easily.

Traditionally, hunters try to call either from above or from the same level or contour as the turkey. Follow that advice when you can, but always remember that it's more important to set up along the turkey's line of travel first thing in the morning. Ideally, you've scouted the bird and you know which way he goes after flydown. Usually, he'll head out to strut right away, so position yourself between the roost and an open field, creek bottom, ridgetop logging road, or oak flat.

Take a minute to clear a comfortable place to sit when you set up; you may be there awhile.

CALLING

Most hunters begin the morning hunt with a quiet, sleepy tree yelp, calling only once while the tom is in the tree. All you want to do is let him know where you are. He may gobble back, but even if he doesn't answer, you can be certain he's heard you. Even the tips of a turkey wing brushed against a tree trunk are enough to let a gobbler know there's a hen nearby. Wait until the tom flies down before yelping excitedly.

If he interrupts your calls, gobbling while you're in midyelp, keep calling; he's definitely interested. At the same time, if a gobbling turkey falls silent, don't assume right away that he's lost interest. Resist the temptation to crank him back up with the call. Instead, get your gun ready. When turkeys shut up, it often means they're on the way to you.

There are two schools of thought when it comes to calling turkeys: Some think less is more, others believe more is more. Neither school is right all the time. The first calling advice I ever heard was: "Yelp three times and shut up." That's old-school thinking, but it's still valid today. Call sparingly, scratch your hand in the leaves occasionally, and make the turkey come looking for you.

In many parts of the country, however, you'll face a problem old-time hunters never knew: too many turkeys. Call too little, new-breed hunters say, and you lose out to real hens. As hunting pro Eddie Salter puts it: "My theory is, a lot of times you call once or twice and you're waiting and waiting and here comes ol' mama hen on the next ridge and, *yawk, yawk, yawk,* big boy's gone with her."

While Salter enjoys his reputation as a caller who fills the woods with turkey talk, he also knows the value of silence: "I've had the opportunity to hunt with a ton of people, and even experts call too much when the bird's already committed and coming in. Really, the best thing to do if you know a bird's on the way is to shut up. I may crank a turkey up and get him hammering, but when he's coming in, I'm gonna let him come **in**. If you keep calling he'll stop right there and gobble and gobble and gobble."

HUNG-UP TURKEYS

Gobblers hang up; that is, they stand there and gobble at you without coming into gun range, for all sorts of reasons. The main reason, of course, is that you, the hen, are supposed to go to them. Also, though turkeys can easily fly across rivers, ravines, fences, and just about anything else, they're notoriously reluctant to cross obstacles to get to a hen.

By calling to a hung-up gobbler, you encourage him to stay in one place, strutting and gobbling. Try shutting up and waiting him out. If you absolutely have to call while giving him the silent treatment, rake the leaves with your hand. Then you'll sound like a feeding hen who's nearby but ignoring the gobbler. It should drive him nuts.

Sometimes you have to move to fool a hung-up gobbler. When birds hang up on Ozarks guide Alex Rutledge, he'll back away from the turkey while calling, as if the hen is walking away. Then, Rutledge stops and sneaks back to his original position, raking leaves to simulate a feeding bird. If he's guiding a client, he'll pull the same trick by walking away calling, then finding a place to sit 100 yards behind his hunter. Thinking the hen is getting away, the gobbler will come closer, walking right past Rutledge's waiting client.

Salter likes to circle behind hung-up turkeys. "If I call and he interrupts my calls, but he doesn't come in, he's telling me he's a killable bird, but some element's bothering him, maybe a stream or a ditch that he doesn't want to cross," says Salter.

"I'll use a crow call to keep him gobbling and move around him, staying about 200 yards away. I like to get on the very back side of the bird because he's already traveled that route one time and he'll come back through there. Most of the time, if I can get all the way around a bird I can kill him."

WEATHER

When you wake to thunder rattling the windows or, worse, the howl of the wind whipping through the trees, fight the urge to bury your head in the pillow and close your eyes again.

Turkeys, after all, don't like bad weather any more than we do. But they cope with it and carry on with their lives. In fact, cold snaps and even heavy snowfalls don't seem to bother them in the least. On the other hand, a chilly wet dawn keeps turkeys on the roost longer and makes them gobble less. So does heavy fog.

Downpours drive turkeys to shelter, although they'll ignore gentler, all-day rains, often heading to open fields and gobbling well into the morning. In fact, one of the best mornings of hunting I ever had was a wet, drizzly morning in Missouri. Turkeys answered calls all morning long.

Poll any 10 experienced hunters, and every one of them will tell you they hate hunting in the wind most of all. When the wind blows, you can't hear the turkeys and they can't hear you. Unable to listen for danger, turkeys turn paranoid. Look for them in the fields or holed up in draws down out of the wind. Call loud and listen hard.

Back before I knew any better, I hunted in a spring storm when 45 m.p.h. winds drove the rain sideways in thick, stinging sheets. Gusts ripped heavy branches off trees, dropping them onto the ground with soggy, crashing thumps.

Through it all, I heard a bird gobbling, the sound snatched away by the wind almost before it registered as a turkey sound. That tom felt the urgency of the season, as if he knew spring is too short and unpredictable to wait for the perfect day. If turkeys can teach us a lesson in life, I believe that's it.

6 CHAPTER

Midday Turkeys

B Y MY COUNT, Toby Bridges and I sat within earshot of a dozen gobblers at the edge of a burned field in northeast Missouri one clear, still morning last April. All around us, turkeys gobbled and clucked back and forth to one another, busily arranging rendezvous in the timber. When Bridges chipped in with some yelps of his own, two toms, invisible no more than 50 yards away in the brush behind us, gobbled back in unison. They answered every one of his calls eagerly, but in between gobbles we could hear the scolding yelps of an old hen who wouldn't let either bird leave her side. Bridges switched tactics and began trading insults with the hen, providing a whispered simultaneous translation from Turkey to English for my benefit. After an hour of heated bickering, the hen tired of the argument, turned snootily on her heel and lead both toms away, their gobbles eventually fading out in the distance. The woods grew quiet.

Left to my own devices, I would have done what many frustrated hunters do: declared the morning an exciting failure and gone home to bed. To quit early, I was about to learn in a most dramatic fashion, is to miss some of the best hunting of the day.

Bridges was far from discouraged. "In 30 years of hunting, I've probably called in more birds after 10:00 or 11:00 in the morning than I have at dawn," he told me as we left the field. "If we can find the right bird, he'll come running. What we do now is shop around 'til we find a hot turkey."

The hills of Putnam County aren't particularly steep, but there certainly are a lot of them. By lunchtime, Bridges had led me up one side and down the other of most of them twice, stopping every 150 yards or so to call.

Steve Pollick uses a box call to draw a gobble from an Ohio turkey. Walking and calling at midday can be an effective way to locate birds. *Photo by Julia C. McClellan.*

"Don't worry," he said confidently over his shoulder as he strode up yet another hill. "We'll pry a gobble out of a bird here yet."

Toiling up the slope behind him, I sneaked a look at my watch: 12:30, just half an hour before Missouri's 1:00 closing. I doubted we'd have time to set up on a bird and call it in even if Toby could make a bird gobble. Since my job on this hunt was to carry the gun and do what I was told, I kept my mouth shut and followed dutifully.

Bridges paused at the top of hill to yelp loudly on his box call and listen for an answer. "Lights are on, but nobody's home," he remarked, not for the first time on that long day. One hundred yards down the logging road, he purred and clucked softly on a mouth call. Immediately a loud gobble rattled back at us through the empty timber, its source no more than 70 yards away.

"That's a turkey!" I blurted involuntarily and altogether too loudly, sort of a human-shock gobble, and we scrambled to set up against the nearest tree.

Three soft yelps and 5 minutes later (including time spent shaking hands and slapping backs) I was, to my complete astonishment, fixing an out-of-state tag to the leg of a 24½-pound gobbler.

Welcome to midday turkey hunting.

Why Midday?

Gobbling, it's true, peaks during the first few hours of daylight. Early morning may be the easiest time to locate a bird and set up, but it can also be the hardest time of day to call a turkey into range. Most gobblers meet hens first thing in the morning at a predetermined spot. After flying down from the roost, toms may answer your calls excitedly while heading off in the opposite direction, urging you to follow along where their hens are waiting. Once a tom is actually with his harem, he has no reason to go look for another hen. In the natural scheme of turkey behavior hens go to the toms, not vice versa. The presence of other hunters in the woods early in the morning can also complicate our plans.

Later in the morning, however, hens wander off to sit on the nest, and gobblers find themselves at loose ends. From about 10:00 in the morning on, if you can locate these lonely toms you stand a good chance of calling them in. Moreover, you'll have very little competition from real hens or other hunters.

Don't give up at noon if your state allows afternoon hunting. Turkeys will gobble and come to a call all day long; shortly after our hunt, Bridges shot an Iowa gobbler at 4:00, using the same tactics he'd shown me.

Midday Tactics

Pro Mark Drury is another hunter who's tagged many birds between 10:00 A.M. and 1:00 P.M. Like Bridges, Drury swears by "running and

Author with a 24½-pound gobbler killed at midday. Notice the high-noon shadows.

gunning" for turkeys. "I think it's just a case of covering the ground and trying to up the odds," he says. "You're trying to find the right tom in the right place. I think running and gunning works best later in the spring, when the leaves are coming out and some of the hens are done breeding, but I'd always rather keep moving and make something happen than sit and call blind." If you run and gun in crowded woods, for safety's sake, wear blaze orange as you move through the timber, making noises like a turkey.

How Drury hunts depends on the land. "If I've got a big national forest to hunt," he says, "I like to cover as much ground as possible. If I'm confined to a smaller area, I'll be more patient. There's a 200-acre farm I hunt, near Warsaw, Missouri, where the fences have been bulldozed all along the perimeter. I'll walk the boundaries and stop and call for an hour in each of the four corners. That way I'm not just hunting that farm but calling to birds on adjacent properties. That 200 acres can make a good morning's hunt."

When he's moving at his preferred pace in the big woods, Drury stops to call for 5 minutes every 200 or 300 yards. On windy days, or any other time there's a lot of background noise (say, while hunting near a busy highway), Drury stops even more often, moving only 50 to 100 yards between calling sites. "When there's lots of background noise, a turkey that couldn't hear you when you called 50 yards back up the trail might hear you from your closer position," he notes.

I described my own hunt to Drury, telling him how Bridges's series of loud yelps 150 yards down the trail went unanswered but that a quiet cluck and purr brought an immediate response. "I've seen that happen many times," he said. "You know the turkey must hear you coming, but he doesn't answer until you're right on top of him. I think he hears the hen coming closer and closer and finally gobbles to say, "Here I am. Don't pass me by."

Some hunters work a variation on running and gunning by hunting their backtrails. By retracing their steps they hope to draw gobbles from birds that may have heard them calling as they walked through the woods earlier, and they don't want to let the "hen" get by them again.

Tony Knight of Modern Muzzleloading in Centerville, Iowa, has the most relaxed approach to midday hunting I've heard of. Knight hunts in the early morning, then returns to the shop on his farm at 8:00 or so and putters around. "A lot of times the turkeys will crank up again and gobble about 10:00 or 11:00. I keep my bibs and boots nearby like a fireman," he says. "When I hear them start gobbling again, I jump into my gear and go."

CALLING

As Mark Drury runs and guns through the woods, he begins with a crow call, then switches to soft yelps, increasing the volume if he gets no response. "I like to start with a crow call because I'd much rather strike a bird without sounding like another turkey. That way, I can take a little more time to set up without bumping a bird that's looking for me." While some hunters prefer to start out with a loud, aggressive call, hoping to shock a bird into gobbling, Drury likens calling to climbing a ladder. "Start at the bottom and go up [in volume] rung by rung. It's hard to go back down if you start out too loud, but you can always make the next call a little louder."

Cutting is a popular call for many hunters trying to provoke a gobble, but both Drury and Bridges stick primarily with yelps. Says Drury, "I'd say 90 percent of the turkeys I call in come to a series of yelps. That's the backbone of turkey calling. If my yelping hasn't brought a response I'll sometimes mix in some cutting at the end."

Bridges agrees with Drury: "A lot of hunters want to master all the sounds of the wild turkey and wind up not making any of them really well," he says. "Me, I'd rather be the best yelper in the woods. I do like to mix in some purrs and clucks, because I think that's more natural; hens don't just yelp all the time, and I think a tom knows there's something wrong if he doesn't hear some clucking and purring in between the loud yelps."

WHEN TO LEAVE THEM

When they're using run-and-gun tactics, both Bridges and Drury will give up quickly on birds they deem unenthusiastic. "I call that first gobble from a bird a 'courtesy gobble,'" says Drury, "If he answers just once and doesn't make any sign of coming closer in 10 or 15 minutes, that's a sure indication to me that he's with hens and won't be coming at all. Then I'll leave him and look for another bird. Of course, if I'm hunting a small area and I can't pick and choose my turkeys, I'll be more patient with any bird I get to gobble, even if he doesn't come in right away."

On another midday hunt with Bridges, we struck a bird on our very first call. Bridges couldn't make the turkey gobble again, so we shrugged and set off on our way. An hour and a half later, we'd made a big loop and were coming back to the spot where we'd first heard the gobbler answer. And there he was, standing on the logging road, still looking for the "hen" he'd heard earlier. If we'd sat down when we first heard the gobble and waited that turkey out, we might have eventually killed him.

Alex Rutledge examines fresh tracks. Sometimes setting up near fresh sign and blind calling works well at midday, especially near open fields.

Some hunters prefer to sit for long periods in good habitat in the middle of the day. They point out that most of the turkeys they kill come in silently. A run-and-gun type of hunter will walk right past any number of silent but callable turkeys and never even know they're there. Perhaps the most pleasant way to hunt turkeys is to combine the two methods; walk and call until you find a place to sit and call quietly for 45 minutes or so.

Which method works best? My theory is this: In areas with high turkey densities, sitting still might be more effective. There are so many turkeys that gobblers don't have to run all over the woods looking for hens. By the same token, running and gunning might work better in areas where turkeys aren't as plentiful and where toms will travel a long way to meet a lonely hen. How you hunt depends on your own preferences, too. If you hate sitting still, walk. If patience is your strength, sit.

"I might get a little antsy sometimes and leave a bird too soon," Bridges admitted to me, "but running and gunning is a system that works for me. If I leave a bird I'll remember where he is and come back to him an hour or so later. Sometimes the commotion of calling to a bird with hens sets the stage for later on in the day. He'll remember the "hen" he heard earlier and come looking for her once his own hens have left him."

Ponder that for a moment. How many times have you unknowingly made a date with a tom for later in the morning, then stood him up by going home to bed? Imagine him out there, mooning around the woods, gobbling his head off forlornly, looking for you. That's a thought to keep you out in the timber long after dawn, isn't it?

Fall Hunting

OUR FOREFATHERS hunted turkeys the year round, but we are, by and large, a nation of spring turkey hunters today. Folks who've never tried a fall hunt disdain the idea of shooting hens and poults. The real excitement of turkey hunting, they sniff, lies in hearing the birds gobble.

I am here to tell you that the sight of 25 turkeys piling over a hilltop intent on kicking your tailfeathers will change your mind about fall hunting in a hurry.

So will sitting stock-still at the scatter point not knowing which way to turn as unseen turkeys whistle to relocate one another all around you. If you ever set up under 60 or 70 roosted birds on a fall morning, you'll hear more varied turkey sounds (including gobbles) in an hour than you'll hear in a whole spring season.

When you finally shoot a 10-pound hen or a bird of the year and roast it whole, you'll start to wonder why we ever bother with those big ugly gobblers in the spring at all. Not only that, the lessons you learn in the fall will make you a better hunter come spring.

SCATTERING THE FLOCK

The classic method of fall hunting is scattering a flock. What you do is, and I'm not making this up, spot a flock, sneak in close, then run into the middle of it, screaming, waving your arms, perhaps even shooting into the air. If you've done it right, turkeys flush in all directions. Then you sit down and call them back.

It's imperative, however, that you really do scatter the flock. If

Eleven states allow the use of dogs in the fall season to scatter flocks. This trained turkey dog then waits patiently inside its camouflaged bag. *Photo by Julia C. McClellan.*

they all fly off together, or, worse, run away as a flock, you're out of luck. You need the turkeys to be looking for each other and trying to regroup for this method to work. While you can bust up a flock any time of day, many hunters like to scatter birds as they're going to roost at night, returning first thing in the morning to set up and call. Others like to slip in to the roost early in the morning and break up the flock right after flydown.

Pick a tree close to the scatter point, set up and wait 5 minutes and start to *kee kee* or use the "assembly call," a long series of 15 or more hen yelps. Think "lost" and try to get some plaintive urgency into your calling. Very shortly, you'll hear birds around you whistling and looking for one another.

It's possible to scatter flocks of gobblers, too. Longbeards fre-

Ray Eye packs out a fall gobbler. *Photo courtesy of Ray Eye.*

quently spend the fall in bunches of six or seven. You can call them with the same tactics you use on the young of the year, but you'll need an extra dose of patience to do it. Scattered toms might not start looking for one another for up to an hour after the flush, and they'll take their time coming to your slow, coarse gobbler yelps.

New York and Virginia are the strongholds of fall hunting with dogs; the concept is the same as a normal fall hunt, but the dog does the legwork. A turkey dog (and yes, it is a breed) covers the woods, sniffs out turkeys, and charges into the flock. After they scatter, the dog remains at the flush site, barking so the hunters can find him and set up. From there on out, the caller takes over, just as in a dogless hunt. The dog, his work done, crawls into a camo bag and waits with the hunter in case he's needed for a retrieve. Fall hunting with dogs, alas, is legal only in a handful of states.

PECKING ORDER

Scattering the flock isn't the only way to hunt fall turkeys.

"Where I grew up in the Ozarks, you might hunt four or five days without seeing a turkey. It didn't make any sense to me to run 'em off once I finally found 'em," says Ray Eye. Rather than scattering turkeys and recalling them, Eye takes advantage of the turkey's highly developed social structure to call in whole flocks of birds.

"Turkeys are just like dogs or deer," Eye explains. "The flock has a rigid pecking order, and each bird has its own secure place in their little turkey world. If you can get close to a flock and sound like a new turkey, they'll try to call you to them. When you don't go to them, they'll come to you, running, posturing, purring, curious to see who you are and where you'll fit into their social order."

In the fall, gobblers, jakes, and hens all gather in separate flocks. Calling like a hen to fall gobblers brings no response; to upset the pecking order, you need to be a new gobbler. Same thing with jakes and hens.

Eye always begins a fall hunt at dawn, close to a roost. "Every morning when they wake up they have to fuss and bicker for an hour, sorting themselves out and getting the whole flock organized," says Eye, "They can't go on about their day until every bird is in its proper place."

If the early morning hunt doesn't produce a turkey, Eye will walk and call, just like a spring hunter trying to strike a gobbler. Eye's basic fall locating call is a long series of plaintive yelps, a generic lost call. When turkeys respond, he answers in kind—replying with hen calls to hens, jake calls to jakes—mimicking the bird's calls and upping the intensity with each exchange. To make Eye's style of hunting work, you need to get close and call aggressively.

One October afternoon I followed Eye, scuttling half-crouched across a northeast Missouri pasture, as we tried to get around a flock of birds we'd spotted heading into a wooded draw. "Sit there," he whispered, "there" being a patch of bare pasture in grass roughly the height of the manicured turf on a putting green. When Eye yelped, the flock of young birds responded with whistles. Eye countered, trading whistled insults with the unseen birds until we could hear them running up the side of the draw, feet rattling the dry leaves, making as much noise as a dozen men sprinting toward us. The flock crested the hill, led by an old hen, who skidded to a halt when she spotted us, then took off on the run. "Shoot that one," commanded Eye, so I did, after which he made fun of me for shooting the only hen in the bunch. Me, I could care less; that hen was a trophy from one of the most exciting turkey hunts I've ever been on, and she was a lot easier to carry out of the woods than a 22-pound gobbler anyway. Incidentally, the flock had scattered at my shot, and 20 minutes later Eye *kee keed* in a young bird for the other hunter who was with us that day.

If your conscience or vanity doesn't permit you to shoot a hen or bird of the year, Eye can tell you how to call up a fall longbeard.

"People kill hens in the fall because they make hen calls," he explains. "If you want to shoot a fall longbeard, you have to talk gobbler talk."

Gobbler yelps don't always sound like the long, low croaks you hear in contests or on instructional tapes. Actually, they're similar to hen yelps, but each yelp is drawn out, and at a slower cadence. Like hens, gobblers will also putt and cutt when they're excited. For gobbler calling, Eye uses a call with a clear tone and a raspy finish.

Spring hunters know gobblers will be near hens, but that's not true in the fall. "Gobblers are no different than mature whitetails," Eye points out, "They keep to themselves. You won't find fall longbeards in the same place you see hens, jakes, and poults."

Eye advises fall gobbler hunters to look for 4- to 4½-inch tracks, big droppings, and black-edged breast feathers. Find the roost and their food source, then try to get in between them on the turkey's line of travel. If you're pushy enough on the call, six or seven mature gobblers might just run to you, beards swinging, ready to fight. Make them really mad, and they'll strut and gobble as they come in, even though it's mid-October and the leaves are glowing red and gold.

FALL TACTICS FOR SPRING TURKEYS

The lessons learned in October can help you tag a gobbler in April.

Eddie Salter, another Hunters Specialties pro-staffer, likes to use the scatter on tough, henned-up gobblers in the spring.

"I go in at dusk and scatter the gobbler and his hens off the roost. I feel like we're athletes playing a sport and that tough turkey has the home field advantage. If I scatter him off his home field, I break him out of his routine, and the next morning when he wakes up he won't have those hens sitting right there with him. He'll act like a completely different bird. Most of the time when you scatter a gobbler like that, you kill him 20 minutes into the hunt the next day."

Turkey pecking-order tactics work year round as well. In fact, Eye first learned to use pecking order to his advantage on a spring morning in the Ozarks, 25 years ago.

"I was watching my brother call to a gobbler with hens out in a field. Marty was doing a fine job of calling, but the gobbler wanted to strut with his hens." Eye, meanwhile, was trying to figure out a way to shoot his brother's bird; pecking order is pretty important in some human flocks, too.

"A pair of toms appeared at the far edge of the field, and one yelped. My brother's gobbler dropped out of strut, ran to the end of the field, chased one bird off, beat the stuffing out of the other, then came back to his hens. I snuck around to that end of the field and made the same gobbler yelp. Marty's came running. He was ready to whip me. Isn't it just like a turkey to bring spurs to a gunfight?"

Whether you hunt in the fall to tune up for spring or to learn more about your favorite bird, you'll quickly discover fall hunting to be very much its own reward.

FIELD & STREAM

The Complete Hunter

Book Three

Upland Bird Hunting

William Tarrant

Gimmicks, Gear, and Garb

MY WORLD is God-made-man. I want my life natural—and all that touches it. Man-made-man is the norm today: plastics, polymers, prosthetics, silicon-enhanced and cloned.

Once boats were powered by wind, sleds were pulled by dogs, and big-game hunts were taken on horseback. Now we've got ear-splitting engines and stenchy fuels, and tomorrow will offer some new device that costs 20 times what it's worth and robs us of 90 percent of our outback pleasure.

So I'm going to tell you how to go afield, but you do what you want. Nobody's told me what to do in the boondocks since the Marine Corps, and I accord you the same latitude.

RULES FOR ATTIRE

There are some rules to this game.

1. The ultimate yardstick for hunters is how well they wear their mud. In other words, fancy doesn't cut it: Function does. Wear what works.
2. The most effective and comfortable way to stay afield, bar any fashion designer's notion, is layered. Wear successive layers of light clothing, which can be shed as the day warms or as your activity increases. If you sweat, you're losing it: The test is that simple.
3. Boots are the single most important item you can buy and wear. They must be sure-footed for traction, supportive of your

unique feet and ankles, and comfortable for a limitless trek. Young guys don't necessarily need them, but older hunters better slip in orthopedic inserts.

Socks worn with boots must wick away moisture (perspiration), move fluidly with the inner lining, and stay fitted. Forgo the socks that bunch and sag and stretch to two extra sizes.

Thanks to modern technology, boots and socks are now made of miracle fibers and materials. If that's what you want, go for it! I don't. Cotton and wool have sustained us for centuries. Why should I abandon them? As a matter of fact, God chose wool, fur, feather, and leather to cover and protect the birds and beasts—whose world you're entering. Why take less than the best God could give them?

LITTLE THINGS

I once accompanied Hawaiian Watson T. Yoshimoto, Weatherby Award Winner and Bird Dog Field Trial Hall of Fame honoree, on a Mongolian hunt for argali sheep. Yoshi had a master list and a specific location for every item in each of his four safari bags. In the dark of night, he could zip one open, insert a hand, and immediately touch a tube of sunscreen—or sunglasses, lip salve, Kleenex, gun oil, anything he needed.

I always marveled at his packing and his book keeping. And on many trips I had to listen to his repeated logic on why I should become equally accountable. I tried, and over many hunts did improve, but never to match this master of inventory location.

TRAVEL LIGHT

There's seemingly no end to what you can tote. I remember the overweight charge on Yoshi's luggage from Moscow to Ulan Bator, Mongolia, could have paid for his new pickup. But I understood why Yoshi needed all that stuff, since every place he hunted was novel and exotic, and every shot he took was an attempt for a world record. Everything had to be right.

Me? I was looking for adventure and something different to eat for the night's kerosene-lighted dinner.

And I still am. So I advise you to do as I do, and travel light. I'm overloaded with a PayDay candy bar and an apple. If I could take only one thing on a hunt, it would be toilet paper. Second place would go to insect repellent.

THE GUN

I'm not going to be much help for you in this category. I use guns to paddle boats, push down barbed wire so I can get a leg over—I'm only 5 feet, 7 inches—and shuck the shells, then stick out the unloaded gun to steady a buddy who's hung up and tottering in a stream.

Mostly what I care about a gun is, will it shoot? Sure, I'd like the least weight, most balanced swing, and a design that fits perfectly in my shoulder, but other than that, so what?

My favorite gun is not a side-by-side heirloom; no, I want an automatic. I use a lightweight Franchi 20 gauge for bobwhite, for example. And I shoot a Remington 12-gauge auto for pheasants, prairie chickens, grouse, and anything else that takes lead to drop.

I shoot predominantly low-brass 7½s for quail and load a 6, plus two 4s, for pheasants. The theory is that the 7½s will drop the quail from flush to 30 yards, and for the pheasant 6 will have maximum spread for the first shot and long range, with tightly grouped 4s for the go-away hope. Lead has been the hunter's mainstay in shot for decades, but some states won't permit it anymore, even for upland game. Check the regulations.

There's not a type of gun I've not carried afield. In my gun cabinet are over-and-unders, side-by-sides, pumps, even single shots. But as you grow, your needs change. Being there eventually becomes more important than scoring there. And where you once handled complicated hardware, now you want it light and simple. For example, I hate new cameras with too many confusing functions and buttons. And as for rental cars, I can sit in the garage and experiment for an hour before I dare pull out.

I once asked an attendant to help me. He said, "You're in an Avis, I'm Hertz." "So?" I said. He stared at me and explained, "I don't do nothin' with other company's cars." I asked him, "Ever think of just being a good Samaritan?" He thought a minute, and I was on my way. He'd showed me where all the secret buttons were hidden.

Another time in a motel I learned you couldn't turn on the hot tub unless you were sitting in the tub: it took your body weight plus the switch. Oh, for the natural simplicity of a farm pond!

THINGS FOR PUP

And as for the law—I mentioned it before, in regard to the shot in shells—bright orange is now required for bird hunting in most locales. You need it on your cap, shirt, vest, and/or jacket—enterprising retailers even sell it on game bags or shell bags.

You and Pup can share the same water and energizer supplies—that is, if you fill some large gelatin capsules, obtainable from your vet, with honey, and you and Pup pop one about every two hours.

Cactus can immobilize Pup just as though he had a seizure. Carry tweezers to pull out the thorns. Such dogs could use rubber or leather boots, which do work. You tape them to the ankle fur. Other dogs may get tantalized with porcupines; you'll need pliers to pull out the quills.

Wire cutters prove an asset when Pup gets hung up in a barbed wire fence. Oh yes, it happens. And the dog won't take too kindly to you piddling around. Immobilize him with a blanket and cut the wires.

Some dog handlers (especially woodcock and ruffed grouse hunters) want a bell attached to Pup's collar. Others are satisfied with an orange nylon collar. And there's an element who want a beeping collar that you can hear or one that transmits a signal to your electronic receiver. They want to lessen the chances of losing a great dog.

The basic tools for hunting Pup (or training him, for that matter) also include a wide nylon collar with welded D-ring and a check cord ending in a swivel snap. Collar and cord will do it all.

Finally, there's some nonsense being advertised out there. How about a raincoat? Can you believe it? Or how about this: an antenna that attaches to Pup's collar—you can see that thing whipping about way out there. But so can Pup's bracemate, and now you've developed a trailer.

Carry your dog to and from the field in your car. Sure, you can put him in your pickup bed, but I worry about his safety back there. See if you can't get him inside. Knowing the nature of dogs, they'd make sure you were inside if they were the driver.

More will be said about gear and guns and dogs as we go from one bird species to another. Why, heck, we may stop the hunt and train Pup a bit.

Let's get started.

Bobwhite Quail

THE MONARCH of game birds is the bobwhite. This quail has an adulation borne of many things. The familiar call at dawn in the hollow behind the home place. You're taking a break from the hunt, sitting in a country graveyard, eating your lunch, then notice a bobwhite perched on a nearby tombstone. The bird is part of us.

Plus, there's the scat, the burst, the missed heartbeat as the covey scrambles up from a dog's encroachment or a kicked boot. Years ago, during the Depression, you could buy a shotgun shell or two at the crossroads store and hope to drop two "pottiges" after work. That way we could also have quail at dinner.

Those were the bobwhite's tattered subjects, but the titular element secured the bird's crown.

177

The Gentry

There are mansions with manicured savannas all over quail country, great plantation houses bought and dedicated and planted and pathed and fenced and framed by tall pine in continual pastoral murals—just for the bobwhite.

Remember when Hobart Ames, the toolmaker from Braintree, Massachusetts, bought the Ames plantation at Grand Junction, Tennessee, arriving each fall in his private railroad car and entourage to have a go at the quailey bird? The grounds are now the home of the National Bird Dog Championship, run exclusively on bobwhite.

I remember a long-ago noon, walking out on the front porch of the clubhouse at the Dixie Plantation as Mrs. Livingston was delivered by her chauffeur in her black 1937 Chevrolet sedan. She stuck out her wrist for anyone to take and walked with caution into the shack.

She stood a while to catch her breath, to find a propelling strength, then spoke in fractured voice: tinkling and cryptic, like thin, breaking glass, as she wished us all to her Continental Championship. And we all bowed. We were rough men in mud-caked boots with red and white demarcations on our foreheads where our brimmed hats sit day on day as we rode in the saddle, handling bird dogs.

Wealth

But I'm talking about Mrs. Gerald M. Livingston because of wealth. It seems wealthy people like bobwhite. One handler told me that Mrs. Livingston owned the land under the Empire State Building. I don't know. Maybe she did, maybe not.

The reason I know she was rich was the black 1937 Chevy sedan. I was there in 1975, and no one else had a 40-year-old car. Only the affluent can afford to keep 40-year-old cars on the road, in mint condition.

Well, such vignettes make up part of the bobwhite's royal trappings. Just like John Olin's plantation at Albany, called Nilo. And the physical plant he built and kept to perpetuate this little bird. Plus the wizard he hired for game management: Francis Frazier, an old-time dog trainer. The big trucks loaded with corn, driving the country lanes, the aft propellers splattering corn everywhere for the demure birds to eat. And Francis tending his flash cameras to learn what predators were eating the quail eggs or killing the chicks. Incidentally, it proved to be opossum.

"Damn the Rich"

I smile when I hear the poor cuss the rich. They don't know the philanthropy spent on birds or bird dogs, or the knowledge learned by an old scion who wants the best quail hunting in the state. That's where we get our advancements. But many people still cuss them.

I remember when Olin wanted to know what was "killing those damned bird dogs in the kennels." Then he called the veterinary school at Cornell University and told them he was writing them a $1 million check to find out the cause, and how to stop it. That's how the world got the distemper vaccine: all because of bobwhite.

So there's no monarch without subjects. And those are en masse for bobwhite, from the sharecropper to the international banker. They all go afield with a shotgun, a dog, and a hope, looking for that little band of birds at dawn, all bunched up, keeping their heads down, their breathing stopped so the dogs won't smell their breath. (Actually, the dog is scenting the feces the birds have dropped—that's what slams a dog to point in a scent cone, the droppings.)

The Hunt

To hunt them best, the savvy hunter knows the time of day and matches that to the schedule of the birds. They arise, look for breakfast, dust to rid themselves of minute vermin. If in season, they seek a mate; otherwise they search for cover, especially with an overhead canopy to thwart hawks. Hawks are their main fear. The federal government protects all hawks; is the federal government the bobwhite's worst enemy?

If you find an early-morning covey of quail still circled and holed up from night's rest, just sail your hat over them. Let them but sense the shadow, and see them duck and freeze. Hawks are their doom.

The Dirt Bird

Bobwhites are the ultimate dirt bird. They demand bare ground. It facilitates feeding, enhances their ability to see insects, keeps their

Field Trial Hall of Famer Wilson Dunn, from Grand Junction, Tennessee, takes a second bobwhite to hand from a future trial prospect.

feet dry, lets them move about easily, and provides them rapid transit lanes and dusting areas.

Quail spend most of each day walking about, scratching the soil, feeding on the round. Many quail can go days without having to fly. They literally walk from their roost and stay to ground until dusk.

Also, in the spring, chicks will be 1 to 2 inches high. If they were hindered by a heavy mass of grass, they couldn't travel or scratch or peck for food. Chicks must also be kept dry, or they can sicken and die. Bare dirt is the best nursery.

THE EDGE

There are two truths about all game birds. One, they don't dawdle at dawn. It's up and at 'em. And two, they feed at the edge. That is, wherever there's a break in cover, some distinct demarcation between one type of cover or feed and another type. This is where you'll usually find the birds.

They'll be dining in breaks between soybeans and lespedeza. A stand of multiflora roses or a plum thicket will form a hub where quail will feed at the perimeter: wherever one vegetation changes to another, or just to plain dirt, that's where you'll find your covey.

WATER

Quail don't require drinking water. They get moisture from insects, for example, or the dew collected on seeds. But you'll find bobwhites at water sites for two reasons. One, they're there because of the edge that is formed; and, two, because the standing water creates a micro-environment fostering succulent plants, grasses, and insects.

Especially when the land is dry, this means that you must hunt wet. Seek out windmills, water tanks, cattle ponds, irrigation ditches, watersheds, and creeks. The quail you'll find there will not have congregated to get a drink but to eat the vegetation and insect life that survives best in a wet environment.

So now we've learned two things. Hunt wet when the land is dry—and always favor the edge. Keep in mind the best theoretical habitat for a bobwhite covey could be likened to a New Mexican arroyo: dry dust with scattered cover. And believe me, I've found them there. Found them in northeast New Mexico, the Oklahoma panhandle, and all through South Texas.

SPEAKING OF TEXAS

Traditionally, the storied mecca of bobwhite has been Dixie. But the great populations there have now been lessened for several reasons, particularly loss of habitat. Great shooting can still be found, but not like the old days.

Today's bobwhite's burned-up Garden of Eden is South Texas. Bud Daniel, who summers in Monticello, Arkansas, and guides Texas quail hunts in the winter, combines knowledge of dogs, game, and habitat with a continuous patter of colloquial witticisms and sundry hilarity that makes for a mighty enjoyable guide.

Bud looks like a rancher, not a cowboy: He wears clean khakis, not crummed-up denim, has high cheek bones, laughing eyes, a square jaw, a grimed hat, leather gloves, and a check cord stiffer than a lariat. He's good with dogs—knows how to get the most out of them yet still protect them from South Texas hazards—such as slate-dry thirst.

Realizing that waiting out a sentence from Bud is like waiting at the DMV for a license plate, we hear him say, "South Texas bird hunting is a good bit different from classic, textbook, old typical-type bird hunting that people know and remember from days gone by. You know, the old covey rising up the bitch's leg, textbook dog work, all that flawless stuff.

"And if you expect to find that every time on every find down here you're going to be disappointed because that doesn't exist in Texas. Why? Because the weather conditions usually are a lot tougher scent-wise and can change dramatically during a brief period of time during the day."

I recall long bursts from a Gatling gun in a grade B Western each time I wait out a Daniel sentence.

He continues, "It's no gentleman's sport hunting bobwhite down here. It's an aggressive sport. There's no pure dog work. Too much open space, lots of wind, tight places with heavy cover that confuses and confounds the dogs to some extent. Plus birds really move a lot more, which means they're on the run.

"So when a dog points, if he's been broke to death by some classic trainer, he's not going to move, and he won't relocate on these birds when he probably should.

"But if a dog relocates too aggressively, sometime you don't get an early rise because the birds get up farther in front of the dog.

"Then, too," adds Daniel, "there ain't much brush down here and that dog is standing out there naked in the line of fire, for those birds are taking off low because there ain't no cover to protect them. You know, there's just so many things different."

At first I don't realize Daniel's stopped talking. Then jarring myself to attention, and once again eyeing the greasewood flats, I ask, "But why would a bird be here in this desolation in the first place?"

WHY TEXAS?

Daniel answers, "Well, I'll tell you. If you get out a book on poultry and see what the proper way . . . what the ideal conditions are . . . to raise and hatch birds or quail or chickens, South Texas is that. We have vast, vast areas, where one spot may be the size of an automobile and as bare as a pool table; and adjacent to that will be a spot that is so thick you can't cuss a cat in it.

"And that's a perfect situation, for a brooder situation, once a bird has hatched. Also the temperature at the time of the hatching season or the nesting season hovers in the 90s, which is ideal for any quail. Ninety-three degrees would be the ideal. We have a lot of that, plus an extended nesting season. Birds are starting to pair off down here in late February.

"Harvest comes, and they start pickin' cotton in July. The birds have that extended time from February . . . why, we'll see birds that aren't more than two weeks old in late November. And that makes a 10-month nesting season.

"So you've got that extended nesting season. And the ideal conditions for raising birds, both temperature and cover wise. Plus birds don't necessarily want to eat seed. And seed in this country is an alternative to insects and green shoots.

"And until you have a killing frost down here, and we've only had two this winter, you seldom find any seed in a bird. And you never find an extruded craw [now this is important] unless it's been bad, cold weather for a long time.

"Birds don't eat like you and I do. I eat because it's good and I like it and it tastes good and I cram full of it. But birds eat for three reasons: One, for energy; two, for heat; and three, for moisture.

"All this is available in South Texas; plus, birds don't have to move a lot to get it.

THE IMPORTANCE OF KNOWING WHY BIRDS EAT

"Now everything a bird takes in goes to the craw first. But the craws are empty here—which tells us that birds don't need feed for heat. And they need very little for energy, because they don't have to move a lot. So a bobwhite in this country is a full 2 ounces lighter than one in southern Oklahoma and 4 ounces lighter than its cousin in Kansas.

"The Kansas bird has food in its craw because it's eating a lot for body warmth and energy. A killing frost in Kansas takes away the bugs and the shoots, so the quail must eat grain. That's all they have left; they have to switch to seed.

"And that's not ideal in Texas. For a bird will carry its lunch through a partridge pea patch to go to a grasshopper. Bugs and green shoots are preferred."

This back-country wizard with his mile-long sentences has me spellbound. How about you? He should . . . because Bud Daniel knows his business like none other I've ever met.

KANSAS

Now the reason Bud Daniel mentions Kansas is because it's the second premier bobwhite venue in America today. And it betters Texas in view: Those barren flats give way to rolling prairie with running streams, great stands of cottonwood, grain by the ton, and maybe the best ground cover and overstory (canopy) in the world.

I was born there, raised there, and left a toenail under every rock there. Southeast Kansas can produce 20 coveys a day, even 20 coveys a half-a-day.

Plus the cover works easily for a bird dog. There's always a breeze, a mud puddle to flop in, a spring to drink from, a deep bed of mixed prairie grass to lie in and rub away the dust and vermin—and no rattlesnakes to speak of.

You learn things in every country. We always knew we'd hit a covey within 100 yards of a cardinal sighting. We also knew to concentrate on the road's borrow ditches and windmills and abandoned structures. Bobwhites love old houses, barns, churches, and schools.

Most important, Kansas farmers are friendly. If you ask nicely, they'll let you hunt their place. Plus, there are miles of state land open to the public.

But in South Texas, almost every square foot of land is leased. You pay to get on, or you must be invited: There's a lot of corporate leasing.

WHAT ELSE?

What else do we need to know about hunting bobwhites? How about firepower and dog work?

Only moderate power is needed to drop a bobwhite. Shoot a 20-gauge, 28-inch barrel, with 7½ shot and you'll be fine. In fact, 12 gauges might almost be too much for the diminutive birds.

Now for the dog. There are several imperatives in adopting a dog for bobwhite hunting. One, the English pointer, English setter, and Irish setter have premier status; then along comes the Brittany, the less popular setters, and all the continental breeds: the German pointers, wirehaired pointing griffons, pudelpointers, vizslas, weimaraners, and the little known munsterlanders and spinones.

The dog must have intelligence, intensity, endurance, heart, biddability, the desire to please, ample wind, the capability of a great race, and a birdiness that borders on the zany. The hunting dog stud book pick of the lot is the English pointer: It gets the most registrations of serious field trialers. This number has especially picked up since careful breeders have concentrated on congeniality in this breed.

You see, old-time pointers harbored many carnal instincts. They'd be out for birds, jump a sty, kill a pig, then race a half mile to wipe out a chicken coop. But breeders like Bob Wehle, from Midway, Alabama, and Henderson, New York, now produce pups that buyers call back to report, "This dog was congenitally trained."

Yes, trained in the womb? Trained in the gene pool? These dogs are not hardheaded, self-willed. They want to please, and they have the functional conformation to do it.

In a recent issue of *The American Field,* the official field trial newspaper, I counted the name Wehle or Elhew (kennel name) 1,400 times. That's how this remarkable breeding is being rewarded. That's how a new bird dog is being brought to field. And there are others accomplishing similar results. Bully to them.

I wish we could get such ingenious and responsible breeding started in other sporting species.

WHAT YOU NEED

I'm now convinced you shouldn't teach a dog what it doesn't need to know. That's a quote from Montanan Ben Williams, the developer of the prairie Brittany.

You see, Ben hunts 40,000-acre parcels and wants a dog with legs to cover that vast area. So for 30 years he's bred this unique Brittany.

I went to see it. Ben puts them down in packs of four to eight. The dogs train the dogs. The only things Ben requires are that they come when called and honor a point. The reason for this is clear enough: If the dogs are a half mile away and don't honor, there could be a hell of a fight.

Never have I witnessed finer performers.

As a matter of fact, Ben—and other considerations in my travels and my training—helped set my requirements for tomorrow's bird dogs.

They should whoa, point, honor point, relocate, hunt singles, fetch if required by the handler, and self-cast for the next covey. I do not want a mechanical dog. I want a dog that thinks for itself and gives me the benefits of its genetic genius.

I hear people say, "I'm going to take my dog hunting." But it's the dog that takes the hunter hunting. If not, then why don't you go alone?

Today, with all our instruments of brutality, we restrict the dog too much—and we remove too much of the fire. We don't give the dog its head. I don't want such a dog. I want a dog that self-hunts because it knows more about it than I do. Why should I give the orders?

My job is to start the dog right, encourage him to excellence, then get out of his way and let him do it.

WHAT YOUR BIRD DOG SHOULD DO

Just off the bat, he should self-cast for likely objectives. He should know the lay of the land, the best bird-producing coverts, what all that means when put together, then cast to use it.

To train a dog to evidence such savvy and maximum efficiency, you merely work it over endless miles of land and tons of birds. More drills. Just train a dog to hunt by hunting him. And know this: There's no dog problem that can't be solved with a bird.

Some wannabes buy these bird-dog-training videos that never once, I mean it, never once show a bird. Start looking. You'll see it. That's like teaching a boy to become a Cy Young pitcher without touching a baseball.

HOW TO HUNT PUP

In this book we don't train dogs, we hunt birds. There's a way to do it, and this is how.

English pointers and setters are not pack dogs. They're usually hunted alone or with no more than two other dogs down. The traditional setting is one lone bird dog, a hunter, and a long tree-shrouded valley you'd die for.

The dog is at race, searching for scent. When suddenly he hits it and either slams to immediate point or, knowing the scent is faint, moves forward until his nostrils confirm, he's entered his power zone. What's that? That's the proximity where his ability to flat hold the birds slams in, pressing the birds to earth—totally immobilized, so they can't fly. Then the dog waits for the gunner.

When the gunner appears the dog tightens up even more, his body rigid, a bone-and-flesh arrow, pointing to the exact spot where the birds are penned down.

Now this is imperative. We've seen it too often, and it places the dog at great disadvantage. The gunner walks up behind the dog and directly past his side.

The emphasis of the gunner's movement naturally prompts the dog to move forward—the gunner's passing body is too great an incentive. So never, ever walk up beside and past a bird dog. Always go way around, ever keeping your eye on the dog and on the place he indicates the birds are stuck. Then you're ready for the dog to move or the birds to launch.

Such positioning has two values. One, it gives dog and hunter an unobstructed view of the rising covey. And two, it puts the gunner out of the dog's life space so the power of the shot will not produce a gun-shy dog.

WHOA

How many bird hunters know that "whoa" has nothing to do with birds. "Whoa" means for the dog to put all four feet flat and not move an eyelash. "Whoa" is yelled to stop a breakaway, to keep a dog out of a sludge pit, or to rein him in before an interstate.

Never does the hunter say anything around the pointing dog. This is nothing but distraction.

An English pointer flushes a single bobwhite. The bird is directly above the end of the hunter's barrel.

When the gunner fires, the dog can do several things. I want mine to follow the flight and mark the landing of the covey and any deadfall. Do you know the sport is short on good judges? I know of instances where a mature dog did just this at a field trial and the judge dropped him because the dog was "not steady on wing and shot." The dog knew more about the game than the judge.

The gunner must also mark all birds down in order to help the dog. The hunter tells the dog, "Alright," then, "Find a bird," and the dog searches the cover. Finally, the dog is dispatched to the covey's relocation, or to singles.

When the dog finds a downed bird, he may or may not deliver to hand. The handler will know. If the dog is just going to locate and not fetch, the gunner needs to accompany the dog. The worst thing we can do is drop a bird and abandon it.

When all birds are placed in the game bag, the gunner then calls the dog and inspects his eyes, nostrils, ear tips, and underbelly. If the dog is thirsty, he is watered from a canteen or directed to a creek. Be especially watchful of the dog's eyes. The gunk that can pile into and behind the eye lids is phenomenal. Let that stuff stay there and you may not have a dog that can hunt tomorrow. All you must do is pull out the eye lids and flush the eyes with water. If gunk piles up at the corners, wipe it out with a Kleenex.

THE NEW BIRD DOG IN THE FIELD

For 30 years I've specialized in hunting Labrador retrievers for bobwhite. The results have been fantastic. And the dogs love it.

Ideally, I put down four all-age Labs and cast them for game. Following along, I can control them with a whistle and watch every signal they transmit. When they make game their whole body tells you. The set of the neck, the cock of the ears, the tenseness of the cape of muscle that bows over the shoulder. The tails rigidly tremble, the flanks flex. You know the birds are coming up.

The dogs barge in, more than leap to flesh. Impervious to harsh cover, they'll invade anything, ignore any pain.

But once again, we require here what we required in the bird dogs: great intelligence, birdiness, biddability, and all the rest.

I wouldn't hunt quail any other way, but it may take you some time to get used to such an idea.

THE POINTING LAB

We Americans are crazy about fads and gadgets. At seminars, people ask me, "How can you train with just a rope and collar? The sports catalogs say you've got to have this and that and that."

Well, my belief is that sports catalogs are designed to sell gear, not train gun dogs.

And so it is with the pointing Lab. Sure the Lab points, almost all Labs do, but it is a sight point they give you. And who wants that? To do it, the dog has to so encroach on the bird that he can stand over it and look down and see it. If the bird has any wildness in it, it'll be gone.

God simply didn't put into the Lab what he put into the bird dog. It just doesn't have the remote power that turns birds' hearts to stone, immobilizes their wings, actually stops their breathing. No, a pointing Lab is not what I want. You choose for yourself.

PEN-RAISED BIRDS

Terry Smith, from Decaturville, Tennessee, died about 14 years ago, in a car accident on a winding Tennessee road.

I'll never get over it.

Terry was the consummate outdoorsman and fitted my primary criterion: He wore his mud well. We were hunting one day at Stuttgart, Arkansas, when the mallards caught Terry returning to our blind. He merely sat down in the water.

I yelled at him, "What on earth—you've got mud and water to your chest."

He said back, simply, "I'm duck hunting."

Terry had come by his family's farm and was rebuilding the house, which he discovered was made of solid cherry. The place had survived the Civil War, and Terry and I spent a great deal of time there.

He'd fix something to eat and we'd sit at the gate-legged table and he'd say, "That's brought on." Which meant whatever it was we were eating wasn't raised there.

And that's the way it is with pen-raised birds. They were made by man, not God, and they're brought on.

Yet what gun-dog trainer could cope without them? Pen-raised birds will let you train your dogs, but they'll never have the scat, the wildness, the panic, and the will to survive at all cost as their wild cousins.

One thing you can do to increase their value afield is to make sure their flight pen is planted in the same type of cover as the release area. The birds then make the transition without harboring a need to escape, and why not? Too often, the new cover they're planted in isn't what they were raised in.

The gun-dog pro knows that his charges will encroach too much on the pen-raised birds and will consequently knock wild birds on a real hunt.

Everything has to be adjusted for these tame counterparts.

Many big-time operations build sheds, called Johnny houses, to keep quail overnight and release them each morning. Gradually, the liberated birds take on wild characteristics. And this is good, because it approximates more the conditions found on a real hunt.

Each evening they are called back to the Johnny house by their "call-back" bird.

Other trainers release birds to the wild and leave them there, letting them eat out of specially built garbage cans situated around the training grounds to provide sustenance.

So the pen-raised bird is a mixed blessing. It'll train your dog for you, but not in actual hunting conditions. You take your best shot with these birds and go with it.

CLOSING HOUR

Sundown comes to every hunting day. Time to quit. And that's where we are with the bobwhite. No bird on earth is as much fun, as exciting, as fulfilling to hunt as this bird. He is the monarch.

I hope we've given you a leg up on your next outing. Remember, bobwhites are found on the edges, around water. They are the ultimate dirt birds, so look for clear areas where they can feel safe and comfortable. You won't find them buried in a tall sedge field.

And before you ever go to seek them out, remember to steel yourself. They come up like rockets and scatter like fragmented hand grenades. That's their defense, designed to scoff at your gun and leave you standing with wilted pride and gaping mouth.

CHAPTER

Pheasant

IF A PHEASANT would suddenly turn human, you'd see him riding a Harley-Davidson, wearing a Wehrmacht helmet and sporting an open, black leather vest with assorted silver chains hanging here and there. Across his forehead would be tattooed the words, *"Make My Day."*

The pheasant is a belligerent and pugnacious bird that lives its whole life on the edge of mortal combat. When in cramped captivity, the pheasant's beak must be cut off or shrouded and his leg spurs kept short, for he can stab like a marlin and kick like a mule.

He keeps about six wives, either to his joy or his headache, and lives in a military caste system. And know this: The cock is no bird to be admired by any women's group. When pressed by a gunner, he pushes the hens to fly to save his own skin.

192

Mike Gould, gun-dog trainer extraordinaire, has kept flight pens with 10,000 of these birds on hand for game preserves he's managed.

He tells the story about how he once had a prime pheasant cock-bird left over after training and decided to reintroduce it to the flight pen. The bird was dead within seconds after entering the pen, killed by his brethren for assuming he could place himself anywhere in the hierarchy he liked. The bird had attempted to retake his old rank, and died because of it.

You don't mess with a pheasant. Remember that the next time you send a Lab pup to fetch one up. The pup can be ruined for life if the bird decides to make a fight of it.

WHAT TO DO WITH THIS SCRAPPY BIRD

We hunt him, that's what. Here's how.

The ring-necked pheasant is a big bird, some 36 inches in length, though 22 to 23 inches can be in his tail. He weighs about 4 pounds and he's mostly meat. He can be found across the United States, though South Dakota has made a fall business of them, with birds and hunters by the thousands. The important pheasant bird-dog trials are usually run somewhere like the Finger Lakes region of Upstate New York.

The birds were introduced to this country in Corvallis, Oregon, in 1886. The American counsul general in Shanghai, Judge Owen Denny, secured the birds and successfully shipped 20 to 30 of them to his brother's farm. Several years later, a wealthy sporting family in Alamuchy, New Jersey, hired a Scottish gamekeeper who brought a few of the birds with him. So now they were started on both coasts, and today they range from Maine across to Oregon, poking south some places as far as New Mexico, and generally following the terminus of the repeated ice glaciers.

I met and fell in love with them in western Kansas. You don't find them in eastern Kansas, and game biologists tell me it has something to do with lack of lime in the soil.

WHAT AN OPENING MORNING

What's really special about pheasants in Kansas is the morning of opening day. You can place a toothpick in the ground in Kansas, drive

Mike Gould, a gun-dog trainer from Kamiah, Idaho, lowers his gun to drop a pheasant. Note the intensity of the English pointer.

away, stop 10 miles distant, get out and look back—straight at it. Which means you can see forever in western Kansas. And there are good people to look at out there.

What I'm leading up to is the church or school or community breakfast. Even on the blackest of nights, you'll see glowing lights in the distance. The nearer you get, the greater and brighter they become. You're driving smack dab into the greatest bird-hunting treat in America: The morning pheasant breakfast.

You stop the car and there will be hundreds of hunters milling about in the dark, some exercising their dogs, others taking a smoke, some yelling at others, all happy, all dressed in bulky hunting clothes. Dust is everywhere, in great slow swirls as car after car passes by. Then a door opens and a great flood of light pierces the dark and silhouettes the surroundings.

You enter. There before you, in jaunty aprons and peached cheeks, are the farm wives, the church women of west Kansas, serving breakfast. You're directed here or there. A donation plate poses at the start of the feed line. You look down a groaning board of grub.

You want 16 pancakes? Take them. You don't want scrambled eggs, you prefer poached? "Well, just a minute and I'll have them cooked for you." There's French toast, fruit in season, slabs of bacon, ham, and plump sausages, plus coffee, tea, milk, and juice. It's the west Kansas pheasant breakfast and the greatest event I've attended in my far-flung hunting life.

The money raised goes for choir gowns or school books or maybe a park bench by the courthouse. It's all good, mighty good. And you walk out of that little white, wooden church, or school, or whatever, and you know, it really doesn't matter if you get a bird that day or not. To me, that's hunting.

THE BIRD IN FLIGHT

The cockbird in hand looks nothing like he does in flight. The hens are dirt colored for concealment, but up close the cock pheasant is as dazzling as a jewelry display in Bangkok. What you notice most is the ruby patch at the eyes, the copper breast, the yellow beak, and the iridescent glory of his head. At a distance you mostly see the white ring about his neck.

Jim Culbertson, my dog-training and hunting buddy in Wichita, Kansas, plus Robby Rupp, a teenager who helped me with the kennels, and I were pheasant hunting on a private road near the Quivira National Wildlife Refuge by St. John, Kansas.

Jim was always ornery. A high-school football coach, he delighted in rousting young bucks. So what we'd do is wait until Robby went to sleep in the back seat; then Jim, who was uncanny in spotting a pheasant's white neck ring in the weeds, would slam the brakes on, bang his hand on the outer door, and yell, "Robby... a pheasant in the ditch ... get him."

And Robby, a 6-foot-tall string bean, all angles, would try to untangle himself, get his gun, and fall out the door. Then Jim and I would laugh, slap our knees with our fists, and tell Robby, "There ain't no pheasant," and laugh and laugh.

We did it often because Jim had such great credibility in finding pheasants and Robby had total faith in him. But one time, when once again there was no pheasant, Jim went into his act, Robby went falling out of that door, and bam, a cock pheasant as big as a bomber and as colorful as Mardi Gras erupted in flight—beating its wings and twittering its long tail—right by my open window. I gulped as I watched Robby bag the best pheasant of the day.

Robby stood by the car's front bumper and displayed that big bird and would not get into the car. Jim started the engine and told Robby if he didn't quit showing off he was going to run over him. Those really were good days.

Hunting is not about killing. Hunting is camaraderie, getting acquainted with other hunters, working new dogs, viewing the country in all seasons, picking up pebbles or unusual pieces of bark to take home. And all the tomfoolery ... that's hunting.

How to Hunt

There are two recognized and established ways to hunt pheasants. Form a row of mates and walk a field in line, pushing the birds before you. When the birds run into blockers at the end of the field, they're forced to take flight.

The other way to go is just you and Pup, and maybe another person with a dog, hunting prime habitat.

The driven hunt is an adaptation of the European method of drivers pushing the pheasants toward a tall stand of trees and having the sports, usually standing on the mowed grass lawns of some grand estate, waiting on the far side of the trees for the high, passing shots. A gun bearer stands beside, ready to thrust a loaded gun into the sport's hands, and to take the one that's just been emptied.

The drivers are usually village boys waving long-poled flags, interspersed with Labrador retrievers, who kick out any sleepers.

There is little sport to the whole mess.

The American drive is more democratic, and fairer to the birds. Yes, the hunters drive the birds, the birds run to the edge of the field and then fly. The drivers walk in a sag, with point guns at each forward edge to get the birds flying out the side of the field. Some pheasants begin loitering before the drivers and at first chance double back. This is where the dogs are supposed to fill the gap.

Now all this can be a pretty hairy undertaking because when the drivers meet the backers and both are armed, there's a lot of shooting going on. Safe shooting is at a premium: Always know where your muzzle is pointing, and never shoot until you're sure that no one is behind your target.

I gave up driven hunts a long time ago, but you should know they are the social event of the west Kansas season. Farmers or villagers will invite all their relatives and friends from several states to join them, rent all the local motel rooms, and have a two-day party. They are a lot of fun.

In the old days, so many birds were taken to hand that the local women would set up shop in their garages and clean birds for so much apiece. Everyone enjoyed the bash, most town people made money, and those invited had great fun.

YOU AND YOUR DOG

I appreciate the solitude and the quiet wonder of nature by trekking along with a dog, or two or three. We know what we're doing. We stop and kick about every hay mound, stack of cut limbs, or piled-up mounds of weeds.

We especially walk the shorelines of duck marshes, where pheasants idle in the tall salt grass out of the wind, but are near the varied harvest afforded by a water environment.

Pheasants have a passion for borrow ditches filled with weeds. Usually there's ample cover, and run-off underfoot. If you come across a barbed wire fence loaded with tumble weeds, this is prime pheasant habitat. So are Osage orange hedgerows. This is impenetrable cover, and pheasants can lounge in there, knowing full well that the leavings of a row crop field are but a few steps away. Row crops: You'll find pheasants filling their craws there all times of day.

DOG WORK

The state-of-the-art pheasant hunt comes after a big snowfall, when there are great mounds of banked snow. The dog moves before you—he knows his business—as he searches for blow holes. Such holes are breathing tunnels for pheasants that have dug beneath the snow and idle there, with the snow being their insulation.

When the dog detects a blow hole he immediately leaps and bores in, nose pointed to penetrate and scoop. The startled bird will burst free with a cackle, frantically cupping the wind with its wings. It's to no avail. The dog will catch the bird mid-air and you'll laugh and suddenly feel warm all over, for you've just seen bird hunting at its best.

THE DOG

Traditionally, all retriever breeds have been called on to find and control pheasants. The Lab performs excellently, although the golden has the reputation of being the top upland game-bird retriever. The Chessie is a bulldozer and can produce birds where others can't due to his boldness and thrust. And that's not to forget the flat coat retriever. This mellow people-pleasing bird hunter will fill your freezer and vie for a spot in your bed.

Only the retrievers are usually worked on drives, but all of the retrievers plus the spaniels and bird dogs can be used for the one-person, one-dog hunt.

A classic pheasant hunt is turned in by the English springer spaniel. How many photos have I taken of this vest-pocket contender, springing several feet off the ground, with the frenzied pheasant striving to rise above the dog snapping at its tail.

At trial the English springer spaniel is tested on pheasants and ducks, so those two birds are regarded as his primary interest and capability.

Realize there's always an extra bonus from any gun dog: They're

An overloaded Brittany delivers a pheasant rooster to the hunter.

not with you just to kick out and fetch birds. The English springer spaniel is the jolliest bird dog on earth. He is in perpetual laughter and keeps you the same way. Lucky is the one with a sure'nuf hunting springer.

English pointers, English setters, and Brittanies are also tested at trial on pheasants. They are recognized masters with their skill and effort. Plus, all the versatile gun dogs from Europe are prized for their capability in handling this bird.

THE GUN

The pheasant gun is any 12 gauge, with 28- or 30-inch barrel(s), modified or open choked, shooting No. 6s and 4s. Birds are usually shot within 40 yards, but at English springer spaniel trials I've seen Chuck Dryke, and others, drop birds with low brass as far away as 80 yards.

I once told Chuck that his gunning was amazing, and he replied, "You ought to see my boy."

I went to Sequim, Washington, just for that purpose. The boy, Matt, shot the skeet range from the hip, riding a unicycle. He dropped all birds.

So it came as little surprise Matt became America's first Olympic gold medal winner in skeet.

But I'll never forget *Field & Stream* challenging the copy I submitted, saying Chuck could drop pheasants at 80 yards. Though I took an oath before them, the story came out, "... 40 yards."

ENOUGH SAID

This rough-out bird, the pheasant, is the common man's sport and meal, though I've hunted him, and dined on him, in banquet halls where French kings once dined.

The pheasant lives just outside the city limits of many towns, and any kid can get to him on a bicycle or by foot. He's easy to hunt, if you've got legs, and though it may take 10 miles to bag one, it's worth it.

The pheasant also does well when raised by hand. When released, he shows more wildness than other pen-raised birds. He is beautiful in hand, fascinating in the wild, and delicious on the table. Seek him out any chance you get.

CHAPTER

4

Chukar

YOU'VE GOT TO LOVE PAIN as much as birds to hunt chukars
(pronounced chuckers), the desert dwellers. Why is that? The
bird lives in remote barrens, usually on 90-degree slopes, in
regions where temperatures often hit 100° F; he's not prone to set to
a point; and when he's not running, he's diving downward with the
wind.

The wild chukar has minimal resemblance to his tame cousin
hunted on preserves. Yet the chukar is one of three game birds in the
United States that can be successfully raised in captivity and released
to the wild or used to stock commercial hunting operations.

Wild chukars are rim-rock birds, looking down from their lofty
perches, probably laughing at most people's futile efforts to climb up

and get 'em. But that can be their undoing in the most delightful bird hunting of all.

You need to train a hunting retriever on hand and whistle signals, cast him up the canyon sides, get him on a ridge where he will start hunting just as a flusher or a bird dog, then whistle him back toward the rim where any chukars nooning up there will be forced to leap off and sail straight down to your waiting gun.

That's right, chukars take off angling upward, but when airborne, dive in a glide to the valley floor.

All this gets even more exciting if you and your friends and your retrievers float-hunt one of the great western rivers such as the Snake. You drift along, checking the rims, and when you feel there's a chance for success (or you hear their *chuck, chuck*), you launch your dog, cast him up the incline, and wait for him to push the birds to you.

The fun part is floating along in that raft, butt and legs flat to rubber—same way you wait in a lay-out boat for ducks—and seeing the birds come zooming down. Hopefully you'll be on smooth water with no rapids when they get within range, and you'll be able to take your harvest.

Of course, you have no bird until the retriever climbs back to the canyon floor, then you direct him to the fall. And that may be on the bank or wherever the bird's floated up ahead of you, or possibly hung up on vegetation and moored where you were when you shot.

The Lab is not the only dog to help bring chukars to hand. All the retrievers, sundry bird dogs, spaniels, and the many versatile hunting dogs can get the job done. It's interesting to note that field trials are run on chukars in Idaho and other western states. The dog of choice there seems to be the German wirehaired pointer. Some hunters believe this dog's rough coat serves as armor against desert hostility.

When you do get this bird in hand, you'll find little discernible differences between sexes. Both males and females weigh about 1½ pounds and are some 12 inches long, with black chestnut rally strips down their sides, a hooked beak, a white head with a black slash that runs through the eye and curves down and around to the chest, and a gray-blue body, with red legs.

There was a time when the desert had few game birds. Then Ira Kent, of Fallon, Nevada, read an article in 1934 about hunting chukars in the Himalayas in India. As he read a description of that country, it reminded him of his own state. So he got in touch with a friend in the import-export business and inquired about getting some chukars shipped from India.

It wasn't long until his intermediary located 100 chukars for $600 in Calcutta. Now let's put that in perspective. My dad was an electric motor winder in 1934 and, drawing journeyman wages, he was making $14 for a 60-hour week. Dad would have had to work 43 weeks to buy those birds! That's a ton.

Those 600 chukar were stowed on a tramp steamer and shipped to San Francisco. Only 13 of them arrived alive, but those 13 were the basis for the majority of chukars you now find in Utah, Wyoming, British Columbia, southern Alberta, Baja, Idaho, western Colorado, Montana, eastern Washington, Oregon, New Mexico, northwestern Arizona, and western South Dakota.

I'm not saying Kent is the sole party who one way or the other seeded all those birds. Other chukars arrived at later dates from other parts of the Mideast. But Kent was the pioneer. He showed it could be done.

Nor did Kent just go out into the desert and let 13 chukars fly to the wind. No, he set up a "poultry" operation and began raising chukars. These were then *sold* to fish and game departments, which released them at selected points.

It's the same old and glorious story of the hunter funding the fish and game departments' costs for stocking game in American wildlife habitats. It's not the hunting protester, not the anti-hunter who denies the natural order of the wild food chain, or others who've not thought things through—it's the hunter, as always.

In Nevada alone, more than 13,600 birds were released in 30 years. In 1941, a hunting season was opened. Chukars require free-standing water, so Nevada then stopped planting birds and invested in guzzlers. The one-thousandth guzzler was completed in early 1996 (they are placed about a mile apart).

Some states didn't enjoy Nevada's success in introducing chukars. Arizona, for example, has tried hard to establish huntable populations, but presently all plantings have been marginal except in the Arizona strip north of the Grand Canyon.

I've listened to many an account of a hunter shooting a departing and downward-diving chukar on the north rim of the Grand Canyon, then walking to the edge and seeing a gray puff snagged on a naked pinion limb 100 yards below. Over the side the hunter goes. I'm

A hunter stops to thank his Lab for good work on this chukar.

telling you, that's dedication. Ever look down the perpendicular side of the Grand Canyon?

One way to get your bird without hanging by an arm from a rock ledge is to hunt the flats. Well not the flats, exactly, but the rims where the edge drops straight down to the canyon floor. And always look for cheat grass. It bursts forth bright and lime green in the spring, grows a foot tall, and then dies. That's how this grass gets its name: It tricks us with a spring promise and ends up cheating on us with a stand of dead thatch. But chukars love it. If you hunt the cheat grass, you'll eventually bump into the desert dweller.

Chukars also favor sagebrush, horsebrush, rabbitbrush, and spring perennials such as Russian thistle, red-stem fillaree, and fiddleneck. Know your arid grasses and desert scrubs, and you can focus your hunts on specific habitats and cut down on your walking. And make no mistake, the chukar is the ultimate walking bird. I've been on hunts that went 10 miles, with much of that being up and down. And what was brought to bag? Maybe two birds.

But again, don't lose hope. Chukars have a trait you can use. A flock may evaporate upon your presence, but a couple of birds will often remain behind to reassemble the covey. Look hard, get your dog in for a close hunt, stay intense. You may find the remaining birds and get the only flushing shot of your life on chukars.

Too many shots are far behind the departing birds. Chukars are just that spooky, and they have the defense of the ledge. Up, out, and down they go with your string of shot biting clear air and eventually dropping to the canyon floor.

The last tactic to use in bringing this bird to table is hunting the water sources. Subpopulations take up residence adjacent to water-holes and leave track coming and going. Follow them, and you might intercept their makers.

It stands to reason with the heat, the habitat, and the inclines, you want to travel light. Wear layered clothing, carry a lightweight gun, pack some salt tablets and energy bars, and keep your dog and your-self well watered.

About that gun. Few hunters double on chukars. And the few who have tripled should be in some kind of hall of fame. Given a choice, I'd recommend carrying a light automatic. Load the number of shells you want, but considering the weight carried in high heat and the fact that I've seldom seen more than one chukar downed on a covey rise, I often insert but one shell.

Side-by-sides or over-and-unders might give you a make-up shot, but, again, why carry the weight of an extra barrel? Twelve-gauge shotguns with 30-inch barrels are preferred for the long-range punch of a fast-disappearing bird.

Boots have got to be the best for chukar hunting. You're walking on volcanic ash, disintegrated granite, pulverized sandstone—in a way, you're sandblasting your footwear. And you're climbing, so the soles should have good lugs—something that won't slip. Your ankles will be strained and contorted, too, so the tops have to be supportive.

Then, too, you need sunscreen, a wide-brimmed hat, sunglasses for all the glare, and a wet bandana around your neck.

Finally, you'd better know where you are and where you're going. Topographical maps can be life saving. You look at the desert and say, "Why, I can see all the way to Yuma. I won't get lost." Ha! Just go up and down a couple of canyons, top out, and tell me where you are. You can get lost fast in the desert.

You'll have fun pursuing chukars if you use good tactics. The birds are beautiful in hand, and they're worth the try. And they have few equals on the table. Enjoy!

Gambel's Quail

W E'VE LEARNED that bobwhite live in close proximity to humans; Gambel's quail do the same. I lived eight years in the Sonoran desert, where they nested each night in my dense backyard pine. Later, I moved to the piñon-and-juniper high desert beneath the Mogollon Rim at Sedona, Arizona, where each evening the birds roosted in the many pinion that surrounded my place.

The roosting ritual requires a landing area where the birds can scan the trees, then glide to a limb and rustle about. They repeatedly give a four-point *gonk* call as if they're never certain that everyone's

checked in. But all through the night you can hear one or more of them emit soft location calls, telling I-don't-know-who, "I'm over here."

I was always cautious in going about the place after dark because those quail would spook to my movements; not seeing well in the dark, they could have hurt themselves flying about.

Gambel's quail are family dedicated, with the rare distinction of having the male tend the hatch. I've actually seen Gambel's males try to lure a hatch away from a hen or abduct the peeps in her absence. If the female dies and leaves a motherless clutch, the male will incubate the eggs.

They are also beautiful birds, with the cock sporting a jaunty black plume that tilts forward and bobs when he walks. The male is gray, with black and white rally stripes down his sides, a fawn back, and a belly distinguished by a black patch. The hen is dirt colored, but she does sport the plume and racing stripes.

Both birds weigh some 6½ ounces and miss being a foot long by 1 inch. Their flight speed reaches 40 miles an hour, and they can hoof it out at 15 mph, but prefer a moderate-paced walk. It's a delight to see the hen leading her brood through short cover, the peeps scurrying along in disarray like erratic little golf balls.

THE HUNT

Experienced hunters agree it would be impossible to shoot out Gambel's quail; that is, render it extinct by overhunting. The primary reason for this is we hunt a phantom bird. You just can't find Gambel's quail if they decide to avoid you. Consequently, there's usually a generous limit allotted each hunter.

If you do chance upon them and fire on the covey, you will seldom get a second chance. You're primarily shooting young birds, and this baptism under fire creates a life-long spookiness.

Why are they so hard to find? The reason is that they will usually run first, then fly over limitless expanses of heavy cover and stumbling blocks—such as lava rocks and arroyos—thus presenting the hunter with incredible challenges. The birds can thrive on the flats, but prefer hilly country that eventually defeats those in pursuit.

VITAMIN A

Game-biology research in Arizona has determined that the amount of vitamin A in a bird's liver determines the following year's hatch. And the quantity of vitamin A depends on the amount of rain falling from October through March. The rains sprout the green seeds, so the birds can eat well early on. Incidentally, Gambel's are 90 percent vegetarian.

This early feeding triggers their reproductive system, so they pair off and hatch. If there's no rain, there's scant reproduction.

Favored spring foods include the flowers and leaves of Indian wheat and exotic filaree, with a lesser interest in the leaves and flowers of mesquite, paloverde, and mimosa with such legumes as locoweed, deer vetch, and lupine. The preference for these winter annuals continues through the summer rains.

In fall, these winter perennials dwindle—which, in turn, triggers a great dispersion of the quail families. This results in an intermingling of coveys, which manifests itself to the hunters as a "horde" of birds on a covey rise.

Gambel's quail can be found during hunting season on warm hillsides where early rains have prompted fresh growth of green annuals. The birds will also frequent salt blocks at this time because of an increased diet of mesquite beans.

A QUEER TRAIT

Gambel's quail are extremely territorial. Kick up a covey in a particular ravine and you may kick up four more in the same spot during season.

The birds have a queer trait when selecting a safe-haven site. If you find, loft, and fire at a covey, the birds will fly to a preselected safe haven. But—and this is the key to their doom—should you sit and wait for their assembly call, then go and kick up the relocated covey at this new site, the birds will freeze in immobility and panic.

Why? Because you've found their one and only chosen hideout, and they have no place else picked out to go.

Consequently, whereas you usually see Gambel's quail take off afoot, now they flounder in great confusion, with some birds flying far and others landing close. You can tell that each of the birds is very concerned and frustrated. This is when you can achieve the maximum harvest, if that's your interest.

FIREPOWER AND PERSONAL COMFORT

Depending on the mood of these birds, one day you'll need a 12-gauge, 30-inch barrel, open-bore shotgun shooting No. 6s, while other times the birds will stick tight and linger so you can take them with a 20-gauge, 28-inch barrel, modified choke, shooting No. 7½s.

Imperative to any Gambel's quail hunt is the best boots you can buy. The terrain is quite uneven, often hard as coleche, with great scatterings of lava rocks, steep arroyos, and punitive cover. Ankle support proves as necessary as foot tread.

Clothing should always be layered, and that's especially true on any desert quail hunt. You'll leave the pickup in a sort of cold nip, but by 9 A.M. you'll already have removed clothing, even down to a T-shirt.

Primary equipment includes water bottles or canteens. An old army cartridge belt with several canvas-covered aluminum canteens will prove vital for both you and Pup.

Call your dog(s) in often, and water him by pulling a bottom lip out to one side and pouring water into the pouch so the dog can lap and ingest all the water instead of spilling it about.

Finally, don't forget tweezers for removing cactus from Pup's pads. Yes, I guarantee you it'll be there.

DOGS

I've seen almost every breed of dog on a Gambel's quail hunt except a flusher. The dog favored by hunters who actually live in the desert is the German wirehaired pointer. These people believe the dog's rough coat turns the cactus and sundry harsh brush. Another bonus with this dog, they say, is that you can take it atop the 2,000-foot, sheer drop-off, Mogollon rim and hunt it on ducks.

Web Parton, a gun-dog trainer from Oracle, Arizona, removes spines from a setter on a Gambel's quail hunt.

Thus, you can have an upland game hunt and waterfowl outing all in the same day.

ADDED BONUS

Hunting Gambel's quail beneath the Mogollon Rim in Arizona can be a beautiful and inspiring experience. The distant spires and turrets and towers of the red rocks, set against the ocher and rouge colors of the never-ending cliff, played out under a spectacular sky continually altered by the radical winds that collide with and bounce off the cliffs, gives you a background that truly could not be bested in any paradise.

There's no hunting in the Grand Canyon, but this is the nearest thing to it, which should give you some idea of the awesome splendor.

Mearns Quail

REMEMBER Ben Rumson, the prickly misanthrope in the musical *Paint Your Wagon?* Ben sang a song with a stanza that went, "The only hell I know is the hell in hello." Mearns quail sing the same refrain in their sky-high Garden of Eden—as far from humans as these quail can get. I love 'em.

Exotic and imperiled, Mearns have adopted a high-altitude habitat that is one of America's finest hunting venues.

The birds' traditional grounds are the northern, high Sonoran desert of Mexico, with a small spillover in Arizona and, less frequently, New Mexico and Texas. You'll find the greatest concentration of these birds east by northeast of Nogales and south by southeast of Tucson.

Mearns generally live 4,800 to 5,100 feet up, in lush-grass, park-like country, among scattered live oaks and pines, with colossal stands of manzanita that are remarkably hearty, as evidenced by trunks as thick as a man's wrist.

LIFE DATA

An understory of grass is vital for this bird's survival, which seems remarkable when we remember the bobwhite as a dirt bird. We'll get into the Mearns' ground-cover preferences in a moment.

It's practically impossible to push the Mearns from its beloved woods. And without 10 inches of rain each summer, there would not be sufficient moisture to sustain the grasses and forbes that make up the birds' necessary food and cover.

Because thick, heavy grass is their preferred habitat, the birds display the remarkable behavior of squatting amid cover for concealment. That works, but if caught on flat, bare dirt, they'll do the same thing—which is totally dysfunctional.

They have, of course, acquired advanced grass-crafting skills, to the extent the hen will nest her clutch beneath thick grass; when departing, she'll flip over a thatched grass door for concealment of the access hole.

RESPONSE TO POINT

When forced to leap from their squat position, the birds, though strong runners, will go only a short distance before squatting again. When flying, they can attain 20 miles an hour in a short time, but will not sustain the flight, typically lifting over the nearest rise, then touching down in cover.

The experience of my dogs, and myself, is to continually push the birds before us, always guessing which way they'll turn when they top a hill.

Mearns emanate a soft congregation call throughout the year, but the call has a misdirection quality, and one can zero in on it only by walking and "talking" with the quail, especially the females.

DESTRUCTION OF HABITAT

Overgrazing of livestock in the Mearns' range, plus devastating summer droughts, are the enemy of this magnificent little bird. I have personally walked through lands so trodden by cattle that the cover is shorter than nap on a pool table.

Considering these quail are especially fond of nut grass—where they must actually dig the nut from the earth to consume it—the disappearance of cover foretells the disappearance of the species. With our present range policy, this bird will one day be extinct in Arizona and other hard-put locales, and the only way we will be able to see a Mearns, or hunt a Mearns, is to enter Mexico.

THE BIRD THAT CAN'T CLUTCH A LIMB

I have mentioned the unique way this bird dines—it digs. To do that demands long, strong nails. A consequence of this foot structure is that the Mearns cannot curl its claws about a limb and nest aloft. Therefore, it is grounded evermore in the tall stands of grass.

If cattle stamp out the vegetation or rip it open to drought so it easily dies, what does the poor bird eat, and where does it sleep? For it to survive, cattle simply must be removed from this bird's range. Doing this will not be easy.

To vouchsafe my findings, no less an authority than Aldo Leopold, who extensively worked the Mearns' range, concluded in a 1957 resource paper that "grazing destroyed the birds' food resources." It possibly was outside the scope of Leopold's interest at that time, since he said nothing about it, but Mearns also refuse to nest on overgrazed land, further diminishing their potential population.

THE DOG

Mearns are too well hidden and squat too tight to be chanced upon by a lone foot hunter. A pointing dog is required.

A close-working dog that works near the gun—either due to genetic disposition or training—will be the greatest producer. Since the birds are so deeply buried and so capable of turning to stone, it takes a meticulous performer to ferret them out. The dog must painstakingly hunt every inch.

That's not to say a Mearns' hunt can't be a fast-paced adventure. I've had a covey rise and depart over hill and, while pursuing it, have kicked up other coveys on the way.

But really, who wants this? Taking one or two of these birds is sufficient. After all, we're talking about a premier game bird, one that is severely imperiled.

Even to get that one bird, you have to avoid treeless areas. The birds just won't be there. Hunt uphill in the morning—that's the direction in which the birds feed—and cover the canyons come evening. Mearns avoid crests.

When kicking out a covey, expect the same startling explosion you get from bobwhites: Mearns do depart, and depart fast. Watch where you drop any birds, because in this heavy cover your dog may need help in finding the fall. It's rare to be able to watch a covey down, as there are just too many promontories for the birds to loft over and disappear.

Understandably, this is not a bird handled well by flushers or other breeds taught to flush. A pointing dog is the ticket. The same gun and ammo used for bobwhites is used here. The same goes for sturdy boots, layered clothing, and toted water for you and Pup.

THE BEAUTY OF IT ALL

This is one hunt that must be recorded with film. Take along a light-weight camera. The country is that gorgeous. It's also heavy with sandburs, so carry your tweezers for Pup's comfort.

One way to maximize your walk through Mearns country is to look for sign: scratched or dug earth with gashes some 2 inches long, 1 inch wide, and maybe 3 inches deep. Some lucky bird found a nut there. These diggings will be all over the place. Look for fresh ones, which will indicate that birds may be nearby.

In ending our hunt, I'll share this with you. This bird is probably the most magnificently marked bird in our country. He has a dramatic white and black series of swirls about his sparkling black eye, which have earned him the name "harlequin" or clown. Clown, because of all the gaudy make-up such performers use. Atop the Mearns head is a russet shock of feathers, most unkempt in appearance, which, along with those swirls, also encompasses his eye.

The back of the bird is striped black and brown, and the breast is salt and pepper. Altogether, the appearance is just dynamic.

The bird weighs 8 ounces and extends 8 inches, but he has a puffed-up appearance, shaped more like a ball than a bird.

The crown jewel in hand: the Mearns quail.

Visit this bird at least once, just to see him. Admire the country he lives in. Shoot him if you must, but make it the shot of a lifetime.

A Couple of Things I Want to Visit with You About

Back in 1900, 90 percent of all Americans lived on farms. As near as I can calculate from the most recent census date, 4 percent are still there today.

The difference this has made in our lives is dramatic. The boy going to bring in the cows 100 years ago heard the covey of quail, saw the cock pheasant flush and sail over the farm pond. While driving cattle in New Mexico, he saw the scaled quail scatter before the herd; while riding fenceline in the Kansas flint hills, he witnessed the great flights of prairie chickens over the gate. The locomotive engineer going cross-country from the Dakotas to Montana delighted in seeing the Hungarian partridge pace his speed.

In other words, we lived with nature, we were neighbors to wildlife. Today we're often far removed.

When you live with wildlife, you learn to respect it, to know its nature, and you get a kick out of seeing if you can outwit it—and that's hunting. To know a bird or animal so well that you can predict what it's going to do, to be there waiting for it when it's finished out its play—that's hunting.

Hunting is not how well you shoot but how smart you think, and how much you revere what you're after. When you reach this plateau, you really respect the game, and you make sure it's always given an even chance.

What I'm leading up to is that the farm boy of the past was hunting birds as soon as Dad cut the stock off a single-barrel shotgun. He toted that gun to school, either carrying it in his arms or tied to a horse's saddle ring, and during recess he hunted just outside the schoolyard. He also hunted all the way home come afternoon.

No one questioned the right to hunt: It was born with you, like your umbilical cord. Nor was any thought given to taking a gun to school, for how else were you going to harvest the bird?

Yes, it was different, and in many respects a simpler and far better world. Everyone lived by subsistence in those days. The chickens in the barnyard were killed, the hogs in the sty, the steer in the pasture, and the wild birds down by the creek.

So think of the advantage the farm youth had then, the mind set that was given him at birth. This made us a different people, living with a different set of facts. Compare that with the hunter of today. What boy at 10 years of age has harvested everything within 10 miles of his place, or participated in the group festivities that sometimes accompanied hunts: the early church service, the picnic before the hunt, the barn dance that evening.

I was part that boy and part of what we raise today. I could duplicate my uncle's best in the field, have Mom tell me just how many birds she needed for company dinner, and fill her order. I lived for the hunt.

You can still do that today. There are enough weekends, enough game, enough vacations accumulated: You've just got to make plans to be in the field.

Don't think we've lost anything, because we haven't. It's still out there, and you should be, too. You can even work in an occasional game preserve for a change of pace and alternate hunts between upland game and waterfowl as populations of these birds wax and wane.

If I hadn't hunted as a kid, I really don't know what I would have done, what I would have been. Hunting's been the primary determinant of my life. It's taught me to accept challenge and defeat, to have the good sense never to underestimate the other party, to always act within the rules of the sport, and to realize the best of me is when I outwit my quarry.

These are good guidelines for living, I think. Anyway, I don't feel those guidelines have ever failed me.

So hunt. Be a better person because of it. And never forget to invite the new kid moving in down the block to participate in the magnificent world of outdoor sport, at your side.

ANOTHER THING

This high country where you hunt Mearns quail is one of the best of all worlds. Take the time to see it, to participate in its many variances. The Western bygone villages of Sonoita, Mexico, and Patagonia, Arizona—such lyrical names—are the hub of a Mearns hunt.

I've not been there for a while, but there are several startling discoveries at Patagonia. There's the Feedlot Restaurant, where once hung a sign that read, "If you can't control your children, leave them outside." The Last Gasp saloon is just across the railroad tracks to the south, and built around that structure is the Stage Stop Inn. The dining room in the inn has never failed me or any guest I took there.

To the west of all this and a little north is Patagonia's bird sanctuary. I've sat there many times in the summer and listened to the faint melodies. North of Patagonia, on Highway 83, is the world-famous Madera canyon, one of America's greatest bird havens.

THAT DAY WITH HISTORY

South of Patagonia on the dirt road to Lochiel is the first recorded site of a black and a white man crossing the Mexican border into Arizona: 100 years before Plymouth Rock.

Estaban, a Moorish slave described as "Black, massive, and spectacular," who adorned himself with fur trappings and strings of tinkling beads, walked between two giant dogs (some say they were coursing hounds), and for a while convinced the Indians that he had magical powers. But was eventually stoned to death by the Zuni for favoring too many of their young women.

Estaban guided Fray Marcos de Niza, the revered Franciscan missionary, into what would one day be *Norte Americana*. I never hunt Mearns without stopping near the cross at Lochiel, where Estaban and Marcos are assumed to have crossed into present Arizona, and pray for the day, the past, tomorrow, and all that's lovely.

If it fills your needs, double back to Sonoita where there's nightlife in a cowboy blow-out bar, with stamp dancing, line dancing, and noise enough to split the building in two.

Heading back to Tucson, stop at the Santa Rita abbey where the nuns celebrate noon mass in choir. I've sat there, entranced and stunned at their beautiful voices, long after the nuns had left.

All this is to say that good hunters are multidimensioned people: Tough but gentle, hard on themselves but not on others, at peace with the world and wanting to share the best of it, fitting best where there is silence and long shadows and the gentle hints of something far more than wind in the rustling leaves.

You'll not go wrong being a hunter. The legacy assures you of that. For without having been hunters for 3 million years, humans would not have survived and civilization would never have existed.

7

Scaled Quail

THERE . . . SEE THAT! Yeah, way up there . . . maybe sixty yards? Looks like clods of dirt rolling along. Well, Pardner, you just spooked your first covey of scalies.

"What? Are they always that far away?"

"Yes . . . or farther. You don't get a point on scalies unless you've overtithed at church and refuse to take the refund."

"What?"

"Is it always this hot?"

"Yeah . . . or hotter."

"You want to know why we hunt this bird? Because of the sport . . ."

So it goes with one of the strangest bird hunts on earth—going after the faraway bird, the marathon bird, the "I don't want anything to do with man" bird.

THE BIRD IN HAND

When you get a scalie in hand—and that may be once or twice in a day's hunt—you'll find they're larger than Gambel's quail: some 11 inches in length and 7 ounces in weight. Master runners, scaled quail have thighs like pit bulls.

The back and wings are gray (some hunters say blue-gray, which may be a regional thing), with an off-white breast and a head crest. Incidentally, that white head crest is the source of their nickname: cotton top. Their other name—scalie—comes from the feathers on the breast, which look remarkably like the scales on carp.

PREFERENCES IN COVER

Scaled quail prefer scant vegetation, and you'll rarely find them in thickets as you would a Gambel's quail. The scalies preference is limitless greasewood flats: miles of monotonous, flat ground, with a few cuts or arroyos the birds don't want to cross—so they run with the depression.

The only other time you might be on scalies' land is in answer to some far-removed developer's ad for "40-ACRE RANCHETTES," with assured installation of utilities, but date unknown.

HOW TO HUNT

To hunt this bird you need maxi-power in dog, gun, and legs. You've got to have a dog with a stretched-out quest, one that doesn't mind quartering an eighth of a mile on a cast and can keep up with birds that'll run even farther.

The dog must be an intense English pointer for my money, with the ability to slam to a point with the same intensity a border collie puts a rank bull in a pen—otherwise he'll never plant these birds.

A Llewellyn setter spots a scaled quail hiding on the other side of a "Mickey Mouse" cactus.

A point has to have that quality to it, that power. It has to make a bird freeze because it senses the power of the dog, no matter how far that bird may be from its hiding place. I've seen it often with border collies: the EYE!

With border collies, first the sheep turns but slightly away. There is at first nervousness, then there is a show of futility, and finally the absolute crumbling to the collie's will. The same should happen with birds, especially scalies. The dog must bury them with a glare.

That's not going to happen on the first point. No, when the birds are discovered, they scatter like the start of a Grand Prix. The dog relocates, actually chasing them like an unbroke pup.

All during this race the covey—which can be up to 100 birds—is losing individuals to each side. But the race goes on until, finally, the birds stop and freeze. Even now the pointer usually can't hold the birds. They bust again. Only after the ensuing race will they eventually give up and freeze before the dog, having no more run in them.

This is when you get your shots. You'll seldom drop more than one or two birds, though, as even now they'll flush far out in front. There is the prospect of hunting down singles, however, and now the dog must change from a long-range pursuer to a steady, close-working pointer.

I've hunted scalies from horseback. I've hunted them on foot. I've chased them with pickups. You gain no advantage, no matter how you go. During my heyday, when I could outwalk a Jeep, I finally gave up and hunted scalies only in conjunction with Gambel's. Simply, the scaled quail is a bird that will humiliate you.

WHY HUNT SUCH AN ELUSIVE BIRD?

If the bird is so tough, why is it hunted at all? One reason might be that there are hunters everywhere, but not enough game. There are places in New Mexico, for example, where if you don't hunt scalies, you don't hunt. So the hunter puts on his boots, grabs his gun, releases his dog, and spends a day in the desert with whatever hope he can muster.

DISTRIBUTION

Scaled quail are located in southeast Arizona, northeast Arizona, and central-eastern Mexico (the Chihuahuan desert) all the way to the east-west mountain belt. The birds also inhabit Texas (west Texas and the panhandle), southeast Colorado, and the Oklahoma panhandle.

FAVORITE VENUE

Scalies' favorite venue is semidesert grassland and adjacent lands where scrub has invaded but not taken over. In fact, whenever the cover gets too heavy, too massive, too tangled, these birds hit the road. They eschew promontories and broken-up country and stick to open plains, mesas, and low, rolling hills.

The birds will use scant vegetation for cover, even nesting under a cholla cactus. You'll also encounter them close to abandoned dwellings, feed crops next to semidesert grassland, and irrigation

You'll probably never see another photo of a scaled quail in a tree. The author's hunting companion flushed this bird to a tree; the author was directly underneath.

sites. Scalies will drink water if available, but it's not necessary to sustain their existence.

The birds' favorite elevation is 3,500 to 4,600 feet, with some extreme differentiations, such as the highlands of northeastern Arizona.

REFINING THE HUNT

So far I've given you a gross picture of chasing these running birds. But they also mess around and give the hunter an advantage or two. For one thing, the alert hunter can hear their calls. And even though most quail calls have a ventriloquist disorientation, casting your dog to such sites won't get you a point, but it will get the birds running.

During hunting season, most calling is done to gather members of the covey. There are also alarm calls, which are fairly impossible to describe in print. Just stay afield long enough, listen carefully, and you'll soon discriminate what the different sounds mean.

Up and at 'Em

You can also try to follow the birds' daily routine. They arise each morning and start foraging along ridges toward water. But they sleep in different spots each night, so you won't find them today where they were yesterday, and they don't go to water every day. After the morning routine, the next thing on their agenda is to scatter across a slight slope and dine. Midday they seek shade, where they dust and loaf until it's time to snack before turning in.

Most scalies prefer to congregate around stands of catclaw, mesquite, mimosa, and prickly air, so pay special attention to such areas.

Scaled quail also issue what I suppose you'd define as a content call. They'll be foraging along and you'll hear a buzz among some of them—like people in an old-world plaza on market day. You can stand your ground, and they may even start to surround you. They won't stay for long, however.

After stringing out a covey, and lofting it several times, then hunting singles, you should sit—even up to an hour—and wait for the reassembly call. While grouping, these birds will fly far beyond your gun's knock-down capability if aroused, so wait, and wait, and wait. Then cast your dog.

By this account you know you need a high-power pointer, along with a high-power gun to hunt scaled quail. Carry a 12-gauge whatever, with an improved cylinder, shooting No. 7½s.

By now your scalie hunt should be finished for the day, so drop elevation, get into the tough and tangled stuff, and seek out some Gambel's quail.

I've had more than a few two-bird scalie hunts. Don't expect much more than a long walk. But it isn't all that bad. In fact, sometimes it's a lot of fun! Good companions and good dogs make any hunt a joy.

To me, getting one scalie can be as hard to do as doubling on woodcock. When you get one, you can be proud, because you will have earned it.

Mountain Quail

YOU AND I just hunted some quail that we couldn't catch up to, and I suppose there was a sense of frustration, or futility, in doing that. So the question is, would you go again? Would you hunt a quail you can't find?

It's the mountain quail, the phantom bird, one that lives in vertical country, where the cover is the toughest, most tangled, thickest mess of all. It's a bird that'll spook on a California mountainside if it senses your pickup leaving Nevada, and it will attempt every subterfuge to avoid detection before it will fly.

We didn't know what we were doing, Cosbone and I. We were two young Marines, putting in our time on the base wrestling team at the El Toro air station near Santa Ana, California.

I was reading the football scores in a newspaper and saw an article about hunting California birds. One bird it highlighted was the mountain quail, a bird it said could be invisible right before your eyes.

That sounded exciting to me, so I talked Cosbone into borrowing a shotgun from a sergeant who lived off-base, bought some shells and licenses, then headed north by northeast to get this ghost quail.

We had no dog (they were not allowed in the barracks), but thought nothing of it. We figured there wasn't anything we couldn't handle. And it made no difference that we had only one gun: we'd just hand it back and forth.

I'd read about a forest of giant trees, and when I told my mother about them, she said I ought to go see them so I could describe them to her.

It was a beautiful drive, up through the Sequoia trees, with the great slanting shadows, and through the breaks you could see a hazy kind of blue horizon, stretching forever. We read a sign by the road that said one of those Sequoias was growing before Christ was born.

I told Cosbone that the hunting article said mountain quail migrated from 10,000 feet in summer to the valley floors of chaparral in winter. We figured we were too high for the birds in this big timber at this time of year, but we'd be losing elevation when we doubled back toward Modesto and started around the north end of Yosemite.

We drove the remainder of that day, and the next morning were northwest of the park and heading south. The article said mountain quail could be found from Yosemite Park to the eastern slopes of the Sierra.

We started asking field hands if they'd seen any mountain quail. Most didn't know what we were talking about. Some pointed farther east, and others pointed back west.

We finally stopped at a one-pump filling station that sold bait, beef jerky, soda pop, fuzzy orange work gloves, fan belts, and a little bit of everything. This station owner knew exactly what we were talking about, and sent us down the valley, where he told us to turn right and we'd find the birds everywhere.

He told us to pay special attention to standing water, for these birds drank a lot, and also to look for the meanest bushes we could imagine, for these birds had tunnels in there and could run like hell through them. He also said the birds were spooky.

You know how you just sense things? We didn't stop where the farm improvements were worth anything; instead, I picked out a sort of galvanized gray clapboard shack with an old car in the yard, drove in, and asked if anyone was home. A guy showed up and looked us over. I told him what we wanted and he said, "Sure . . . just go out back there and poke around. Go far enough and that's all public land. You may find something."

We told him we were much obliged—as I said, we didn't know what we were doing—and started mountain quail hunting. What I want you to know is if we had known what we were doing, we'd never have thanked anyone for pointing us to mountain quail.

We walked and climbed and sweated and sat and then, when we heard some bird calls in what we later learned was manzanita—catch it on fire and it'll blow up like a can of gasoline—we tried to bust through it. It wouldn't budge, so we got down on all fours and peeked through the cracks, and sure enough, there were some birds movin'. When Cosbone yelled, "Get 'em," they all vanished.

We sat and looked at each other. There was no way this hunt could be done. Finally, we decided that if the birds were in this manzanita, we'd split up and come in from both sides. That'd bottle 'em up. Ha.

We couldn't find them to start with, and when we did we had to crawl on our bellies through their tunnels. When we came out the other side, or met in the middle, the birds were gone.

I was from Kansas and Cosbone was from Nebraska, and we were accustomed to birds that played the game right, birds that'd jump up right before you and yell, "Get me if you can." Those birds would give you a chance. They weren't this sneaky nonsporting kind.

The plan was to camp out and eat mountain quail, but we never saw one. We substituted red beans and caught a few fish that we cooked and ate with lemons squeezed over them.

We were just kids being kids. We went off half-cocked and ill-prepared. The point is that we went. We now had one leg up on hunting a very elusive bird. If someone stopped us now and asked about hunting mountain quail, we could sure tell them more than we could have a week back.

That's the way it is with all hunting. Each outing teaches something important, reinforces what you've learned before, and gradually you start to get it right. And you never forget the good times getting there—even crawling around in manzanita tunnels and running head-on into Cosbone.

We were back at El Toro watering the football field come Tuesday morning. Then that afternoon it was back to wrestling practice, with never a mention of mountain quail.

WHAT WE SHOULD HAVE KNOWN

Process servers and bounty hunters may have perfected the techniques to bring the wily mountain quail to hand. The average bird hunter never has.

It's best to hunt the more obtainable valley or California quail (same bird, two names), which occupies the same area during hunting season, and pick up the odd mountain quail.

NO DOG

Don't think a dog will do you any good. Dogs can't get through those tangles either. A retriever would be the only dog that could help you, and that would be to fetch any deadfall you might have lucked out on.

To put all this into sharper perspective, you should know the mountain quail is the largest of all North American quail. Measuring some 11 inches in length, the same length as a blue-wing teal, they weigh in at 8 ounces, which is two more than the bobwhite.

DESCRIPTION

A magnificent bird, I feel it out-glamours all others. The male has a chestnut throat and flanks with black and white markings, a gun-metal head and neck, a chestnut forehead framed by tawny side stripes, an olive back and—this is important—a long, straight, drum major head plume.

This plume is twice the height of a plume on any other quail and is composed of two straight feathers, appearing as one, that stick straight up. Compare this with the topnot quail, which have a teardrop plume composed of several feathers all compacted to resemble a great teardrop that bobs over the forehead.

The hen is similar to the cock, but more dusty in overall appearance.

HABITAT

Favored habitat of these birds during hunting season is dry mountain flanks, brushy wooded areas, chaparral, and manzanita. You'll find them among juniper, willow, wild rose, cottonwood, mountain sage, bush grass, antelope sage, and rabbit brush. They'll roost in a piñon tree or any shrub that's over 5 feet tall.

Mountain debris such as fallen timber, charred remains from a fire, and logging leavings get their nod during the summer months at high altitudes.

HABITS

These quail prefer vegetable food, opting first for seeds, fruits, greens, buds, and sometimes roots. The males have a loud, distinct, clear call and will sometimes answer a hunter's whistled inquiry. The male also shares the male Gambel's penchant of doting on the young and even sitting on the nest.

HOW TO HUNT

Experienced hunters physically climb, drive, or ride horseback to get above the canyon walls that quail often prefer. It's a process of walking the ridges, listening for volunteer calls, looking in bare spots, and then whistling in hope that a male will answer.

A dog can only help you by bringing deadfalls to hand. Therefore, the favored hunting dog is the retriever.

Once you hear the quail's call, you drop to all fours and start inching down the drop-off—going slow to minimize falling rock and gravel, going slow to maintain watch for any signs of birds relocating within the dense brush.

Don't think the birds won't know you're coming: They will.

Ken Osborn, a flat-coat retriever specialist from Sacramento, California, takes a break before continuing his hunt for mountain quail, which scramble vertically.

They'll be tensed for escape, so be ready. Chances are they'll run, but pray for that scant surprise of a covey flush (usually some 12 birds).

The one constant in all this is not the size of the covey, or the denseness of the cover, but the verticality of the descent. It'll be tough, straight up and down.

RESPONSE OF THE BIRD

Since this is a fast-trigger bird, the covey will usually kick up at some 40 yards. A full-choked 12 gauge with long-carrying No. 4s or 6s is in order. But if the terrain is just too much for you—and it is for me—carry a lightweight two-tubed gun instead. Try a No. 7½ in the first barrel and a No. 6 or 4 in the second.

Should you get a bird, I'd advise you to forgo the barbecue and get it to a taxidermist.

DISTRIBUTION

California is not the only home for these birds. They can also be found in northern Baja, eastern Washington, Idaho, Nevada, and Oregon. They always choose the best weather, like snowbirds who can afford to winter at Yuma. They'll migrate upward in spring and return to the valley floor in winter. This makes them one of four migrating upland gamebirds: They have the same vertical route as blue grouse, while mourning and white-wing doves cover the country when they move.

A FINAL WARNING

With all that crawling about you're prepared to do, let me leave this last thought with you. The mountain quail's favorite California habit is also the place of choice for the diamondback rattlesnake. You'll find him in the manzanita, too. Have fun.

CHAPTER

California Quail

THIS QUAIL seems to love people—or at least what people have done to the land. You'll find him in your backyard, gardens, farmers' crops, city parks, and anywhere there is water. What's more, you can find plenty of these birds. During hunting season it's not unusual to bump into California (or valley) quail in flocks of 500. Wouldn't that blow your mind to see that many birds rise?

Apart from suburban life, you'll find California quail thriving in coastal brush to inland chaparral. To maximize your contacts, hunt for them in creak bottoms, irrigation ditches and tailing ponds, tangled brush, open woodlands, chaparral, grassy slopes, windblown stacks of dry vegetation, canyon rims, grain fields, and vineyards.

Description

California quail have a black plume atop a bold head pattern outlined in white, with a gray breast, striped russet sides, and a scaled belly. The hen, as always, has less distinct patterns.

This quail weighs some 7 ounces and measures 10 inches in length. It cruises at 40 miles an hour when relocating, but if shot at will hit speeds up to 60 miles an hour.

Behavior

The bird is a strong runner but will flush to a dog and a gun. As with Gambel's and mountain quail, the male helps with the young, and should the female disappear, he will incubate the eggs.

Habits

Only 3 percent of the bird's diet is vegetable, while the rest of his intake is made up of seeds and greens. The bird has a distinct call that seems to say *Chi-ca-go,* and seems mighty proud telling you about it.

Range

California quail inhabit lands from Baja through Washington and inland to Idaho and Nevada. They nest on grass, roost on limbs, rise early to eat and drink, and then, like bobwhites, seek over-story to dust, loaf, and sleep out of harm's way.

Hunter Rated

Hunters favor these birds over others because of their sportiness. They shock you with explosive rises, quick take-offs mixed with all types of tactics, including putting some upright obstacle between the two of you. The birds will land only to run and fly again. You're not going to come by them without a well-thought-out, concentrated effort.

Favored Bird Dogs

A pointing dog works California quail picture perfect. He often sees them, hears them, and smells them all at the same time. Everything is going for him, which will prove nerve-wracking for a pup. But a seasoned dog will revel in it. And what about those massive, thunderous

This Brittany pup can't believe how many valley quail are running directly in front of her.

coveys of 500 birds? That dog will be telling his grandchildren about this hunt for a long time.

TRAINING

All the dog must do to help bring this bird to hand is honor the scent cone. The moment he detects birds, he must stop, put all four feet flat to surface, and not move an eyelash. Should he doubt the incoming communications and edge forward, crowd the birds, or even take a step, it's likely he'll bump the covey before the gunner is ready. California quail dogs must be rock-bottom steady. Any pointer or setter gives you the best assurance.

I've seen Brittanies, most of the German pointers, plus the standard English pointers and setters afield for California quail. As always—I mentioned this up front—desert hunters favor the German short-haired pointers because their dense, wiry coat acts as armor in a land that stabs, sticks, and pricks.

RETRIEVERS

I've often said the trained retriever can be cast out and around the covey, then worked back to push birds straight to your gun. Much of that is the experimental stuff that I enjoy doing, and a guy out for dinner is better off just putting a meat dog on point and getting his shots.

GUNS AND AMMO

Distant covey rises are common with this bird. Carry a gun bored for modified choke, shooting No. 7½s, or switch to full bore and No. 6s if the birds are coming up too far in front.

When hunting desert birds, it helps if you love steep hills, sheer cliffs, dusty creek bottoms, high chaparral, brush piles, and any other kind of mess that saps your energy, desiccates your body, and belabors your knees until you can't lift them two inches.

Of course, you could always buy a home in their range and hunt in your backyard. Settle in your hammock with a cool one, and keep looking. Your dog can be sleeping beneath you, so both of you can move fast on any sightings—or that clear call of the California male telling you, "Hey Sport, you've got to be kidding."

Prairie Chicken

PRAIRIE CHICKENS are birds of constant winds, inhabiting the great, mixed-grass prairies of mid-America. This is land with few outcroppings of rim rock, or even table rock, where the wind has scraped the dirt clean or the buffalo herds rubbed it naked long ago.

The only trees found on the plains are cottonwood, sandbar willows, maybe some salt cedar, and an occasional sycamore—and then only in the creek bottoms, safe from drought, and free from fire that the wind hurls across gaps in the land.

The country is not noted for rain, but when it comes it's mad about it, pounding the land with hail and heavy water, with the wind trying to knock down all the fenceposts. Snows hit this area hard,

too, and it takes some time to melt because of the deep cold and the insulation of the grasses.

Only cattle are found on these prairies. Nothing else ever came there or happened there. On the edge of oddities is the realization that Remington, the great New York cowboy and military artist, tried homesteading at Leon, Kansas, running a herd of sheep.

The good people of the community convinced him to return home after several roof-lifting parties that cut against their stern ideas of propriety. Remington's property was close to a place called Cow Creek ranch, where I lived for a time with my gun dogs.

I never tired of it there. There were bass in the pond, good grass for the cattle and horses, vast vistas, and no one calling but the mailman. I caught a cattle rustler there and felt for a minute like I'd earned kinship with Earp and Dillon.

But back to the birds.

CHARACTERISTICS

Prairie chickens are big birds, and there are two distinct members of this species. There's the greater prairie chicken, found sketchily from Canada to the Gulf Coast, with the greatest population being in Kansas; and the lesser prairie chicken, which is more concentrated in Oklahoma and down through Texas.

The "greater" of the two is 18 inches long, and the "lesser" is 2 inches shorter. They respectfully weigh 2 pounds, 3 ounces, and 1 pound, 12 ounces (all figuring done on males).

A yearly ritual sees the males gather on booming grounds for courtship rituals, with the hens looking on. The males stamp their feet, puff up their neck feathers, posture, fight, drum the air with expanding air sacs on each side of their necks, and fan out their tails. It was all this that gave the American Indian his macho pose and his powwow. What Indian dancer doesn't have the bustle harking back to the chickens' expanded tail feathers? And how about the Indians' circle of drums, forming a booming ground?

The greater cocks are mottled brown and gray, with black-rimmed stubby tails that expand for showmanship and ritual. They have several feathers on their heads that become upright and rigid when posturing, and on each side of the neck is a booming sac that is bright orange when displayed, but otherwise concealed by long tufts of feathers.

The lesser cocks are lighter in color with red air sacs.

Both subspecies rely heavily on grasshoppers, supplemented with leaves, fruits, and insects, for their survival. Winter sees them switch to seeds and waste grain.

HOW TO HUNT

It's a rare event to get a point on chickens. You can try. I have. But early in life I switched from bird dogs to Labs that just ran through the country and bumped them up. It wasn't that gross. You can read a Lab and know exactly what he's thinking, what he's planning, and what's confronting him. It's all there: the angle of the neck, the perk of the ears, the trembling tail, the tense stance, up on the toes, looking down for sign. Plus it'll glance back impatiently, checking to see exactly where you are, actually managing a look of disgust, dancing and maybe whining a bit to hurry you up. All this means the birds are about to break. You see, the dog and you are bonded, joined at the hip, ESP. The dog itches, you scratch. You're one soul, one mind, one heart.

Ideally, you sight the chickens from far away, cast the Lab to them, then whistle the dog back into the birds. But that's the ideal: Usually the birds break out to the side and re-enact *Gone with the Wind.*

Prairie chickens post sentries, compounding their security by nooning on top of knolls with unlimited views of their surroundings. Canada geese do the same thing on winter wheat. Again, you can try concealment: Drop down and crawl through the grass, then come up the steep side—if there is one—and have the strongest wind imaginable at your back, to cover your noise.

But there's another way, a better way. You can ambush them on their way to breakfast.

THE WONDER OF SOYBEANS

You spend a great part of summer getting up before dawn and driving the country roads in chicken country. Finally, you begin to spot the great early morning flights. The birds must leave their roosting grounds—the great knolls—and cross farm-to-market roads to get to grain.

Pick the flight you feel you'll have the greatest success with, and that'll be the flight heading for a soybean field. Along that road there'll probably be a fence row, and mixed into the barbed wire will be lots of tumbleweeds or other vegetable debris.

The opening morning of chicken season, you, your dog, your buddy and his dog wait in the wan light for the first flights. As they come, you check legal shooting time, getting ready, rubbing your palms.

Now they rise and come straight at you, maybe 30 yards straight up, angling to the wind. And *wham, wham, wham* the guns bark, and the momentum of the shot birds carries their dead weight on past you—maybe 200 feet behind you—and you cast the dogs for the retrieves.

FIREPOWER

To get this bird, shoot a 12 gauge with heavy-duty No. 4s or 6s. Your barrel should be 30 or 32 inches, bored full choke. My friend, Jim Culbertson, the Wichita, Kansas, high school football coach, is an amazing long-distance shot, and I have seen him repeatedly bring prairie chickens down at 80 yards. Maybe you can, too, though shots under 40 yards should be the norm for most shooters.

It's been my experience that prairie chickens are tough and that it takes a full, heavy charge to drop them.

I've seen chickens knocked sideways and keep flying. Also, you never know the exact line the birds will take from roost to field. They may be off 30 yards from the line they held yesterday, so you must have enough gun and heavy enough charge to make up for this distance. This means, then, that chickens can be long-range targets.

They aren't the only birds in those prairie hills, either. A friend of mine said he wanted to hunt Kansas and asked if I knew anyone who could direct him about. I sided him up with Culbertson.

The next morning they entered a prairie chicken field and the hunter asked Jim, "What would be here in all this desolation?"

Jim answered, "Everything."

"Everything?" the guy countered.

"Yeah," said Jim, "Here you'll get bobwhites, pheasants, prairie chickens, and in season, doves."

The hunter scoffed but followed Jim. By noon he had all three legal birds in his bag (doves were out of season).

Have fun with chickens. They'll keep you coming back for more.

CHAPTER

11

Hungarian Partridge and Sharp-Tail Grouse

T HESE ARE TWO REMARKABLE BIRDS that provide great dog training in summer and excellent hunting come fall and winter. They're found on the Dakota prairies, on into central Canada, and even up to Alaska. Paul Johnsgard, the eminent ornithologist, talks of a *plains* or *prairie* sharp-tail and differentiates its regions. That's vital for him, but cutting it too slim for our purposes. Yet, his *plains* and *prairie* bird is the one we most generally encounter when hunting from northern New Mexico, up through the Dakotas, and on into Alberta.

I've been privileged to know Dr. Johnsgard. I even charred a perfectly good steak on the backyard barbecue on my old Kansas farm, yet went ahead and served it to him anyway. I recall his enthusiasm in discussing grouse and quail waned after dinner, but he was so far out of my league that I probably missed the nuances that indicated I was a poor host and he could have used a Pepcid.

SUMMERING ON THE PRAIRIE

For the past 100 years, most big-time bird-dog trainers following the field-trial circuit—mostly from Dixie—have summered on these prairies, getting their charges into continued contact with these two launch-and-sputter-and-land-and-fly-again birds.

I'll explain. It's the nature of young birds from each year's hatch to hide in dense cover, essentially wait too long before a dog's inquiry, then launch, only to fly a short distance and land. The dogs are told to relocate by the handler, and the birds are bumped again. This gives a novice pup repeated opportunities not only to honor wing and shot but to pay keen attention to the birds' departure so he can take the gunner to the birds' new hideout. This bump and run is repeated over and over until the thoughtful trainer calls off the quest.

Remember, it's hot there in the summer, and all the participants in this ritual—horses, trainers, helpers, dogs, and birds—all tire and dehydrate. Add that to the fact that the spear grass is hearty and high at this time of year—just level with the dog's mouth and nose—and the pros must maintain constant vigilance.

Spear Grass

Know what spear grass does. It's a grass that produces awns built upon a small, sharp spear. That spear can penetrate a dog anywhere, but most vitally in the respiratory channel. Beneath the point of the spear, stiff fibers (spears) catch tissue and migrate through the body as muscle or tissue is contracted and expanded.

The late M. Wayne Willis, my long-ago hunting buddy and world-class outdoor artist, had one of his Llewellyn setters get spear grass in a front leg. It migrated through the dog's body—you can some-times follow the abscesses or possibly track them by x-ray—and exited at the hip. All this happened while a veterinarian was chasing it with surgery to the near death of the dog and at a cost of thou-sands of dollars. The dog survived but was off its game ever more.

Looking Close

Sharp-tails and Huns live in punishing cover, ground so rough an Eng-lish springer spaniel (a dog of choice for many) must actually leap, dig in, and root out the quarry. Take silver buffalo berry as an exam-ple. It's tangled and thorny, and an English springer spaniel will emerge with cut lips, bleeding nose, and matted eyes.

But put a class bird dog on these birds and he'll point from afar, then let the gunner walk about and kick them up; or if the dog's point is loose and lacks power, the birds (especially the Huns) will run before they fly.

When either sharp-tails or Huns do make their move and loft, they give gunners an explosion and swiftness that even outmatches bobwhites. The birds hold a tight pattern, which can prompt a gunner to flock shoot and miss the whole shebang. Both birds will be found during hunting season in mixed prairie grass, row crops, and weed fields. The sharp-tail will generally enter heavier brush than Huns will.

HUNGARIAN PARTRIDGE

The Hun is the third bird successfully imported to this country, the other two being the chukar and pheasant. Despite its name, the bird did not actually come from Hungary but from Russia, Sweden, and Germany. Hungary provided a scant part of the release.

Interestingly enough, the bird was introduced near the spot where the pheasant was let go: Oregon.

Hun cocks weigh about 13 ounces, measure about 13 inches, and

are identified on the wing by their rust-colored outer tail feathers, the inner tail feathers being gray.

In hand, the bird shows a brown cap and ear patch with a cinnamon face. The breast and upper belly are gray highlighted with chestnut crescents. The bird's back is gray to brown, with darker wings that reveal white streaks. As always, the female is similar but more drab.

These birds are generally located in great grasslands and semi-desert venues. They prefer bunchgrass and sagebrush areas near cultivated crops. They avoid woodlands, but take to brushy areas. During winter the birds form a roosting circle—heads to the outer perimeter—just as do bobwhites. This gives them 360 degrees of vigilance, plus group body heat to keep flock members warm. If conditions get really rough, or the snow is deep and the temperature plummeting, they can burrow under snow and stay snug.

When first detected by predators, the genetic disposition of these birds is to scat, to run in an erratic course that defies good aim with a gun. The eventual covey bust is more dramatic than even that of the bobwhite. And once aloft, the birds may cover a half mile before setting—only to take off running, again.

Any attempt to follow the birds and poke around their relocation is futile. By the time the hunter covers anywhere from an eighth to a quarter mile, the birds are long gone.

Another tactic of the elusive Hun is to beat toward a prominent hill and land on the far slope. That way the hunter has no idea which way the flight turned upon landing or whether the birds ran in a straight line. Another maneuver they use to outwit the hunter is to stick close, let the hunter pass, then backtrack.

During times of rest, the bird prefers knolls where it can survey the landscape. Yet they can surprise you and hide in row crops where you've entered to jump sharp-tails. If found in grain, the birds will do the same as pheasants: run to an edge and loft. No bird likes to exit to a bare stretch of dirt, cement, or asphalt.

SHARP-TAIL GROUSE

These birds are a whole different deal. Sure, you'll find them almost anywhere you find Huns, but sharp-tails give you an entirely different escape. Once they're airborne, they set a straight course, alternately

beating their wings, then setting them to soar, until they glide to their next haunt.

Sharp-tails can be found all the way from Canada to southern Colorado and laterally from Michigan to Oregon.

The adult male measures some 18 inches, has a wing span of 20 inches, and weighs about 2 pounds. The bird strongly resembles its southern cousin, the greater prairie chicken. By holding strange-looking birds in hand and trying to figure out what they were, I've even come to believe that the two birds occasionally cross breed.

The pure-bred bird has a black line from the bill through the eye. Both hen and cock bear striking resemblance: their cheeks and throat being white, bellies and sides white with black darts, and backs mottled black. Their wings are dark brown with a white pattern. Both birds sport a yellow comb above the eye, and on each side of the male's neck is an invisible air sac that can be seen only when inflated, at which time it appears pale purple. Both sexes are feathered to the base of their toes, and the white underparts are the outstanding characteristic noted in flight. These birds got their name due to their narrow, pointed tails, which are white edged.

Now you may think you've seen some heavy-duty dancing, but until you come upon a dancing sharp-tail, you ain't seen nothing yet. This guy gets with it.

You'd think he'd gone nuts with all his frenzy. But what he's doing is making it mighty plain he'll fight any male competitors anyplace, anytime, anywhere. All the antics are intended to attract a mate.

So the male jumps, cackles, rattles his erected tail, calls out a great repertoire of sounds, and inflates his eye combs and neck sac.

When picking out a housing tract, sharp-tails prefer brushy and woody cover with mixed stands of hardwoods and conifers. If the copse contains aspen, they'll pay double rent. Aspens are their favorite trees. Another area they look for is clumped stands of woods and relatively sparse, far-flung forests.

Sharp-tails do not roost in trees overnight during winter. Instead, they scoop out snow burrows and, lacking snow, do the same thing in soft or moist earth.

These birds will eat grain as long as it lasts, but when the snow is deep they'll turn to buds of trees, twigs, and various tree fruits. They'll fly past miles of nature's abundance to dine on catkins and buds of birch and aspen.

DIFFERENCE IN SEASON

Especially during hunting season, and at other times, these birds prefer to congregate on knolls and keep an eye on the surrounding countryside. But as noted, once you roust sharp-tails from their lookouts they will give you a direct flight to their predesignated bail-out.

During summer the bird-dog trainers praise these birds for helping to get their dogs ready for the fall field-trial circuit back in the states.

WOLF WILLOWS

Big-time pointers and setters run a continuous race, what I call a stretched-out quest. So here's this broad, flat ground for them to have a go at it. Interspersed here and there on these flats are depressions blown out by constant prairie winds, or dusted out by itching buffalo years past.

The rains came and filled in these depressions, thus supporting the growth of what the Canadians call *wolf willows*. This, of course, is a misnomer: The trees are aspens and several varieties of poplar.

Dogs learn to run to these wolf willows because the sharp-tails hole up there: escaping from the prairie heat, secure in their humid environment, hidden from view by the stands of trees.

TRAINING

When the young birds are eventually flushed from these clumps of timber, they make an erratic, twittering flight, eager to set down in any stand of grass or copse of brush at the first opportunity.

Most important, the covey does not stay together. Instead, the birds scatter in flight and, upon landing, provide the dog and trainer invaluable opportunities to locate and handle singles.

What it all means is this: The dogs get constant bird work from young sharp-tail grouse. This is a rare event, especially since the trainers are putting their dogs on wild birds.

HUNTING

Let's say you come back in the fall to hunt these birds. If it's a hot opening day, the birds will stick to those buffalo willows. Then it's a matter of hunting those willows and following up on singles that fly to the nearest cover.

But let opening day be cool, and, Ha! The grouse leave the bluffs and keep a mighty distance between them and anything that moves. Now the birds are scattered on the prairie, not holed up in a stand of woods, and they are mighty elusive. Slam a car door and see what happens.

By the following weekend, after the opening-day hunters have had their fill, the birds can be found in hedgerows, along edges of cultivated crops and, yes, once more on their hilltops, surveying their surroundings.

DETAIL

To maximize your success when conditions get this way, you'll need a long-range, heavy-hitting gun, with high-impact shells—No. 4s, 5s and 6s.

You'll also need marathon legs, good lungs, and lots of water for you and your dog. Call the dog in often, give him drinks, and he'll run all day. But let the dog heat up and you'll find there's not enough water in the Missouri River to cool him down.

Sharp-tail and Hun grounds often contain pheasants, so you have a chance for a three-way bag.

Remember the spear grass: If it's a factor at this late date (during hunting season), the dog can possibly work during the early morning hours. Later than that the spears harden and become a menace.

Blue Grouse

THE BLUE GROUSE is my bird. I love this bird, love him as much for what he is as for what he does, and where he does it. One summer, while hunting at 10,000 feet, Mike Gould and Gary Ruppel, his sidekick and a puppy specialist from Kiowa, Colorado, introduced me to this bird. Mike's an innovator, a custom gun-dog trainer, who had a miracle Lab named Web. You know, this dog could practically survey the land, identify all of nature's flora and fauna, read minds, and hold psychiatry sessions with you lying on the forest floor, absorbing that high, bright Colorado sun.

In those days, Gould's kennels were in Carbondale, Colorado,

although he's since relocated to the Nez Perce country of Kamiah, Idaho.

Mike had a string of classy Elhew English pointer pups, and he wanted them in constant contact with wild birds. So he camped on the flat tops, 10,000 feet up in the Rockies, and daily cast Web to find a covey of blues. That'd only take a minute; then Web would stand there, looking at the birds, waiting for Mike's pups to show up.

Just a minute: Because Web was able to stand there like that, some people might say that this bird is like a fool's hen. But think a minute. In such total isolation, why should the birds fear encroachment? Let one shot be heard and you'll not find this covey until next spring. That's how foolish a blue grouse really is.

When Mike arrived with his pointers and Gary brought in his various pups in training and all dogs were on point, Web would retire, and Mike would steady Web's pack, do whatever was necessary—like picking one dog up and bringing him in closer—and then walk about and loft the birds.

Mike and Gary would keep the pups steady and give them multiple opportunities to watch the covey remnant and singles down. No shots were ever fired.

It wasn't necessary to rework a covey or even locate the singles, since Web would already have another covey located. Mike called Web a *strike* dog. And Web is the only Lab I've ever met so named, and so employed. He was one in a million. God rest his glorious soul.

LET'S LOOK AT THIS BIRD

The blue grouse is the largest of its species in the western states and provinces. He ranges from Alaska, down through western Canada, into eastern Washington, Oregon, and California. He's also found in the mountain country of Montana, Idaho, Nevada, Arizona, and Wyoming.

Females measure about 18 inches long and males average 20 inches, though they can go to 22.5 inches. Males and females are alike in appearance, both having squared tails with grayish tips.

The males' backs are gray with pronounced vermiculation, highlighted with brown and black peppering. The flanks and undertail coverts show white markings, and feathering reaches down the legs to the toes. Males also have bare skin over the eyes, which are yellow

A blue grouse in hand.

to yellow orange. Males can also display a bare neck patch that varies from deep yellow to purple. Females also have these bare-skin spots, but their overall body color is more brown.

Now I'm talking here about brown this and brown that and brown everything. But to have the dog fetch to hand and stand there and admire the bird close, well, it's brown, like a hen pheasant or prairie chicken.

But wait a minute. A field-trial mug on my desk shows some 40 separate blue grouse tail feathers. Let's look at one: It may appear brown, or even black, but it's general hue is really cadet gray—gray with chevrons of repetitive, mottled brown and black with a 1-inch band of black at the tail's end and a final swipe of gray. So what's brown, especially when we call this a blue grouse? You go get one and tell me.

But mind you, there are eight subspecies of blue grouse, and the one I'm in constant contact with is the dusky blue, maybe that's why I see cadet gray.

HABITAT

The favorite resting site of these birds is male aspen stands. In late June or July you can determine the sex of an aspen tree by looking at the buds. The buds of the male are larger than those of the female and much richer in protein, fat, and minerals. Blue grouse seem to avoid the female trees when it comes to dining.

If you want to increase your chances of sighting blue grouse, follow the range of the true fir and the Douglas fir. As a matter of fact, the blue grouse range is coincidental with that of the Douglas fir. Blues range from 7,000 to 10,000 feet in fall and winter. Fall? I've found them at 10,000 feet in August.

MIGRATION

The deal is, blues migrate. They winter at the highest elevation that stands timber. This is high and cold country, where their principal

A hunter and pointer take time out from a blue grouse hunt. The 10,000-foot elevation can affect dogs as well as people.

diet is needles. They concentrate on true and Douglas fir, consuming seeds, buds, needles, and twigs. I don't know much, but I've heard of only one other creature filling up on needles in the winter and that's the black bear just before it hibernates. But then, I'm a hunter and not a naturalist or zoologist.

When spring arrives, the mating urge drives the blues down the slope. There are reports that they travel up to 30 miles, and their descent won't stop until they find relatively open and dry cover, characterized by shrubs with lots of bare ground. That reminds me of bobwhites. The migration, on the other hand, makes you think of the mountain quail. Remember?

Blue grouse choose both elevation and cover that will provide their young with insects during the first 10 days of their lives. An optimal diet includes ants and beetles. As the young mature they switch to berries. Come August, they all head back up the mountain.

COURTSHIP

Before the chicks are born, the cocks must woo the hens—which, for blue grouse, is an elaborate ritual called hooting. The males hoot from ground clearings or high tree branches, boasting *this is my turf; stay out.* As the cock's behavior is designed to drive away males, it must also attract a mate. This calls for a great production of movements, calls, and body posture.

Possibly the most complicated and dramatic of all bird courtships, it can be likened to a counterculture orgy. It doesn't occur during hunting season, though, so we'll forgo the details; but I tell you, it's something.

HOW TO HUNT

There are several ways to hunt blue grouse: Put bird dogs on him and shoot over points; send flushing Labs or springers in and roust him out of his hideaway; or just take off, cross-country, hoping for voluntary flushes. I've done all three. Because of the elevation and the inclines, it's tough hunting for an older hunter, but the young can take it in stride. Besides, there are plenty of fallen logs to sit on so you can regain your composure.

Blue grouse will also run to a cliff and launch downward to the valley floor. They loft high, which causes many to shoot where they think the bird is going. Since the bird usually dives suddenly, it's generally best to shoot under.

I've found blue grouse with sage hens, so you can have a mixed bag. As a matter of fact, the sage hen's territory generally coincides with that of the blue grouse.

Since you can get a point on these birds, No. 7½ shot serves the purpose. If the birds are spooky and rising early, switch to No. 6s or 4s. A lightweight 20 gauge is the gun of choice because of its reduced weight. Carry it either in automatic or two tubes.

Keep water with you, though you'll come upon freshets and rivulets. And even in that high wilderness, you can suddenly encounter a constantly running, store-bought water pipe—erected by whom?

THE BEAUTY OF IT ALL

Nowhere will you have a more beautiful hunt. In early morning you can watch the sunrise touch each successive peak, then slide down to the valley depths. There's always a wafting breeze cresting the cliffs, and you'll see the harrier hawk smoothly handle the currents above you. The distant vistas are captivating.

The whole panorama can be so beautiful that you'll be hard put to weigh it all out. Are you having the best of all hunts? Or are you experiencing a magnificence in nature that no other place could match?

CHAPTER 13

Sage Grouse

THE SAGE GROUSE is one big bird that doesn't live on Sesame Street. Startling to confront the first time, the sage grouse seems like a desert turkey without glitz: just a big, old plain bird, dust colored and gangly. Cockbirds can weigh 8 pounds and be 30 inches in length, roughly the size of a specklebelly goose.

I find this bird a dud to hunt and a flop in the pot. Why? I'm not that fond of sage, and this bird practically lives on it. Since I won't shoot anything I don't eat, I leave this bird alone.

The last time I shot a sage grouse and tried to cook it, I left it on the stove for seven days. Each time I poked it with a fork it proved

tougher than a cavalry saddle. I gave up. Who's to say you won't have better luck or that you're a better cook?

The sage grouse struts and displays to intimidate competitive suitors and to attract hens (yes, they are polygamous). This ritual is performed on large strutting grounds (called leks), where the cock inflates himself to exaggerated proportions with the highlight being the white, puffed-up oval of feathers that runs from his upper back down both sides of his neck and then falls in pendulums several inches before his chest. All this is showcased with an absolute, upright position and a spread, spiked tail. The olive green sacs on the back and breast are expanded and collapsed, with a resulting popping sound.

Distinguishing characteristics aflight are a black belly patch and long, sprig tail. The overall color is a dark gray-brown.

WHERE THEY LIVE

The birds range from Canada through Washington, Oregon, and California—nowhere approaching the Pacific—and inland through Idaho, Utah, Colorado, Nevada, New Mexico, Wyoming, and Montana. There's also a smattering of birds in the Dakotas and a wee bit in Nebraska.

The birds will be anywhere there is sage grass. This grass must stand above the snow line for both cover and feed in the winter. Cocks are the first to leave these wintering grounds and head for their leks. The distance between their winter homes and strutting grounds can be 100 miles, which might qualify grouse as migratory.

Following the hatch, peeps favor ants, weevils, beetles, and grasshoppers, on essentially moist grounds. During summer, all grouse feed heavily on dandelions.

HOW TO HUNT

When hunting season opens, sage grouse will be found anywhere you find chukars and blue grouse. A dog is imperative for the hunt, since grouse are seldom brought to hand without a point. You might kick up a surprised grouse, but the rule is, no point, no game.

Dogs don't take to sage grouse all that fast. At lower elevations there are intense heat and miles of barren flats to contend with. Plus, when the dog enters the bird's scent cone, he's encountering a very strange odor.

Any bird dog will do. Cast your favorite. Even Labs can flush the sage grouse under certain conditions. The most success will come over a long-winded, ground-covering, full-bored nose pointer or setter. Don't forget the Brittany and all the European versatile pointers, however.

When a sage grouse lofts, it's like a B-52 getting airborne, or so it seems. The bird is actually flying faster than a bobwhite and picks up speed as he beats and then glides down a slope. It takes a big-time impact to bring one of these birds down, and you'd better look sharp, for these birds blend in perfectly with the ground cover.

Dog and hunter can walk for only so long. But take heart, for now you can scout a waterhole and make a hide. If birds are using the place, you'll find tracks. The usual routine sees sage grouse visit water several times a day. If nooning, the birds loaf just outside the water tank area.

I use the term *water tank*, but running water is also found in irrigation troughs, tailing ponds, creeks, seeps, and so on.

There'll be broad expanses where you'll not find a drop of water. So you'll need to tote what you drink, plus a supply for Pup.

Since you're shooting over points, you can reduce your burden. Select a 20 gauge with low-brass No. 4s and 6s. Should you drop one, don't you think Pup should mutiny if you insist that the dog fetch such a huge bird all the way back to the truck?

Keep in mind that you can get lost in these great featureless flats. Ever think of carrying a helium-filled balloon you can hoist over your pickup? I have, and it works.

Carrying a compass and a Global Positioning System (GPS) isn't such a bad idea, either. Just make sure you know how to use them.

14

Woodcock

YOU'VE SEEN HIM in a thousand brandy commercials—the gray sideburns and crushed hat, the squared mustache constantly evened with the back of an index finger. He's wearing a great waxed coat with wide elastic sewn into the handkerchief pocket so two follow-up shells can be brought quick to hand. Then there are the flared breeches, the cavalry boots, and the Llewellyn setter, wet to the skin, shivering by his left leg.

It can mean but one thing: Gentry drink brandy and hunt woodcock.

A WORM, ANYONE?

Surprisingly, we had woodcock in Kansas, and nonelite as I was, I'd get one now and then when going for quail. Lord knows, I never set

out to hunt a bird that spent its life with its nose stuck in mud siphoning for earthworms.

I remember Darrell Kincaid, an oil man, retriever enthusiast, and pump-gun expert, created a club where if you could double on woodcock in his presence, Darrell would put you on an honor roll and give you a silver hat pin. I never did do well in front of Darrell. For certain, I never got the woodcock pin; once I even fell backward out of Darrell's duck boat.

DOG TRAINING

I love any wild bird that's a benefit to gun-dog training. Woodcock migrate twice a year: north to south and south to north. When the birds come north in early spring, a dog handler can get in some exceptional bird work. The birds stick, the dogs learn to honor their scent cone—even if they don't like the smell—and they learn, as well, the necessity of being steady to wing and (blank) shot.

IN APPEARANCE

The woodcock is a dirt-colored bird with eyes set high and far back in the head so it can see 360 degrees while eating. The bird has a big head to accommodate those wide-spaced eyes and to support that railroad-spike proboscis.

The woodcock, which you'll learn is called a Timberdoodler—for his phenomenal flight—weighs just over 6 ounces and measures 11 inches in length. It flies only 13 miles an hour, but that doesn't mean a thing. This is a master aerialist that occupies only that piece of air that your shot never encounters. I mean this guy can put a grapevine between you and he in one billionth of a second. There was a time I called the woodcock the bark bird, for I had so much of the stuff flying around.

HABITAT

The fact that the woodcock lives in swamps, mud bogs, marsh skirtings, wide creek meanderings, and other generally bottomless places means the vegetation abounds. It is this vegetation that conceals his flight, no matter where he's going or how fast you're shooting. I don't know if anyone ever got a video camera on a woodcock upside down, but I swear he's capable of any type of flight—even penetrating and exiting tree trunks.

APPEARANCE

Now get this: We're talking about a shorebird here, but hunting him as upland game. He comes to hand Van Dyke brown, with but a hint of a tail and rounded wings. The bird is nocturnal but is available for daylight hunts. He explodes on the rise with whistling wings and disappears before you can get your gun shouldered.

DOG WORK

Any dog that hunts close will do well on woodcock. A woodcock will let a dog stand beside him all day, but once a hunter appears, it's adios. Since the bird sleeps during the day, its bed is understandably deeply concealed and has endured the test of time. A dog must hunt close to puzzle out the bird's bedroom.

Though must gun dogs will point a woodcock, few will fetch it to hand. It stinks. Look closely when a woodcock falls to your gun, as you may have to retrieve it yourself.

GUNNING

The bird favors heavy timber and masses of limbs, and he has the ability to fly where any other bird would kill himself. You must seek him out with a lightweight gun: a 20 or 28 gauge shooting No. 7½s. If limbs soak up the light shot, then go heavier because you might be able to knock some of the stuff down and still have enough firepower to get the bird.

Be careful of your footing—this is slide-and-fall country. Sometimes dogs get into boggy mud that cakes to their feet, so that they spend undue time scraping at the stuff, even chewing at it with their teeth.

RANGE

Woodcock can be found from the Great Lakes down through Louisiana and on eastward to Georgia, then up through New England. The woodcock is not a resident of Florida.

The woodcock's courting flight is unique and spectacular. In early morning and at late dusk, you'll come upon the cock in an open grassy spot, where he alternates his display of strutting with a skyward zoom that culminates in a spiral back to earth. The mute twittering sound that you often hear during this spiral is apparently made by the wings.

No other bird may prove as testing for you as a woodcock. These birds are hard to find, hard to manage, hard to hunt, and hard to bring to hand. But they're also hard to overlook.

CHAPTER

15

Ruffed Grouse

WHILE IN THE COMPANY of ruffed grouse hunters, I've often felt a silent consensus: *If we weren't hunting ruffed grouse we wouldn't be hunting at all.*

The ruffed grouse has taken on many dimensions, even to becoming a national mascot: The bird was involved in many incidents that became the basis of our national pride.

He was there to greet the Pilgrims. He was in the outskirts of Philadelphia at the signing of the Declaration of Independence. And he could be heard across the sweep of the White House lawn, drumming in the brush of the Potomac, when Lincoln signed the Emancipation Proclamation.

The Northeast doesn't circumscribe the bird's total range, either.

The ruffed grouse is found from Alaska, through all the Canadian provinces, completely across the upper states of America, and as far south as Tennessee and the Carolinas. So he was there at the firing on Fort Sumter as well as at the surrender at Appomattox.

Rules of Tradition

There are many upper-crust "requirements" accompanying a ruffed grouse hunt. The dog better be a white- and black-ticked Llewellyn setter. The gun should be a side-by-side, dainty and lightweight as a fawn's leg. At no time would a gentleman shoot anything more lethal than No. 7½ shot.

Despite these "rules," I love ruffed grouse, and I love to hunt ruffed grouse. And I bring them to hand with Labs, curs, and all sorts of beloved canines, shooting heavy guns with industrial-strength shells. You see, I'm not upper crust, so anything goes!

Other Dimensions

But there is this: Since all my life I've hunted the barrens of the West, you put me in those eastern timber tangles and I'll hope for a chainsaw to clear a path. I just don't like the idea of missing anything I've worked so hard to get, as a ruffed grouse.

Okay, maybe my reference to a chainsaw is a little crude, so let me put it all into perspective. To hunt is a privilege. I don't mean some right given by the state, but given by God for his placing the game here and giving us Genesis as our guideline.

Furthermore, hunters have many obligations to the game they pursue. Foremost, they must study it, learn everything about it: where it lives, what it eats, how it hides, its physical needs for each time of the day and for the season.

Only when hunters know the game so well they can predict what it's going to do and dupe it into their gun range do they have the right to go for it.

What a hunter hunts is based only on the individual's ability to go afield, knowing how to survive there, how to use the equipment of the hunt, and honor the game sought more than anything else. Ultimately it is the hunter's obligation to sustain the game during times of peril.

THE BIRD

No bird is honored more than the ruffed grouse.

The male grouse can weigh in at approximately 1¼ pounds and measure 19 inches in length. It is gorgeous in display, with a pronounced fanned tail of many concentric rings and a great brown stripe near the terminus of the fan. About the cock's neck is a huge ruff, and his wings protrude and droop to the ground.

Scrutinize him in flight and you'll see brown spots at the bottom, back of the neck and a patch of brown and white at the inside, bottom of the wings. The legs have no feathers.

Remember, the ruffed grouse has two distinct color phases: inclined toward red in the South and toward gray in the North.

Once again we have the grand display of the grouse courtship. Here the ruffed grouse seeks a hollow log, or several of them, mounts one, then "drums" by beating the air rapidly with his wings. The ruffed grouse also struts, especially to rush at an encroaching male.

The bird subsists on fruits, leaves, and buds, with the young preferring insects. Grouse live in open woods and parks during spring and summer, and conifers in winter. Stands of balsam, poplar, and paper birch overlie its habitat. As with other woods birds, you can't go wrong checking stands of aspen in search of ruffed grouse.

Wintertime sees the birds roosting in evergreen trees or burrowing under snow. They require standing water.

HONORING THE SCENT CONE

Delmar Smith, the man who made the Brittany a field-trial dog in America, was campaigning in New England, having entered a horseback trial for ruffed grouse.

His Brittany had been trained to stop at the absolute, outermost hint of a scent cone. The dog did. Delmar dismounted and walked the bird up, firing his blank pistol.

One of the two judges coaxed his horse forward and told Delmar, "In a lifetime of hunting ruffed grouse, that's the most perfect job I've ever seen for a man on horseback handling a grouse."

That night, traveling down the road, Delmar confided in me, "That man shouldn't have been surprised. All you have to do to get good points on ruffed grouse is make sure the dog doesn't crowd the bird's space."

That's the ultimate rule when hunting ruffed grouse. Don't let the bird feel as if you're pushing him. He can't stand it, won't stand it, and will loft away quickly in a whir of wings.

FEEDING

Don't forget to drop in on the bird's favored restaurants during hunting season. Have your dog check all stands of aspens, willows, catkins, hazelnut, wild cherry, and apple. There the birds eat buds, fruit, leaves, and twigs.

Remember to cast Pup about and have him investigate snow banks closely. Who knows if the birds have burrowed in to keep warm. If they have, stand back because you're going to get a mighty launch.

COLOR AND BELLS

Since grouse frequent heavy cover, it behooves both hunter and dog to outfit themselves with bells. Of course, if you've got a rock-bottom steady bird dog that will not move on point, then what are you going to hear? So the hunter must walk about, following the tinkling bells, but finally, if the bells disappear, the hunter must shout out. The one thing you don't want is a lost dog.

Dress yourself and Pup with lots of fluorescent orange clothing. We want both of you to see each other as much as possible, and we surely want both of you to be conspicuous to any other hunter.

RAINY WEATHER

Ruffed grouse live in perennially bad weather. Seven-day rains are common. And rain hunting is a lost cause. Bad weather is especially hard on ruffed grouse because it destroys the apples. If fall is late, however, the apples will still be clinging to the trees, and the grouse will have no way of harvesting them. They avoid open orchards at such times.

You should also know that ruffed grouse don't want to eat hard

A ruffed grouse hunter refreshes his setters at a stream before going back into the heavy cover.

apples: They prefer them mushy and fermented, which is another reason they wait for the apples to fall.

The alternative is for the hunter to concentrate on intertangled and impenetrable cover. That's a downer, day after day, with everything dripping wet.

So pray for apples on the ground, or dry weather.

In any case, know there are some hunters who demand you look good doing it.

Mourning Dove

THE FIRST TIME I went afield with my old friend, wildlife painter Wayne Willis, it was for mourning doves. Since Wayne was in charge, he loaded me up, then drove a few miles south of town, staying on the main highway. Soon he stopped, exited the car, and started walking into a weed field with dilapidated road signs and soybeans planted on the far side.

Wayne carried a Browning 20 gauge in his right hand and a galvanized bucket in the other.

I assumed his plan was to enter the bean field, sit on the bucket, and shoot doves. But there were so many doves trading back and forth enroute that Wayne had his legal limit in the bucket before he ever left the weeds.

How could I forget it? He'd throw up the Browning, steady the forepiece with the hand holding the bucket, sweep, shoot, then scoop up the fall. We had no dog to do the fetching.

I knew the national average for doves was four shots per bird. Wayne was the one person who didn't know it, shooting one shot for one bird eight straight times.

THE ABUNDANT BIRD WITH THE MAXIMUM HARVEST

The mourning dove is the most abundant bird, with the maximum harvest, in the United States: Some 20,000,000 a year are brought to hand. If the national average is actually four shells per bird, that's 80 million shells.

These birds may be found from Canada into Mexico. I've had them on my property everywhere I ever lived, and right now they are roosting in my chimney in the blast furnace of south Nevada.

THE NEST

Doves build nests that couldn't pass the least stringent housing inspector's test. Their nests show all the planning of a floodjam, with sticks jutting every which way, shattered leaves, feathers of any kind—just airy, flimsy, chaotic, slapstick, negligence.

Unless this nest blows down, I'll show you what's expected of it. Mature doves can lay two eggs in this nest three to four times a year. The young grow up fast, so the egg laying just keeps going on.

The kicker is that this year's young may also mate and lay two eggs, meaning some 10 doves could have been hatched to one set of parents, and at least one of their young having mated with a dove from another family.

We may worry from time to time about loss of some particular species in the wild, but I don't think we'll ever include mourning doves.

RANGE

I've encountered doves from sea level to 8,000 feet. I've found them in deep coniferous forests, deserts, hedgerows, grain fields, truck farms, orchards, deciduous timber stands, and any place people frequent.

Spring sees the birds nesting in lower elevations, and depending on wealth of feed and water, the birds may be laying their last eggs in September.

CALLED ON ACCOUNT OF RAIN

If there is one truth about doves, it's this. I've never completed a dove season. Why? Because a rain inevitably pushes the birds away. I mean it. No matter where I've been, it's the same old story. Dove season is great, every day gets greater, then one night a cool rain will sweep through the country and before you can get to the field that morning, the birds are gone.

They are the most fair-weather birds in the world. Yet, and get this, I've lived in freezing country where late-born doves won't migrate. So some doves can take the cold and others bottom up at the first cool mist.

HOW TO HUNT

Doves will present an infinite variety of hunts to the individual who wants to experience all their craftiness. I like to take a stand by a pond or tank and shoot them as they come to water. Such pass shooting results from knowing about their daily activities. Once you learn their flight lanes, the key is to then make a hide and catch them going to grain fields or visiting gravel sources for their gizzards.

To make your hunt even easier—to maximize your success—choose a sesame seed or sunflower seed field. Now you just set up on their two favorite foods.

Kansas is a haven for doves. And here they come, being able to attain 60 miles an hour just for the fun of it, only now they've got that tail wind behind them, and move over jets! You think you have coordination, eyesight, muscle control, and balance. Hah. Get ready for some lessons in humiliation. You'll leave the field knowing you are the saddest shot who ever mounted a stock. Think seriously about seeing an eye doctor.

It's not because doves cruise at 60 miles an hour that you can't hit them. It's because they are aerial acrobats like none other. Study the doves and you'll see how testy a target a butterfly could be if it

A German short-haired pointer dives into the water after a dove that has dropped into the cattails.

flew 60 miles an hour. They sashay, dip, slide, climb, twist, reverse (I swear they do), and twirl. If there's anything a bird can't do on the wing, doves do it.

They also have an uncanny detection system, seeming to know exactly where you'll be found. At the slightest hint that they're right, they'll slam into a repertoire of maneuvers the Thunderbirds couldn't unravel.

Pass shooting is the most difficult, I assure you, and can be practiced only by the hunter who's spent all summer learning their flight lanes.

The Party Shoot

There is one type of hunt that has more popularity than any other, and that's party shooting grain fields in the South. You know, the good ol' boys: They've planned this hunt for months, invited everybody for miles about—even relatives from three states over.

A great groaning table may be hidden in the trees, festooned with sodas, lemonade, iced tea, corn on the cob, red beans and rice, fried chicken, berry pie, and more.

Around the field itself, all the shooters have taken a stand, hoping to get the best place depending on the direction of the wind. Every type of gun imaginable will be aimed skyward. All gauges, all makes, all chokes, and all shells. And there'll be a Lab tied to every ankle.

Migratory Doves

Doves are migratory game birds and under federal jurisdiction. Make sure you check out all the regulations before you hunt them. When the shooting is fast and furious, some people can be tempted to shoot more than they should. Don't do it!

Some hunters try to take their doves over a dog's point. That seldom happens. Doves flock in groups of two: love birds. In other words, they're not covey birds.

When a migration comes, they'll join up, but that's done quickly, and then the birds are gone.

Doves won't run before a dog, they'll flush, hearty and quickly. They'll startle you, so you just don't get all that much sport with a bird dog.

The Bird in Hand

I know you can get the bird in hand and laud its iridescent coloration; make great distinction. But I see the bird in flight: a gray bird with a heavy breast, small head, and pointed tail. It walks with a bobbing head, like a pigeon.

Bush Whacking

For bush whacking doves, choose a 20- or 28-gauge shotgun. The winds will demand the size of shot and charge of powder.

There isn't a farm boy who hasn't knocked a dove off a telephone line. But it is illegal to shoot in a public right-of-way. Remember that.

REMEMBER THIS, TOO

When pond or grain field hunting, the hunter needs a retriever to fetch from water or to search vast areas for a downed bird. This can be accomplished if the dog handler follows a few simple rules.

The dog must be kept cool at all times. Dove hunting is a hot-weather activity, though, so here's what we do. Leaving home, the dog should be transported in a cross-ventilated or air-conditioned vehicle. If this isn't possible, the dog should be stored in a crate with at least a 25-pound block of ice. He'll love it.

THE ICE BLOCK

When you get to your field or pond, walk, *I mean walk,* to your set-up, which is usually under a tree. Carry the ice block with you. Place it on the ground and let it start to melt. Now scoot the ice over and tell Pup to lie down in the puddle.

Before you do anything else, give Pup a drink. Then, 15 minutes later, refresh him again. Do the same thing in another 15 minutes. The point is, if you can keep Pup cool, he'll fetch for you all day. But if Pup ever gets hot, there's not enough water in Lake Mead to cool him down. If you reach that point, Pup will quit fetching.

Here's how it works. Pup's got a hot mouth to begin with. When his temperature goes up, his mouth gets hotter. Once the saliva gets hot, it turns to a gunk with the ability to pick up almost anything: grass, pebbles, grit, feathers, seeds, and so forth.

KEEP A WATER-SLICK MOUTH

Particularly annoying to Pup are dove feathers. They're flimsy, fuzzy, and easily soaked on their fringes. Now Pup rubs the side of his face in the grass. Grass! Now he's got more grass, plus feathers.

So the cycle goes. But if enough water is on hand, you can break the cycle. Pup once again attains a water-slick mouth. And when that happens, he'll be all too happy to fetch for you.

PUP AFIELD

If a puppy is in the field, hide the doves that are already in your possession. Store them in a water cooler, a gunny sack, whatever. Just don't let the puppy get feathers stuck all about and be put off doves for life.

As a matter of fact, of all the bird hunts available, a dove hunt would be the last hunt I'd choose to introduce a puppy to the sound of the gun, the taste of feather, the heat of the day, and the predictably long and boring waits for anything to happen.

Puppies want action; they have an attention span of seconds or minutes. When starting one, keep everything fast-paced and happy.

FIELD & STREAM

The Complete Hunter

Book Four

Bow Hunting

Bob Robb

Choosing the Hunting Bow

HUNTING with a bow and arrow used to be the simplest of sports. All you needed was a recurve or longbow, a back quiver full of cedar arrow shafts fletched with real turkey feathers and tipped with a large broadhead that took some hand sharpening, a leather shooting glove, and a farm with deer on it.

Today, you still need the deer-infested farm, but other than that, the face of bowhunting has changed dramatically since the late 1960s, when the first reasonably priced compound bows became available. Walk into any well-stocked archery pro shop today and you'll approach sensory overload as you're bombarded by an endless array of high-tech compound bows, arrow shafts, broadheads, bow sights, and other accessories.

It all centers around the bow. Obviously, before you begin bowhunting you'll need a bow of some sort. The question is, How do you sort through all the hype and hoopla to find the right one for you?

M. R. James, one of the founders and former editor of *Bowhunter* magazine, once wrote that choosing a hunting bow was a lot like choosing a wife—it all boiled down to a matter of individual taste. His observation was, and still is, right on the money. Virtually every major bow manufacturer in business today builds top-notch hunting bows. They have subtle differences—how they look, how they feel in your hand, how they shoot for you may not be the same as they look, feel, and shoot for your best hunting buddy. Selecting a new bow is going to be a personal decision, one that should be based on your own tastes tempered with an objective look at performance and cost.

TRADITIONAL VERSUS COMPOUND BOWS

During the early days of the compound bow—the late 1960s and early 1970s—virtually all archers began their careers shooting either

Traditional bows, such as this Hoyt Skyhawk recurve, are the foundation on which modern bowhunting was built. *Photograph courtesy of Hoyt.*

The Browning Afterburner is a good example of a modern-day compound bow. It features two hard cams, Fast Flite string-and-cable system, is affixed with modern bow sight, peep sight, arrow rest, stabilizer, and bow quiver, and has a split-limb design. *Photograph courtesy of Browning.*

a longbow or recurve—lumped together and called "traditional" bows—then stepped up to a compound bow. Today just the opposite is true. Beginners start with a compound that lets them master the skills needed to become a good shot before ever thinking about stepping back into time and shooting a traditional bow.

That's not to say that traditional bows are no longer good for anything. I know serious traditional archers who have track records that would make the best compound shooters green with envy. It's just that it takes much more time, effort, and commitment to become a skilled "instinctive" shooter with unsighted traditional bows than it does to become proficient with a compound bow. If, after you've achieved basic bowshooting skills with a compound bow, the thought of emulating the original archers tickles your fancy, then go ahead and try your hand at traditional archery. But not before.

COMPOUND BOWS: WHAT ARE THEY?

Simply stated, a compound bow uses a system of round or eccentric wheels and cables that work together as the bowstring is pulled back to reduce a given bow's "holding weight" well below its listed "draw weight." This is a huge advantage for the shooter over using traditional bows, which give you no such mechanical advantage. Here's how it works.

With a traditional bow, the shooter draws the bowstring back, reaching the bow's peak draw weight—the heaviest amount of pressure needed to draw the string back—at full draw. There he must hold it on his fingers until he's ready to release the arrow. Let's say that's 70 pounds. That's a lot of weight! With a compound bow, however, the shooter gets a distinct mechanical advantage from the wheels and cables. A compound bow with a peak draw weight of the same 70 pounds and a "let-off" of 65 percent also forces the shooter

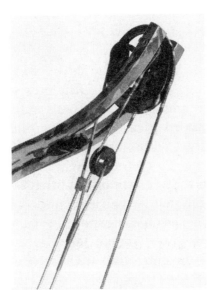

Modern compound bows rely on wheels and cables to reduce their holding weight well below the listed draw weight.

There are three basic types of compound wheel designs: round wheel, hard cam, and half cam. The round wheel, pictured here, is the most forgiving and quietest of the three.

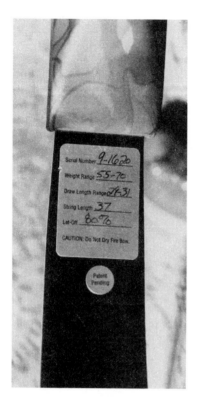

Modern compound bows feature an adjustable draw weight and adjustable draw length, making it easy to fit them to the individual shooter.

to put 70 pounds of pressure on his fingers as the bow is drawn back to about the halfway point. Then, this 70-pound peak weight is slowly reduced as the shooter continues to pull the bowstring all the way back to full draw, where he has to hold only 35 percent of the bow's peak draw weight on his fingers until the time of release. That's only 24.5 pounds of pressure! With such reduced pressure on your fingers, you'll be able to aim longer at the target without muscle fatigue, meaning you'll shoot more accurately.

In the early days of compound bows, the common let-off was about 50 percent. Today, let-offs commonly fall between 65 and 80 percent. High-let-off bows are increasingly popular despite the fact that the Pope & Young Club will not recognize animals taken with bows with a let-off of above 65 percent for entry into their record book.

Compounds have other advantages over traditional bows. For one thing, they allow you to shoot a faster arrow, which reduces trajectory, which in turn makes it easier to hit the target at unknown distances. They also generate more kinetic energy, which helps a broadhead-tipped arrow penetrate more deeply. And modern compound bows are designed for use with the latest high-tech accessories, such as bow sights, arrow rests, and release aids that foster precise shooting at distances that make traditional archers green with envy. It's no wonder that more than 90 percent of all modern bowhunters shoot a compound bow.

Here, then, are things you'll need to know as you go about selecting that new compound bow.

DOMINANT EYE

The most basic decision you'll have to make is whether or not you'll shoot your bow right- or left-handed. That's not a function of whether or not *you're* right- or left-handed, but whether or not you're right- or left-eye dominant. Normally the dominant eye is on the same side of the body as the dominant hand, but not always. Here's how to find out.

Hold your hands at arm's length, then form a small hole between the thumbs and forefingers. Keep both your eyes open, and center a distant object through this hole. Slowly draw your hands toward your face while staying focused on the object in the center of the hole. Your hands will naturally come back to your dominant eye.

DRAW LENGTH

The most important thing you can do when choosing a compound bow is to select one with *exactly* the right draw length for you. Draw length is defined as the distance from the bowstring at full draw to the back of the bow handle (the side farthest away from you as you hold the bow). A common mistake many bowhunters make is choosing a bow with a draw length that's too long for them. This creates shooting problems and will not permit you to shoot to your accuracy potential.

You can gauge your draw length in a couple of different ways. The best way is to pull a light-draw-weight bow to full draw with a long arrow on the bowstring, anchor it using the same anchor point you'll use when shooting, and have a friend mark the shaft at the back of the bow handle. Measure the shaft from that mark to the string groove on the arrow's nock, and that's your draw length. (Draw length is not the arrow length you'll need, however, so don't confuse the two.)

Your draw length will vary according to whether or not you shoot with a release aid or your fingers. You'll also find that your draw length may change over time, as you become more comfortable shooting compound bows in general. A good rule of thumb is that you'll shoot more accurately under hunting conditions with a bow set for a draw length that's slightly on the short side for you.

DRAW WEIGHT

Draw weight is defined as the maximum level of force needed to draw the bow back to the full or cocked position. Modern compound bows come from the factory with adjustable draw-weight ranges of between 10 and 15 pounds. The most common two are bows with draw weights between 55 and 70, and 65 and 80, pounds. That means that these bows can be adjusted within that draw-weight range to whatever setting the archer chooses.

A few years ago, when compound bow design was not as efficient as it is today, it was necessary to draw a lot of weight to shoot a reasonably fast arrow. Then, many bowhunters were pulling between 75 and 85 pounds. Today, however, bows are much more mechanically efficient and, coupled with today's modern arrow shaft design, produce faster arrow flight with less draw weight, with comparable kinetic energy. For example, it's easy to achieve a raw arrow speed of between 240 and 250 feet per second today with a draw weight of just 55 to 65 pounds. That's plenty of speed for most bowhunting situations.

That's not to say that raw arrow speed isn't important in bowhunting. It is, especially when shooting at game at unknown distances. A faster arrow has a flatter trajectory, which means you have more leeway in judging the exact distance to the target. It's just that when you pull more draw weight than you can comfortably handle you sacrifice bow control, which is the real key to accurate shooting. If you have to strain to pull the bow back, you'll have tense, taut muscles, which make it much more difficult to relax and "lay them in there."

To measure the correct draw weight for you, take these simple tests. Standing flat-footed, hold the bow at arm's length and pull it back. If you have to "cheat"—lift the bow up above your head—to achieve full draw, it's too heavy. Next, do the same thing from a seated position, as if you were sitting in a tree-stand seat. Finally, do it from a kneeling position. Being able to draw your bow with a minimum of movement, even from weird angles, is important when bowhunting. Extra body movement can spook an animal, so the less the better.

WHEELS AND CAMS

Modern compound bows have two wheels or cams, one at each end of the bow limb. There are three basic wheel designs, each offering advantages and disadvantages.

Round wheels are smooth to draw, very quiet, and foster accurate shooting. Most target shooters use a roundish wheel. However, round wheels are the slowest of the three basic designs, which is one reason they've fallen out of favor with today's bowhunters.

At the other end of the spectrum are full, or hard, cams. These egg-shaped eccentrics store the most energy of all the basic designs and thus produce the fastest arrow flight. For that reason they're very popular with bowhunters. However, cams tend to be a bit noisy and are the most difficult design to consistently shoot well.

Half-cams are the compromise, with part of the design round, part egg-shaped. This design produces a smoothness and reliability comparable to that of a round wheel, but also provides increased arrow speed, though not so much as that of a hard cam. Half-cams are an excellent choice for bowhunters.

Although most compound bows feature the same wheel or cam design at both ends, in the late 1990s the one-cam bow became the "rage" in compound bow design. One-cam bows have an oversized energy-storing cam on the lower limb, but instead of another cam on the top limb, they have a concentric wheel, called an idler. The advantage of the one-cam design is that it eliminates the problem of wheel timing, an important but difficult to control factor in bow tuning. (More about bow tuning in Chapter 7.) Modern one-cam designs are just as fast as comparable two-cam models, are quiet, feature a high let-off of between 70 and 85 percent, and are inherently accurate to shoot. Look for one-cam bows to continue their rise in popularity in the near future.

BOW HANDLES

Bow handles are generally made of aluminum or magnesium, two lightweight, strong metals. Modern handles feature an offset, or cutout, design, which makes it easier for the arrow fletching and broadhead blades to clear the riser during the shot.

The most important thing a bow handle can do for you is feel comfortable in your hand. Some shooters will sand or file a handle down a bit to fit their hand more precisely. Others will add tape, or premade plastic, or wooden grips to alter the feel. When you are

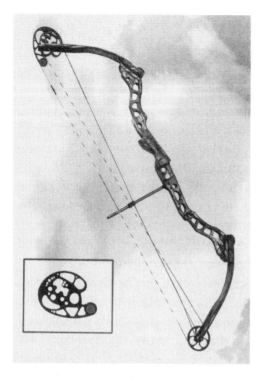

The one-cam bow, like this Matthews Conquest, has become increasingly popular in recent years. It features an oversized energy-storing cam on the bottom limb and a roundish "idler" wheel on the top limb. *Photograph courtesy of Matthews.*

shopping for a new bow, pick up several and see how each feels. The one that feels best is generally the bow you'll shoot best.

BOW LIMBS

Bow limbs come in both straight and recurve designs. Both work equally well, the only difference being how you like their looks. Two basic limb materials are used today—laminated wood and fiberglass. Generally speaking, glass limbs are the most dependable and trouble-free. However, wood limbs are excellent, too, and weigh a bit less. You can't go wrong with either material.

For many years, bow limbs were of a solid design. Today, however, many manufacturers are building bows with "split limbs." Split-limb bows have limbs with the center section of both the upper and lower limbs removed. This creates a bow that's lighter in weight than the solid-limb bow. Some manufacturers claim that split-limbs also reduce noise and increase arrow speed a bit. Others say that split-limb bows are less reliable than solid-limb bows, more difficult to tune, and not as consistent. I have a fair amount of experience with split-limb bows, and although I shoot them well and have taken some fine animals with them, I have personally gone back to a bow with solid limbs. To each his own.

STRINGS AND CABLES

For many years, Dacron was the material of choice for bowstrings and metal was the material used in cable systems. In 1985 Brownell & Co. introduced a synthetic material called Fast Flite (technically called "Spectra"), which is stronger and stretches less. That, in turn, gives us more arrow speed and less problems with wear and breakage. Today most bow companies offer complete Fast Flite string-and-cable systems. Another string material, Vectran, sold by both BCY Fibers and Brownell's, does not stretch or creep over time, as Fast Flite will. It is a bit less tolerant to abrasion, however. Both are excellent choices.

You'll also see most hunting bows affixed with a pair of string silencers. These are small pieces of rubber or pile material attached above and below the nock, about midway between the nock set and wheel. String silencers help dissipate the vibration—and hence, the noise—of the bow at the shot, reducing potential game-spooking noise. They don't noticeably affect bow performance, don't cost a lot, and are a recommended addition to your hunting bow.

BOW LENGTH

Another important factor is the overall length of your bow. Generally speaking, bows with a shorter axle-to-axle length produce more raw arrow speed than longer bows. (The axle is the rod that holds the wheel into the end of the bow limb.) Today, short bows with axle-to-axle lengths of between 36 and 41 inches are the most popular. There are several reasons for this besides the faster arrow speed. For one thing, most bowhunters use some sort of mechanical release aid instead of releasing the arrow with their fingers. Shorter bows lend themselves to this use. Conversely, longer bows are better for fingers shooters, because they reduce the amount of "finger pinch." Shorter bows are also easier to maneuver in the field, both among the limbs and branches encountered while you are in a tree stand and through brush while you are hunting on the ground.

Shorter bows are more subjective to the problems of hand torque on the riser during the shot, which can result in poor accuracy. For that reason alone you don't want a bow that's much shorter than 36 inches unless you're an expert shooter.

STABILIZERS

Stabilizers are elongated metal bars that screw into the front of the riser. They help reduce hand torque (twisting) of the bow handle at the shot, helping accuracy. They also help counterbalance the bow's rearward weight, helping counter a bow's tendency to "jump" forward at the shot. The added weight of a stabilizer also helps you to steady the bow as you aim and release, and the stabilizer helps reduce vibration and noise during the shot.

Stabilizers were once solid pieces of metal. Today the trend is toward hydraulic stabilizers, which improve performance. Generally speaking, the longer the stabilizer, the better it will work. Most hunting stabilizers are between 4 and 10 inches long. For many years, I shot my bow without a stabilizer. Today, however, I use a relatively short (5-inch) hydraulic stabilizer. That's not necessarily because I like the extra weight or having a long rod sticking off the front of my bow, but because I can consistently shoot better with one.

OVERDRAWS

For years, a popular way bowhunters achieved more arrow speed was to use an overdraw. An overdraw is an arrow rest bracket that extends 2 to 6 inches back behind the riser, allowing you to shoot shorter, and therefore lighter, arrows. However, overdraws have their problems, the biggest being that they make it imperative for the archer to maintain excellent shooting form throughout the shot sequence to avoid torque, which will throw the shaft off-target. The longer the overdraw, the more exaggerated this problem can become.

I know several bowhunters who have shot an overdraw well for years, but I personally don't like them. They are an advantage for shooters with extremely long arms, though. For most of us, a better way to achieve a small overdraw effect is to use an arrow rest that bolts directly to the riser, then "wraps around" the rear of the handle to produce, in effect, an overdraw about 1 inch long.

THE PERFECT HUNTING COMPOUND

You can read all the books and magazine articles and listen to an endless stream of advice, but the bottom line on choosing the perfect hunting bow is this—you like it. It's a bow that simply feels good in your hand, looks good to you, and makes you happy to own it. It's set

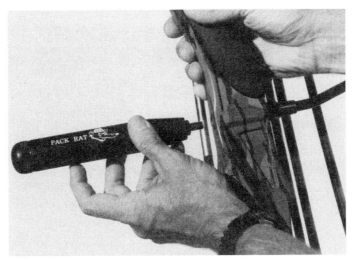

A stabilizer is an elongated metal bar that screws into the front of the bow. It helps reduce hand torque, counterbalances the bow's rearward weight, and reduces vibration.

The bottom line when choosing a new hunting bow is simply this—does it feel good to you? Do you like it? Can you shoot an accurate arrow with it?

at the correct draw length for you, at a draw weight you can comfortably pull back, with a let-off you can hold for a reasonable length of time. To it you can attach modern accessories like a bow sight, quiver, and arrow rest. Today, virtually all major bow manufacturers build excellent hunting bows backed with a solid warranty.

A COMPOUND BOW

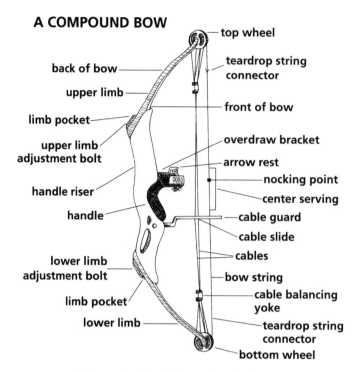

top wheel
teardrop string connector
back of bow
upper limb
front of bow
limb pocket
overdraw bracket
upper limb adjustment bolt
arrow rest
nocking point
center serving
handle riser
cable guard
handle
cable slide
cables
lower limb adjustment bolt
bow string
cable balancing yoke
limb pocket
teardrop string connector
lower limb
bottom wheel

Illustration by Christopher Seubert.

The best place to buy your bow is from a reputable archery pro shop. Here you can "test drive" several different makes, models, and designs, and get expert advice on the features and benefits of bow designs and accessories applicable to the kind of bowhunting you'll be doing. Most important, the resident pro will help you set up your bow the right way, making sure the draw length and draw weight are correct, help you select the right arrow shafts, and then help you tune your bow until it's shooting darts. He'll also be there when you have problems and need a little help in working the kinks out of both your bow and your shooting form. Choosing a new bow in this manner—not unlike shopping for a new car—can be time-consuming, but the end result is that you'll have a bow that you have confidence in, shoot well, and will enjoy for years.

CHAPTER

The Modern Arrow Rest

THE DIFFERENCES between the basic bow-and-arrow setups used to shoot at game and targets just a decade or two ago and the hot-rod setups so popular today are astounding. In just thirty years the archery industry evolved from a recurve bow, wood or aluminum shaft, glue-on broadhead, finger tab or shooting glove crowd to a short-axle compound bow, advanced aluminum, carbon, or aluminum–carbon composite shaft, screw-in broadhead, release aid bunch. If you'd been asleep for twenty years and just woke up, you'd have a hard time recognizing one of today's most popular bow-and-arrow setups.

Few archery items have evolved over the years as dramatically as the arrow rest, yet rests are often overlooked and underrated by archers more concerned with raw arrow speed and other accessory items that have more "sex appeal." Take it from me: using the wrong arrow rest is a formula for consistently poor shooting.

ARROW RESTS IN THE "OLD DAYS"

In the beginning, archers with longbows did nothing more than rest the shaft across the fist of their bow hand, usually protecting against friction with a leather glove or, sometimes, nothing more than an adhesive bandage or strip of cloth tape. Then, in the 1950s, the then highly evolved recurve bow was designed with an arrow shelf that was carved into the grip. Archers covered these shelves with pieces of low-pile carpet, cloth, or leather, and found that shooting "off the shelf" was a big step up in consistent accuracy.

It was in the 1960s that archers began using the first removable arrow rests. These simply designed rests were usually little more than a horizontal plastic (or, sometimes, hair or feather) shelf for the arrow to rest upon, and a plastic or nylon side plate for the shaft to rest against. Rests were soon developed that permitted some horizontal

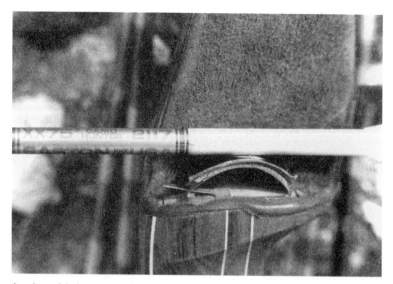

In the old days, archers shot their arrows "off the shelf" without the aid of modern adjustable arrow rests.

side-plate adjustments, which greatly aided in the bow-tuning process and made accurate shooting at longer ranges a reality for skilled archers. Most of these rests attached to the bow with double-backed adhesive tape. These types of inexpensive arrow rests are still available today.

Arrow rests took a giant step in the evolution process in the mid-1960s with the introduction of the Berger Button. Actually invented by tournament shooter Norman Pint, but named for well-known tournament shooter Victor Berger, this button cushioned the shaft against side-to-side oscillation as it was released, which in turn tightened arrow groups dramatically. When used in conjunction with the popular adhesive-backed Flipper or Flipper II arrow shelf, this combination became the standard against which all other rests of the late 1960s to early 1970s were judged. Although you won't find any Berger Button–and–shelf rests today, you will find many similar arrow rests, which today are called by the generic name cushion plunger.

A variation of the cushion plunger of the 1970s was the springy rest, which was nothing more than a threaded brass barrel connected to a coiled, one-piece spring-wire plate-and-shelf unit. Springys were sold in a variety of spring gauges and tension weights to accommodate different bow weights and arrow stiffnesses, and could be adjusted horizontally. These simple, rugged rests were popular with bowhunters of that era, but are as rare as a four-leaf clover today.

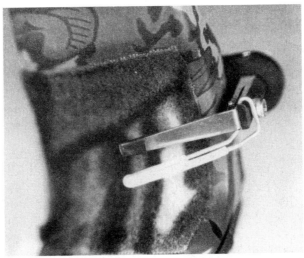

The cushion plunger rest, which revolutionized arrow rests in the late 1960s to early 1970s, could be adjusted both side to side and up and down. The Cavalier Super-Flyte rest is a type of cushion plunger rest, and remains popular with modern fingers shooters.

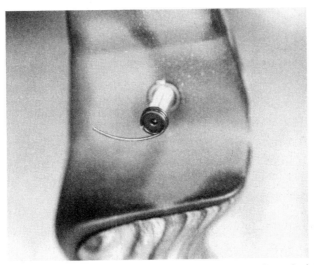

The springy rest was nothing more than a threaded brass barrel connected to a coiled piece of wire. It was popular in the 1970s.

In the 1980s we saw the rise in popularity of the prong, or launcher-type, arrow rests. These rest types were actually invented in 1967 by southern Californian Fred Troncoso, a professional musician and serious tournament archer who founded Golden Key-Futura a

The Golden Key-Futura 3-D Rover is a classic example of a modern arrow rest. *Photograph courtesy of Golden Key-Futura.*

year later, making not arrow rests, but the first rope release aids and a nock-aligner device. "I was shooting tournaments with Roy Hoff, and he got me started making rests back then," Troncoso says. "I first just whittled rests out of wood and plastic. The first prong-type rest came about after I acquired my first Sable center-shot bow in 1967, which had a little wire rest, so I made a prong-style rest to fit this bow. This was before release aids were around, but it worked great anyway. But no one was really interested in them, they were too radical and complicated at that time."

Troncoso kept tinkering with his new arrow rest design, "just trying to improve my own shooting," he says. "I just wanted to beat everyone else." Troncoso's first patented arrow rest was the Match One, patented in 1973–1974, followed by the Pace Setter Vee-launcher type rest a year later. "Even though my wife won three national field championships using this new rest, people still weren't that interested in such a new, radical design," Troncoso says. "After all, the arrow fell off if you turned the bow on its side! Sometimes it just takes a while for a good idea to catch on."

It wasn't until 1982–1983 that Troncoso's Vee-launcher rest first became accepted by a significant number of archers. Back then these rest types were commonly called wraparound rests because the rest unit attached to the Berger Button hole tapped into the off-side of the bow's riser, then "wrapped around" the back side of the riser. Initially there were two basic styles of this rest. The Vee-launcher type, like the old PSE Hunter Supreme and Martin Slide Rest, featured a solid metal post with a V-shaped cutout in which the arrow was rested. The Shoot-Through rest featured a pair of upthrust metal prongs, between which the shaft was rested. The Townsend Lodestar and PSE-CF-TM Hunter were two early examples.

The evolution of the arrow rest continues at a fast pace. Basic designs remain the same, but variations on the theme are widespread. Today's archer has more different arrow rest makes, models, and designs to choose from than at any time in history. Such diversity is good, but it can also breed confusion. Which rest is the right one for you?

MODERN ARROW RESTS

Today, arrow rests come in a seemingly endless array of styles and designs that, often as not, confound the novice. Common questions are, Why is rest category A better than category B? What features do I need on an arrow rest? Can I use the same rest for target shooting as I do for bowhunting?

Before choosing an arrow rest, you have to have a basic understanding of how arrow shafts bend, or oscillate, when released. It may not appear to be so, but high-speed photography has shown that arrows bend a surprising amount during the shot. The amount and type of bending are a direct result of shaft stiffness and the way the shaft was released. It is not until the shaft has traveled downrange that it recovers from this oscillation. Clearing the arrow rest at the shot is very important for accurate shooting.

Basically, when you release an arrow with your fingers, it oscillates from side to side as it leaves the bow, the first large bend it takes being away from the bow's handle. This type of release lends itself to the cushion plunger style of arrow rest, because as the shaft bends away from the bow it is bending away from the arrow rest, too. Conversely, a shaft that has been released with a mechanical release aid tends to bend up and down, not side to side. This lends itself to the use of a Vee-launcher or prong-type arrow rest. That's because when the bowstring is released the first large bend the shaft takes is upward, away from the rest's two metal prongs.

"Our surveys indicate that somewhere between 80 percent and 90 percent of today's archers—and that includes both bowhunters and target shooters—use some type of release aid," says Bob Mizek of New Archery Products, a leading manufacturer of both arrow rests and broadheads. "That means that the basic shoot-through rest design is the basic type of arrow rest that most of them will be using. To that end, you're seeing a lot of the industry's research and development efforts in the arrow rest segment directed towards this type of rest."

"Without a doubt, the biggest part of the business is for bowhunters, and that's what we concentrate our efforts on," says Huey Savage of Savage Systems, another large rest maker. "They need an arrow rest that's reliable, quiet, and that will be unobstructive for vane clearance. When you think about it, the arrow rest is an asset only until the arrow is released. After that if it were totally out of the way we would be much better off.

"And because most archers are shooting a release these days, the shoot-through–type rest is by far the most popular and practical for them," Savage continues. "We offer some arrow rest models with cushion plungers in them, but they're not high-ticket or high-volume items for us."

DESIRABLE DESIGN FEATURES

A look at the many different arrow rests offered for sale today will turn up everything from simple to complex. Some rests have few adjustment features; others—notably those designed with the serious target archer in mind—have more screws and adjustment knobs than a rocket ship.

In recent years, the industry trend has been toward rests that can be micro-adjusted—that is, with vertical and horizontal adjustments that can be made in small increments. The goal is to permit precise vertical and horizontal rest adjustments so that an archer can perfectly tune his bow-and-arrow combination. However, many of these rests ultimately disappoint bowhunters, who find that their complex adjustment systems are difficult to work with and that the many tiny adjustment screws and knobs often rattle loose or slip during hunting season, which of course changes their shaft's point of impact.

Fortunately, the pendulum seems to be swinging away from complex and back to simple. Manufacturers have learned that bowhunters—their bread-and-butter customer base—want simpler designs that require less maintenance during the course of a hunting season.

"We feel that basic arrow rest design is returning to a more simplistic style," says Mizek. "Our conversations with our bowhunting customers show that they want, first and foremost, reliability in their arrow rests. Second, they need to be able to make both vertical and horizontal adjustments easily, but then once they have been made, not worry about it again. They want simplicity without giving up the features. We know we can make everything super adjustable, but the reality is that often you end up with a bow-and-arrow setup that, once it's tuned and the arrow rest set, you never use the adjustment features of the rest again. We're trying to make rests simple to set up, quick to dial in, and built so they won't get beat up during tough field use and will hold up in extreme weather conditions."

"The number one factor in an arrow rest for bowhunting is reliability," says Troncoso. "Simplicity is also crucial for bowhunters. And yet, savvy bowhunters want the micro-adjustability that permits them to precisely tune their bow-and-arrow setup. After all, all archers, be they target shooters or bowhunters, like to tinker with their equipment, and want to be able to tune their bows as precisely as possible. They're always looking for a little extra edge in their equipment, and this is one factor that gives it to them."

THE CUSHION PLUNGER: OBSOLETE?

With 80 to 90 percent of all bowhunters using a release aid and, therefore, some type of shoot-through arrow rest, is the cushion plunger style of rest now headed for the scrap heap?

Not necessarily. "I find that, when it's all said and done, using a reliable cushion plunger rest—especially one that offers a bit of downward give—can be an excellent choice for bowhunting, even with a release aid," says Lon Lauber, a well-known bowhunting writer, highly accomplished bowhunter, and winner of several Alaska state field and broadhead target shooting championships. "Especially on what I sometimes call a 'he-man' hunting trip, like backpacking for deer or elk, hunting in Alaska, and so on, the simplicity of these types of rests, the ease at which they can be adjusted in the field with a minimum number of tools, and their almost indestructible construction makes them a good choice."

"We've found that we can still sell a quality cushion plunger style of arrow rest," says Mizek. "The Centerrest, for example, with its downward give, sells about 60 percent to fingers shooters, but about 40 percent to release shooters. That tells us that there are still many, many bowhunters out there who value the rugged simplicity of this type of rest enough to put them on their hunting bows, even if they're shooting a release aid. So really, cushion plungers aren't fading away at all."

THE CARBON ARROW CHALLENGE

Although large-diameter aluminum arrow shafts continue to dominate the market, more and more archers are discovering the benefits of small-diameter carbon arrow shafts for both target shooting and bowhunting. They're also discovering the challenges posed by these small-diameter shafts in terms of choosing and using an arrow rest.

"Tuning a bow with a hundred different arrow rests when using aluminum arrows is a pretty straightforward task," says Savage. "But when using the small-diameter carbon shafts, shooters are finding that they need to make precise adjustments both with their rest and in the way they position their arrow nocks. It takes the right rest to shoot carbon shafts well."

"No doubt about it, carbons are coming on," says Mizek. "And with them comes a fletch clearance problem. We've also seen trouble with the highly abrasive carbon material rapidly destroying the shrink tubing used for many years to help silence the sound of a shaft as it is drawn and shot across the metal prongs of a shoot-through rest. To date no one has been able to solve that problem, although using stick-on felt seems to work well now, and it definitely holds up better than shrink tubing.

"One other thing we see that is starting to make a difference with fletch/arrow rest contact problems is that the smallest-diameter carbons are beginning to fade somewhat in popularity, with the larger-diameter carbon shafts like the Easton A/C/C, Gold Tip, Beman ICS, and Game Tracker with internal components instead of overserts, coming on in popularity," Mizek continues. "These slightly fatter shafts help tremendously in eliminating fletch clearance troubles."

ARROW REST COSTS

"While there are several price categories of arrow rests, we believe that today's archer who's not a beginner won't get sticker shock if a quality arrow rest falls into that $25–$40 price range," says Mizek. "Beginners may buy something a bit cheaper, but much higher than that you'll find some resistance."

"Top target shooters will pay anything for a rest, because they want the ultimate in performance," Troncoso says. "But with the mass market, and that includes bowhunters, rests selling in the $20–$40 range are the mainstay of the business. The key for us as a company is to have a quality rest that falls into every price category, so the shooter can spend as much or as little as they want and still buy our products."

DOWN THE ROAD

What's down the road for arrow rests, in terms of design? Manufacturers tell us not to hold our breath waiting for a new "radical" design anytime soon.

"There is a tapering off point for everything, just like the efficiency of bows," says Troncoso. "Most quality products are built on a variation of some tested theme. But creativity will tell. For example, we have some arrow rest designs that we're working on right now that, while we could bring them to market today, we don't want to saturate the market with too many new products at once. You also have to educate the public to the benefits of a new rest before it will sell well for you, which both takes time and some of the focus off your existing product line.

"I think two things are important in any archery product design and development, not just arrow rests," Troncoso continues. "First, for dealers to be able to sell the product, customer awareness is critical. The best manufacturers support their product lines with advertising and promotions. And two, you have to be a shooter to design quality new products. Our family goes hunting primarily to think and brainstorm about how we might tweak this or that to make it better.

"So who knows? Maybe on our next trip to the woods, one of my sons will come up with some crazy idea that will work, like I did with the prong-type rest back in the sixties," Troncoso says. "We'll all just have to wait and see."

CHAPTER

Effective Aiming Systems

EW THINGS IN LIFE get my goat more than poorly designed and cheaply made hunting accessories. Over the years, few things have disappointed me more than one of the many different bow sights I've purchased and taken into the hunting woods. Lousy bow sights have cost me more than one opportunity at game. That's why I made a myself a promise years ago—no fragile bow sights will ever find themselves attached to my riser!

Fortunately for bowhunters, there are more excellent hunting bow sights available at reasonable prices today than ever before. Bow sight design and manufacture are both evolving rapidly, the result being that innovations like easy-to-see sight pins and/or stadia wires, easily adjustable sights featuring fewer moving parts, and compact construction are becoming common. Accessory and sight companies such as Advanced Archery Products, Chek-It, Cobra, Fine-Line, Fisher, Keller, Saunders, Sight Master, Sonoran Bowhunting Products, Specialty Archery Products, Sure-Loc, Timberline Archery, Toxonics, and Tru-Glo, among others, all make excellent hunting bow sights today. Many large bow companies—Browning, Hoyt USA, Martin Archery, and PSE, to name a few—also offer excellent hunting sights.

SIGHTING SYSTEMS

A bow sight is part of a total sighting system that can include a peep sight or kisser button, as well as some add-on sight accessories such as small lights for illuminating the top sight pin in dim light.

While some compound shooters hunt without a peep sight, every year more and more are discovering the peep sight advantage. A peep forces you to keep your head erect and anchored consistently, presenting the same sight picture shot after shot. "I see more and more

A peep sight will help you shoot a more accurate arrow. Be sure to use it with as large an aperture as possible.

bowhunters shooting a peep today simply because it helps them shoot more accurately," says Sam Topel, President of Fine-Line, Inc., the industry's leading manufacturer of peep sights and himself an accomplished bowhunter. "One reason is that most all top 3-D shooters are using peeps, and bowhunters feed off their success. It also takes much more practice time to become a good shooter without a peep than with one, and time is something most bowhunters don't have in great abundance these days."

The key to using a peep sight for bowhunting is to make sure the aperture is as large as possible. This lets in the maximum amount of light, critical when you're trying to find your pins or stadia wire at dawn or dusk. This large hole won't noticeably affect hunting accuracy. In the "old days," I used to take a Fine-Line Zero Peep Sight and use a quarter-inch drill to drill out the aperture hole as much as possible. Today, Fine-Line has eliminated this hassle with its Sta-Brite peep, which has a huge hole already in place. Some peeps, like the Fine-Line Pick-A-Peep, come with adjustable apertures to make this process easier. Game Tracker's popular Dusk Vision Peep Sight uses four small neon polycarbonate fibers that gather light, which helps illuminate the viewing window in low light conditions. The Shurz-A-Peep, Golden Key Line-O-Peep, and Pete Shepley Peep Sight are excellent peeps as well.

When it comes to bow sights, there are four basic bow sight types—fixed-pin, movable-pin, crosshair, and pendulum. Each has advantages and disadvantages, and each has a place in a bowhunter's repertoire under certain circumstances.

FIXED-PIN SIGHTS

By far the most popular sight type today, fixed-pin sights offer tremendous flexibility in that several sight pins can be added or

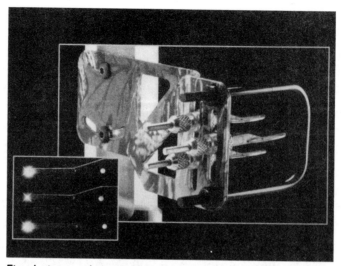

Fixed-pin type bow sights are the most versatile and popular design used today. Those with fiber-optic pins, like this Tru-Glo Glo-Brite pin sight, are the best choice for most hunting situations.

removed as your needs dictate. Each of the pins can be set for a precise distance, and shots taken when not at these distances—as most shots at animals are—are sighted at "between the pins." Easily switching between pins set at different distances is also a big advantage when game is moving, allowing the hunter to track the animal and change pins instantaneously. Because of the simple design of most fixed-pin sights, they can be made with few moving parts and constructed like a rock.

The choices between the sight pins themselves are varied. Small-diameter pins are best when distances are long and light is good; larger-diameter pins are better in lower light. For many years the only pins available were either $\frac{5}{32}$ or $\frac{8}{32}$ inch in diameter, but now some sights, like the Sonoran Hunter, feature thin, 0.026-inch wire pins.

The first sight pins designed to help bowhunters see in dim light, such as the Saunders T-Dot and Dot Sight Pin as well as the Meprolight Tritium sight pin, are fast being replaced by the new wave of fiber-optic sight pins. These pins use a colored polycarbonate fiber strand that gathers the maximum amount of available light in dim light conditions when deer and other big game animals are most active, transferring it along the length of the fiber strand until it brightly concentrates in the fiber tip. This makes shots possible earlier and later in the day than ever before without the use of electronic lights. Companies making quality fiber-optic sights today include Browning, PSE, Sonoran Bowhunting Products, Montana Black Gold, Tru-Glo, Toxonics, Savage Systems, Original Bright Sight, Fine-Line, Cobra, and Scout Mountain Equipment, among others. Bowhunters can also purchase fiber-optic sight pins separately from companies such as Tru-Glo, Timberline Archery, and Game Tracker. Fiber-optic bow sights and sight pins are the wave of the future. They are the smart choice for most all bowhunting situations, but especially for tree-stand bowhunters expecting their best opportunities for a shot on the cusp of daylight.

Also available today are various lighted sight pins, which are not legal in all states but offer excellent low-light visibility. Cobra offers lighted sight pins, as well as the Light All sight light, which screws into the top of the pin guard and shines a light down on the sight pins.

CROSSHAIR SIGHTS

Crosshair sights are also excellent for bowhunting. They function the same way pin sights do, with horizontal stadia wires moved up or down to place the arrow on target at a specific distance. Their vertical stadia wire helps keep the shooter from inadvertently letting the bow cant left or right during the shot, and also helps when shooting between the pins.

Crosshair sights give the shooter both a vertical and horizontal reference point, making them very accurate sights. The Fine-Line version is the bestselling crosshair sight of all time.

When crosshair sights first appeared, many were flimsy and broke easily. The best, however, such as those from Fine-Line, Cobra, Montana Sights, Hoyt USA, Game Tracker, and PSE, are built to take the inevitable bumps and bruises a bowhunter will give them. Another disadvantage to early crosshair sights was their deep black stadia wires, which are almost impossible to see in critical low-light situations, especially when using a peep sight. Many bowhunters paint the stadia with fluorescent paint to overcome this handicap. Today several crosshair sights, such as the Fine-Line Ultra-Glo, Timberline Archery Natural Light Crosshair Scope, and Seneca Range Finder Sight, feature fiber-optic stadia, making them easy to see in poor light. Fine-Line also has a crosshair sight with stainless steel stadia wires, which are easy to see in almost all light conditions.

MOVABLE-PIN SIGHTS

The theory behind bow sights with movable pins is that by moving the single sight pin to adjust to the target distance, the archer could always aim with his pin dead on the target, thus eliminating the guesswork of shooting between the pins. The ideal situation would permit the archer to dial in the distance to the target with a range finder before coming to full draw.

Movable pin sights have their proponents. Some open-country western bowhunters—where shots can range from in-your-face to "way out there"—depend on the combination of a laser range finder and movable pin sight to help them make precise shots at all distances. Some tree-stand whitetail hunters like these sights, too, setting their sight pin for a different specific distance when they change their tree-stand locations.

The downside to movable-pin sights is when the animal is moving, or appears suddenly out of the brush, and the distance is not known. Then the bowhunter is forced to guess, and would probably would be better served with a fixed-pin or crosshair sight. However, movable-pin sights do have a place in some bowhunting situations. I've used a Sight Master movable sight a fair amount and have found it works very well. Martin Archery also makes quality sights of this type.

PENDULUM SIGHTS

If ever there was a bow sight designed for the tree-stand hunter, it is the pendulum sight. Here a single horizontal cross wire or pin is permitted

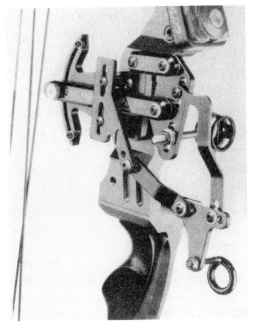

Movable-pin type sights allow the shooter to move the single sight pin to the exact setting at which the target is located. This eliminates the guesswork of shooting between the pins.

to freely pivot on a hinge so that it rises as you take aim closer to the base of your tree and drops as you aim farther away. Together with a fixed vertical stadia wire, the two give a precise aiming point out to 30 to 35 yards, the exact distance being directly proportional to arrow speed. Beyond that distance the system breaks down. Some pendulum sights attack this problem by adding a couple of fixed horizontal pins or stadia wires to give the shooter an aiming point at longer distances.

The better pendulum sights will allow you to adjust the length of the pivoting arm, thereby fine-tuning the sight for your individual bow's arrow speed. However, sights without this feature give acceptable accuracy at the distances at which they are designed to be used. One disadvantage of some pendulum sights is that they tend to be a bit noisy, and their moving parts can break or stick. You'll find that tree-stand bowhunters who use pendulum sights would rather, as the old commercial used to say, fight than switch. There are several good pendulum sights on the market, including those by Keller, Saunders, and Advanced Archery Products.

IMPORTANT HUNTING SIGHT FEATURES

When it comes to hunting bow sights, the KISS principal—Keep It Simple, Stupid—applies. Bow sights with the fewest movable parts, that have the least number of screws and knobs, that need the fewest

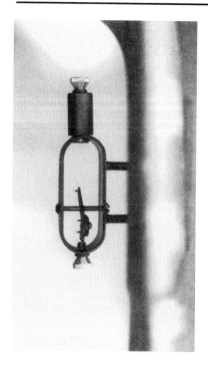

Pendulum sights were designed with tree-stand hunters in mind. Their single pin freely pivots on a hinge, allowing the elevated hunter to aim right on the target out to 35 yards without making any sight adjustments.

number of different Allen head wrenches to adjust and secure, and that are compact and relatively lightweight, are the ones that will cause you the least grief over time.

The better sights have simple vertical and horizontal adjustments. Many of today's sights also permit the entire sight pin block to be moved as a single entity while maintaining the solid integrity of the sight. This is a great feature, especially if you sight the bow in, then bump the sight bracket or find the bow goes out of tune just a bit and are forced to adjust the arrow rest or move the nock point slightly to regain the tune you want. You then must resight in only one pin—usually a midrange pin—and the others are going be very close to exactly on the money. This will save you a bundle of time.

One often-overlooked hunting sight feature is a rugged pin or stadia wire guard. A pin guard cannot be too beefy. After dinging pins for many years, I have often cannibalized a bow sight I didn't particularly like just to get its oversized pin guard for one I did like to shoot.

"I can remember back in the old days hunting with an old Merrill pin sight," says Jim Velasquez, president of bow quiver maker Sagittarius, a former tournament shooter, and an experienced bowhunter. "Once I was chasing a big bull elk and fell, totally trashing all my sight pins to the point I couldn't hunt any more. Ever since then I've

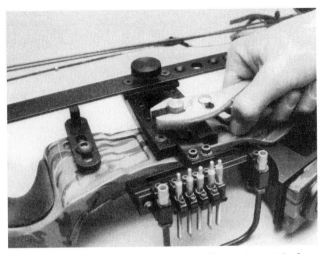

The best bow sights are ruggedly made, with few moving parts to rattle or shake loose in the field. Using a dovetail sight mounting system allows the sight to be removed for transport, then reattached quickly and easily.

believed that without a good pin guard a bow sight was useless for hunting." Some bow sights feature a beefy clear plastic pin guard that does two things—protects the sight's fiber-optic sight pins and allows in additional light for easier aiming in low-light situations.

Hunting sights must also attach securely to the bow's riser. Some attach directly to the riser with two large screws; many more use a dovetail mounting system. The dovetail system provides the most flexibility while still holding the sight in place like cement. With a dovetail mount, you can easily remove the bow sight for transportation, then reattach it quickly and easily. One helpful hint is to use white paint or an indelible marker and mark the edge of the both the male dovetail and female dovetail bracket with the sight attached. This way you can be sure that the sight is replaced in precisely the same position every time, assuring a consistent point of impact. To minimize noise I like to pad both the riser and the bottom of my sight's dovetail bracket with a small piece of stick-on felt before bolting the bracket down.

Choosing a Hunting Sight

There's no secret formula in choosing a hunting bow sight except to select one that fits your shooting style, hunting technique, and personal preferences. With sight design and technology changing rapidly, the best way to see what's out there is to visit a well-stocked archery pro shop and look over several different makes, models, and designs. Ask the shop owner to let you shoot a couple of different sights on the indoor range. If two or three appeal to you about the same, make your decision based upon the KISS principle.

However, KISS doesn't include the word *cheap*. To avoid heartbreak at the wrong time—like when a good buck finally walks into range after a season of searching—buy the best bow sight you can afford. Then take your time and precisely adjust the pins or crosshair stadia wires until you know exactly where your bow is shooting at various distances. Doing so will help you enjoy shooting your bow and will increase your chances of success in the hunting woods.

4

Arrow Shaft Selection

OWHUNTERS LOVE TO TALK about their "stuff" and spend countless hours debating the merits of this arrow rest versus that, the advantages of bow sight A versus sight B, and so on. Yet when it's all said and done, the object of the entire exercise is to place a broadhead-tipped arrow shaft into the vitals of your quarry. Central to that task is a perfectly straight, correctly spined arrow that will fly with dartlike precision from your bow despite the attempts of a broadhead to steer it off course.

Fortunately for bowhunters, there are now more top-quality arrow shafts and shaft components from which to choose than at any time in history. Getting a shaft to fly straight and true with a broadhead attached has never been easier.

BASIC SHAFT COMPONENTS

A modern arrow shaft is made up of several components: the shaft itself, nock, fletching, and arrow tip insert. To build a shaft that will fly straight and true, each component must be made to work in perfect harmony with the others.

Although some traditional bowhunters continue to shoot arrows made of select wood, more than 95 percent of today's archers use arrows made from aluminum, carbon, or a combination of the two. We'll talk more about materials later in this chapter, but one thing you need to remember about arrow shafts is that they must be as straight as can be to fly true. Shaft makers will guarantee their shafts to be straight up to a certain tolerance, usually of between ± 0.004 and 0.001 inch. I've found that to fly perfectly straight with broadheads attached, shafts must have a straightness of at least ± 0.002 inch.

When selecting a shaft for bowhunting, you must choose one with the correct "spine." High-speed photography has shown that shafts bend tremendously when shot from a bow. Spine refers to the

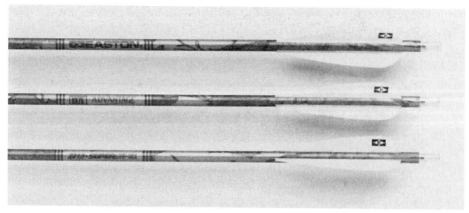

Aluminum arrows have dominated the arrow shaft market for decades, and continue to provide high performance and good value for bowhunters.

amount the shaft will bend during the shot. Shafts of the proper spine will bend less and recover from this initial bending more quickly than those of improper spine, which results in more accurate arrow flight. The correct spine for your own bow is a function of several things, including your bow's draw weight and eccentric (wheel) design, your draw length, the arrow point weight, the type of arrow release you use (fingers or a mechanical release aid), and the shaft material itself. Fortunately, all shaft manufacturers produce shaft selection charts, which helps simplify the selection process.

Adequate fletching is critical in steering your shaft on a straight course. It is the job of the fletching to overcome the tendency of a broadhead's blades to try to steer the arrow, a formidable task. There are two basic fletch materials to choose from: natural feathers or plastic vanes. Feathers are softer and therefore more forgiving of any slight contact they might have with the arrow rest or bow's riser during the shot. They also weigh less and are a bit faster than vanes. However, vanes are much tougher and are impervious to water and other climatic changes that can severely hamper the performance of feathers. For those reasons vanes dominate the market.

Most shafts today use three vanes glued to the shaft in a slightly helical, or offset, pattern. This encourages the arrow to spin like a perfectly spiraled football pass, not like a wobbling knuckleball. Most aluminum arrows are fletched with 5-inch-long vanes or feathers, while smaller-diameter carbon shafts generally are fletched with 3½- to 4-inch-long vanes or feathers. On rare occasions, four vanes or feathers are used.

There are two ways to attach nocks and arrow points to an arrow shaft. The first is by "swaging," or gluing, them on. One or both ends

Arrow shafts must have adequate fletching to stabilize the shaft while in flight. There are two choices—plastic vanes (top) or natural feathers. Vanes are more rugged, feathers are quieter and a bit faster.

of an arrow shaft are tapered to a solid point, over which a nock or an arrow point is then glued. Swaging was popular with traditional archers, but few bowhunters follow this practice today. Instead, modern archers use adapters that permit broadheads and target points to be screwed into the shaft, and tunable nock systems.

Aluminum screw-in arrow point adapters fit snugly into the hollow core of the shaft, where they are glued in. They are convenient, they are easy to use, and they make changing target points and broadheads quick and easy. They add a small bit of weight to the overall shaft, but not enough to worry about. The key to using them properly is to make sure they are glued into the shaft as straight as can be.

Tunable nock systems are a million times better than old-style, glue-on nocks, and are one of the great advances in modern arrow shafts. Why? To achieve dartlike arrow flight, it is important that minimal—and preferably, no—contact be made between the fletching at the arrow rest or bow riser during the release. This is achieved by positioning the nock so that the fletching clears these two obstacles. Once the nock is glued on, that's it—the fletching is going where it's going, regardless. With a tunable nock—one that can be turned, or pivoted—the nock can be adjusted slightly to ensure perfect fletch clearance. This is a time-saving and convenient function, especially when you are tuning a bow or changing arrow rests or your style of release.

One of the most important innovations in bowhunting in recent years is the proliferation of tunable arrow nock systems. These systems permit the archer to fine-tune the position of the shaft on the arrow rest, helping to eliminate any fletch contact with the rest or bow handle. Here two Easton tunable nock systems flank a shaft with an old-style glue-on nock.

Arrow shaft components are little things, yet without the right components properly matched and attached to a shaft of the correct spine, you have been defeated before the battle has ever begun.

DOUG EASTON: ARROW SHAFT PIONEER

A discussion about modern arrow shafts would not be complete without mention of arrow shaft pioneer Doug Easton, whose arrows helped make shooting a bow popular for the masses of people who did not have time to mess with the intricacies of wooden shafts.

In 1922 Easton was a resident of the San Francisco Bay area, an avid archer and bowhunter who built his own first hunting bows and arrows in his teens. He experimented extensively with wooden arrow shafts, and many top competitive archers set records using his cedar arrows. In 1932 he moved his arrow-building business to Los Angeles, where he grew frustrated with the lack of consistency and uniformity between each piece of wood. He began to experiment with other shaft materials, and after extensive testing and research, produced the first Easton aluminum shafts in 1939.

There are many different choices of arrow shaft weight in a given spine classification. Lighter shafts will fly faster, giving flatter trajectory. Here I look at the impact of two different weight aluminum arrows of the same spine when shot into a target using the same sight pin. The lighter shafts are faster and flatter, making them a better choice for most hunting situations.

After World War II Easton's production of aluminum arrows shifted into high gear. Easton developed a process of drawing 1-inch aluminum tubing down to the desired shaft size and continued improving shaft quality using thermal processes. These then-innovative production techniques led to the first trademarked aluminum arrow, the 24SRT-X. By 1948 Easton was producing 16 stock sizes of aluminum arrows.

In the early 1950s Easton developed the now-standard system of labeling aluminum arrow shaft sizes, in which the first two numbers represent the shaft diameter in sixty-fourths of an inch and the second two numbers indicate the shaft wall thickness in thousandths of an inch. (A 2413, for example, has a diameter of 24/64 inch and a shaft wall thickness of 0.013 inch.) In 1958, Easton developed the XX75 shaft, which was available in 22 different sizes. The company continued to grow, and eventually moved to a new plant in Van Nuys, California, in the late 1960s.

With Doug Easton's passing in December 1972, his son, Jim, took over as company president, and under his direction the company continued to explore the use of new materials and manufacturing processes to develop the next generation of arrow shafts. In the mid-

1980s Easton expanded its operation to include a modern manufacturing facility in Salt Lake City, Utah, which today houses one of the largest aluminum anodizing operations in the country.

New products continued to come from the Salt Lake City facility. In the early 1980s Easton introduced the then-radical concept of wrapping a thin-walled aluminum core with layers of lightweight, high-strength carbon fiber. The result was an extremely strong, stiff, lightweight, and durable arrow shaft. By 1984 the first of its kind was used by Olympic archers to capture gold and silver medals. This concept lives on today in the form of the A/C/C, A/C/E, and Hyper-Speed shafts. Another version, the X10, accounted for all but two of the medals awarded at the 1996 Olympic Games. And in 1991, the XX78 Super Slam aluminum arrow shaft system was introduced. It featured new camouflage patterns and processes, a new adjustable nock system, and new methods of drawing aluminum tubing to thinner wall thickness with extreme consistency.

Today Easton's aluminum arrow shafts continue to dominate the market in terms of overall sales. "From a cost/value standpoint, aluminum is hard to beat," said former Easton president Peter Weaver. "For a very low cost you can get an arrow shaft that's very consistent in weight, in spine, is easy to build into an arrow shaft, easy to tune into a bow, and durable enough to be straightened. Aluminum arrows are a proven product, and they have darn good utility."

CARBON SHAFTS COMING ON

For decades, aluminum was without question the king of the hill when it came to arrow shaft material. At the time, few bowhunters thought that new shaft materials might some day challenge aluminum's dominance, although aluminum arrows are still the market leader in terms of overall sales, carbon (graphite) shafts have come on like gangbusters the past few years. While Easton discontinued marketing their P/C pure carbon shaft when they acquired carbon-arrow maker Beman in 1995, they continue to develop and aggressively promote both the Beman line of carbon shafts and their aluminum/carbon composite shaft line, the A/C/C.

"With the A/C/C, we're refining what we think is a superior use of materials, optimizing what you can get out of both aluminum and carbon," said Weaver. "When you take the hoop strength of an aluminum core, which gives a precise foundation for component fit and sizing,

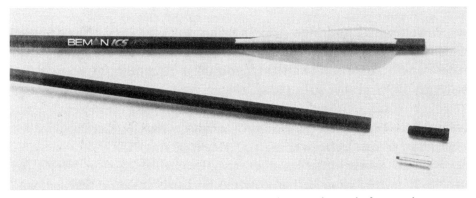

Though aluminum arrows dominate the market, carbon shafts are becoming more popular because they offer more arrow speed and better penetration than comparable aluminum shafts. *Photograph courtesy of Beman.*

and reinforce it with carbon fiber, you're now utilizing the carbon fiber in the best way possible."

Carbon shaft sales are growing because they can provide several performance advantages over aluminum shafts. One is raw arrow speed, achieved because carbon shafts of the same length and spine as a comparable aluminum shaft weigh much less. Another is durability. Carbon shafts are just plain tough, able to withstand much more abuse than aluminum and aluminum/carbon composite arrows. With carbon, the shaft is either as straight as it came from the factory or it's broken—and it takes quite a wallop to break them. (When aluminum is involved, as is the case with the A/C/C, the shafts can bend, often imperceptibly, and these slight bends can destroy accuracy.) And third, carbon shafts outpenetrate any other shaft on the market. Although there is no empirical, scientific research to back up this claim, there's no question in my mind that this is a fact.

Still, many dealers have been slow to stock and/or aggressively promote carbon shafts, which means that many bowhunters have not yet been exposed to them. In most cases, those dealers who do sell carbon arrows are carbon shooters themselves who understand both how to build quality carbon shafts and how to tune bows to shoot these small-diameter arrows. "Using carbon shafts is a bit different than using aluminum arrows," says Jerry Fletcher, owner of Fletcher's Archery in Wasilla, Alaska, an experienced bowhunter, and the 1998 Alaska state field archery champion. "For example, I've found that when tuning carbons, a 'perfect' paper tear isn't always the best in terms of the groups you'll shoot. Also, arrow rests that work well with aluminum arrows often don't work well at all with carbon shafts. And you sometimes need a bit more weight-forward balance with a carbon shaft than you do with aluminum to get consistently tight arrow groups at longer yardages with broadheads." Fletcher recommends a weight-forward balance of between 12 and as much as 18 percent with carbon shafts, whereas the standard for aluminum arrows is between 7 and 10 percent.

Several manufacturers curretly offer pure carbon shafts for bowhunters, including Beman (owned by Easton), Game Tracker/AFC, Gold Tip, Carbon Impact, Carbon Tech, and CAE (Custom Archery Equipment).

CARBON SHAFT STYLES AND COMPONENTS

Early carbon shafts were so small in diameter that archers had to use an "outsert" to affix screw-on broadheads, field points, and nocks to them. Outserts are carbon components that glue on over the shaft, creating a slightly larger-diameter part than the rest of the shaft. This attachment system is still used by some manufacturers.

Early on, there was some trouble with attaching outserts to carbon shafts in a perfectly aligned manner. This, of course, adversely affected accuracy. Today, however, outserts are built to exact tolerances, and the bugaboos of attaching them to the shaft have largely been eliminated. If there is a downside to using outserts today, it is that a broadhead outsert requires the use of a shaft that is an inch longer than the arrow length would be if internal components were used. Failure to do this results in a shaft that, when drawn, will see the outsert skip over, and sometimes off, the arrow rest. Also, the overhang from the outsert often catches on the batting of a target, making it difficult to pull the shaft out of the target.

One of the downsides to some carbon shafts is the fact that they are so small in diameter. That means the fletching ends up being very close together where it is glued onto the shaft, which in turn makes achieving perfect fletch clearance when using popular prong- or launcher-type arrow rests more difficult than when using larger-diameter aluminum shafts. It takes careful tuning to avoid this problem.

Two companies—Gold Tip and Beman—began using internal components à la aluminum shafts in their pure carbon shafts in 1997. By 1999 virtually all other carbon shaft makers had followed suit. They can do so because the finished shafts are a bit larger in diameter than other carbon arrows. I began shooting these shaft types in 1997 and have been impressed with the way they perform. They fly like darts, they are consistent, and the larger diameter makes it easier to keep fletch contact off the prongs of my shoot-through arrow rest than with other, smaller-diameter carbon arrows.

As is the case with aluminum shafts, archers can use an adjustable nock system with all carbon shafts on today's market. This allows for a precise nock alignment regardless of the type of arrow rest you choose and makes it quick and easy to reset the nock position should you desire to change arrow rests.

FUTURE TRENDS

One trend among today's bowhunters is that more of them are shooting expensive shafts. Modern bowhunters want the best shafts they can shoot and are willing to pay for them. This is evident in the increased sales of carbon arrows over the past half-decade, with more and more bowhunters switching to carbon every year. Carbon shafts cost a few more dollars than aluminum arrows per dozen—top-of-the-line carbon arrows sold for nearly a hundred bucks a dozen retail in 1999—but discriminating bowhunters realize that in the overall scheme of what it costs to own top-quality archery equipment and go bowhunting, a few more dollars spent on arrow shafts is money well spent.

"One of the things we see in archery is an aging demographic. People in the sport are a bit older and have a little more money to spend on equipment," said former Easton president Weaver. "They're definitely starting to move up the ladder in terms of arrow shafts. The guy who shot GameGetters 10 years ago is shooting XX75s and XX78s today, and in some cases A/C/Cs—3-D archery has really helped promote them. More bowhunters have started shooting A/C/Cs than we initially thought would."

Going hand in hand with that trend is a shift to using shafts with tunable components, especially tunable nocks. Weaver's data shows the same thing. "I think we are getting a more knowledgeable group of archers out there," he said. "Maybe that's because we don't have as much influx of new archers as we did years ago, which may be a problem for archery in general, but it is creating a more knowledge-able shooter as a percentage of the marketplace. These people appreciate the features of adjustable nocks, easily replaced components, a choice of different arrow shaft sizes, and so on."

318

My Beman ICS shaft, tipped with a Barrie Archery Ti-125 broadhead, passed completely through this record-class Alaskan caribou bull at 45 yards. He went only 50 yards before piling up.

So, what's on the arrow shaft horizon? Only time will tell. But one thing's for certain—today's manufacturers are not standing still when it comes to shaft development.

"We continue to work on improving our aluminum shafts, but we're continually looking at anything and everything out there, stuff like boron, Kevlar, and so on," Weaver said. "Kevlar, for example, doesn't have any value by itself. It adds lots of strength and weight, but it doesn't have any stiffness. But that's the process. We look at all materials out there, all the resin systems, all the composites, thermoplastics, and so on. Nothing is sitting on the horizon right now that we're aware of that will appear tomorrow as the all-new, breakthrough new material. Where we've come with aluminum, aluminum–carbon composites, and pure carbon are really the only choices today that offer reasonable performance values to the consumer. But if we can find something that will work better, you can be sure we'll use it."

Broadheads for Bowhunting

TODAY'S BOWHUNTER has a wide array of high-performance equipment from which to create the bow-and-arrow setup with which he will head into the deer woods each fall to try and "make meat." But without a strong, razor-sharp broadhead that will surgically slice through an animal's vital organs, arteries, and veins, causing a quick, humane death, all the work, planning, and hope is for naught.

Fortunately, today's market offers a huge array of choices when it comes to quality broadheads for hunting deer and other big game. Understanding what's available and the advantages and disadvantages of each style and design is the first step in selecting the right broadhead. You should also keep in mind that, like other archery equipment, broadheads continue to evolve. Never overlook new developments, but at the same time look them over with a skeptical eye. Make sure that a new type or style of broadhead will do the job you need it to do before switching from a proven winner.

Here's a look at what's available.

FIXED-BLADE HEADS

Traditional broadheads have been cleanly killing deer and other big game since the days of primitive man. This system—in which two, three, or four nonreplaceable blades are attached to a center ferrule that is either glued on or screwed into the arrow shaft—are still found in the deer woods annually. These generally have a cutting tip design and are relatively heavy, weighing between 140 and 175 grains, with some weighing as little as 125 grains and some as much as 220 grains.

Most bowhunters who use this type of broadhead today are traditional shooters who hunt with either recurves or longbows. However, there is a group of compound shooters who use this type of

Traditional fixed-blade broadheads, such as this Simmons Land Shard 160, have been killing deer and other big game for centuries. Most people who use this design now are traditional archers. *Photograph courtesy of Simmons.*

broadhead, too, believing that when deer hunting from a tree stand—where shots are generally less than 25 yards—a super-strong, deep-penetrating head that cuts a huge hole is more important than a light-weight head designed more for aerodynamics than strength.

REPLACEABLE BLADE HEADS

The replaceable blade head is the most popular basic style of broadhead found in the woods today. Like all good equipment, it has evolved over the years, the design changes mirroring the advances in efficiency found in modern hunting bows and arrow shafts.

When bowhunters shot slower recurve bows loaded with heavy arrow shafts, a large, heavy, two-bladed cutting-tip type of broadhead with blades that had to be hand-sharpened made all the sense in the world. When compound bows came on the scene, an arrow speed of 220 feet per second was hot stuff. To match this increased speed, broadhead size dropped until the three-blade, 125-grain head became the most popular. With today's highly efficient compounds sending their shafts off at somewhere between 240 and 270 feet per second—some even faster—the most popular broadhead size sold, according to major manufacturers, has dropped to 100 grains.

The big advantage to replaceable-blade broadheads is that bowhunters don't have to hand-sharpen their own blades. Instead, they can quickly and easily replace used blades with inexpensive, fresh, scalpel-sharp blades in seconds. In fact, manufacturers recommend *against* the shooter sharpening these blades at all. Their tests show that the only thing you can do is dull them. The best replaceable-blade broadhead designs also incorporate secure locking systems that prevent the blades from coming loose on impact. They're just as dependable as the old-style non-replaceable-blade broadheads ever were.

Replaceable-blade heads come in two basic styles—cutting tip and

Replaceable heads feature a solid ferrule and blades that can be quickly and easily replaced with new, scalpel-sharp blades. Both cutting-tip and chisel-point styles are available in this configuration.

chisel point. Years ago, it was believed that the cutting tip design—in which the head's sharp blades extend all the way to the broadhead's forward tip—penetrated better than the chisel point design. The blades on chisel point heads do not extend to the broadhead's forward tip, instead stopping a bit short of that mark. The nose consists of a piece of metal shaped like a chisel point, with some manufacturers sharpening its edges. However, recent research has shown that the difference in penetration between the two designs is negligible.

MECHANICAL HEADS

The tendency of broadhead blades to act as airfoils that can steer an arrow wildly out of the bull's-eye is the big reason expandable-blade, or mechanical, broadheads have increased in popularity in recent years. Their development goes hand in hand with the proliferation of today's super-high-speed bows and lightweight arrow shafts with small fletching, a combination more difficult to precisely tune with the large-diameter, fixed-blade and replaceable-blade broadheads that have been a mainstay of bowhunting since its earliest days.

A mechanical broadhead features blades (usually two or three, but sometimes more) that are connected to the ferrule by a hinge system, which allows them to be folded forward into the ferrule before the shot. Upon contact with an animal, the blades are driven out and backward until they lock into the ferrule. The blades are now in the

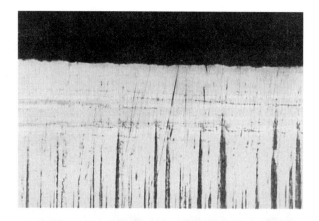

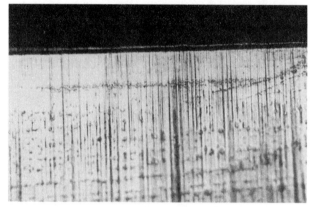

Just how sharp are new replaceable broadhead blades? These microscopic photos, magnified 200 times, show the edge of a new surgeon's scalpel and the edge of a new replaceable Thunderhead broadhead blade. The broadhead blade has the smoothest, sharpest surface. *Photographs courtesy of New Archery Products.*

same cutting position as those found on fixed- and replaceable-blade broadheads, and thus perform the same cutting function.

The advantages of this system are many. First, by removing the airfoil of the fixed blades and creating a low-profile arrow tip, expandable-blade broadhead-tipped arrows fly almost identically to arrows with target tips of the same weight. The superior aerodynamics of these heads were designed to be used with high-speed compound bows pushing small-diameter, lightweight arrow shafts—specifically carbon and aluminum–carbon composite arrows—with small fletching at 250 feet per second or more. Their low profile also makes a bow/arrow/broadhead combination easier to precisely tune than when using fixed-blade

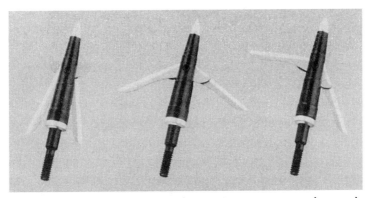

Mechanical broadheads are becoming more popular each year as companies refine their designs and improve manufacturing processes. They are not legal in all states, however.

broadheads. Expandable broadheads also achieve a wider cutting path through an animal than most other heads of the same weight. The most popular fixed- and replaceable-blade broadheads have a cutting diameter of between one and 1¼ inches, but most expandables start at 1½ inches, with the majority in the 1⅞- to 2½-inch range. In bowhunting, the bigger the hole, the better off you are.

My personal experiences with mechanical heads is limited, extending more to the testing grounds than the field. I have taken whitetails and black bears with them, with excellent results. My feelings, at least at this point in time, remain mixed. I've found that most expandables tune and fly well, and I have had many glowing reports from friends who have used them when whitetail hunting. The large-diameter exit hole created by the expandable's ultrawide cutting surface is awesome and a definite advantage. However, there are poorly designed mechanical heads out there that can cause you grief when their blades fail to open on impact as advertised. Mechanical heads should not be used with bow-and-arrow setups that produce relatively low raw arrow speed because it takes speeds approaching 240 feet per second to ensure that you'll achieve adequate penetration and the blades will open properly. And be advised that some states do not allow mechanical broadheads during big-game hunting seasons. So, before deciding that these sleek missile-like heads are the cat's meow, check the regulations to make sure they're legal where you hunt.

WHAT TO LOOK FOR

Regardless of the style and type of broadhead you select for hunting, there are several factors to consider. Foremost is quality construction.

Manufacturers who spend the extra few bucks to make sure that their manufacturing tolerances are tight and only use high-quality materials produce broadheads that are consistent shooters and hold together on impact. This is not the case with all broadheads. For example, I once weighed six dozen identical broadheads from a popular manufacturer to see how close to the advertised 125 grains each weighed. To my surprise, almost all weighed between 130 and 135 grains, with some weighing as much as 140 grains. This kind of inconsistency will result in inconsistent arrow flight and make tight arrow groups impossible to achieve. Yet to read this manufacturer's advertising, you'd think they were carefully making high-performance rocket ships with the latest high-tech, space-age materials.

Some manufacturers do try and cut corners, but the smart ones know that serious bowhunters are willing to spend the extra few dollars for top-quality broadheads. For example, when Barrie Archery—a company with a long track record of producing excellent broadheads—introduced a 100-grain replaceable-blade head with a titanium ferrule that cost nearly 10 bucks apiece at retail, the skeptics howled that they'd never sell enough to make ends meet. Yet Barrie couldn't make them fast enough and soon expanded the titanium line to include additional weight sizes of 85 and 125 grains.

When shopping at your local archery pro shop, ask to examine the new broadheads you are considering. Take them out of the package and check them for quality construction. Assemble the heads, screw them into an arrow shaft, and give them the spin test, spinning them rapidly on their tip and checking for the tell-tale wobble that

Top-quality, bullet-proof construction—not price—should be your first consideration when shopping for broadheads. Though this Barrie Archery Ti-125 broadhead costs about $10, its titanium ferrule helps make it the toughest replaceable-blade broadhead available. *Photograph courtesy of Barrie Archery*

Giving your broadhead-tipped arrow shafts the spin test to check for wobble where the broadhead and shaft meet is a good way to check both broadheads and the arrow shaft for slight imperfections.

can mean a bent ferrule. Make sure that all the components—specifically the blades, blade-locking collar, and ferrule—mate tightly together. Ask to weigh them on the shop's grain scale.

Second, use a broadhead that flies well with your chosen bow-and-arrow setup. I have found from time to time that a particular broadhead make and model just would not tune perfectly with my bow unless I made adjustments to the bow itself—change the draw weight, shorten the draw length, change arrow rests—that I wasn't happy making. When that happens, it's time to go to Plan B and use a different broadhead.

One of the problems with some modern archers is that, in the search for the fastest possible bow-and-arrow setup they can shoot, they are going to lighter and lighter broadheads. Sometimes they'll choose heads that weigh as little as 75 grains. This isn't necessarily bad, except when the ultralight broadhead does not provide enough front-of-center (FOC) balance to the arrow shaft.

Without the proper FOC balance, the shaft will not fly perfectly. Front-of-center means that rather than balancing at the shaft's midpoint, the arrow should instead balance a bit forward of that midpoint. To determine FOC balance, measure your overall arrow length with the broadhead attached. If the length is 30 inches, your midpoint is 15 inches. Mark this spot on the shaft with a felt pen. Now move one finger forward under the shaft until it balances itself per-

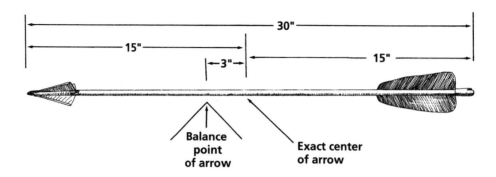

fectly on your finger tip. That is your balance point. Mark this spot with the felt pen. The ideal FOC balance on an aluminum hunting arrow shaft is generally somewhere between 7 and 10 percent of the arrow length—in this case, a balance point somewhere between 2 and 3 inches forward of the shaft's center point. With some light-weight carbon shafts, a bit more exaggerated FOC of between 12 and as much as 18 percent can produce better arrow flight.

Third, never hunt with broadheads unless the blades are so sharp they scare you. Dull blades will not slice cleanly through arteries and veins, the kinds of cuts that bleed freely and are slow to clot. We owe it to the game we hunt to try and kill them as quickly and humanely as possible. Razor-sharp broadhead blades are the only ones that can get the job done.

The last consideration in selecting a broadhead for bowhunting should be price. Too many bowhunters try and save a dollar or two when purchasing broadheads, when in reality the broadhead is the one piece of bowhunting tackle that should never be compromised. At the moment of truth, the last thing you need to worry about is whether or not your broadhead will fly straight and true, penetrate deeply, and hold together should it inadvertently strike a leg or shoulder bone.

Today's bowhunter has more quality broadheads from which to choose than ever before. The relatively new mechanical broadheads are growing in popularity, but they are still in their infancy and are not the right choice for everyone. The key to both success and satisfaction is in carefully selecting the right broadhead design, style, and size to match both your current bow-and-arrow setup and the conditions under which you'll be hunting.

CHAPTER 6

Shooting Accessories

YOU'LL NEED several accessory items to complete your bow-shooting system. These smallish pieces of equipment may not seem like much at first, but once you've been shooting your bow a while, and have been on a few bowhunting trips, their importance will not seem trivial. Here's are several accessory items you'll want to consider.

FINGER TABS, RELEASE AIDS

A fundamental decision you'll have to make is whether or not you'll release your bow with your fingers or with a mechanical release aid of some sort. We'll talk more about each style in Chapter 8. Regardless of the style you choose, you'll need accessory items to help you.

If you're a fingers shooter, you'll need a finger tab or shooting glove to protect your fingers from the abrasive bowstring. At one time leather shooting gloves were the cat's meow for fingers shooters, and they are still popular with some traditional archers. Most compound shooters use a finger tab, which is held in place by a plastic ring that fits over the middle finger and can be slipped over both bare fingers and gloves. Tabs can be rotated over the back of the hand, freeing your fingers for work, then quickly rotated into place when it's time to shoot.

Most tabs slide off the string with a facing of calf's hair, leather, or plastic. All work well. I personally like the calf's-hair tabs best, even though they will wear out and have to be replaced from time to time. Plastic and leather tabs wear longer and work very well, too. Most tabs also come with a thick plastic finger spacer to help prevent your pinching the arrow shaft between your fingers when you draw and shoot, something that can adversely affect arrow flight. Make sure any tab you buy has this spacer.

Archery industry estimates show that between 80 and 90 percent

328

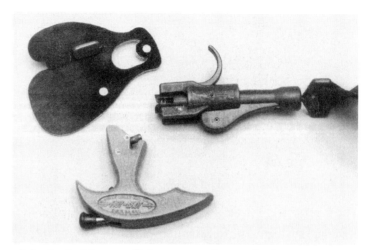

A basic decision you'll have to make is whether to release the bowstring with your fingers, or with a mechanical release aid. Fingers shooters will need some sort of tab, such as this Martin calf's hair tab (upper left). Release shooters have several designs to choose from, including the Pro Release wrist-wrap model (upper right) and Hot Shot thumb-triggered version (bottom center).

of modern bowhunters release their arrows with some type of mechanical release aid instead of their fingers. The reason is simple: A release makes it easier to shoot a consistently accurate arrow. This fact was first demonstrated more than a quarter-century ago, when simple releases started replacing finger gloves on the competitive target circuit. As release design evolved and manufacturing techniques improved, quality releases became more readily available and affordable. Today archers can choose from a myriad of designs and styles in price ranges from a few bucks to over a C-note.

How does a mechanical release produce more accurate arrow flight than a finger release? Simply stated, when you grip the bow string at a single point, as you do with a mechanical release, you achieve a more consistent release than you do with a finger tab or shooting glove sliding off the same string. Also, arrows shot with a release tend to flex and vibrate less at the shot, which makes the bow easier to tune properly, especially with broadheads. And since these arrows do bend less, you can tune the bow with a lighter arrow shaft than can be done with the same setup using fingers. This, in turn, translates into higher raw arrow speed and flatter trajectory, making distance estimation less critical.

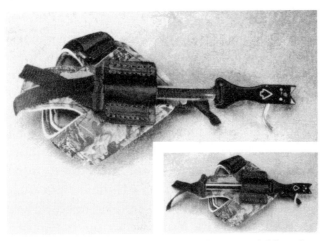

The wrist-wrap, caliper-type release aid like this Golden Key-Futura Top Gun is the most popular hunting release design. *Photograph courtesy of Golden Key-Futura.*

Three factors stand out as the reasons for the increase in release aid popularity. First, in today's go-go world, our discretionary time has shrunk. People have less time to tune and practice shooting their bows. By using a quality release aid, these archers can shoot more accurately more quickly than they can with fingers. Second, as bow manufacturers continue their quest for high-speed, energy-efficient bows, more quality bows are built with a short axle-to-axle length. This design favors the use of a release aid over fingers. And third, release aid manufacturers continue to improve their products, offering the consumer an annual wave of new high-quality releases in a variety of designs over a wide spectrum of prices.

Most release aids grab the bowstring with either a set of metal caliper jaws or a rope. Although there are several variations on this theme, these releases can be defined by the way they are triggered. In this there are three basic designs: index finger-triggered, thumb-triggered, and back-tension-triggered. (Back-tension releases are triggered by contracting the back muscles, not by a trigger hit with either the index finger or thumb.) The basic caliper-type, index finger-triggered release has dominated the market for many years. Most shooters using this type of release choose one with some sort of wrist strap, which makes smoothly drawing the bow using the back muscles easier than using a release without the strap.

"The index finger-trigger-fired caliper release is the most popular design by far," says Vince Troncoso of Golden Key–Futura, a leading release aid manufacturer. "They're about 70% of our total sales. For bowhunting, the caliper-type releases really dominate things. The target guys are more into the rope releases and what I call 'therapeutic releases', like the back-tension releases that help guys with target panic. For the most part, bowhunters stay away from these styles."

However, the market may be changing a bit as more shooters gain experience using release aids. "We're starting to introduce new release designs besides the more traditional trigger/caliper style as we see that different people want and/or need different styles," says Jeff Barhoover of Cobra Manufacturing, a maker of release aids and bow sights. "For example, we're experimenting with some new things, such as offering a thumb trigger on a caliper-style release aid."

Both archery pro shop owners and manufacturers say that while most archers are price conscious when it comes to purchasing a new release aid, trying to save an extra few bucks on a release can lead to poor accuracy and long-term disappointment. "There are some releases out there built from inexpensive imported parts and powdered metal using questionable machining practices," says Barhoover. "In order for a release aid to function properly, you have to hold machining tolerances to a hundredth of an inch or less. Many of these cheaper products do not, yet they are touted as low-cost alternatives to more expensive models. In the long run these $20-and-under releases will disappoint the consumer."

"A quality hunting release is moderately priced, in the $30–$60 range, with serious target archers willing to spend up to twice that," says Golden Key's Troncoso. "Any target-type release built with a high degree of precision is going to be a high-dollar item. Shooters should stay away from the bottom-of-the-barrel releases."

The best way to start shooting a release is to visit your local archery pro shop. There you can play with several different models and designs, get expert advice, and shoot a few arrows on the shop's indoor lanes to get a feel for each. The pro shop can also help you set up your bow and help you tune it using a release (bows must be retuned and resighted in when switching from a fingers release to the use of a mechanical release aid, and vice versa).

A mechanical release aid may not be Robin Hood pure, but using one *is* the best way to achieve consistently accurate arrow flight.

ARM GUARDS

An arm guard may not seem like much, but it is one of the most important accessory items a bowhunter can use. Arm guards are designed to keep the bowstring from "slapping" the inside of the forearm of your bow arm when you release the arrow. This is a common problem with beginning shooters, but rarely happens to those who have some experience. The big value of an arm guard in bowhunting is not protecting your arm, but protecting the bowstring itself.

How so? In cool or cold weather, you'll be wearing thick, heavy clothes. The oversized or baggy sleeves of a heavy shirt or jacket can inadvertently catch your bowstring at the shot, causing your arrow to be launched like a drunken duck. That's why a bowhunter needs an arm guard. It doesn't have to be fancy or expensive. Most arm guards cover the inside of the forearm, have a Polarfleece or slick face, and are attached to the arm with three or four stretch strings and Velcro. You can get a good one for under $5.

QUIVERS

Quivers are used to store, protect, and transport your arrows to and from the field. All quivers feature a hood to hold and protect your broadheads, and a series of arrow shaft grippers to hold the lower end of the shafts. There are two basic types of quivers: those that attach to the bow, and non-bow-attached quivers that are carried either on the archer's hip or back.

There is a small debate about which type of quiver is best for bowhunting. On one hand, a famous bowhunting personality swears that using a bow-attached quiver is a formula for disaster, causing excessive bow torque, an overbearing weight imbalance, and missed shots at game. On the other hand, bow-attached quiver makers swear this isn't so. Because there's been no definitive, scientifically valid way to prove or disprove either theory, the controversy rages on.

What's the answer?

"If you ask the question, does a bow-attached quiver affect accuracy, yes or no, the answer would have to be yes," says Randy Ulmer, a several time 3-D and field shooting world champion, as well as a highly accomplished bowhunter. "But does it make any real difference in bowhunting? I'd have to say no, it does not.

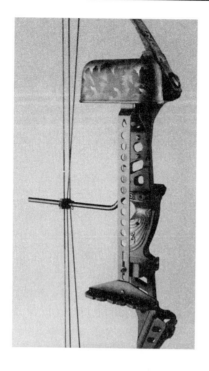

Most bowhunters use a bow-attached quiver to carry and protect their arrow shafts. *Photograph courtesy of Browning.*

Jim Velasquez, president of bow quiver maker Sagittarius, is a serious and accomplished bowhunter who has done some testing of this subject. He also believes a bow quiver's effects on hunting accuracy are minimal.

"Years ago, we made a shooting machine, because we wanted to see what the differences would be with and without a bow quiver and without human error affecting the shooting," Velasquez says. "We shot in excess of 400 arrows out to 40 yards, using four, six, and eight arrows in the quiver. We saw a very insignificant difference in point of impact in comparison with no quiver attached to the bow. When we went down from eight arrows to one arrow in the quiver, we did see a small, but very insignificant, point of impact change, but it wasn't enough to make any difference in a person's ability to hit a kill zone in hunting situations."

All quiver makers emphasize that if you hunt with a bow-attached quiver, it is important that you tune your bow with the quiver attached and practice shooting that way, too. Tuning a bow without the quiver, then randomly attaching one the day before hunting season begins is a sure formula for inaccurate shooting. They also emphasize that all parts and screws must be tight, which will help dampen any noise produced at the shot.

Choosing the right bow quiver is a very important, yet often overlooked, component of an accurate bow-and-arrow setup. Sam Topel, president of Fine-Line, one of the country's leading quiver manufacturers, believes that rugged simplicity is the secret to his company's long-standing success.

"There are few innovative things happening with bow quivers today," Topel says. "The secret is to find a quiver that helps balance your bow, minimizes vibration, and protects the arrow shaft. For example, our Fine-Line Hunter protects the shaft at both ends thanks to our unique nock bar. It's the only quiver that holds the shaft by the nock, and doesn't rely on the torque of the broadhead in the quiver hood foam to keep the shaft in place. It weighs just 12 ounces and can be put on or taken off the bow in seconds. And because it does not grip the arrow shaft itself, you can use any size arrows without worrying about whether or not the rubber grips that hold the shafts on other quivers will fit right."

Range Finders

The more you bow hunt, the more you'll realize that the No. 1 reason people miss shots at game is that they misjudge the distance to the target. Just how critical is accurate range estimation? Even from the fastest compound bow, an arrow shaft traveling 300 feet per second will drop more at 30 yards than a bullet from a .30-06 at 300 yards. With this same superfast compound, if you misguess the distance to a deer-sized target standing broadside at 40 yards by ± 3 yards, you're going to miss the 8-inch-diameter heart/lung "kill zone," even if your shot was perfect.

For that reason, all bowhunters should practice estimating range with their naked eye. But this is not a bombproof method, and it breaks down even for the most skilled bowhunters out past 35 or 40 yards. That's where a mechanical range finder comes in.

There are two basic range finder types. Optical range finders, popularized by Ranging, use the triangulation principle. That is, they have two windows and a combination of prisms and lenses that produce two separate images the user sees when looking through the sighting window. As you view the object, you turn a dial with your finger until the images coincide and appear as one. You then read the distance on the dial. These units have to be calibrated before use and in skilled hands are very accurate out to 50 or 60 yards.

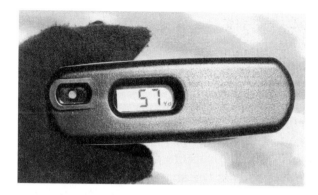

The laser rangefinder is a superb bowhunting tool. It allows archers to know the exact distance to the target with the push of a button.

The best range finders today are the laser models. With the press of a button, these units send out a beam of light, which is reflected back to the unit. Distance is calculated by the unit measuring the time it takes for this reflection to go out and back. Laser range finders have proven themselves in military applications and are accurate to ± 1 yard at distances of a quarter mile or more. Bushnell offered the first laser units for bowhunting, the Yardage Pro 400 and Yardage Pro Compact 600. Nikon, Simmons and Tasco make similar units, although their design and bulk make them a better choice for firearms users than archers. Laser range finders are powered by a 9-volt battery and are relatively expensive, costing somewhere between $250 and $350.

Range finders are usually used to take readings off objects, not animals, calculating exact distance to an object that you expect an animal to walk past. When it gets there, you don't have to guess where to hold your sights. You know. Such knowledge translates into more perfect hits, the goal of all bowhunters. For this reason I never head afield without a laser range finder.

TARGETS

Unless you do all your practice shooting at a local pro shop or outdoor range, all bowhunters need at least one target for practice. There are several different types and designs.

For field-tip practice, the choices are endless. Styrofoam targets with replaceable bull's-eye cores are popular, lightweight, and relatively inexpensive. These targets will wear out faster than most other types, but the replaceable center helps extend their life for just a few bucks. Foam targets are best used with aluminum or wooden arrow shafts because small-diameter carbon shafts have a tendency to blow

Life-sized 3-D targets, like this McKenzie Targets mule deer, are excellent for bowhunting practice. *Photograph courtesy of McKenzie.*

right through them. Foamlite, Stanley Hips, Arrow Stop, and American Whitetail are four companies that make good foam targets.

Better still is a bag-type target, a longer-lasting target type featuring a heavy burlap or coated material target face and filled with a cotton batting or similar material. The best of these targets can withstand hundreds and hundreds of shots without breaking down, regardless of the shaft material. Bracklynn, Morrell, Dead Stop, Arrow Brake, and Southern Archery all make good ones.

You'll need a special target for broadhead practice. Continued broadhead shooting into regular targets will simply destroy them in a hurry. In some cases, these targets may not even stop a broadhead-tipped arrow. American Whitetail makes a line of fine broadhead targets, but the best I've used is The Block by Field Logic. It can take hundreds of broadhead hits from the fastest bows and still perform.

3-D targets are extremely popular for bowhunting practice. These are three-dimensional replicas of big and small game animals, from deer to elk to bears to turkeys and a variety of small game. 3-D targets are made from a high-density, self-healing foam and offer the best pre-season shooting practice of all. McKenzie Natra-Look and Delta Targets are the leaders in 3-D target manufacturing.

7

Tuning Your Bow

BOW TUNING has become something of a mystery with present-day bowhunters. Some people make it out to be a process that only a magician can do. Others, turned off by the thought of dealing with the mechanics of their compound bows, don't even worry about it.

Tuning is the process of adjusting (with the proper arrow being used) the arrow rest, pressure point, string height, draw weight, and nocking height of the bow to achieve optimum arrow flight. Sounds difficult, doesn't it? In truth, tuning a modern compound bow isn't all that tough. Anyone with the right arrow shafts, bow accessories, and a few simple tools can do it. Why bother with bow tuning at all? Because only a well-tuned bow will produce consistent dartlike arrow flight, which in turn produces optimum accuracy and penetration of game—both critical to success in the field.

Let's face it: Most of us are bowhunters, not bow technicians. Although we enjoy shooting our bows, we'd rather be in the field, hunting, than in the shop tinkering with equipment. But we also know that getting into the in-your-face range needed for a good bow shot at game is tough. It doesn't happen every day. When we do get there, we want to make sure that our bows will deliver the accurate arrow necessary to close the deal. Without a well-tuned bow, the chances of that happening are slim. And that's not acceptable.

To tune your bow, you'll need a few basic tools. These include a bow square, nock pliers, and the various Allen wrenches necessary for adjusting your bow's limb bolts and the adjustment screws of your arrow rest. You'll also need a target butt to shoot into and a paper rack to shoot through. A bow scale, to measure the bow's exact draw weight, is helpful but not necessary.

Of course, you can always take your bow to your local archery shop, where the resident pro can help you tune your bow-and-arrow setup. He'll have all the right tools and will be able to assist you in getting everything in synch. I recommend that all novice archers take this route. In fact, most pro shops include initial bow tuning as part of the purchase price of a new bow. However, knowing how to tune your own bow is beneficial. It not only gives you a good idea of how everything works together to produce perfect arrow flight, but you'll then be able to periodically check your bow's tune during the course of the year, making any small adjustments needed with a minimum of fuss and muss. You will also have the skills to make emergency field repairs when the nearest pro shop is either closed or too far away to be of practical help.

Matched Equipment

Unless you have the right arrow shafts of the correct length with the proper spine for your bow, tuning is impossible. The manufacturer's shaft selection chart is the place to find this information. You also need arrow points of the same weight. It should go without saying that your arrows should all be built the same, with identical fletching, nocks, and screw-in arrow point inserts. The goal here is to shoot arrow shafts that are both built from the same components and are as close to the same weight as possible.

You'll also want an arrow rest that is adjustable both in and out, and up and down. Rests with micro-adjustment features are the easiest to tune. Generally speaking, a shoot-through, or Vee-launcher, type of rest works best with a release aid, and a cushion plunger rest works best for fingers shooters. It's also important to have all your bowhunting accessories—including bow sight, peep sight, string silencers, bow quiver, and stabilizer—attached when you tune the bow.

Step-by-Step Bow Setup

To ready your new bow for tuning, do the following:
1. Check the tiller, making sure that both upper and lower limb tillers are the same. You can do this while adjusting the bow's draw weight to the setting you desire.
2. Make sure the bow is set at your exact draw length. If not, adjust it. (In most cases, you'll need a bow press to do this. If you don't have one, take the bow to the pro shop).
3. Attach the arrow rest, following the manufacturer's instructions. Then, adjust the rest's "center shot" (the left/right position of the rest) to a dead-on setting. To do this, nock an arrow

Checking the bow's tiller with a bow square is one of the first steps to tuning. To begin, make sure both the upper and lower tiller measurements are equal.

and place it on the rest. Holding the bow at arm's length, use the bowstring as a reference point while looking at the tip of the shaft. This should be hidden by the bowstring. If it sticks out from the string, move the rest back in. If it's in toward the bow handle, move the rest back out.

4. Using the bow square, place a nock set on the bowstring. The bow square will allow you place the nock set precisely. Start

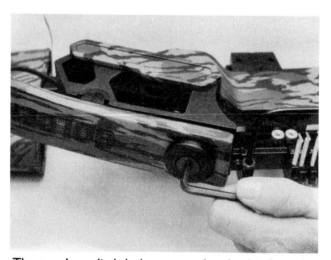

The two large limb bolts are used to both adjust the tiller and set the bow's draw weight. Draw-weight and tiller adjustments should be made before the tuning process begins.

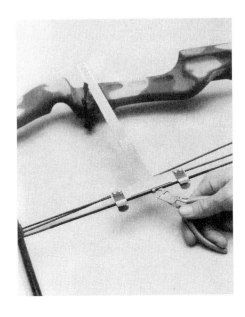

Attaching a nock locator is done prior to tuning. A bow square and set of nock pliers are needed for this task.

with the nock set ¼ inch above center and, using your nock pliers, crimp it down medium-hard. You may have to move it later, but this should get you close.

5. Attach your bow sight, peep sight, stabilizer, string silencers, and quiver to the bow, following the manufacturer's instructions.

6. Turn your arrow nocks. This means turning the nock so that the fletching will not contact either the arrow rest or bow riser during the shot. You can do this visually by placing a shaft on the string, setting the shaft on the rest, and eyeballing the fletching from the rear to find obvious contact points. A good test for fletch contact is to spray a fine white powder (foot powder works well) onto the arrow rest and riser, then shoot an arrow. Check the riser and rest for places where the arrow wiped the powder off. Remembering that minor fletch contact is inevitable, you can make adjustments from here to alleviate the problem.

7. Conduct close-range paper testing.

Paper Testing

Paper testing, or paper tuning, is the best method around for gauging arrow flight. Using the paper-tuning method, you can tune arrow flight with either field points or broadheads. When setting up a new

Once the bow has been tuned, mark both the limb bolt and limb-bolt bracket with an indelible marker so you can make sure that the limb bolts haven't shifted.

hunting bow, I tune it first with field points, then go out and shoot a bit, getting used to the bow and setting my sight pins for the distances I like—20, 30, 40, and 50 yards. Then, a bit before hunting season, I retune the bow, this time with broadheads, then go out and reset my sight pins. You'll probably have to make a few minor tuning adjustments when switching from field points to broadheads. They should be just that—minor adjustments. Sometimes you don't need to make any changes at all.

To paper-tune the bow, you'll need a frame to hold the paper and paper to shoot through. There are commercial frames available, but you can make your own out of plywood or do what I do when I'm in the field—use an old cardboard box with the bottom and top cut out. The box should be at least 18 × 18 inches, although I like a box that's 24 × 24 inches. I tape my paper over the holes—old newspaper works okay, but I prefer white butcher paper—then set the box on a stump, small dirt mound, pair of saw horses, or some other support that will prop it up solidly at chest height. Three feet behind the paper rack, place a target butt to stop your arrows.

The illustration on the following page, provided by arrow maker Easton Technical Products, helps explain the paper-tuning process. The goal is to achieve a perfect bullet-hole tear through the paper. Keep two things in mind here. One, you will find small imperfect

Paper Tuning Arrow Test

The Paper Tuning Arrow Test is a good basic bow tuning method for all three types of shooting styles—Recurve with finger release (RF), Compound with finger release (CF) and Compound with release aid (CR).

- Firmly attach a sheet of paper to a frame type rack approximately 24" x 24" (60 x 60 cm).
- Position the center of the paper about shoulder height with a target mat about six feet (1.5m) behind the paper to stop the arrows.
- Stand approximately six feet (1.8m) from the paper.
- Shoot a fletched arrow through the center of the paper with the arrow at shoulder height.
- Observe how the paper is torn.

A. Tear A indicates good arrow flight. The point and fletching enter the same hole.

NOTE: Try the following instructions in order, one at a time.

B. Tear B indicates a low nocking point. To correct, raise the nocking point 1/16" (1.6mm) at a time and repeat the procedure until the low vertical tear is eliminated.

C. Tear C indicates a high nocking point. Clearance problem or (for release aid) a mismatched arrow spine. To correct, lower the nocking point 1/16" (1.6mm) at a time until the high tear is eliminated. If the problem remains unchanged, the disturbance is probably caused by a lack of Clearance or (for release aid) a mismatched arrow spine. CR only—if no

Clearance problem exists try:

1. A more flexible arrow rest blade or reducing downward spring tension on launcher rests.
2. Decreasing or increasing peak bow weight.
3. Reducing the amount the shaft overhangs the contact point on the arrow rest.
4. Using a stiffer arrow shaft.

NOTE: The following instructions are for right-handed archers. Reverse for left-handed archers.

The best way to tune your bow is to shoot arrows through blank white paper. Attach a sheet of paper to a sturdy frame (24 × 24 inches is ideal). Position the center of the paper about shoulder height with a target mat about six feet behind the paper, to stop your arrows. Stand six feet from the paper, and shoot a fletched arrow through the center of the paper. **Tear A** indicates ideal arrow flight, with the point and fletching entering the same hole. **Tear B** indicates a low nocking point, with the point entering the paper above the fletching. To correct, slightly raise your nocking point until the tear resembles tear A. **Tear C** indicates a high nocking point. To correct, lower the nocking point until you achieve tear A. If lowering the point does not work, you may have a clearance problem. *Illustration by Christopher Seubert.*

tears on some shots, even when the bow is perfectly tuned, due to hand torque on the riser. When you are paper-tuning, take your time and use as close to perfect shooting form as you can. Two, not all bowhunters find that they get the best accuracy with the perfect bullet-hole tear. Many like to have an arrow that tears slightly high and to the left of center (for right-handed shooters.) The final judge on your bow setup is how well it groups broadhead-tipped arrows at the end of your own maximum personal shooting range.

Some people claim they can tune their bows so that both their field points and broadheads hit exactly the same place. Don't believe it. I've tuned a lot of bows over the years, and the number I've had that could do that you can count on one hand and have some fingers left over. It's not important that they do, though. What is important is that you achieve dartlike arrow flight with broadheads, then set your sight pins so they correspond exactly to how your shafts are flying with the broadheads attached. After all, you won't be shooting at game with field tips. Who cares where they hit when the season's on?

Prior to hunting season, begin shooting your broadhead-tipped shafts at targets, both to set your sight pins and to make sure that each broadhead-tipped arrow in your quiver flies straight and true.

First, I make sure both my arrow nocks and broadheads are perfectly aligned with the shaft. To check the broadheads, give the shaft the "spin test." Simply hold the shaft vertically and place the tip of the broadhead on a hard, flat surface. Now lightly hold the shaft near the fletching and spin it on this point like a top. Watch the area where the shaft's insert and the broadhead meet. If it appears to wobble, there's an alignment problem and you can be sure this shaft will not fly as accurately as possible. This wobble can be caused by a couple of things, including a broadhead ferrule that did not come perfectly straight from the factory, loose blades, a shaft insert that is not perfectly aligned inside the shaft itself, or a slightly bent arrow. To correct this I change to a different broadhead and try the test again, and am not satisfied until there is no discernible wobble. If I find a bad ferrule or shaft, I discard it.

Next, conduct an accuracy test. Some people alternate shooting one shaft with a field point, then one with a broadhead, at different targets, until three shafts of each kind have been shot. They then compare the group size of both three-shot clusters (group size is measured between the inside points where the two shafts furthest apart struck the target). Your broadhead groups should be close to the same size as the field point group—no more than a couple of inches larger. You should shoot your test groups at least five times, and shoot them at your maximum effective shooting range.

If you don't want to go through all that, just shoot your broadheads. If your groups are nice and tight, you're getting good broadhead flight. One thing to watch for is the same arrow always grouping farthest away from your group's center. If it is, you may have a problem with that particular arrow. If you find a "bad arrow," try a different broadhead and see how it groups. If the arrow continues to be a poor shooter, discard it.

Once I find half a dozen arrow shafts and broadheads that group well, I mark them with an indelible felt-tip pen, giving both the shaft and the broadhead the same number. That way if I ever take the broadheads off the shafts for transportation, cleaning, or replacing the broadhead blades with new ones just before hunting, I can match them up again. During my practice sessions it seems I always find one or two shaft/broadhead combinations that really fly like laser beams. These I designate my No. 1 and No. 2 arrows, and I make sure they are placed in my quiver in such a way that I will automatically use them first in the field.

Paper-tuning your bow is not black magic. It can be time-consuming and sometimes frustrating. However, the best advice anyone can give you about putting together a new bow-and-arrow setup is this: Don't head afield without tuning your bow to give you precise, laser-beam arrow flight. This will breed accuracy, which helps give you confidence in your ability to make the shot when the chips are down. And that's what it's all about.

CHAPTER 8

How to Shoot Your Bow

YOU DON'T HAVE TO be a star athlete to shoot a bow accurately. In fact, I know quite a few successful bowhunters who have trouble tying their boot laces in the morning, are always tripping over things in the woods, and are so mechanically impaired they find changing the batteries in their flashlights a real chore. If the truth be known, I'm one of them. These folks will probably never win a major target shoot, but they are excellent field shots who, when the chips are down, consistently place their broadhead-tipped arrows into the boiler room of whatever animal they're hunting.

Their formula for success is really pretty simple. They all shoot matched tackle that has been precisely tuned, and they have their sight pins set the way they want them. They learned the basics of bow shooting from someone who knew how to teach them. And they spent countless hours practicing before the season, fine-tuning their muscles and skills.

Although accurate bow shooting is not that tough, there is a risk of learning to shoot a bow incorrectly. Unless you begin slowly with proper instruction, you can develop poor habits and lousy shooting form that could plague you all your life. That's why I recommend that beginning bowhunters spend some time at their local archery pro shop, where the resident pro can teach you the correct way to shoot from the get-go. Bad habits are difficult to break. It's always better to learn from someone who knows how to do it right and has experience helping beginners get started.

If there is one key word in accurately shooting a bow, it is this—*relax*. Don't be taut and tense. Instead, relax both your muscles and your mind as you shoot. The best bow shots keep their muscles working naturally for them, not tensely against them. They also relax their minds, forgetting about stress and strain. There's no pressure on you to outshoot the next guy here. You're simply trying to do the best you

344

Many youngsters shoot their first bows in group events, where bows don't fit and arrows are mismatched. Novice shooters are better served using matched tackle that fits them properly, and receiving individual instruction from a qualified teacher.

can do. A relaxed shooting form breeds consistency, the key to accurate shooting.

Before going into how to hold the bow and release the string, here are some questions you may want answered.

How Soon Should I Begin Practicing?

The best bow shots I know shoot at least a few arrows almost every day, all year round. Shooting a bow is an athletic skill, and the way to be the best shooter you can be is to keep your form sharp and muscles tuned. However, for a variety of reasons, most of us can't shoot on a daily basis throughout the year. If that's the case with you, you should begin shooting at least a little bit three or four months prior to hunting season. This will give you plenty of time to iron out kinks in your form as well as find and fix problems with your tackle. It is unethical to simply grab your bow out of the closet, shoot a few practice arrows a week or two before opening day, then head afield. We all owe it to both the game we hunt and our fellow bowhunters to take enough time to prepare our shooting skills so that when the time comes, we can make an accurate shot and clean, humane kill.

Too Much of a Good Thing?

You're determined to master this bow-shooting thing, and so you think the best way to do that is to shoot a bazillion practice arrows, right? Not necessarily. In fact, it is easy to practice *too much* with your bow and arrow. Overpractice is one of the best ways I know of to develop sloppy shooting habits. That's because your arm, back, and shoulder muscles will become sore and fatigued with too much shooting. When that happens you'll see your groups open up and shooting form falter, which leads to a lack of confidence.

When you feel tired, take a break. Most beginners have trouble shooting more than 20 to 40 arrows before fading. When I have been shooting for a few months, I find I can shoot perhaps 80 to 100 arrows in a day's time before I wear down. Also, it is a good idea not to shoot a lot of arrows day in and day out. Taking a day off helps your muscles recover and, just as important, your mind to recover, too. When I begin my own serious preseason practice sessions 4 months before opening day, I shoot only a dozen arrows the first few times out. As time goes by the number of arrows I shoot during practice sessions increases. I also try never to shoot a lot of arrows 2 days in a row. If I shoot 50 to 80 shafts one day, the next day I might only shoot 10 to 15—if I shoot at all.

When you are practicing, take your time between shots. Shooting a bow is not a game of speed, like basketball. Instead, like golf, it's as much a game of calculation and mental preparation as it is physically making the shot. I like to shoot an arrow, then take a few minutes before the next shot. This gives me time to relax my muscles and go through my mental checklist of proper shooting form. When you shoot too quickly, it is easy to get into a groove of making the same shooting form mistakes over and over until they have become ingrained habits and thus difficult to break.

One final note on bow-shooting practice. Highly trained athletes have their good days and their bad days, and so will you when it comes to shooting your bow. Some days it seems that your arrows are magically drawn to the center of the target. On others, it's tough to find your posterior with both hands. Don't worry about it. When I'm having "one of those days," I quit shooting and go do something else. There's no use fighting it, so why try? It's better to retreat and come back a day or two later, mind refreshed and muscles relaxed.

How Far Away Should I Practice?

There's a tendency for beginning bowhunters to want to fling arrows from long distance. Heck, it's fun. But the best way to improve your shooting skills is to begin practice sessions at relatively short range. Somewhere between 10 and 15 yards is good. After your shooting form improves, move out to 20 yards. When teaching beginners how to to release an arrow, instructors often have their students stand in front of a target only 10 *feet* away and shoot with their eyes closed so that they can mentally visualize their form and not worry about where the arrow is hitting.

As you become more skilled in your shooting, move farther away from the target. Soon you'll be able to consistently make good shots at 40 yards or more. We'll talk more about establishing your own maximum effective shooting range in Chapter 9. For now, suffice it to say that practicing at longer distances is the best way to force yourself to concentrate on every facet of accurately shooting your bow. Once you begin making good shots at 40 yards, you'll be surprised how easy those 20 yarders become. I'm a firm believer that bowhunters should practice shooting well past the distances at which they anticipate taking shots at game. Not that they should ever shoot at an animal past their own "comfort zone." It's just that once basic shooting form and skills have been mastered, long-distance practice is the best way to improve your overall ability to make the shot at any distance.

BOW SHOOTING BY THE NUMBERS

In the military they tell you to do certain things "by the numbers." That means there's a right way (*their* way!) and a wrong way to accomplish the task. Shooting a bow is the same. The basic steps are stance, draw, anchor, aim, release, and follow-through.

Stance

Most top bow shots prefer a sort of open stance, with their back foot set at about 90 degrees to the target and the front foot set at about 60 degrees. Spread the feet 12 to 18 inches apart, and get comfortable. The torso should be straight up and down—don't lean forward or backward. As you lift the bow, you should not have to cock your head to see the sights. The key is to have your bow set up so that it will fit your stance, not the other way around.

Proper hand position on the bow handle cannot be overemphasized. When placing the hand on the bow, do so in a consistent manner shot after shot. Variations in hand placement and pressure can cause inconsistencies in arrow flight, which will hurt accuracy. Keep

Using the proper stance is the basis for good field shooting skills. This will translate into good shooting from a tree stand, where the only difference is that you have to bend forward at the waist.

a natural, relaxed wrist. The major pressure should occur in the webbing between the thumb and forefinger. Lightly grip the bow with the index and middle fingers, taking care not to choke the handle. Avoid pressuring the handle with your palm, as this will create torque, which will definitely alter arrow flight.

If you shoot with your fingers, the most common method of string hand placement is to use the first three fingers, placing the index finger over the arrow nock and the other two under the nock. If you use a release aid, the position of the hand will be dictated by the style of release you're using.

Drawing the Bow

To draw the bow, simply raise your bow arm into shooting position and smoothly draw the bowstring back to your anchor spot. Remember that you shouldn't have to "cheat"—that is, lift the bow above the vertical to get it drawn back. If you have to cheat, you need to reduce the draw weight until you can properly draw the string back. Over time, as your bow-pulling muscles strengthen, you'll be able to pull more draw weight than in the beginning.

It is important to keep your bow arm relaxed during the draw. Once you get the bow up and drawn back, the bow arm should lock

A consistent anchor point is crucial to good shooting.

into place in a relaxed fashion. The shoulder should be pulled down, forcing the humerus into the shoulder socket. You should also rotate your forearm so that the wrist is in the vertical position, which is the best position for maximum bowstring clearance. Experiment with different bow hand, bow arm, and foot positions as you take your stance and draw the bow until you find the combination that's most comfortable.

Anchor

A consistent shot-to-shot anchor point is critical to consistent accuracy. There are several ways to anchor the bowstring. When shooting with fingers, I like to place the tip of my index finger in the corner of my mouth. Some people place the thumb knuckle under the chin. Anchor points with mechanical release aids vary by style of release. When shooting a wrist-strap caliper-type release—the most popular in use today—most shooters place the big knuckle of the thumb solidly under the rear of the jawbone. It really doesn't matter where you anchor the bowstring, only that you do it the same way every time.

If you use a peep sight, as most present-day compound shooters do, bring the bowstring back until it touches the tip of your nose when you draw and anchor. Having the peep properly placed between the strands of the bowstring will do two things. First, it allows you to clearly see your sight pins through the peep without cocking your head to one side or the other. Second, it acts as a secondary anchor point, which helps reinforce your primary anchor point.

Aiming

Aiming the arrow is not rocket science. You simply select the right sight pin for the distance, place it in the center of the peep sight, put it on the center of the target, hold it steady for a moment, and release.

The keys to aiming are consistency and smoothness. Smart bowhunters place their pin on the target the same way every time. Some like to line up their spot, then move the sight pin up from the bottom of the target to the right location before releasing. Others like to come from the top down. Both work well, but you'll find your shooting is better if you do it the same way every time. Also important is to smoothly move the pin on target instead of in a herky-jerky motion. Shooting a bow should be fluid, not break dancing.

You'll also find that it is impossible to hold the sight pin completely steady on the target. It's going to bounce and jump around some. Don't fight this. Professional tournament champion and top-notch bowhunter Randy Ulmer advises shooters to let the sight pin "float" over and around the target, releasing the arrow when it floats over the right spot. "Through practice, you'll just know when the exact moment to release the arrow comes," Ulmer said. "If you fight it, you'll get so tense trying to do something that is really impossible that you'll never be as accurate a shot as you can be."

You'll also find that you cannot focus your eye on both the target and the sight pin at the same time. You'll shoot best if you focus on the sight pin, not the animal. This is what top-notch competitive pistol shooters do. As I settle my sight pin, I focus on the target first, picking the spot on the animal I want to hit. I then let my subconscious remember that spot and focus on the sight pin as I place it precisely where I want my arrow to go.

On the target range, you'll be able to shoot from marked distances that correspond to the common sight pin settings of 20, 30, 40, and 50 yards. In the field, however, you'll often find that, often as not, you'll be shooting at an animal that is an odd distance away. Instead of 20 or 30 yards away, it's actually 25 yards, for example. If you use a common pin-type bow sight, you'll then have to do what I call "shooting between the pins."

On shots such as this, I simply split the difference between my pins when aiming. That is, instead of putting the 20-yard pin on the spot I want to hit, I raise it slightly above the spot, keeping the 30-yard pin just below it. This places the space between the pins vertically dead-on the target. Also, by drawing an imaginary line between the two pins I can line up the shot horizontally. This may sound weird at first, but it works. Be sure to practice this aiming skill during your practice sessions so you'll know how to do it when the time comes.

The Release

A smooth, consistent bowstring release is paramount to accurate shooting. If you shoot with your fingers, simply relax the fingers and let the string go, smoothly slipping away. Do not throw the string hand open or pluck the string like a guitar, two common mistakes.

Because releasing the string consistently shot after shot with fingers is so difficult, mechanical release aids have become the method of string release for more than 80 percent of today's bowhunters. With the simple squeeze of a trigger or press of a button, the machine that is the release sends the string off with the same amount of pressure shot after shot. That this translates into more accurate shooting is evident in the world of serious target shooting, where release shooters were given their own classification after they began beating fingers shooters virtually every time out.

Release shooting isn't a no-brainer, though. It is easy to punch or jerk the trigger or button, which defeats the purpose of the exercise. Approach the triggering mechanism the same way every time. To prevent accidentally setting off the trigger of my release prematurely, I keep my finger behind the trigger when drawing the bow, and don't place it on the front of the trigger itself until my sight pin is settling onto my spot.

Follow-Through

In all athletic endeavors—a golf swing, shooting a basketball, throwing a football—follow-through is critical to success. The same is true with shooting a bow. Follow-through makes sure you won't drop your bow or force it to the side before the arrow has cleared, which will send the shaft off-target.

To follow through, concentrate on continuing to aim at the target after the string has been released. Sounds simple, doesn't it? Yet follow through is one of the most difficult pieces of the accuracy equation for most archers. In the excitement of shooting at a big-game animal, the tendency for most of us—myself included—is to drop that bow out of the way so we can watch the arrow strike the target. That is a surefire formula for missing. Instead, concentrate on keeping the bow arm straight, looking for the spin of the fletching through your peep sight. It is this conscious follow-through that will ensure that all your practice and preparation up to this point will not have been in vain.

PRACTICE IN THE FIELD

There's more to successful game shooting than practicing at bull's-eye targets set at known distances. You'll need some realistic field practice, too. I begin by shooting on the target range from positions other than standing straight up. These include kneeling, sitting on a stool, and twisting my torso into odd angles from all three positions. This helps me simulate realistic shooting positions encountered when hunting from the ground. To prepare myself for tree-stand hunting, I climb onto the deck of my house and shoot down at targets. I also set a tree stand at the same height as the stands I'll hunt out of in fall, with targets scattered near the stand at various distances.

"Stump shooting" is another terrific way to practice field shooting. Here you simply walk around the woods, shooting blunt-tipped arrows at rotten tree stumps, tufts of grass, mud banks—whatever

Bowhunters need to practice shooting under simulated field conditions. Shooting from the knees and under brush is great practice.

you can safely shoot at without destroying the arrow. By pretending these targets are actually big bucks or bulls, you can not only hone field shooting skills, you can learn how to accurately estimate range. This technique also teaches you your limitations.

Finally, don't overlook shooting at 3-D targets. These are realistic targets built to the same size and shape as a variety of game animals. Some bowhunters purchase their own 3-D targets (they're pricey!), but many archery clubs have 3-D target ranges already set up. Here they hold both informal practice days and tournaments, which are great fun and excellent practice. Your local archery pro shop should be able to direct you to any 3-D courses in your area.

CHAPTER 9

Bowhunting Gear

IN HIS CLASSIC WORK *A Sand County Almanac,* Aldo Leopold called the new generation of hunters "gadgeteers" for their love of new technology and propensity for using it in place of old-fashioned woodsmanship. This was back in the 1940s! What would Leopold think of today's sportsmen and their mind-boggling array of high-tech equipment?

No doubt about it, today's hunters like their "stuff." Smart and experienced bowhunters, however, have learned to take it all with a grain of salt. They eyeball each new gizmo with a careful eye. As Euripides said back in 412 B.C., "Man's most valuable trait is a judicious sense of what not to believe." You, too, should be skeptical of gadget manufacturers who claim their products can do amazing things.

That said, several product categories do offer modern bowhunters superior performance and the reliability of the sunrise. Here's a look at some of those you'll want to consider.

CAMOUFLAGE

Despite all the hype, camouflage will not make you the invisible man. Yet judicious use of camouflage will definitely help your bowhunting scorecard. But with all the different patterns out there, how do you decide which is best?

Although there is still much debate about how much color big-game animals can see—if any—most authorities agree that deer, elk, and bears see the world in black, white, and shades of gray. For that reason, I believe the two things that give us away to big game animals the most are scent and movement. I once told Bill Jordan, who invented the various Realtree and Advantage camo patterns, that I had the perfect pattern that would put him out of business. "Tell me," he said, "and we'll make it." My idea? Take the old red and black check-

TreBark Sniper: One pattern that will make you almost invisible. *Photograph courtesy of Trebark.*

ered wool shirt your granddad wore in the woods. In the red squares, put black writing; in the black squares, put red writing. One should say, "Watch the Wind," the other, "Don't Move." Bill said something like, "Don't *ever* tell anyone that!"

That said, it is important that bowhunters cover the shiny parts of their exposed skin, including hands, ears, and face with gloves, a face mask, or a camouflage cream such as CarboMask. I prefer camouflage with a more open pattern as opposed to one with a tight pattern. At a distance, the tight patterns tend to look like a solid dark blob, while the open patterns help break up your outline. I also try to match the prevailing foliage color whenever possible.

I always wear camo when bowhunting, and I believe that together with playing the wind and not moving at the wrong time, it will help me stay hidden. That additional confidence alone is worth the price of admission.

OPTICS

All bowhunters need a quality binocular. There are many makes and models of binoculars out there, and serious hunters should purchase the best optics they can afford. Higher-priced optics have higher-

Trail timers can provide valuable information on game movements. This Cam Trakker even takes the animal's picture when it walks past.

quality glass, which translates into a clearer picture, especially when light conditions are poor.

Binocular prices vary widely. For example, the very best 10 × 40 binos from such companies as Bausch & Lomb, Zeiss, Leica, Swarovski, Leupold, and Steiner will run between $750 and $1,000. Similar binos from Simmons, Nikon, Tasco, and Bushnell cost somewhere between $150 and $200. You can find them for half that price, too. When considering price, remember that you're making a purchase that will last you a lifetime. Factored over many years, the initial price of a top-end binocular isn't really all that much.

Smallish compact binoculars are not recommended. That's because they are too small to use enough available light in low-light conditions—when game animals are most active—to make them very useful. Standard-sized binoculars in powers such as 7 × 35, 8 × 30, 8 × 40, 10 × 40, and 10 × 50 are the most useful all-around sizes. If you hunt in the West, where judging game at long range is important, you'll need a tripod-mounted spotting scope. Scopes with a variable eyepiece in 15–45X and 20–60X are my favorite.

TRAIL TIMERS

One of the most useful items I've played with in recent years is a trail timer. These gizmos use a beam of light that, when broken by an animal passing through the beam, records the date and time of passage. Inexpensive models cost less than $25, but record only one passing.

Camouflaged day packs are an absolute must for toting gear. *Photograph courtesy of Crooked Horn Outfitters.*

Models costing between $100 and $300 can record several hundred passings before you have to reset them. The Cam-Trakker and Trail-Master even take the animal's picture.

Trail timers can help you determine when animals are passing along certain trails or when black bears are hitting bait stations. They also let you know how much activity is occurring on a given trail at a given time. Such data can be useful in deciding where and when to set up. I use them even in the off-season as I try to piece together the patterns deer and other animals are using on a specific piece of property.

DAY PACKS

You're going to need some sort of pack to carry your stuff. Obviously you'll need a different size and design of pack for backpacking trips as opposed to day trips to a tree stand.

For most day hunts, either a fanny or day pack will suffice. Fanny packs are worn across the lower back and secured with a web belt. Day packs are worn over the shoulders, like the ones your kids tote their school books in. Whichever you choose, make sure your pack has enough room for your basic accessories, some drinks and snacks for all-day sits, and extra clothes. I also carry a screw-in step in my pack, which allows me to hang it next to my tree stand. This makes it accessible with minimum movement and keeps it out from under my feet.

Choose a fanny pack made from quiet fabrics such as fleece or

Stealth Cloth. Zippered closures are quieter to open and close than Velcro. Wide belts and shoulder straps help spread the load, and exterior web straps that allow you to strap on a heavy jacket while hiking are a great feature. There are several excellent bowhunting pack makers, including Badlands, Crooked Horn Outfitters, White Buffalo Outdoors, and Fieldline.

TREE STANDS

The tree stand is the bowhunter's best friend. We'll talk more about using them in Chapter 10. Basically, there are six types of tree stands: portable, climbing, ladder, tree sling, tripod, and homemade.

Portable or fixed-position stands are the most popular type. They feature a platform and seat attached by metal pole, all of which is attached to the tree trunk on top with either chain or nylon webbing, and supported on the bottom by either screw-in T-screws or built-in spikes. Tree steps or ladders are required to climb the tree when using them. There are more different makes, models, sizes, and styles of fixed-position stands than there are of any other. Fixed-position stands are also the most versatile, because they can be used safely in virtually any type, size, and height of tree. Many bowhunters like smaller fixed-position stands because they present a smaller outline against the tree trunk than larger stands. To use them you'll also need some tree steps or a portable ladder system.

Climbing stands are popular in areas where there are lots of tall, straight trees with few limbs, such as oaks, birch, and the like. They are designed for quick, quiet climbing without the use of tree steps or ladders. They generally have two pieces, with the hunter raising and securing the top piece with his arms, then lifting and securing the bottom piece with his feet. They are usually heavier and bulkier than fixed-position stands.

Climbers are excellent when the hunter is scouting on the move, prepared to set up and hunt hot sign that day. They are quick to set up, allowing the hunter to find his tree, assemble the stand, and climb into position in a matter of a few minutes. This also makes small adjustments in stand location during the hunting day both easy and practical. The downside is that they are impractical to use in trees with lots of large limbs or crooked trunks. You also must remember to connect the bottom section to the top section with a safety rope or cord. If the bottom portion slips off your feet and

Ladder stands are easy to set up and very stable. They're common on private lands, where they don't have to be taken down and moved constantly.

falls to the ground without the safety cord, you'll be left hanging—literally.

Ladder stands are basically metal ladders secured to the tree, with a small seat/foot rest built into the top of the ladder. Ladder stands are easy to climb and are most popular on private land, where their bulk and weight are not a factor with hunters who leave them set up all season. Ladders are growing in popularity each year because they are easy to setup and generally very safe. When you begin securing the ladder to the tree, you must take care that it will not roll off the trunk at the top, a potential problem on small-diameter trees with slick trunks. Ladders also generally only permit you to get no more than 12 to 14 feet off the ground, with many only rising 10 feet up. They also create a large silhouette against the tree trunk.

Tree slings permit the hunter to sit in a sling held in place by several nylon web straps and/or rope. Slings allow the hunter to remain close to the tree trunk, reducing his outline, and also quietly maneuver around the tree trunk and change his shot angle, depending on the direction from which game is approaching. These are graduate-level stands that take some getting used to. They are popular with

Homemade tree stands that you stumble across in the woods should never be used. They can be dangerous, as rotting wood will give way when you least expect it.

bowhunters because of their versatility and the small outline generated against the tree trunk. Most hunters use a pair of screw-in tree steps as foot rests once the sling has been set up, which makes waiting more comfortable.

Tripod stands are most popular in Texas and portions of the Southwest, where the tall trees needed to use more conventional tree stands are few and far between. Tripods are just that—three legs joined at the top, on which a rotating seat or shooting house is placed. These are monstrous stands and stick out like a sore thumb unless they are set up inside or adjacent to a small tree like a cedar. If they are set up and left for a long period of time, though, game generally will get used to their presence. Hunters sitting in a open-area tripod with a seat on top must take great care not to fidget because they have little or no cover around them. Tripod stands are stable, safe stands, and easy to get in and out of. They work well when set overlooking large green fields, feeders (where legal), and open-country water holes.

Homemade stands are those constructed by hunters of wood, nails, and whatever else they may have lying around. Extreme caution should be used before climbing into a homemade stand you're not familiar with. Rotting wood and loose steps have been the cause of more than one serious accident.

One final note about tree stands and their use: Never, ever use a tree stand without wearing an approved safety belt or harness. Every year several people are killed, and hundreds more seriously injured, in tree-stand accidents. Most were not wearing a safety belt or harness at the time. You don't want to be one of them.

ANCILLARY GEAR

There are several small items you'll need for basic tree-stand deer hunting. Other hunting trips for other game will, of course, require refinements in this list, which includes:

- **Small hunting knife:** For field-dressing your deer.
- **Pruning shears:** For snipping off small branches.
- **Compact saw:** For trimming large branches. Browning, Uncle Mike's, and Game Tracker make good ones.
- **Pull rope:** For hauling your weapon and day pack up and down the tree. Nylon parachute cord works well.
- **Bow holder:** Either hooks that screw into the tree trunk or holders that clamp onto the stand's platform keep your bow handy and your hands free.
- **Headlamp:** Better than a flashlight, it keeps your hands free for climbing up and down the tree in the dark.
- **Flagging:** Can be used to flag the trail into the stand so it is easy to find in the dark, or as an aid when tracking bow-shot game. Fluorescent stick-on dots that glow in the light of a flashlight also work for this.
- **Wind detector:** A talc-filled puff bottle or butane lighter works, but tying a piece of thread with small downy feather on a tree branch will allow you to monitor subtle wind changes constantly. Knight & Hale's Wind Floater, a small pouch filled with downy-light fluff pieces, is an excellent wind detector.
- **Walkie-talkie:** Compact radios are great for communicating with your buddies, calling for help to drag out your deer, and in case of emergencies. Motorola is the leader in sportsman's radios for this type.
- **Butane lighter:** For wind checking, but also as a survival item.
- **Hunting license/tags:** Required to be on your person by law. I carry mine in a plastic baggie for protection against the elements.
- **Pee bottle:** 'nuff said.

10

CHAPTER

Basic Bowhunting
Techniques

VOLUMES HAVE BEEN WRITTEN about bowhunting various big-game species. We don't have the space to delve into the nuances of successfully bowhunting everything from deer to elk to bears, but we can lay down the groundwork for bowhunting just about any big-game animal in North America. How? Simply put, there are some basic truisms in all bowhunting. These apply regardless of what you're hunting or where you're hunting it.

First, remember the goal of all bowhunters: to put themselves into a position to take a close-range shot at an undisturbed animal. To that end, you must spot the animal before it sees, hears, or smells you. Once you find it, you must not only get close enough for the shot, but also be able to draw your bow and release your arrow undetected.

There are four basic bowhunting methods: hunting from a stand, spot and stalk hunting, still hunting, and calling. Before you actually go hunting, though, it's best to understand a little bit about how to penetrate an animal's sensory defenses.

DEFEAT THE SENSES

Most big-game animals, but especially ungulates such as deer and elk, live in a world of smell. They depend on their sense of smell as the first line of defense against predators, which includes bowhunters. Most experienced bowhunters will tell you that if your quarry spots you or hears you, you might get away with it. But if they smell you, the party's over. They will turn tail and run as fast as their little legs can carry them.

To help defeat an animal's sense of smell, many bowhunters use cover or masking scents. I have never found these to be all that effective, though. Smart bowhunters will, however, take great pains to

362

Some bowhunters use masking, or cover, scents to help them defeat a deer's sense of smell. These can help, but are never foolproof.

eliminate as much foul-smelling human odor as possible. They do this by bathing with a nonscent soap, washing their clothes in the same, and storing their clothing in a plastic bag so it won't pick up odors at home or in the truck. They may go an extra mile and wear scent-blocking clothing and rubber-bottom boots, both of which have worked well for me at times. Above all else, they are meticulous wind-dopers. That is, they are constantly monitoring the wind direction. They know that the most important thing they can do to be successful is to keep the wind in their face so that it does not blow their smell to the animal's radarlike nose. Rule number one in all big-game bowhunting is simply this: Keep the wind right at all times.

Smart bowhunters also don't ever make human-like noises in the

Using a small puff bottle filled with unscented talc is a good way to monitor the wind.

woods. That includes talking, coughing, banging metal on metal, wearing scratchy, noisy clothing like denim and nylon, slamming car doors near stand sites, and so on. They do their best to slip through the woods on cat's feet, knowing that the hearing of most game animals is so much more acute than a human's that we really can't comprehend it. If the game hears you coming, it will simply slip away. You'll never even know it was there.

Finally, successful bowhunters don't let their quarry see them. That means blending into their surroundings with the judicious use of camouflage, eliminating shiny objects from their gear, and meticulously camouflaging their stand sites. It also means moving slowly, carefully scanning ahead for an animal before taking the next step. Watch a cat stalk a bird in your backyard and see how slowly it moves. Cats would make excellent bowhunters.

TAKE A STAND

Taking a stand is the most effective bowhunting method ever devised. That's because you're letting the animal come to you, not going to it. This, in turn, means that you don't have to move at all as the game approaches, both helping you stay hidden and giving you a chance to size the animal up and get ready to make the shot. The effectiveness of stand hunting is evident when you realize that more than 90 percent of all whitetail bowhunters hunt from some sort of stand, and more than 80 percent of all Pope & Young record book whitetails have been taken by archers hunting from stands.

Stands are also conducive to short-range shots. If you set a stand in a relatively thick area on a known travel route, deer and other game will pass by your stand well within your own comfortable shooting range. Most stands are set to give the archer shots of between 15 and 25 yards. Another advantage of stand hunting is that even if the animal walks past your stand and you either don't get a shot or choose not to take one, the animal can proceed undisturbed. That means it will never know someone was in its living room and hence will have no reason to change its habits. You can then confidently hunt the same stand again and again.

There are two basic stand types—tree stands and ground blinds. Ground blinds are simply that—blinds built on the ground in places where game is likely to appear. Tree stands are more common—and more effective. There are two reasons for this. One, they elevate you off the ground, which is a tremendous help in keeping animals from smelling you. Second, by elevating yourself above the animal's line of sight, it is easier to draw and shoot your bow without being seen. One final word on stands: For your stand to be effective, you must be comfortable. You have to spend countless hours sitting in your stand. Unless you do this without doing the hully-gully, you'll never get a shot. The game will see you moving, and it will be all over before it ever begins.

The downside of stand hunting is the same thing that makes it so effective: it's static. If you place your stand in the wrong place, you are going to be bored silly. That means you have to scout the hunting area to locate places where game is likely to pass during legal shooting hours.

I key in on two basic types of places to set tree stands: food and funnels. During the early whitetail season, for example, food sources such as mast crops—which for most whitetail hunters means acorns—as well as food plots, green fields, honeysuckle, persimmons, standing corn, alfalfa fields, and so on are dynamite stand sites. In any given area, deer have what we call "preferred food sources," which refers to a specific food source that, when available, the deer flock to like kids to candy. Find out what this is in your hunting area, then scout until you find where it's available, and you'll have a great place to set a stand.

In whitetail country, when there's corn on the ground, you can be sure there will be deer close by, as evidenced by these large tracks.

Funnels are areas along an animal's travel route where the nature of the cover is such that it pinches, or constricts, the likely places the animal will pass through on its daily journey. Likely funnel locations include along fences, fence crossings, saddles, creek bottoms, and edges where thick cover meets thinner cover. I like to hunt funnels located between thick bedding cover and a preferred food source.

Rutting areas are also good places to set stands. Whitetail scrapes and rub lines can be excellent rut-hunting stand sites. Wallows are good places to set a tree stand for elk. But remember this: During the rut, males go to the females, and females daily go to food. That's why food sources are such dynamite stand sites all season.

In dry, arid country, water holes can be superb stand sites. Water hole hunting is more important to western bowhunters pursuing pronghorns, elk, mule deer, and Coues deer than it is to eastern whitetail hunters.

Regardless of where you set your stand, there are a few basic tenets you must follow. First, set your stand so that you can approach and leave it with little chance of game seeing, hearing, or smelling you. Second, you have to be able to get a clear shot from your stand. That often means pruning brush and/or tree limbs to clear shooting lanes. Only remove necessary branches, however. You want to clear some lanes, but not alter the look of the woods so much that game can recognize the changes, or cut down so many limbs that you remove all your own cover. (Trust me, deer *do* look up. You need some cover up there!) Set your stand on the downwind side of the trail you think the game will approach from. Even though you're off the ground, the chances are good they'll smell you if they come in from upwind. Many bowhunters set more than one stand in a good spot, choosing the specific one they'll hunt on a given day according to that day's wind direction.

SPOT AND STALK HUNTING

Spot and stalk hunting is best used in open country like that found in the West, where the nature of the terrain and lower animal densities can make it a better choice than stand hunting. However, spot and stalk hunting can be effective in semiopen country, too. I've taken several animals—elk, blacktail deer, mule deer, and wild hogs—in country where visibility was much less than a quarter mile.

In this game, you find a spot that gives a good overall view of the

Spot-and-stalk hunting involves the use of optics, like binoculars and a spotting scope, to locate game to stalk. Topographic maps are a big help on western spot-and-stalk hunts.

country and use your optics to locate game to stalk. It can take hours and hours of meticulous glassing, but once you find the animal you want, it's time to plan the stalk.

And plan you must. Too many bowhunters simply dive off the hill with no real plan and ultimately blow their chance. It's best to first try to anticipate where the animal is heading. Use your binoculars to try to dope the wind by watching blowing grasses or hanging moss. If you see deer or elk moving and can get ahead of their path with the wind right, you might be able to intercept them by hiding behind some natural cover.

If I can't pick them off this way, I like to wait until the animal has bedded for the day, then put on a stalk. Step one is to plan a good stalking route, again using your optics to guide you. Identify easily recognizable landmarks both along this route and near where the animal has bedded. This is critical, because things never look the same once you get to them as they did through your glasses. Also, look for other animals. Many a stalk has been blown by stumbling over an animal you never saw.

Remember thermal currents, which are critical in stalking bedded game. Generally speaking, thermals take the wind down the slope in the early morning and late afternoon and evening, and carry the wind up the slope from mid-morning through late afternoon. When stalking, use the thermals to help keep your scent from the game.

Spot-and-stalk hunting can pay big dividends in open country. I shot this record book mule deer at 21 yards after stalking him in his bed along the edge of the thick junipers he called home.

The key to a successful stalk is to not move too fast. You might hike fast or even run to initially get into position, but the final stalk should be made at a snail's pace. Deliberately set your feet and hands down one at a time. Move any dry sticks or potential rolling rocks out of the way before taking the next step. When you get the urge to rush in and get it over with, remember the question Larry Jones, a call maker, video producer, and one heckuva bowhunter, asks himself when the urge to hurry overtakes him: "Why am I in such a hurry to blow this stalk?"

As you get close to the animal, relocating it can take some time. Use your binoculars to pick apart the terrain and look for a piece of the animal, like an antler tine, shiny nose, twitching ear, or white rump patch. Once I've found him, I slowly creep in to my own maximum personal shooting range, and go no farther. That's where I want to shoot from. Trying to get any closer only ups the odds that something will go wrong. If I have a clear shot at the bedded animal's vitals, I'll shoot. If not, I'll wait for him to stand up, which will give me a better chance to hit both lungs.

STILL HUNTING

Still hunting is one tough way to bowhunt. Unlike spot and stalk hunting, in which you first spot the animal before meticulously planning how you're going to stalk it, in still hunting you simply slowly sneak along, making no noise, and hope to spot an animal before he spots you.

Successful still hunting is tough. New Yorker Bill Vaznis, a well-known outdoor writer and accomplished whitetail bowhunter, makes a habit of taking a nice whitetail buck from the deep woods near his upstate home each year by still hunting, though. "I try and find the deer when they're up feeding, but I've also found them in their beds," Vaznis says. Vaznis knows the country intimately, which means he knows where the deer are likely to be before he ever begins. That gives him an advantage. In unfamiliar country, scouting can give you the confidence you need to still hunt effectively. When there's fresh sign around, you'll expect, not hope, to see game.

Vaznis is a careful still hunter, taking only a step or two before carefully scanning ahead with both his naked eye and his binoculars. He's looking for a piece of a deer, not the whole animal. He also listens carefully for the sound of a deer walking. He makes sure the wind is either in his face or blowing crossways. When the wind is swirling badly, he doesn't still hunt, knowing the odds are stacked against him. He makes sure he's wearing silent clothing, favoring wool over synthetic fabrics. If there is crunchy snow on the ground, the wind's wrong, or the leaves are dry and crackly, he hunts from a stand. But when it's cool enough for the deer to be moving, the ground is quiet, and the wind is steady enough to keep game from smelling him, Vaznis prefers still hunting to stand hunting. "Taking a deer this way is the most satisfying type of hunting I do," he says. "But things have to be just right or you're wasting your time."

CALLING

You can call a variety of big-game animals into bow range, including deer, elk, bears, pronghorns, and wild hogs. Calling is an exciting form of hunting in that it can offer all the advantages of stand hunting—basically, you're taking a stand while trying to bring the animals to your location—while still being a very active game.

There are two basic ways to approach game calling, says David Hale, half of the legendary Knight & Hale game-calling team and a superb bowhunter. "You can call blind, meaning you haven't seen an animal nearby but hope one hears you and comes in," Hale says. "Or, you can first locate an animal, get close to it, then try and call it in for the shot."

Hale has successfully used a variety of calls to lure in deer, including grunt calls, doe bleats, and fawn distress calls. "Of the three, the grunt call is the best all-around call," he says. "Bucks will respond to it all season long, but it is especially effective during the rut. The doe bleat is best early in the year and will draw in mostly does but also bucks that happen to be hanging around. Fawn distress calls, which are more squalls than quiet calls like grunts or bleats, simulate the sound of a fawn in trouble. Using them is a great way to bring in does, especially early in the year." Distress calls can also scare the dickens out of deer, so they should be used judiciously. Elk can be similarly called in, but instead of grunt and bleat calls hunters use bugles and cow calls.

Another method of calling that can work well on whitetail and blacktail deer, and occasionally on elk and mule deer, is antler rattling. This involves banging a set of antlers together to simulate two bucks or bulls fighting over a doe or cow. To that end, antlers are best employed during the rut, particularly the prerut period, before the actual mating begins in earnest.

"While I have rattled in my share of bucks, I have also seen nega-

Rattling can be an effective whitetail hunting tactic at times, especially during the rut.

tive reactions when rattling," Hale concludes. "But the grunt call is something else. I've never seen a deer noticeably spook from my grunting, and I've had several bucks not pay any attention it, too, and just continue to walk on past. But I have had so many bucks change course and come into range in response to my grunt calls that I never head into the deer woods without one anymore."

11

Making the Shot

AFTER ALL THAT TIME, practice, and effort, it's finally come together. A nice buck has just come into view. For some reason, your knees are knocking together, your palms are sweaty, and your body is shivering, even though it's 70 degrees out. How can that be?

The excitement and anticipation of making the shot when bowhunting is an adrenaline rush that's hard to describe to those who have not experienced it. If it didn't happen, there would be no reason for hunting at all. After 30 years and countless opportunities, I still get "the shakes." That's good. It means the inner fire still burns brightly. But it can also be bad. Learning to control your overactive adrenal glands is a big part of making the shot on game.

You need confidence to be able to make the shot under pressure, when a big-game animal comes into range. Such confidence is born through diligent practice sessions.

CONFIDENCE

You can't make the shot under pressure without confidence in both your equipment and your ability to use it. That's why you were so careful when you chose your bow, arrows, and accessories, took the time to meticulously tune your setup, then spent so much time practicing during the off-season, both on the target range and during those realistic field-shooting situations that simulate actual bowhunting.

It's important to note that accurate shooting is just one facet of a successful bow hunt. You have to be able to get close enough to your quarry, precisely estimate the distance to the target, and control the shakes (more commonly known as "buck fever") as well as shoot an accurate arrow to be able to place your tag on a deer.

There are no shortcuts. In bowhunting, there is no substitute for experience in all aspects of the game. In the beginning, you're going to make mistakes that cost you game. That's OK. Don't be afraid of those mistakes. Instead, use them as learning opportunities. You'll move at the wrong time, and a deer will nail you. You'll misjudge the range, and shoot over a buck's back. You'll forget about wind direction, and the deer will smell you and bound off. A million and one things can go wrong at any given moment when you're trying to make the shot on game. The more days you spend in the woods, the more times you're close to game, the more your confidence level will grow—to the point that when the deer you want finally shows itself, you're going to drill it.

MAXIMUM EFFECTIVE SHOOTING RANGE

Deciding when to turn an arrow loose is the most important decision a bowhunter can make. The whole philosophy behind ethical bowhunting is not just to shoot some arrows, but rather to take only high-percentage shots at calm animals that are both positioned properly and within your own maximum effective shooting range.

Just as athletes competing in the same sport have different skill levels, each bowhunter has his or her own personal shooting ability. No one else shoots at game exactly the same way, or with the exact same degree of skill, as you do. No two bowhunters perceive, or even see, the target identically, even under the same conditions. It's an individual thing. One of the most important things in all of bowhunting is for each individual to recognize his own shooting abilities—and inabilities—and to stay within himself at all times.

Most game taken with bow and arrow is shot at 30 yards or less.

Your own personal maximum effective shooting range (MESR) is the limit you set on yourself in terms of how close you have to get to an animal before you'll take a shot. To determine your MESR, shoot several arrows at a standard paper plate, then keep moving back until you aren't hitting this heart/lung-sized bull's-eye every shot.

After all, bowhunting is by its very nature a short-range, get-in-their-face game. But though they never talk about it in public, I know bowhunters who have taken game in the wide-open spaces of the West at 60 yards or more, their arrows slicing through the center of the animal's chest as neat as you please. These bowhunters are afraid to tell anyone how far their shots were, hoping to avoid others' accusing them of being poor sportsmen. In reality, these individuals have earned the right to take longer shots through constant practice; careful tuning of, and uncompromising confidence in, their bow-and-arrow setup; a familiarity with the terrain they hunt; and an intimate knowledge of the habits of the animals they pursue. In fact, they have more right to take a 50-yard shot at game than many less-skilled bowhunters have in shooting half that distance.

You can determine your maximum effective shooting range (MESR) on the target range. Use either the kill zone on a life-sized 3-D target or an eight-inch paper plate—which is about the size of the average deer's heart/lung area—as your target. Shoot your broadheads from farther and farther back until you quit placing all your arrows inside the bull's eye. When you begin missing, you're past your MESR.

Remember that this is your MESR under ideal conditions, which

The best shot placement practice of all is shooting at life-sized 3-D animal targets. Champion target shooter Kathy Caudle is an avid bowhunter who practices long and hard on 3-D targets.

are rarely replicated in the field. Each shot presents a unique set of problems that must be overcome, distance being only one of them. Rain, fog, steep uphill or downhill angles, thick brush, and other factors all must be taken into account when deciding whether or not to shoot. On several of my bow hunts, poor light was the determining factor in my not taking the shot. On another occasion—a bedded mule deer buck on a grassy slope—the 30 yards my range finder told me was the exact distance between us was in no way the reason I didn't shoot. A strong, gusting crosswind of perhaps 30 mph made it hard to steady my bow and would have pushed my arrow to the side a distance of which I was unsure. To try and minimize the wind's effect, I tried to sneak closer. Impatience made me hurry, and at 20 yards I rolled a softball-sized rock right into that buck's back. Had I been pitching horseshoes I would have been a winner. Instead I had an excellent view of that 26-incher's backside as he bounded off into the timber.

Another often-overlooked factor in deciding whether or not to take the shot is the attitude of the animal. Is it calm or tense? Alert animals can literally "jump the string," a term used to describe the lightning-quick reflexes of deer and other animals that allow them to literally jump out of the way of your arrow before it arrives. It may be hard to believe that a whitetail can move fast enough to cause a complete miss at 20 yards, but high-speed photography has shown this to regularly be the case.

For that reason, you want to shoot only at calm animals. And that's another factor in the distance equation. For years I believed that getting the animal in close enough to literally reach out and touch it was the way to go. Then I learned about what I call a big-game animal's internal radar. It seems that whenever they get closer to me than 15 yards, they just sense something's up. Their acute senses can hear the slightest sound, their eyes will pick up the smallest movement, and they'll tense up, ready to jump at the slightest commotion. That's why I try to take the first good shot I can get between 20 and 30 yards. I don't want the animal any closer than that.

SHOT PLACEMENT

With a rifle or slug gun, it usually doesn't matter what angle the deer is standing at when it's time to shoot. The power of the projectile enables it to smash through bone and lots of heavy muscle into the vitals, and its shocking power can knock the animal literally off its feet. An arrow doesn't have that bone-smashing penetrating ability or shocking power, instead relying on massive hemorrhage or the collapse of the heart or lungs to dispatch the animal. Thus, there are two—and only two—acceptable shot angles: broadside or slightly quartering away.

These two angles offer the only trouble-free access to the deer's vital heart/lung region. Sending a razor-sharp broadhead through both lungs of even the biggest, toughest animal will drop it so quickly it will amaze you. For example, I once shot a 700-pound Alaskan grizzly bear—one tough cookie—through both lungs at 35 yards. The bear spun around, bit at the entrance hole made by the razor-sharp blades of my broadhead, and sprinted off, falling graveyard dead in less than 30 seconds. However, animals hit in the wrong place with an arrow can run seemingly forever, making recovery difficult if not impossible.

Aiming for the lungs is the right shot in almost every instance. They present the animal's largest vital target and are bordered on three sides by other vitals—the spine above, liver behind, and heart below—giving you a little leeway. Where to aim? On broadside shots, as your vertical reference aim for the distinct vertical "crease" in the hair just behind the animal's front leg; for your horizontal reference, aim about halfway up the chest cavity. When the animal is quartering

slightly away from you, for your horizontal mark again aim halfway up the chest, but for your vertical mark aim for the opposite front leg. Don't take a shot if the animal is strongly quartering away, though, as your arrow could glance off a rib bone and deflect back away from the lungs and liver and into the paunch.

The best shots are at animals standing completely still. However, animals walking slowly offer good shots, too. You have to time the shot so that the front leg is moving forward and out of the way of your arrow when it arrives at the chest. Never shoot at running game, or animals facing directly at you, quartering to you, or facing directly away from you. The odds are too long that something will go wrong.

AFTER THE SHOT

Though you know you've made a perfect shot, the hunt is anything but over at the time of release. Until you've recovered the animal and put your tag on him, you cannot consider it a successful ending.

Despite a perfect hit, the animal will probably race off before falling. In the thick country where most game is arrowed, this means you are going to have to track him.

Though the adrenaline is rolling through your veins like the proverbial railroad train, there's much to do right after the shot. Most important is to watch the animal for as long as possible, both to see its posture and where it goes. Visually mark a landmark at the spot near which it disappears. This will be helpful when taking up the trail.

It is also important to stay as quiet as possible. One of the advantages a bow has over a firearm is its silence, which generally does not spook an animal the way the loud report of a firearm will. Don't add to the animal's excitement by making unnecessary noise. Being quiet also helps you follow the animal with your ears. Unless the wind is blowing hard or there's a noisy stream nearby, I've heard the animal go down many times before ever leaving my stand.

Get control of yourself. Look at your watch and note the time. Mine has a built-in stop watch, which I click on immediately after the shot. This helps me know exactly how long it's been since the hit while I'm waiting to take up the trail. Use your compass to take a reading on the animal's direction of travel from your stand to the last place you saw it. This reference can be a big help, especially when you are hunting from an elevated tree stand, because the lay of the land always looks different from ground level.

Though I've been bowhunting a long time, I'm still amazed at how many times a well-hit animal leaves little in the way of a blood trail. Some blood trails are so easy to follow that a blind man could recover the animal. Other times the trail is so faint, Dick Tracy would have trouble putting it all together.

Some hits are teasers. Many nonlethal hits, such as a hit in the thick muscles of the leg, can result in a lot of blood for the first 25 to 75 yards, and then the trail disappears like a wisp of smoke on a strong breeze. It may then turn into the occasional drop of blood here and there, leading you on a fruitless tracking job that will last as long as you want to keep it up. Blood volume, while always encouraging, is not a definitive indicator that your hit was a lethal one.

For many years, the rule of thumb following a bow shot has been wait for at least 30 minutes before taking up the track. Generally speaking that's a good rule to follow. Even though the shot looked perfect to you, the animal may have jumped the string without your knowing it, causing the arrow to arrive slightly off-target.

Game that has been hit poorly will generally do one of two things. Those hit in the paunch area will run off, then move at a slow walk for 100 to 300 yards before lying down. Unless forced from its bed, an animal will usually remain in place until it dies. This means waiting at least overnight on an evening shot and until late afternoon or the next morning on a shot taken in early morning light.

Waiting long enough under these circumstances cannot be overemphasized. If you spook the animal and it runs another half-mile to a mile before bedding up again, your chances of recovering it drop dramatically. It will usually leave no blood to speak of, and following tracks is almost always impossible. Of course, all this assumes that weather conditions permit waiting. When it rains, you have to take up the track before Mother Nature washes away all the evidence.

On most game, your arrow will have passed clean through the animal. The shaft will usually be lying very close to the spot of the shot. Find it, and carefully examine it for blood, hair, and other sign that will tell you where the animal has been hit.

The best feeling in the world is to locate an arrow covered with bright red, bubbly blood. This means a lung hit. Very dark red blood can mean a liver or kidney hit, but may also mean a leg hit. When this occurs, wait several hours before following. Greenish residue means a paunch hit. Wait as long as conditions allow when this occurs, but generally at least 12 hours. There will also be times when you can't find the arrow. This does not mean the hit was bad, only that you can't find the shaft. Forget about it, and search for blood sign.

Follow the trail alert and ready for anything. Move as quietly as you can. I always follow a blood trail as if I were still-hunting the spookiest deer. Try not to spook other animals that may give away your presence to game that is not yet dead. Avoid loud talking, banging equipment, or other unnecessary, boisterous noises.

As you follow the trail, mark it with the fluorescent flagging you should always carry in your hunting pack for just such an occasion. Toilet tissue will also work. You don't have to mark every speck of blood, but mark the trail often enough so that you can see the last flagged spot. (Be sure to go back and remove all your flagging after you're done.)

Look for blood splotches on branches and brush as well as on the ground. Also, watch for tracks, overturned leaves, and other signs of an animal passing through the area. I carry a small ¼-inch steel tape

Success at the end of a blood trail is the sweetest feeling in the world. Here Alabama guide Larry Norton and I pose with a nice eight-pointer we didn't have to track more than 100 yards.

in my pack to measure the animal's track, in case I lose the blood trail and have to continue the job by following tracks alone. This helps me identify the target animal if its tracks get mixed up with those of other deer.

The best blood trail often ends surprisingly, like a small creek vanishing into the desert floor. When that happens, mark the spot and make a tight circle of 10 to 20 yards as you try and pick it up again. If you find nothing, widen the circle. Use your head. Study the lay of the land, and try to guess where the animal has gone. There are no hard and fast rules when tracking game, but mortally hit animals will rarely go uphill; they will go sidehill and climb slight inclines, and almost always head for the thick stuff.

Get down on your hands and knees and look for the tiniest speck of blood on the bottom of a leaf that has been overturned by the animal's hoof. More than once I've picked up the track after losing a good blood trail that petered out by finding a single speck of blood many yards from the last good blood sign. When the blood trail begins to thin, it's time to use other tracking skills, such as following tracks themselves, in combination with intermittent blood specks. Take care not to obliterate blood sign by walking over it.

If the blood trail ends and you can't find any more signs, start searching for the animal itself. Now's the time to get others to help if they're available. If not, use your compass and map out a grid that you'll walk thoroughly. Leave no stone, log, gully, or brush pile unturned as you double- and triple-check all the possibilities. Don't give up until you've either found the animal or are 1,000 percent sure it's nowhere to be found.

FIELD & STREAM

The Complete Hunter

Book Five

Shooting Sports

Thomas McIntyre

Introduction

THERE IS A SHOTGUN GAME for almost any way that can be devised for making a target fly. Games with names like "Crazy Quail," "Rabbit Run," "Flurry," "Tower Shooting," "Starshot" (which looks like SWAT assaulting a Ferris wheel), and dozens more are played, with new ones being concocted on a regular basis. All the games, though, are essentially variations on the themes of what are called, rather sternly, the shotgun *disciplines,* of which there are three: trap, skeet, and sporting clays.

Trap, as we've seen, is by far the oldest of the disciplines, dating back in its earliest forms over 200 years. As well as being an Olympic

Olympic trapshooting. *USA Shooting*

Olympic skeet. *USA Shooting*

event, in both singles and doubles (i.e., "singles" being only one target thrown at a time; "doubles" being two), trap is certainly the most widely practiced of the shotgun disciplines—hardly a city or county in this country does not have some kind of trap field somewhere.

Skeet, also an Olympic shooting event, is nearly as widespread, even though it is more than a century younger. Before skeet even had a name, it was introduced as a "form of practice that is of real aid to the field shooter" because it claimed to simulate more accurately than trap the various lines of flight that a game bird might take, the clay birds in trap flying only away from the shooter. In skeet, the targets go away, come at, and cross in front of the shooter at varying angles, with singles and doubles being combined in the same round of shooting. Skeet is also, in keeping with its stated intention of honing hunting skills, the one discipline that has competition classes for the so-called sub-bore shotguns, specifically the 20 and 28 gauges and the .410. The only question is, Where did the name "skeet" come from?

Although it has been practiced for less than 20 years in this country, sporting clays has experienced a rate of growth more explosive than any of the other shotgun disciplines before it. Begun decades ago in England as a way for shooters (i.e., *hunters*) to replicate, even more than with skeet, the conditions of game shooting (i.e., *hunting*)

Sporting clays has experienced tremendous growth in recent years. *National Skeet Shooting Association*

during the off-season, sporting clays utilizes courses laid out over several acres of natural terrain and usually containing 10 to 14 stations that throw targets—varying in size from standard to minis (which in the air resemble black olives breaking Mach I)—in singles, pairs, and bouncing along the ground like some cwazy rabbit.

Before we look at the shotgun disciplines individually, we need to examine some of the fundamentals of shotgun shooting. As Americans, our shooting tradition comes out of the frontiersmen's use of their rifles to bring down large game, so it is not a great overstatement to say that the proper use of a shotgun is just a little foreign to us. And it is no overstatement to say that the only thing shooting a rifle and shooting a shotgun have in common is that they both involve firearms.

Rifle shooting is all about getting a "solid aim" and "lining up the sights." Movement is the bane of rifle shooting, but it is at the heart of shotgunning. Like the Sundance Kid, the shotgun shooter who does not move, and move properly, isn't going to hit a thing.

As we all learned in Shooting 101, unlike the single projectile of the rifle, the shotgun fires a large number of projectiles or pellets (shot), often several hundred depending on the gauge of the gun and the size of the pellets (a 12-gauge 1⅛-ounce load of No. 8 shot, for instance, would contain approximately 460 pellets). This shot forms a spreading "pattern" as it leaves the barrel, giving the shooter a greater chance of hitting a target in flight than he would have with a rifle bullet: Think of trying to kill a fly with a swatter rather than with a knitting needle. In order to cover a target with a shot pattern, a shooter cannot shoot at where the target is (because it is moving), but must send his shot ahead of the target to intercept it in flight. This involves swinging the shotgun barrel past the target so that it is pointing at a place in the air the proper distance ahead before firing. *(Shooting Tip: Following through, or continuing the swing after firing, is necessary to avoid unconsciously stopping the swing short.)* This, of course, is called lead, with shooters adopting one of three basic styles of leading—sustained (pointing ahead of the target and staying ahead through the swing), pulling away (pointing first at the target, then swinging past it), and swinging through (starting with the muzzle behind the target and *swinging through* it to get the lead). Each style has its advocates, and all shooters can do is try to find which works best for them.

As you may have noted, I have not used the term "aim" anywhere in conjunction with shooting a shotgun because a shotgun is never aimed (at least never should be) in the way a rifle is. A shotgun is all about *pointing* in just the way you point your finger at something, rather than aiming it. For this reason, a shotgun has no sights to align, at least none on the gun. The "sights" on a shotgun are the shooter's eye, lined up with the barrel. In order to point a shotgun properly, therefore, it is necessary that a shooter's "dominant eye" be the one that is lined up with the barrel; otherwise the barrel will always be off the target. For almost all of us one eye is, for lack of a better word, *stronger* than the other, and this is the eye that directs our vision. Usually, if we are right handed, it is our right eye, and if we are left handed, our left eye. But sometimes it is just the opposite, and many shooters never bother to learn which is their dominant eye.

The simplest test for determining your dominant eye is to pick out some small object (a doorknob or coffee cup will do) 10 or 15 feet away and look at it with both eyes open. Quickly extend your arm and point at the object with your index finger. *Freeze!* Now close one eye, then open it; then close the other eye. With one eye you should see your finger move off the object, while with the other it remains on it. Whichever eye, right or left, stays on the target is your dominant eye. Another method is to make an aperture with your two hands, then quickly raise and look through it. Now close one eye and then the other, and see which one is looking through the aperture.

If your dominant eye happens to be your right eye and you are right handed, you have no worries! The same is true for left eye/left handed. If you find, however, that you are "cross dominant," then you have several options (relax, one of them won't involve having to shoot in a frilly summer frock, patent-leather pumps, and a string of cultured pearls—unless you really want to). If you are just learning to shoot a shotgun, then learn to shoot from the side of your dominant eye; this, you will find in time, will be the most natural way of pointing. If you've been shooting for some time before learning of your cross dominance and have the patience and determination, you can still retrain yourself to shoot from the other side. If you don't want to go through that, then you can make your nondominant eye assume dominant duties.

The best way to do this involves blocking the center vision of your dominant eye while retaining the peripheral vision so vital to picking up targets in flight. Because you will always be wearing safety glasses when shooting your shotgun (see Chapter 5), an excellent method is to obscure a spot on the glasses that covers the pupil of your dominant eye. You want this spot to be no larger than necessary,

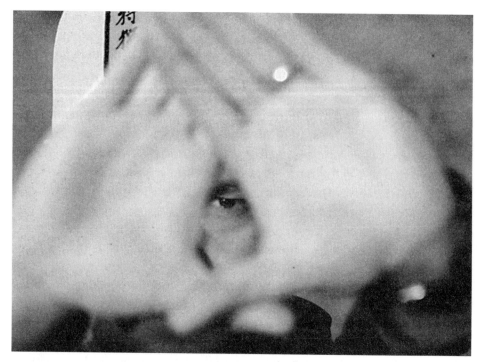

Finding your dominant eye. *Photo by Elaine McIntyre.*

so, **first making sure the shotgun is unloaded,** mount the gun to your shoulder and look down the barrel. While you are doing this, have another person place a small disk of frosted adhesive tape, no bigger than a dime, on the lens of your safety glasses directly over the pupil of your dominant eye. This will cause your nondominant eye, the one aligned with the shotgun barrel, to assume pointing duties. You can also daub a film of lip balm or something similar on the lens of the glasses over your pupil, or sometimes just slightly squinting your dominant eye will switch control to your nondominant one. At all costs, though, avoid shooting a shotgun with one eye completely closed.

Curiously, when your eye is properly aligned with the barrel of the shotgun, it should not be the barrel that it sees but the target. There is, in fact, no way of hitting a target in flight with a shotgun if you are looking at the barrel, anymore than a pitcher could hit the strike zone if he were looking at the baseball as he threw it. As in throwing a ball or pointing a finger, the eye goes to the target and the ball or finger, or shotgun barrel, goes to where the eye is looking.

Patching over your dominant eye. *Photo by Elaine McIntyre.*

Proper mounting of a shotgun is needed to make this possible. Finding a shotgun with the right dimensions, in length of pull (the distance from the trigger to the center of the butt: For a shooter of average build, usually around 14½ inches), drop at the comb, and drop at the heel (these are, basically, the amount of "bend" in the stock down from the line of the rib on the barrel or barrels: Varying according to the physique of the shooter, drop can be roughly anywhere from 1½ to 2½ inches), is very important, but is not a substitute for a shooter's knowing how to bring that gun to the shoulder.

The first element of a proper mount is a proper stance. On a trap or skeet field you can often witness shooters contorting themselves into outlandish postures—shoulders hunched up, chins thrust forward, backsides pouted out like Donald Duck's, assuming a crouch like that of the mighty jaguar about to pounce upon its unsuspecting prey, the gentle jungle tapir—and acting as if they actually know what they are doing. The fundamental stance for a shotgunner is very much like that of a boxer: The feet should be about shoulder width apart with the forward knee slightly bent, the hands raised ("put up your dukes!"), the elbows a comfortable distance away from the the sides (not sticking straight out, Funky Chicken style), the shoulders

Low-gun position.

relaxed, the forward hand well forward, and the upper body leaning just far enough forward to have, as the saying goes, "nose over toes."

In most shotgun sports, shooters have the option of starting with their guns in a "low" position (the butt resting between elbow and hip) or mounted to their shoulder before calling for a target to be thrown. For the new shooter, having to think about calling for a target, bringing the gun up, disengaging the safety, locating the target, getting on it, leading, and firing can be very complicated. A mounted gun can often help simplify matters and enable someone just starting out to break more birds and acquire greater confidence. *(Shooting Tip: In trap almost all shooters will want to begin with a mounted gun.)* As shooters gain more experience, they sometimes find that they can be even faster by moving slower, and so they will start from the low-gun position. The repetition of mounting the gun every time they yell "Pull!" makes them mount the gun correctly. Practiced shooters, for whom mounting the gun has become part of their muscle memory, may also find that starting from the low-gun position can help them pick up (that is, see) the target more quickly after it leaves the trap house, and so acquire it more smoothly.

In either way of holding a shotgun, the muzzle should cover the spot in the air where the shooter wants it to be when beginning the

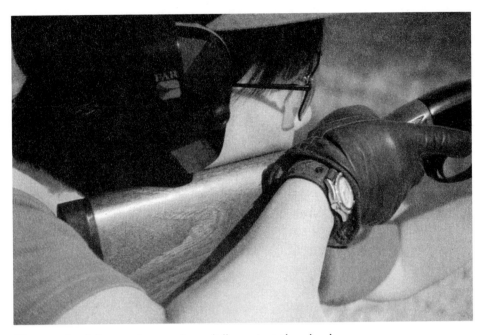

The comb of the stock must be solidly against the cheek.

swing on the target. In bringing the shotgun up, the shooter first pushes the gun forward, raises the rear of the stock by lifting it with the trigger hand, and then pulls it firmly into the shoulder without tensing up. The shotgun's comb (the top of the rear stock) should come up solidly against the shooter's cheek without the shooter having to tilt the head over onto it, making sure the eyes remain level. Through all this, the forward hand remains essentially motionless, while the muzzle has not moved from where it was pointed at the sky. The shotgun should be at roughly a 45-degree angle to the line of the shoulders, compared to the perhaps 15- to 20-degree angle at which a rifleman holds his weapon across his chest, with the raised elbow of the trigger-hand arm creating a hollow in the shoulder for the shotgun butt to nestle in. *(Shooting Tip: Frequent, even persistent,* empty-gun *practice of the mounting routine at home is one of the best learning methods available, as is "dry-fire" practice for all the other shooting sports.)*

The shotgun should be swung by the pushing or pulling of the forward hand on the gun's fore-end. The speed of the swing can be controlled by how far out on the fore-end the forward hand is. Extended all the way, the barrel swings slower, but often more smoothly, whereas pulled closer in, the swing accelerates, often helping to overtake fast flyers. *(Shooting Tip: Mount the gun pointing directly at, or even just slightly past, the spot where you expect it to be when you pull the trigger. Then, without changing your foot placement, turn your body back toward the position where you expect first to pick up the target when it is thrown; this lets your body uncoil like a spring and is faster, and much less awkward, than trying to twist your body around in pursuit of a clay bird in flight.)* As important as following through on your lead is keeping your cheek planted on the comb, even after the shot. Other than that, never load your gun before taking your firing position, and never take off the safety before you are ready to fire.

Now it's time to step up to the line, but first let's look at what we will be stepping up to the line with and learn a little about its history.

CHAPTER

Guns and Chokes

T HE USE OF FIREARMS to shoot pellets, or shot, is a very old application of the gun. Early shot was laborious to make, and the result was crude, often being nothing more than chopped-up pieces of lead sheet. The shooting it provided was equally crude, with pot hunters using their shotguns to splatter flocks of wildfowl on the ground or water and bagging not just two birds with one stone, but often tens of birds with one shot. "Sport" was hardly a consideration until the shotgun became more reliable and more refined. When gentlemen had proved to themselves that shooting game on the wing, or "shooting flying," as it was known, was possible, then it became fashionable.

A flintlock mechanism.

Shooting flying did not become a reality until the perfecting of the first really trustworthy firing mechanism, the flintlock. The Norman artist and gunsmith Marin le Bourgeoys is generally credited with having de-bugged the flintlock by incorporating the frizzen and pan cover in a single piece of steel—thus helping to keep the priming powder dry—and internalizing the lock's works. So when a fowler swung on a bird in the air and touched off his shot, the gun might actually fire, and with a fast enough lock time (the interval between the dropping of the flint on the frizzen and the ignition of the powder charge behind the load of shot) the shooter might be confident that the shot would reach where he was pointing in time to meet up with the bird.

Yet another advancement in the practice of wingshooting came about in 1769. It was then that the Englishman William Watts devised a method of manufacturing shot of uniform size. His method involved dropping lead in molten form from a high tower through sieves with varying-size openings (depending on the size of shot desired) into vats of water. The sieves were made to vibrate, causing the lead to form into globules that were further rounded into perfect little spheres by their passage through the air. (Watts, it is said, came to his discovery by way of a dream.)

Flintlocks and uniform shot worked well enough until shooters began to notice that the flash of the priming powder in the pan would often alert birds that a load of that shot was heading their way and cause them to veer radically. One wildfowler who was tired of seeing ducks flare every time he pulled the trigger was the Reverend Dr. Alexander John Forsyth, minister of Belhelvie parish, Aberdeenshire, Scotland. As a solution to the problem, in 1807 he patented the percussion "scent-bottle" lock, which used fulminate—an explosive substance derived from dissolving metals in acids—instead of flint and priming powder to ignite the blackpowder charge in a gun. In Forsyth's system, the priming charge of fulminate (usually fulminate of mercury and saltpeter) was held in a closed chamber and was struck and detonated with a "plug or sliding-piece so as to exclude the open air, and to prevent any sensible escape of the blast." Thus internalized, the ignition of the powder charge was not only invisible to passing birds but far more efficient than any previous system.

The next major development in shotgunning was the choke. Since the projectiles in a shotgun leave the muzzle in what is essentially a spray, like water leaving a hose, it stood to reason that spray could be regulated hydromechanically as well. Think of the nozzle on a garden hose and you have the basic principal of the choke: The more the constriction (up to a point), the "tighter" the spray, or "pattern," of shot and the longer its useful range. While Fred Kimble, an old-time Illinois market gunner, is often said to have been the inventor of the choke (he *was* a great popularizer of it), it was actually the Amherst, Massachusetts, gunsmith Sylvester H. Roper who on April 10, 1866, first patented an effective choke.

Roper's design consisted of an attachment that screwed onto the muzzle of a single-barreled shotgun and reduced the diameter of the bore. It worked, although not as well as the permanent choking that could be done in the shotgun barrels of the time. And yet, with modern advancements in technology and design, the interchangeable choke that screws on, or rather "screws in," the muzzle has today become the standard method of choking shotguns.

To make possible the rapid-fire shotgun sports we know today, a method of loading had to be devised that was faster than pouring powder and shot down the muzzle of a shotgun. The result, of course, was the breech-loading shotgun along with the shotgun cartridge that had primer, powder, wad, and shot in one self-contained package. The first breech-loading percussion gun was patented in 1831 by the Parisian gunsmith Augustus Demondion, whereas the patent for a priming system integral with the base of a cartridge dates back to another Paris gunsmith, Houiller, in 1847. Smokeless powder began being used in shotgun shells even before the close of the Civil War. By 1874, the first ejector double-guns were available, followed the next year by the first hammerless shotguns, made by Anson and Deeley in England. Brass cartridges began to be replaced by paper; the slide-action, or "pump," shotgun and the autoloader appeared on the scene; and somebody found an electrical outlet in which to plug the throwing machine.

Today we can choose from five types of shotguns for use in the shooting sports. These fall it two categories: the break-actions and the repeaters. The break-actions include the single-barreled, the double-barreled side-by-side (or, simply, double), and the double-barreled over-and-under (over-and-under or even stack barrel). And there are two types of repeaters: slide-action (also called a pump, as stated above), and the autoloader (auto, or, more correctly, semiauto). Let's briefly review the pros and cons of these guns.

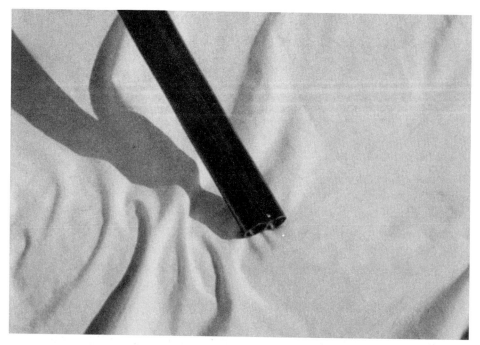

Double barrel—the classic shotgun design.

The double is the classic shotgun design going back to the flint-lock shotguns of Joseph Manton, the 18th-century patron saint of English best-gun makers, his being the first great recognizable talent and brand name to be sought after. As a game gun the double is a superb choice (I'd rather take my own quick-handling Browning dou-ble out after wild quail than any other gun I own), but it is probably not the gun for serious competition (if it were, you'd see them being used, and you simply do not). The over-and-under is a much better choice, perhaps even the best, for the shooting sports for two funda-mental reasons. First, the single-sighting plane along the barrel of the over-and-under allows shooters to see more of the target area and to pick up the target faster, their vision unobscured by the width of two barrels; and second, the gun's straight-line recoil lets shooters keep their eyes on the target without having the barrel jump up in the face, an important factor when shooting doubles—targets, not guns. An added consideration, more so for single-barreled guns than for double, is that the increased weight of the stacked barrels helps pro-duce smoother, more controlled swings.

If the over-and-under is not the best choice for a shooting-sports

Over-and-under shotgun—the preferred choice for most shooting sports. *USA Shooting*

gun, it is only because it runs neck and neck with the autoloader. Modern autoloaders, if well maintained, are as reliable as break-action guns (or rather, *almost*, nothing being more reliable than a good-quality break-action). Their action directs recoil back in a straight line, reducing muzzle jump, whereas the automatic process of ejecting the empty hull and loading a new cartridge greatly softens the gun's kick. The pump, however, lets the shooter absorb all the recoil and slows the second shot by making the shooter have to work the action before firing. It also presents the shooter with the risk of "short shucking" a shell—that is, failing to move the slide far enough back to eject the empty hull before pushing it forward to load the next cartridge. Nonetheless, many top competitors have shot very well with the pump; but with continuing improvements in the autoloader, trying to compete in anything but Singles or Handicap Targets in trapshooting with a "trombone" gun is a little like tying on hiking boots to run a 100-yard dash.

For the serious trapshooter uninterested in shooting doubles, there remains the single-barreled shotgun with its specialized stock and rib. Long-barreled and tightly choked, it is meant for breaking

Remington Model 1100 Synthetic shotgun. *Remington*

Remington Model 870 TC trap. *Remington*

birds at distance. But how long is long, how tight is tight, and what does "at distance" mean?

There may be an application for a barrel nearing a yard in length and for severe choking on a shotgun destined for shooting trap; but too many shooters believe that long barrels and tight chokes are the answer to all their needs in the shotgun-shooting sports. I think that anyone taking up the shotgun sports, or even those who have been in them for a time, should proceed with caution before running out to buy a shotgun with a 34-, 32-, or even 30-inch barrel and a fixed full choke, unless he is entirely sure, without fear of contradiction, that this is the right gun for his shooting situation.

Chokes, of course, come in differing amounts of constriction, which are labeled Cylinder, no constriction; Improved Cylinder, a tightening of .010 inches from the bore's standard diameter (.729 inches in the case of the 12 gauge); Modified, .020 inches; and Full, .035 inches. Besides these basic four amounts of constriction, there are such subtle distinctions as Skeet, .005 inches, running through Light Modified, Improved Modified, Light Full, all the way to Extra Full which cranks the barrel diameter down .040 inches. The function of any choke is to deliver the optimum dispersal—that is, the spray, pattern, or "spread" of shot at a desired range. For hunting purposes, this is usually defined as all the shot, evenly distributed, placed within a 30-inch circle at 40 yards, but this is not necessarily the case with the shotgun sports.

PATTERN/PELLET DENSITY & ENERGY GUIDE

Look up distance to your game for recommended pellet. Pellets appropriate for longer distances may also be used at shorter range. Use of pellets at distances surpassing their listing is not recommended.

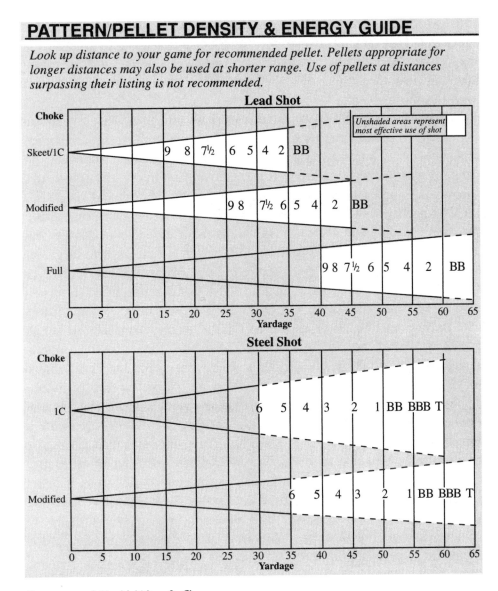

Courtesy of *Black's Wing & Clay.*

In the shotgun sports, targets have their own ideal yardages at which they can be most easily broken, depending on which sport is being played, so the choke needs to be matched to that yardage. As Chuck Webb, gunsmith, skeet shooter, and general manager of Briley, one of the country's oldest manufacturers of custom and after-market interchangeable chokes, puts it, picking a choke is "like choosing a golf club." And yet most people seem to want to use too much choke and too much barrel in most of their shooting, like wanting to hit every golf ball on the course with a driver. Another consideration is the way the target presents itself, so to explain yardage and presentation and how they relate to choke selection, let's turn to the situation found in trapshooting.

In the trapshooting game known as Singles, which will be explained in greater depth in the following chapter, a shooter stands at a position 16 yards from the low building called the traphouse and calls for a target to be thrown. The trap machine inside the traphouse throws the target, and in the time it takes the shooter to react—to pick up the bird, swing, and fire—and for the shot to reach the target, the target is, on average, around 32 yards from the shooter. Now, what a shooter wants is for the load of shot when it reaches the target to be filling that optimum 30-inch circle, both because there are fewer holes in the pattern that the target might slip through and because a trap target, as it flies away, presents itself either "edge-on" or "dome-on." Both presentations happen to be the hardest profiles to break because of their narrowness and because the edge and the outside curve of the dome are the most durable parts of the target, so that a lot of shot is needed to break birds when they fly in these positions.

Is a Full choke, then, the best choice for delivering the largest, densest pattern of, say, No. 8 shot at that 32-yard range? More likely it would be the choice at 45 yards. Then how about Modified? Maybe this is the one to use at 40 yards. According to the choke chart put out by Gil Ash, a noted shotgunning authority, at 32 yards, a Light Modified would probably be the right choice for trap. In trapshooting there is another game, as we shall also see, known as Handicap, in which shooters fire from positions that can go as far back as 27 yards from the traphouse; but even all the way back there, you're still not likely to need more than a Modified choke.

The point is not to get caught up in the mythology that more barrel and more choke are always better; they may even be worse. If you buy that 34-inch trap gun with the Extra Full choke, it may not be easy to have that choke opened up later on. An essential part of any choke is the taper, or "cone" or "lede," of the barrel that precedes the parallel-sided constricted section at the muzzle. This taper needs to be ¾ inch in length in order to let the shot make a smooth transition from the barrel to the choke. Opening a choke from its original diameter may shorten this taper and cause the shot load to become disrupted and not leave the shotgun in the uniform cluster necessary for

Interchangeable chokes.

proper patterning. The sensible choice, especially when new to the shooting sports, is to buy a gun with barrels, or a barrel, no longer than 28 inches; interchangeable chokes; and more or less standard (i.e., average) dimensions and features. Then take the gun out, set up a patterning board, and test various chokes and loads at different yardages until you find which combinations work best in your gun for the different types of shooting you plan to do. This may be time consuming, but for anyone serious about the shooting sports it is a much faster, cheaper, and far less frustrating way of finding how your gun shoots than through round after round of abysmal scores, with more zeros attached to your name than to the national debt.

CHAPTER

Trapshooting

A T THIS POINT, there is not much more that can be learned about shotguns without actually shooting one, and about the best way to do so is in the most time-honored of the shotgun sports, trapshooting.

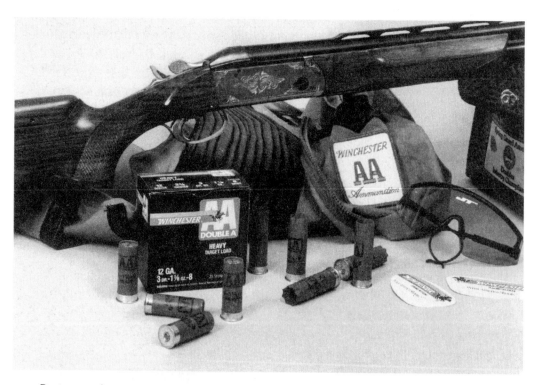

Basic trapshooting equipment. *Winchester*

Trapshooting has been old hat, literally, almost from its inception. In the early 1800s, many shoots, well attended by the à la mode betting men of the period, were held at the Uxbridge Road public house, "Old Hats," near London. The pub earned its sobriquet because the live wild pigeons used in the matches were placed in holes in the ground that were then covered by old hats. When the shooter called for a bird, a puller yanked on a string attached to the hat, allowing the bird to fly up. In other locales the holes were covered with wooden planks that were pulled up. Eventually a box, whose sides and top would fly out and lie flat when a string was pulled, was used to contain, or "trap," the bird. The first place where such traps were used, and the first genuine pigeon-shooting club, was at Hornsey Wood House in England, the club said to have been founded in 1810.

Despite almost continuous complaints about the inhumanity of using live animals for target practice, live-pigeon shooting remained an enormously popular sport throughout the 19th century and into the 20th (the English Parliament outlawed it in 1921). It continues today, both legally and illegally, in many countries, including the United States, with substantial purses being available for top guns and handsome sums being wagered on the contests. No two pigeons fly alike, and it is this unpredictability that for good or ill makes live-pigeon shooting such a fascinating, and certainly a highly challenging, shooting sport. By the middle of the 1800s, though, trapshooters were looking for alternatives to real pigeons, both because of mounting public distaste for their pastime and because of the disappearance of their feathered targets.

This scarcity was more pronounced in the United States than in England because of the dwindling number of passenger pigeons, which were the American trapshooters' primary target. One of the first substitutes for pigeons, just after the Civil War, came out of Boston where a Charles Portlock is said to have introduced glass balls as targets. Portlock, who supposedly drew his idea from the glass floats used on Japanese fishing nets, devised a spring-loaded mechanism to launch the balls, though not, some say, in a very satisfactory manner.

The glass balls were first clear, then stained green, blue, or amber (the better to be seen); then feathers were pasted on them. They later came to be stuffed with feathers, with some even being filled with gunpowder, all to create more spectacular effects when the balls were broken. The balls were relatively easy to hit, at least compared to live pigeons: Captain Adam H. Bogardus, one of the 19th century's great shotgunners and the first man documented to have killed 100 pigeons straight, in the late 1870s broke 5,681 balls without a miss during an exhibition; Annie Oakley in that same event distinguished herself by breaking 4,772 out of 5,000. However, the balls often didn't break, the shot glancing off them, so they were given a raised, checkered pattern on the outside to catch the shot better and break more easily.

The next, and permanent, alternative to the glass balls for trap shooting (and, in fact, for the rest of the shotgun sports) was the clay pigeon or clay bird, or as it is now known, the clay target, and breaking was sometimes also a problem for the early designs (although another noted shotgunner of the 1800s, the trick-shot "Doc" Carver, broke 60,616 during an exhibition in 1885 that lasted from Monday until Thursday evening). Sometime around 1870, disks made of (no peeking!) *clay* began to be thrown for shotgunners, but these often proved too soft, breaking up in flight, or too hard, merely ringing, it's been said, "like a bell" when struck. Apparently, a number of individuals, among them a George Ligowsky of Cincinnati, Fred Kimble, the man who didn't invent the choke, and an Englishman named

Clay targets come in a variety of sizes.

Laporte 285 Twinlap trap machine. *Laporte*

McCaskey, began working independently on improving the clay target, as well as coming up with better mechanical throwers to get the "birds" airborne. The final result, and the one trapshooters break today, was a domed saucer made from petroleum pitch and gypsum. The clay target's dome shape created aerodynamic lift, in the same manner as the upper curved surface of an airplane's wing, allowing it to sail smoothly for a considerable distance.

The official clay target shot in trap today can be no larger than $4^{5}\!/_{16}$ inches in diameter and $1^{1}\!/_{8}$ inches in height. The machine for throwing clay targets is still known as the trap, but today at most trap ranges it is operated electrically rather than manually. (Some traps have become so technologically sophisticated that they are able to be activated by an individual shooter's voice and no other sound.) A trap must throw a target between 48 and 52 yards (44 and 52 for doubles), measured "on level ground in still air," according to the book of rules for trap. This is roughly at 65 miles an hour, or about the flight speed of a pheasant.

The trap is set in the so-called traphouse where it is concealed from the shooters, the machine oscillating back and forth while stopping and starting at irregular intervals so a shooter can never be certain at what angle the target will leave the trap. Sixteen yards back from the trap, as described earlier, is the firing line, with five shooting positions, or stations, arranged in an arc, three yards between each position. Each position has individual yard markers running from 16 yards to 27 yards behind it. A shooter must stand behind the 16-yard marker in position when shooting regular Singles. Five shooters, or a "squad," shoot in sequence, with the shooter in position No. 1 firing once at his first target, followed by the shooter in position No. 2 firing at his, and so on, rotating through the lineup until each shooter has fired five shots, at which time the shooter moves to the next position in the order 1, 2, and so on, with the shooter in position 5 going to position 1. At the end of a round, each shooter will have fired five shots from each position for a total of 25 shots.

A target can be scored either "Dead" or "Lost." A target is Dead, and therefore is scored as a hit, if a shooter breaks any visible piece of it, or disintegrates it, but is Lost if no piece of it is broken or if a shooter manages only to raise dust off it. A Dead target is scored with an "X,"

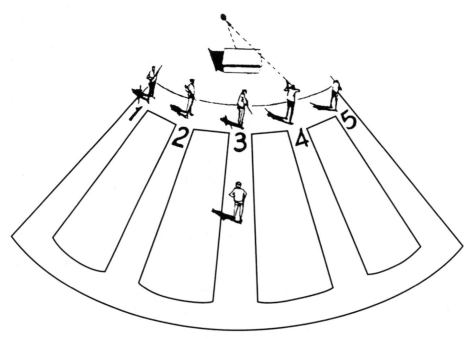

Layout of trap field. Courtesy of *Black's Wing & Clay.*

whereas a Lost one is designated by the notorious "O," the ol' goose egg. (Targets in skeet and sporting clays are scored in the same manner.) To score a hit, the shooter must also break the target within bounds, which in the case of trap means within an angle of a little more than 84 degrees, the vertex being the trap machine.

Organized trapshooting using live pigeons began in the United States probably in the 1820s, and it wasn't until the 1880s that clay birds began to replace animate ones. Over the next decade, the sport was formalized along the lines described above, and what we would recognize as the first trapshooting tournaments began to be held.

Two events marked the year 1900 as a pivotal one in trapshooting. One was the founding of the American Trapshooting Association, the name changing in 1923 to the Amateur Trapshooting Association (ATA). The ATA, with a current membership of over 50,000, is the governing body for trapshooting in this country.

The second event was the first Grand American World Trapshooting Championships, the ATA's main tournament, held in June 1900 in Interstate Park in Queens, New York. (Because there were only 20 competitors in that first tournament, it did not refer to itself as the "world" championships but chose the simpler, and somewhat more modest, title Grand American.) For the next 20 years, the Grand American was held in various cities, including Chicago and St Louis, until in 1924 it found a permanent home in Vandalia, Ohio, north of Dayton. Today, the Grand American is described as among the "oldest and richest sporting events" in America, "the largest participation sporting event in the world," and the world's "largest shooting event"—outside of global conflicts, one assumes. However it is described, the Grand American, over the course of 10 days, manages to draw more than 6,000 competitors, going after $175,000 in prize monies, and 100,000 spectators to Ohio in the swelter of August!

Whatever the impact of the Grand American and the ATA, trapshooters across the country today shoot at over 80 million targets each year—and those are just the ones that are registered by the 1,200 ATA-affiliated gun clubs. The total number might be something closer to a half billion, if one includes all the nonregistered targets that get shot at by the millions who visit trap ranges several times a year and who help to make trapshooting a $250-million sport in this country.

Most people, of course, are shooting 16-Yard Singles, as just described, although some are shooting Doubles, in which two clay targets are thrown simultaneously. The third trapshooting event is, as mentioned earlier, Handicap Targets, in which a shooter starts at the 19-yard mark and is then assigned longer yardages, depending on proficiency, going all the way back to the "fence" at 27 yards. The scoring percentage over at least 1,000 targets is the measure used to determine the shooter's handicap.

Another rare form of trap is known as International (sometimes European), Bunker, or Olympic, although it is not shot in the Olympics—only Singles and Doubles are—and is considered perhaps the most difficult of the shotgun sports. Found in only a handful of trapshooting ranges around the country, International uses 15 traps set in a trench, five stations, and a six-person squad of shooters with five shooting and one on deck, two shots allowed at each target, which must fly 77 yards (or roughly a lot faster than a regular trap target), with misses announced by the blast of an air horn. Well, believe me, if you're reading this book, you've probably never shot it, and I would have no idea where to begin to tell you how.

To shoot the saner brands of trap, though, there are a few things to keep in mind. The first is that in trap the bird is continually increasing the distance between you and it as soon as it leaves the traphouse. This means that it is to your advantage to get onto a target as quickly as possible. It is helpful, then, to anticipate where the target may first appear when it leaves the traphouse and have your gun pointing near that spot. You cannot, of course, guess the exact spot, but you do know that the bird is not going to appear out of the cinder blocks from the back of the traphouse or somewhere out there at the top of the treeline or in the clouds passing over the sun or 90 degrees off to your left. You want your gun pointing in what is essentially the middle of the target's possible flight path. If you are standing at the center, or No. 3, station, then where to point is very simple: about a foot high, directly over the middle of the traphouse. Going back to the No. 1 station, you want to point about a foot over the front-left corner (as seen from the shooting position) of the traphouse; No. 2, between the No. 1 and No. 3 holds; No. 4, between No. 3 and the front-right corner; and No. 5 above the front-right corner. This will not put you precisely on every target every time, but it will keep you close enough to the target that you will be able to pick it up in a minimum amount of time and with a minimum amount of movement. *(Shooting Tip: You will want to adjust your stance at each station to give yourself the widest range of stable movement for covering the target's flight, so that if it goes left, for example,*

Remington Premier STS 12-Gauge Pigeon (cutaway). *Remington*

you won't be out of position by having your body turned too far to the right.)

Now, as far as choosing which shotgun to use to learn to shoot trap, there are really only a few factors you need to take into consideration, most of which we've already looked at. One thing to remember about trapshooting, though, is that it makes no allowances for smaller gauges, the rules stating only that a shotgun must be no larger than 12 gauge. A cartridge used for trapshooting may be loaded with no more than 3 drams equivalent of smokeless powder and $1\frac{1}{8}$ ounces of lead shot no larger than No. $7\frac{1}{2}$, as defined by the Sporting Arms and Ammunition Manufacturers' Institute (SAAMI), a load that is pretty well standard for the 12 gauge. So unless you are very small in stature or extremely recoil shy (and if loaded to full capacity, a 20 gauge, for instance, isn't going to "kick" a whole lot less than a 12 gauge, particularly if you start out with a light 12-gauge load), there's no reason not to use a 12 gauge. Besides, if you ever happen make it to the Grand American, you'll have to use a 12 gauge.

For the expert, a gun designed exclusively for trapshooting can be among the most specialized of shotguns, frequently having a barrel measuring 32 inches and even longer. It is often, if only, used for 16-Yard or Handicap, single shot and can be configured with a raised "Monte Carlo" stock and a high, ventilated rib that in profile looks like a suspension bridge (being of most use to shooters who like to adopt a very straight, "heads-up" posture). Choking varies but tends toward the tighter side, which may not always be to the average shooter's advantage, as has been discussed, but this is the expert we are talking about here, not the average Joe. Because a pure trap gun, really applicable to no other shotgun sport, can represent an investment of $2,000 to $3,000, and at the farthest end of the spectrum many times that, just be certain of how much of an expert you actually are before you run out to buy one.

CHAPTER 4

Skeet

WHILE THE ORIGINS OF TRAP are Old World and old hat, skeet can trace its ancestry to an Andover, Massachusetts, dog kennel and a group of bird hunters looking for a way to pass the time after the close of the 1915 season. In a pasture they drew a large circle and marked off 12 evenly spaced positions. They then placed a trap machine at high noon, throwing toward 6 o'clock, and shot at two targets each from stations No. 1 through No. 11, using up the last three shells from their boxes of 25 by standing in the center of the circle and shooting at the clay birds jetting overhead. They informally called this new sport, aptly enough, shooting "around the clock."

While the trap machine had to throw a target only one way, the shooters, as they moved from station to station, had 12 distinct angles from which to try to hit it. After a while someone noticed that by using a circle, the shooters were, half the time, shooting back toward buildings and houses, so they bisected the circle and added a second trap machine at 6 o'clock, throwing back toward 12 o'clock. On this semicircle, which now resembled a section of an orange, they placed eight stations. The layout for a skeet field evolved into the following official dimensions: The circle has a radius of 21 yards, with stations 1 through 7 set equidistant on the outside of that radius precisely 26 feet, 8⅜ inches apart; station 8 is set in the center of a base line, or "base chord," drawn between 1 and 7. Of the two traps set in "skeethouses," one, the "high house," is set 3 feet beyond the marker for station 1 and 10 feet off the ground; the second, the "low house," is set 3 feet beyond marker 7 and 3½ feet above the ground.

The sport itself consisted of shooting at two single targets (the trap machine was set to throw 60 yards), one from each house, then a

413

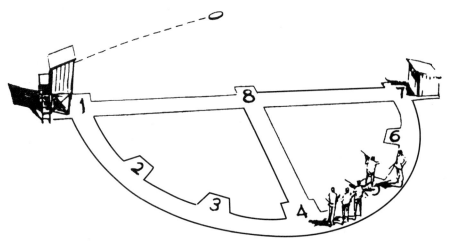

Skeet field layout. Courtesy of *Black's Wing & Clay*.

crossing double, with, again, one from each house, at stations 1 and 2 and 6 and 7. At stations 3 through 5, only a pair of singles were thrown. At 8, the shooter had a pair of singles, one from each house, that he had to break before they passed the stake marking the "target crossing point" at the center of the base chord. Some quick math shows that this accounts for only 24 shots, although a round of skeet consisted of 25. The extra shot was taken immediately after the first miss, at the same target as the one missed; if no targets were missed after 24, it was added to the infamous No. 8 low house—more on which later. (In International Skeet, which is the type shot at the Olympics, the optional target is eliminated by reshuffling the singles and doubles at each station; targets fly 72 yards, and guns must be kept in the low position until a target appears, and that target can appear at any time within three seconds of the shooter's calling "Pull!")

Articles in sporting magazines about this new sport (which had yet to be given an official name) began to appear in 1920, and by 1926 the basic rules had been formulated. Still, it needed to be called something catchy, so a contest to name the game was held. The winner, out of 10,000 entries, was a Mrs. Gertrude Hurlbutt of Dayton, Montana, who submitted the word "skeet," taken from the old Scandinavian word for "shoot," and walked away with the munificent prize of $100. Well publicized, skeet grew rapidly, and in 1946 the National

Skeet Shooting Association (NSSA) was formed as the nonprofit governing body of the sport. Today NSSA membership is some 20,000 with over 2 million people a year shooting skeet at one of the association's 1,000 affiliated ranges. Every October the biggest event in skeet shooting, the World Skeet Championships, is held in San Antonio, Texas, attracting more than 1,400 participants.

The great allure of skeet, initially, was the premise that it provided more realistic off-season practice for bird hunters than did trap. Frankly, I believe this aspect of the sport is overrated, perhaps even extremely so. Skeet certainly does not make anyone a *worse* bird shooter, but what it does make one, above all, is a better *skeet* shooter. A look at the basic dimensions of a skeet field show that it is unlikely you are going to shoot at, let alone break, any target beyond 25 yards, and most targets at probably less than 15 yards. The targets fly unerringly on prescribed paths, so it is entirely possible to take out your pocket calculator and determine what the exact physical lead should be for any shot before the target ever appears in the air. And a good bit of the time those targets are coming more or less toward the shooter, "back lipped," as it is called—that is, with their

Shooting skeet.

undersides, the most vulnerable part, exposed. If ducks, or any birds, flew this way and came only when I called for them and had my shotgun up and ready to shoot, then, yes, skeet would be great practice for hunting birds, except that birds like that would have become extinct ages ago.

All this is to say that the value of skeet does not lie in its pedagogical qualities for making us better hunters. It is perfectly all right to enjoy skeet as nothing more than what it is (a sport of shooting at clay targets), rather than because it is supposedly something that is "good for us."

A skeet gun and skeet choke are probably more applicable to hunting, though, than a trap gun is, particularly the more specialized trap guns. Skeet guns have 26- to 28-inch barrels, as a rule, and are choked much more open. Many hunters, particularly of upland game, look for these features in their shotguns. The best chokes for skeet are, logically enough, Skeet or even Cylinder. As in trap, 12-gauge shells can be loaded with a maximum of $1\frac{1}{8}$ ounces of lead shot, ranging in size from No. 9 to $7\frac{1}{2}$. Unlike trap, skeet does make provisions for the smaller gauges, the 20, 28, and .410; these guns are allowed to fire $\frac{7}{8}$, $\frac{3}{4}$, and $\frac{1}{2}$ ounce of shot, respectively. Many shooters like to compete in all four gauge categories and so will often choose shotguns fitted with four interchangeable sets of barrels so they can maintain the consistent feel of shooting the same shotgun, no matter the size of the shell.

Lead, while important in trap, figures more in skeet. The assorted methods of leading have been described, and although it is possible to give specific distances for leading specific targets, such numbers are not very helpful since the perception of lead is a highly subjective matter, with no two shooters able to estimate a fixed distance exactly alike. A shooter learns leading through shooting. It also helps to have a qualified observer watch a shooter and see if the person is in front of or behind the proper lead. (As explained earlier, one way to regulate lead is by positioning the forward hand on the fore-end: The farther the hand is extended, the slower the lead, whereas drawing the hand in can sometimes help pick up the lead on faster birds).

Of all the shots in skeet, those at station No. 8, particularly at the low house, can appear utterly impossible to beginning shooters. There seems to be no way to pick up the bird as it leaves the skeethouse, find the lead, and break it before it passes the crossing stake, and there isn't. Breaking the targets at No. 8 is almost entirely mechanical and is accomplished by the shooter's pointing the muzzle just below and slightly to the outside of the opening in the skeet-house. Then, when the shooter calls for the target and it appears, the shooter simply swings the barrel of the shotgun along the line of the target's flight, and when the muzzle is pointing overhead, pulls the trigger. When a shooter finally catches the timing, the target will vanish almost every time into a cloud of fine black dust, creating what is one of the more satisfying experiences in all the shooting sports, even if it is mostly a trick.

CHAPTER 5

Sporting Clays

$\mathbf{A}$NYONE THINKING OF taking up sporting clays should be given fair warning: This sport may be habit forming.

Some years ago, Jim, a Texas dove-and-quail hunter, got talked into shooting a round. ("Jim's" name has been changed to protect the guilty.) Finding trap and skeet boring, he did not hold out much hope for sporting clays. After that first round, though—shooting from a series of stations at targets that flushed or crossed or soared or decoyed or *ran*—he walked up to the course manager and told him he'd be back.

Great, said the manager. The course was open several days a week, and . . .

"No," said Jim, "you don't understand. I'm going to town to get more shells. I'll be *right* back."

Poor Jim became so addicted to sporting clays that he has now become a Level III instructor (the highest level) in sporting clays, and shooters who are not careful might just find themselves as hooked on the sport as he. This may help to explain why sporting clays, often (sometimes ad nauseam) described as "golf with a shotgun," has been since its introduction into this country in the early 1980s probably the fastest-growing shooting sport. The National Sporting Clays Association (NSCA) has around 16,000 members and estimates that 300,000 shoot sporting clays regularly and 3 million shoot at least once a year on well over 1,000 different courses.

Sporting clays had its beginnings, innocently enough, in wing-shooting. In the beginning, apparently in the early 1920s, with live-pigeon shooting banned, British bird hunters began firing their bespoke guns at clay targets thrown to simulate the various flight patterns of the wild game they encountered in the field. At first, they did this to keep the rust off, if not improve, their hunting skills and to carry over the pleasures of the hunt into the closed season. As with so many harmless pastimes, though, this shooting was soon codified into a genuine sport with rules, competitions, and the inevitable winners and losers.

Shooting sporting clays.

Sporting clays. Clockwise (upper left): middi, standard, battue, rabbit. Center: mini.

In 1925, according to Britain's Clay Pigeon Shooting Association, one C. W. Mackworth-Praed won the first British Open Sporting, posting a score of 63 out of 80, venue unrecorded. By 1932, the Open was being held at the West London Shooting Ground, remaining a fixture there for generations. In 1963, the Open had its first American champion, S. Gulyas, breaking 84 out of 100.

By the sixties and seventies, based on the research of Georgia attorney Hugh Sosebee, Jr., and Dr. Robert Maurer, assorted flavors of "hunter's" clays were being shot from the East Coast to Sequim, Washington. It was sometime in 1983 or 1984 in the Houston area that the first rounds were shot of what actually called itself sporting clays and adhered to British rules—such as 100 targets per shooter per round, the targets being standard, rocket (similar in diameter, but thinner and faster), rabbit (same diameter, but rolls on the ground), battue (standard diameter, very thin, does wingovers), middi (3½-inch), and mini (2⅜-inch, resembles a hummingbird in a hurry) and shot from fixed stations in singles, and following, report, and true pairs with size 7½ shot or smaller. Today, sporting clays is shot on literally thousands of courses across the country and around the world.

As a measure of how challenging sporting clays can be, out of millions and millions of rounds shot, there have been only a handful of recognized perfect 100 × 100 rounds. In the National Sporting Clays Championship tournament, for example, a score of 190 out of 200 can often win the top prize, whereas in trap or skeet such a score wouldn't even get a shooter into the finals.

In order for you at least to feign comprehension of sporting clays the first time you step onto a course, you should know that the average recreational round generally consists of 100 birds for each shooter, shot at 10 different stations. There are, of course, variations of anywhere from 5 to 15 stations, or as few as 50 targets per round. Some courses have minimums, such as 200 birds per round, which may be shot by a single individual or divvied up among several shooters.

Shooters move through the course in squads, usually of five or six maximum. If you come alone or with just a friend or two, you may be grouped with other shooters to form a squad. Depending on the size of the squad and the course, a round can take from 45 minutes to 2 hours to complete. The score is recorded by the shooters on a score sheet with a hit marked with that universal "X" and a miss with the dreaded "O."

The stations are often named things like "Flighting Doves," "Flushing Quail," "Fur & Feathers," and so on, to indicate the type of winged game they are supposed to represent, although increasingly a target is thrown simply because, in one experienced shooter's words, it is a "neat target," and not for its theriomorphic qualities. Stations are, therefore, more likely to be just "Station 1" these days, rather than "High Driven Pheasant."

Once standing in a station, the shooter demonstrates both firearm safety and proper etiquette by not loading the gun until in position to shoot and ready to call for a target. The shooter should also never walk up to the station, or turn or walk away from it, unless the action of the gun is open and visible as such to the other shooters. The action should remain open between stations, and a shooter must be certain that the gun's muzzle is pointed in a safe direction at all times.

Etiquette also suggests that a shooter always have enough shells for each station, and have them handy, when stepping up to the station to prevent delaying the round by fumbling around while reloading. If the squad ahead is shooting slowly, don't crowd or disturb them with loud conversation. By the same token, if your squad is holding up another, let them "shoot through."

If someone's having a bad round, don't pour it on while he's shooting (that's what beers in the clubhouse are for). Likewise, if someone's smoking the course, don't jinx him by saying something stupid, like, "Gee, you can't miss!" because that's exactly what he'll do on the next shot. Also, refrain from offering free shooting advice unless asked.

Beyond basic gun safety and common courtesy, sporting clays remains a blessedly unregimented game. Of late, the only major rules question has been whether shooters have to adopt a low position with their gun, or if they can shoulder it before calling for a target. Presently, either position is acceptable.

Finally, there is the matter of cost. Not counting shells, a round of 100 birds at one of the tonier sporting-clays clubs in New York costs $100, after you've paid a $10,000 to $15,000 membership fee, in the hinterlands a 50-bird round might cost no more than $15.

If you can handle the financial end, then the single biggest obstacle to beginning sporting clays is bringing yourself to step onto a course the first time. Many novices, particularly women and younger people, are intimidated by the thought of a bunch of shotgun-wielding men snarling at them for *invading* the game. In fact, men these days are more than pleased to see new shooters; so in the words of the T-shirt: No fear!

If you've never shot clay birds (and frankly, even if you have), your first time on the sporting-clays course (or the trap or skeet field, for that matter) will be most profitably spent with an instructor. Gil Ash, who was mentioned earlier in connection with chokes, is a Level III instructor who conducts classes with his wife, Vicki, around the country. He recommends that beginners start out in an all-day group session, to provide a more intensive experience and to allow them to benefit from the instruction given other students, as well as from that which they receive.

Don't worry about a shotgun. (If you take away no other insight from this book, remember that the shotgun, or rifle or handgun, is secondary to beginning any of the shooting sports: Don't get hung up on the idea that you have to own the "right" firearm before you begin to shoot. Don't be afraid to begin with whatever you have, as long as it reasonably meets the requirements of the sport; and as you gain experience, you will come to know what you need.) A good instructor should have several shotguns to choose from, letting you find which suits you best. If you have your own gun, even if not an "official" sporting-clays model, bring it—as long as you are comfortable and can shoot doubles with it and it's open-choked, preferably Cylinder or Skeet. (Daniel Schindler, another Level III instructor, believes most clays shooters, like most trap and skeet shooters, overchoke, the "meat and potatoes" of sporting clays being 40-yard, or less, shots.)

Don't worry about your score, either, or even very much about breaking birds. A broken target is the result of the application of a series of fundamental shooting techniques and by itself is of far less import than grasping those fundamentals. Hits will outnumber misses soon enough.

Although we've discussed them previously, it is worth going over the fundamentals of shooting one more time, particularly as they apply to sporting clays. The first, of course is stance. Ideally, your body ought to be pointing, in the shooting position, toward the spot where the target can most easily be broken when the target reaches it. Because targets may travel in two directions at the same station in sporting clays (as doubles do in skeet), though, your stance should be relaxed and well balanced, but flexible.

In mounting the shotgun, the most fundamental thing you have to learn to do with your gun is raise, mount, and swing it in tempo with the target, *without* looking at the gun itself. It is "physically impossible," to quote Gil Ash, to look at the gun and the target and to expect to break the latter in any way but by accident. The key to hitting, again according to Ash, is "focusing on the front of the target" while bringing the comb of the gun firmly to your face.

Doug Fuller, 1997 National FITASC (*Fédération Internationale de Tir Aux Armes Sportives de Chasse,* the swifter, more rigid French version of sporting clays) champion, believes most misses can be diagnosed by the shooter's having lifted his head off the stock. Other faults include swinging the gun with your body rather than with your forward hand, or simply stopping the gun during its swing.

Properly mounting a shotgun can be practiced at home—**once again, always with an unloaded gun**—by bringing the gun up and tracing the line between the ceiling and the wall with the muzzle, your eye on the line, or by keeping your eye on a light switch or the corner of a picture frame as you mount the gun and point it at the spot. Hold the position for 10 seconds; if you look at the gun in that time, start again. Merely raising and mounting a shotgun for several minutes each day will build shooting muscles.

The best practice is, naturally, on a course. Sporting clays is first and foremost about fun, and the true fun lies in shooting a shotgun and knowing you can hit a target—seeing a bird break. If you shoot enough and break enough birds and you know why, then even the misses can be fun—because you realize they are nothing more than a learning experience, just another part of the game.

If you find yourself in a shooting slump or would like to post higher scores, the first thing to check is the basics: Are you still focusing on the front of the target? keeping your face on the stock? moving the gun with your hands and not your body? not stopping your swing? If none of these, let your instructor evaluate your shooting to see if the problem may be something you are unaware of. If all of your fundamentals are sound, then it may at last be time to look into a better gun to boost your percentage of hits.

The "perfect" gun is no substitute for proper technique in sporting clays or any other shooting sport. A shotgun with a good, for you, general fit, more open chokes, barrels not over 28 or 30 inches (too many shooters crave long barrels for those glamorous 50- and 60-yard crossing shots, which comprise a very small portion of sporting clays), and recoil you can tolerate through 100 shots are all you need in order to begin.

Later, when you want to move beyond that 70th or 75th percentile in your scoring, a handmade shotgun with an exact, custom fit, special triggers, trick chokes, and so on, *may* make a difference. Until then, there are a number of reasonably priced guns out there, one of which will certainly suit any sporting-clays shooter for years to come.

Any shotgun you choose won't be a hit without shells. Bargain-priced "field" loads may be no bargain; and "heavy" loads, over the course of 100 or 200 birds, are likely to damage the shooter more than the targets. Start with light target loads of 7½ to 8½ shot, then move up to more power as you see fit (this holds true for skeet and trap, as well).

Some shooters prefer paper-hulled shells because they perceive less recoil with them. Why? Theories include the shell's paper base-wads absorbing recoil, the paper crimp's opening easier, or the wad's sliding more smoothly against the waxed-paper wall of the hull—or all of the above, or none.

A day's worth of recoil is about the major health hazard connected with sporting clays, and the major health benefit is (as with all the shooting sports) mental, letting us (literally) blow away accumulated stress. Except for some "practical shooting" events we'll talk about in a later chapter, a round of golf—probably of *miniature* golf, at that—would provide a better workout. All it takes to participate in sporting clays is the stamina to shoot a shotgun, which means women (whom the Ashes estimate make up nearly a quarter of their new students), children, and even those in wheelchairs can enjoy it. Conditioning comes from repeatedly shooting that shotgun (though, as has been noted, mounting an empty gun, or curling 8- to 10-pound dumbbells, at home can also help build endurance).

The best way to think of sporting clays, in the words of one shooter, is that it "is a simple game shot by complicated people," which can be said of all the shooting sports. The less complicated we try to make ourselves, the more we can let clays reduce our stress—knocking targets out of the air does a far better job of this than chasing little white balls on the ground.

FIELD & STREAM

The Complete Hunter

Book Six

Deer Hunting

Jerome B. Robinson

Illustrations by Christopher J. Seubert

1

Big Buck Country—
How to Find It,
How to Get There

BIG BUCKS are older bucks, and they don't attain maturity by making mistakes. Consequently, the biggest bucks are usually the most difficult to find, and the areas in which they seek refuge are exactly where hunters are least likely to be encountered.

Where hunting pressure is high, mature bucks retreat during daytime hours to places where their experience has taught them that people do not go. They head for mountain ridges, plunge deep into swamps, lose themselves in the middle of huge fields of standing corn, or seek the cover of brushy river bottoms. If you want to find big buck country, examine your hunting territory and ask yourself where you would go if you were an old buck that did not want company. Then go there yourself. Go quietly and move slowly. Stop often to sit and watch. Look for large deer droppings, large deer tracks, ground scrapes, and rubs on trees where a buck has polished his antlers. Watch, too, for large, single deer beds.

As you assemble these bits of information, you will be defining the area a big buck uses. Eventually, you will have enough information to identify spots that offer good views of places the buck uses frequently. Those are the places you should hunt.

CROSSING WATER

Much of big-buck country that is difficult to reach from a road can be accessed by using a boat and crossing water. I frequently use a canoe or other small boat to cross a river or a lake to reach sections of deer country that are otherwise difficult to reach. Invariably, I find myself in big-buck country, and I usually have it all to myself because few deer hunters use boats.

When you're in remote country, move a few yards back into the woods along the shore of a lake or river. Chances are you'll find a well-beaten game trail that parallels the water's edge. That should tell you something about where deer move frequently.

Lake shores and river banks are natural boundaries in overlapping deer home ranges. Does and fawns amble along the waterways, browsing on the lush vegetation that grows in such places, and bucks patrol the same trails, often leaving their scrapes and rubs as evidence of their regular passage.

Wherever you can locate a section of lake shore or river bank in remote country that is not easily accessible from a road, you have discovered big-buck country. Not all big-buck country is remote, however.

WHERE THERE ARE DOES
THERE WILL BE BUCKS

I once hunted deer along a river in Wyoming and found plenty of good bucks living in brushy river-bottom cover that bordered on alfalfa fields within plain sight of ranch buildings and roads. Large numbers of antlerless deer could be seen grazing along the alfalfa edges at dusk and dawn, and we reasoned that with a good food supply and a doe herd available, there had to be big bucks nearby.

We used canoes to come down the river and hunted in the thick river-bottom brush on pieces of public land that were identified on our maps. Buck signs were everywhere, and six of us tagged heavy-antlered bucks in just two days. The bucks were not in remote country—it was just good deer country that was not being hunted because you needed a boat to reach it and most Wyoming deer hunters use horses, not boats, to reach their chosen hunting areas.

Using a small boat or canoe to cross water often gives you access to big-buck country that is hard to reach from the road.

Go Farther, Go Higher

Likewise, if you hike uphill until you reach a point where going any higher seems like too much effort, you have reached the point where most hunters turn back and big bucks begin to feel safe. Push yourself to go higher and you will enter big-buck country.

The edges of large forest swamps are used heavily by deer until they are disturbed by hunting pressure. Once disturbed, the big bucks move farther into the depths of the swamp where few hunters will pursue them. Going beyond the point where other hunters give up will put you in big-buck country once again.

Hunters who hang up big bucks consistently know where big bucks live and make the extra effort needed to hunt in those places.

Hunters who consistently hang up trophy bucks are usually in the woods earlier than most hunters, hunt farther back from roads, and stay deep in the woods until the end of legal shooting time. They know where big bucks live, and they make an extra effort to hunt in those places.

CHAPTER

The Art
of Seeing Deer

Oᴺᴇ ᴏꜰ ᴛʜᴇ ꜱᴇᴄʀᴇᴛꜱ to successful deer hunting is learning to see deer before they see you.

The trick is to move slowly, stop often, and constantly study your entire view. That view changes every time you take a few steps, bringing new things into your angle of sight, so don't just plunge ahead thinking you have seen all there is to see. The coloration of deer blends into their surroundings, and their shapes are often broken up by the background, making the animals very hard to spot when they are still.

When looking for deer, don't look only for the shape of an entire deer—look for a piece of a deer. Learn to spot anything that seems out of the ordinary, and then study it. Rather than an entire deer, watch for the straight line of a back, the crook of an angled hind leg, the shape of an ear jutting out from behind a tree trunk, an antler moving slightly as a buck surveys his surroundings.

Learning to know where to look for deer is part of the challenge of hunting.

Kɴᴏᴡɪɴɢ Wʜᴇʀᴇ ᴛᴏ Lᴏᴏᴋ

Remember that resting deer may be lying down with only their heads showing above a bulge in the ground or other obstruction. Often

Rather than looking for the entire deer, look for a piece of a deer. Learn to spot anything out of the ordinary, and then study it

Where is it looking? What is it looking at? A doe staring into the distance may be watching a buck that is traveling with her.

they will be bedded next to stumps, logs, and fallen branches that obscure their outlines, so check such places carefully. (Be sure to use binoculars for checking unknown objects; never your rifle's telescopic sight. You may be looking at a person, and your scope is mounted on a loaded firearm that is aimed at whatever you view through the scope.)

ARE THERE OTHER DEER NEARBY?

If you see a deer, freeze. Are there other deer nearby that you haven't seen? Sometimes you will be tipped off that more deer are in the vicinity by watching the attitude of the deer you have spotted. Where is it looking? What is it looking at? A doe staring into the distance may be watching a buck that is traveling with her.

Bucks sometimes travel in pairs or small groups of bucks of various sizes. Dominant bucks often have a subdominant buck or two tagging along with them. Thus, when you spot a buck with small antlers, don't assume it's alone. Stay still and watch. You may discover there is a larger buck with it.

Unfocus Your Eyes

Sometimes it helps to "unfocus" your eyes when watching for deer. Your unfocused gaze will often pick up movement you might have missed if you were looking intently at one spot. When you are over-looking a broad reach of terrain, just keep your eyes open and slowly sweep your view. If something moves, your eyes will automatically zero in on that spot and you can determine what it was that caught your attention.

Be Alert to Other Animals

While watching for deer, be alert to the movements of other animals and birds. Why is that blue jay squawking and flitting from treetop to treetop? Is it announcing that it sees something moving through the forest? What is that squirrel running from? Why did that crow swerve in flight? Did it notice something on the ground below? Learn to ask yourself these questions, and try to discover the answers. Sometimes you will discover a deer in the process.

On cold mornings, when your breath steams, watch for telltale plumes of vapor from the warm breath of a deer that may be hidden where you can't quite see it. Whenever you see an obscure deer-colored object, use your binoculars to check it for hair texture.

Watch for Slight Movements

One frosty morning in Maine, I almost blundered into a big 8-point buck. He was completely hidden by vegetation in a thick clump of alders close to the bank of a north woods river. I had paused for a look around and suddenly noticed movement at ground level under the trees. I could see something small moving with a regular rhythm, but could not determine what it was. A grouse bobbing its head? It didn't look like that. A squirrel digging? I didn't think so.

I raised my binoculars and focused on the spot. The movement was a deer's hoof pawing the ground! Now I could see it clearly. The hoof would paw the ground several times, then stop, then a moment later paw again.

The deer's wet, black nose came into view as it sniffed the pawed place, its hot breath rising as steam. I still couldn't see the deer because its body was screened by vegetation, but the pawing action made me think *buck*. I kept the glasses focused on the spot, and the next time the deer lowered its nose to sniff the pawed place, I saw the tips of antlers catch the sunlight.

It was a buck, all right, and it was less than 100 yards ahead. I dropped to a sitting position and waited, watching. A breath of air moved through the forest from behind me, carrying my scent ahead. Suddenly, the buck caught my scent. He took a step forward, raised his head, and looked right at me. Now I could see him clearly. His entire head and neck and the forward part of his shoulder were in view.

He began to move as I raised my rifle, and as he turned broadside, I slid the crosshairs behind his shoulder and squeezed off a shot that dropped him in his tracks.

I went to his side, and as I was kneeling beside him admiring the heavy 8-point rack and rugged body, I noticed long, raking marks across his ribs and a bloody hole where an antler had punctured the base of his neck. Suddenly, I heard a buck utter a deep, guttural grunt from the other side of the alder clump. Another one! Now the raking scrapes and bloody puncture wound on my buck made sense. Before I came along and nearly walked into him, he had been fighting with another buck and had paused to paw the ground and work up his rage before returning to the battle.

I remained kneeling by my buck, watching. The other buck grunted again, so this time I made a soft grunt in reply. That was all it took. The buck came lunging through the thicket toward me, making all sorts of noises.

As he came into view, he apparently caught my scent mixed with that of the dead buck. He stopped short, then whirled and charged back the way he had come. But as he turned I got a good look at him, and he was magnificent. My big 8-pointer was no match for that buck. No wonder he had paused for a time out!

Checking a slight small movement had paid off for me that time. I saw the buck before he saw me, and I got a shot I would never have had if I hadn't frozen and studied what the woods were telling me.

CHAPTER 3

What Deer Tracks Tell You

TRACKS TELL YOU the story of deer movement in your vicinity. If you learn to read tracks accurately, you will gain knowledge that can put you in a place where a buck wants to be.

Can you tell buck tracks from doe tracks? You can't always, but you can make a darned good guess according to the size of the track, the manner in which the hooves contact the ground, and where the tracks lead.

Size alone does not determine whether the track was made by a buck or doe. Plenty of big does have bigger feet than some bucks. But bucks and does place their feet on the ground differently, and they often travel by different routes; the combined information their tracks provide will give a strong indication of the maker's gender.

BUCKS CARRY WEIGHT FORWARD

Consider this: In autumn, mature bucks put on significant weight in their necks, which throws their balance forward so that they put more weight on their front feet than does do. This causes a buck's toes to spread as he walks and shifts his weight back onto the heels of his front hooves. The result is a distinctly different track, showing spread toes and dewclaws jabbed forcefully into the ground.

Thus, when you encounter a large, open-toed walking track with distinct dewclaw jabs at the heels, you should suspect that it was

In autumn, a mature buck leaves walking front-foot tracks that show spread toes, and its dewclaws jab forcefully into the ground because the buck carries his weight more on the heels of his front feet.

made by a mature buck. If there is snow on the ground and the tracks show long drag marks, indicating the deer barely raised its feet above the ground when walking, you can be even surer that you're looking at buck tracks. During the rut, bucks exhausted by the stress of breeding, fighting, and constantly searching for does drag their feet while walking, so their tracks sometimes look almost as if they were wearing skis.

Does show open toes and dewclaw jabs when trotting or running, but when they slow to a walk the toes close and the track becomes heart-shaped or takes the form of two straight slots with little or no dewclaw jab.

WHERE DOES THE TRACK GO?

Where the track goes will also tell a lot about who made it.

Does and little deer travel on established deer trails a great deal of the time. Bucks, however, have their own routes, which often cut across the bigger, heavily used deer trails. Bucks are often loners, so when you find the tracks of a large, single deer striking out over country, crossing the more heavily used deer trails and moving at a steady marching pace, you should suspect that the maker is a mature buck in the rut, striding cross-country in search of a doe in breeding condition, or estrus.

What happens to the track when it comes to a very low limb? Does usually duck under and continue on their way, but a heavily antlered buck has his rack to consider and usually goes around a low obstruction rather than under it to keep his antlers free.

READING THE SPOOR

When there is snow on the ground, pay particular attention to the sign left when deer pause to urinate. Females spread their hind feet slightly, and their urine falls from under their tail in a scattered, splash pattern between or on top of the hind tracks. Bucks, however, urinate from under their belly, and the steady stream of urine bores a clean hole in the snow somewhere between the front and hind tracks.

Droppings can also indicate the gender of the deer. When bucks are in the rut and on the move, they defecate while walking, scattering their droppings over 10 to 25 feet. Does, however, stop to defecate, and their droppings fall in a clump.

There is no mistaking the track of a really big buck. Medium-sized bucks are more difficult to distinguish from large does, but the indicators I've mentioned will help you tell buck tracks from doe tracks most of the time.

AGING TRACKS

The condition of the track tells when it was made. Pay particular attention to changes in the weather, because it will affect tracks. If you know what time it started to rain or snow or what time the temperature dropped below freezing, you will be able to make an educated guess as to the age of a track. Was it made before or after the rain or snow began? Was it made before the ground began to freeze or after a skim of frost had formed?

Really fresh tracks made in deep snow are often filled with flakes that have fallen back into them, but you can determine their freshness by the condition of the crumbled snow around the edges. If it is very fresh, the snow around the edges will be rough and fluffy and have a bluish cast. As the track ages, the roughened snow around the edges is smoothed by moving air or sunshine. It loses its fluffy appearance and becomes grayish in color.

Fresh tracks made in soil also have loose crumbs around the edges that wear away with age. Tracks made in clay will retain clear definition until the next rain, but the roughness at the edges of a fresh track dries up and wears away within a few hours.

FEELING TRACKS WITH YOUR FINGERS

Tracks made in leaf litter are often indistinct to the eye, but you can learn a lot about them by pressing your first and second fingers into the track and feeling its shape and size. If the track is large, open-toed, and bearing heavy dewclaw jabs, you will be able to feel those characteristics and make an educated guess about the deer that made them.

When you first encounter a fresh set of large tracks, *do not* immediately bend over and start studying them. Instead, stand still and give your surroundings a long, hard scrutiny. The track maker may be within sight and may be looking back at you. The track will wait, and it should not be studied until after you have made certain that its maker is not nearby.

Fresh tracks are seductive. They make you want to follow them. But don't overlook what you can learn from older tracks.

Tracks made in leaf litter are often indistinct to the eye, but you can learn a lot about them by pressing your first and second fingers down into the track and feeling its shape and size.

LEARNING FROM OLDER TRACKS

Older tracks tell you the history of deer movement in your area. From them you can learn where deer travel most frequently, where they feed, and where they bed. Old tracks will lead you to rubs where bucks have polished their antlers and to scrapes where bucks have pawed the ground and left scent to attract does that are coming into estrus. With this information, you will have a much better idea of where you are most likely to encounter a good buck.

When you find a fresh track worthy of your attention, resist the temptation to follow it exactly. To do so, you would have to keep your eyes on the ground and might miss seeing the deer when you catch up with it. Also, deer watch their backtracks. They are very aware that they may be being followed, and their senses are alert to anything that might be coming along behind them.

HOW TO FOLLOW TRACKS

Instead of dogging a track, hunt parallel to it. Follow the track just long enough to get a good idea of the direction in which the deer is traveling. Then swing off about 100 yards on the downwind side of the track and move in a parallel direction. Move slowly, stopping often to study your surroundings. If you fear the deer has changed direction, you can move back upwind until you strike the track again and can reassess its direction.

Just before a buck beds down, he usually turns downwind so he can get the scent of anything following his track, and he moves to an area of slightly elevated ground that offers cover and a view of his backtrack. By traveling parallel to his track 100 yards or so to the downwind side, you are moving in a position that is likely to take you straight to where the buck has bedded. Keep your eyes peeled.

If the buck's track crosses in front of you, headed downwind, freeze. Assume the buck is moving to a bedding site nearby, and search closely for it. Scrutinize every piece of heavy cover and every elevated position.

TRACKS GOING DOWNWIND LEAD TO BEDS

Whenever tracks lead you to believe the buck is moving toward its bed, you are in a perfect position to use a grunt call or rattling antlers to bring the buck from his bed to you. (See Chapters 9 and 10 on calls and rattling.)

If you don't see him, back up 100 yards on your own track, then begin paralleling his track again as it leads downwind. If the buck senses your pursuit and evades you, backtrack him to his bedding site, and remember that spot as a place to check another day when you can come in from the downwind side.

CHAPTER

How to Dress
for Deer Hunting

I F YOU'RE COLD, you won't be able to sit long on a deer stand. If your clothes are bulky, you won't be able to walk comfortably through the woods. And if your clothes make noise, you won't be able to move with the stealth that successful deer hunting requires. So when you dress for deer hunting, keep these three objectives in mind: warmth, comfort, and quietness.

Once, two friends who had not done much serious deer hunting joined my group on a trip to Maine. They brought the most amazing collection of clothing I had ever seen, including entire suits for different days and different weather conditions. A look in their tent revealed arctic windproof snow pants that were so bulky they couldn't walk in them, huge orange jackets rated to –20° F, enormous stuffed hats, down-filled mittens, electric socks, and great big Mickey Mouse boots that caught on everything they tried to step over.

Well, Maine can be cold in deer season, and you have to prepare for snow and ice and cold rain, but these outfits were ludicrous. Not only were they too bulky to allow comfortable movement, the outfits were so well insulated that my friends would sweat if they tried to walk any distance. And worst of all, the clothes made noise.

I was sitting quietly on a ridge one snowy morning when I heard unusual noises sounds, sort of yipping sounds, below me, coming my way. My first thought was that there were coyote pups nearby, chasing each other through the woods.

But it wasn't coyotes, it was my friends. Rather, it was my friends' clothes. The outer shells of their insulated suits were made of nylon, and as they moved through the underbrush, branches whipped and zipped against them, creating the yipping sounds I had heard from a couple of hundred yards away. No way would they ever get close to deer in those outfits.

One deerless week in those outfits convinced my friends that their clothing choices had been disastrous. When they returned the following year, they dressed like the rest of us, in layers of soft clothing that can be added or taken off as the weather dictates.

When you dress for deer hunting, keep these three objectives in mind: warmth, comfort, and quiet. Dress in layers of soft, loose clothing.

WHAT TO WEAR

I have settled on the following clothing as my regular deer hunting outfit.

- *Next to the skin:* polypropylene long underwear, sock liners, and glove liners. "Polypro," as it is often called, wicks moisture from your skin so that sweat does not build up when you exert yourself.
- *Second layer:* Thick wool/polypro-blend socks. Insulated rubber boots. Light or heavy wool pants, depending on the weather. Wool or fleece shirt. Thin wool or fleece gloves. Wool cap with earflaps.
- *Top layer:* Loose-fitting wool or fleece jacket. Wool or fleece is warm, light, and quiet. It doesn't rustle or snap against brush.
- *Extras:* In a fanny pack or day pack, carry a down or polyester vest that you can put on under your outer layer when you stop to sit for a long period. Take the vest off and carry it separately when exerting yourself. A lightweight waterproof rainsuit can be rolled up and stuffed in your pack on inclement days.

For an extended hunt, you will need two such complete outfits so that one is always dry. Sock liners can be rinsed out each day and dried quickly with heat. Take one new pair of heavy socks for each day you expect to be away.

The Rut: Buck Behavior and How to Take Advantage of It

MATURE BUCKS rarely travel with does and antlerless deer except during the rut, or active breeding period. The rut can begin as early as September and continue through January, though peak breeding activity occurs in November in most northern states and later farther south.

As the rut approaches, bucks that have been traveling together in tolerant small groups throughout the summer and early autumn become aggressive and begin fighting to establish dominance. The largest, heaviest bucks have the advantage and usually emerge as the winners of pushing contests they enter into with smaller bucks. When bucks of relatively equal size and strength confront each other, however, the pushing contests can become violent and sometimes escalate into mortal combat.

Although fights to the death do occur, they are rare. Sometimes two heavily antlered bucks jam their racks together with such force that they cannot be separated, and the bucks starve to death locked in their fatal embrace. More commonly, big bucks inflict damaging wounds on one another, striking each other with their hooves, raking each other's shoulders and ribs, and puncturing each other's ears, necks, and bodies with their antlers.

It is rare to see bucks in battle, but the signs of their struggles are commonly found as the rut begins. The ground will be torn by hooves over a room-sized space, and tufts of hair will be found on the forest floor and stuck on underbrush. Often one buck will force the other into a blowdown that limits his maneuvering room and prevents him from turning to deflect the other's antlers.

Sometimes these royal battles occur in the presence of a doe, but usually dominance is settled before the breeding season gets into full swing. By the time does are entering estrus, most bucks are avoiding contact with other bucks of equal size, although they often continue to tolerate the company of inferior bucks or large subdominant bucks that do not challenge their claim to breeding rights.

WITNESSING A BATTLE

I once witnessed a battle between two equal-sized 8-pointers that were pushing and shoving each other around in an open stand of hardwoods one November day when the rut was well advanced. A doe was standing nearby, feeding but paying little attention as the two bucks clashed antlers, pawed the ground, and glowered at one another.

Suddenly a little fork-horned buck appeared on the scene. At first he eyed the battle from a distance. When he determined that the big bucks were fixated on one another, however, the little buck trotted in, nuzzled the doe, then mounted and bred her not 20 yards from where the bucks were fighting. When they finished, the little buck and the doe disappeared together without the fighting bucks ever noticing them.

ANTLER RUBS

The sparring begins as soon as bucks lose their antler velvet in early autumn. Once this takes place, you begin to see bright marks on saplings along deer trails where bucks have rubbed their antlers. The size of a rubbed sapling sometimes indicates the size of the buck that rubbed it. Bigger bucks tend to rub on trees of larger diameter. When you see a rub on a tree 3 inches or more in diameter, you are in the home range of a large, mature buck.

The size of saplings rubbed by bucks while polishing their antlers can tell you something about the size of the buck that did the rubbing. Bigger bucks rub bigger saplings.

The Estrus Period

The active breeding period begins when does begin entering estrus, or breeding condition. Individual does come into estrus at different times, but the condition lasts only about 24 hours. If the doe is not bred during her first estrus period, she will come into estrus for 24 hours once again 28 days later.

During the first month of the active breeding season, dominant bucks search constantly for does that are entering estrus. When a buck finds a doe in breeding condition, he will usually stay with her for about 24 hours and may copulate with her several times during that period. While they are together the buck goes wherever the doe leads, and he will usually fight or drive off any other buck that threatens to come close to her. As her estrus period passes, the doe becomes unwilling to accept the buck and leaves him. The buck then strides out across his range, searching for another doe that is ready to breed. Dominant bucks frequently breed more than a dozen does in a season.

BUCKS GET LESS WARY

As breeding season progresses and more and more does have conceived and avoid contact with bucks, fewer does enter breeding condition. The bucks now have to search even more diligently to find those that remain.

Consequently, as the rut continues the buck barely eats or rests. He loses weight rapidly and becomes gaunt. His entire purpose is to find does in breeding condition. In his exhausted, sex-crazed state, he becomes less cautious, less wary. Now he is using every sense to locate does, and he becomes particularly susceptible to scents and sounds indicating a doe in estrus is nearby. (See Chapters 8–10 on using scents, calls, and rattling antlers to attract bucks during the rut.)

Bucks seek does by checking feeding areas. They travel routes that cross well-established deer trails, searching for the scent of does in breeding condition. When a buck catches the scent of a doe in estrus, he follows her trail with neck extended and head close to the ground, sniffing the doe's tracks and places where she paused to urinate. The buck occasionally curls his upper lips for a few seconds, savoring the doe's scent, and may utter a guttural grunt from time to time.

SCRAPES

In areas most frequented by does, bucks make numerous ground scrapes to advertise their availability. They paw back the leaves and

Scrapes are made by bucks that are in breeding condition. They are usually made beneath a hanging branch, which the buck licks and brushes with scent from the glands in his forehead. Bucks return to refresh scrapes regularly during the rut.

bare the earth in a space beneath a low overhanging branch. They lick the overhanging branch and rub it with their forehead glands and antlers, leaving scent. Then they urinate on the tarsal glands inside their rear knees to leave scent in the pawed space. As they leave, they stamp their footprint clearly in the center of the scrape.

Bucks return to these scrapes regularly during the breeding period to refresh them and to check for signs that does have visited the scrape and urinated near it, indicating a willingness to breed. Much of the scraping activity occurs at night in areas where hunting pressure is heavy. Nevertheless, any place where numerous scrapes are found close to one another is an excellent place to encounter a buck.

During the peak of the rut, bucks are also seized by the inclination to thrash bushes and saplings with their antlers in mock battles. These antler-torn shrubs and saplings are found along well-used deer trails, indicating a mature buck passes there regularly. The thrashed vegetation is one more sign by which a buck communicates his presence and availability. Scent from his forehead glands clings to the battered bushes, advertising his desire to breed.

DOMINANT BUCKS DIE EARLY

The rut leaves mature bucks thin and exhausted. With winter close upon them and food scarce at the end of breeding season, there is little time to regain fat before the rigors of winter begin to take their toll. If subsequent temperatures are severe and the snow gets too deep to paw back and expose food, mature, dominant bucks often succumb. Consequently, large, dominant bucks often have shorter lifespans than subdominant bucks that enter winter fatter and less stressed from fighting and breeding.

CHAPTER

Hunting from Stands

IN AREAS where hunting pressure is heavy and lots of hunters are moving through the woods, it is often best to hunt from a stand. Other hunters will keep deer moving, and your chances of seeing a deer from a stand overlooking the junction of heavily traveled trails are good. Likewise, in areas where hunter activity is slight and deer are moving on their habitual routes from bedding areas to feeding places, your knowledge of their habits will help you locate a stand in a good place to intercept them. The stand can be in a tree or on the ground. The more important consideration is not its height but its location.

WHERE TO LOCATE YOUR STAND

The best way to determine where to locate your stand is to do lots of preseason scouting. It is also important to remember from one year to the next where deer moved during previous autumns. Check tracks, droppings, antler rubs, and ground scrapes to discover where deer habitually travel on the routes from bedding areas to feeding areas, and locate your stand overlooking a place that shows the most deer activity.

LEARN AUTUMN FOOD SOURCES

Bear in mind that feeding locations change as deer adjust their diets from summer food to foods that become available in autumn. Deer that feed on lush green vegetation in summer may switch to acorns and beechnuts in the fall, so scout out where the heaviest concentrations of those mast food sources are located, and choose stand locations accordingly.

If you hunt deer in farm country, locate your stand overlooking a trail that leads to a crop the deer will be feeding on in late autumn. Some of the crop fields deer use in summer will have been harvested or plowed under by fall and so will be of no further use to deer. You want your stand to overlook trails that lead to cornfields, alfalfa fields, or green winter wheat fields that still offer desirable food in late autumn.

HAVE MORE THAN ONE STAND

Don't have just one stand. If you hunt the same territory year after year, you will gradually accumulate more knowledge about where deer move according to changing food sources, weather, and hunting pressure. As you determine the places deer use frequently under various circumstances, look around for good spots that overlook these areas and offer cover and clear shots in several directions.

When you find these choice locations, spend some time and build a comfortable stand that you can return to when conditions indicate deer may be using that area.

TREE STANDS

Tree stands are commonly favored by bow hunters because they must make a physical movement—drawing their bows—before they can shoot. This eye-catching movement can alert nearby animals, so the bow hunter puts the stand high in a tree above the vision of most deer.

Firearm hunters gain the same advantage when they make their stands in trees. Deer are less likely to see them, and the hunter's scent is somewhat dissipated before it drifts to ground level.

A wide variety of comfortable, strong tree stands that provide a solid seat for a hunter perched in a tree are available in sporting goods stores and through catalogs. Tree-climbing models, which enable the hunter to shinny up and down trees, can be mounted in a

Deer are less likely to see hunters in tree stands because they do not expect danger from above and are not in the habit of looking up.

tree with little difficulty and can be moved from one place to another quickly and easily.

BUILDING YOUR OWN

Personally, I prefer to build tree stands out of wood and leave them in place permanently. Rather than just having a seat perched in a tree, I am more comfortable on a larger wooden deck with a comfortable seat surrounded by a low railing.

Look for a clump of trees with trunks at least 8 inches thick 20 feet above the ground overlooking an established deer-feeding area or a junction of well-used trails. Then seek permission from the landowner to construct a deer stand there. On the site, build a ladder that reaches a place at least 20 feet above the ground. Next, construct a frame of 2 × 4s spiked to the tree trunks, deck the 2 × 4 frame with 1½-inch thick boards, and make a comfortable seat in the center. Erect a railing of lumber or strong branches 3 feet above the deck and cover it with camouflage material that will stop the wind and hide you from view. Now hang branches from the railing to break up the outline of the stand. As a last step, tie a rope from the railing that reaches to the ground so you can pull your unloaded rifle up into the stand at the beginning of your hunt or lower it to the ground when you are ready to leave.

STANDS AT GROUND LEVEL

As much as I enjoy the view from a tree stand, I must admit that I am an impatient hunter and find it difficult to sit in one place for a long period if I am not seeing anything. Consequently, a great deal of my hunting is done from stands that I rough together on the ground.

The stands are nothing fancy—usually just some loosely arranged branches piled around a tree trunk to break up my outline and a comfortable place to sit that allows me to turn and face in different directions. The location of these stands is based on wind direction and where I expect a buck to come from.

I have a number of these favorite stands at various locations in the few square miles of woods that I hunt most often. When I am hunting new country I make one of these rough stands whenever I find a place that fits my criteria. (It must overlook an area or junction of trails that shows heavy deer use and offer a clear shot in several directions.)

As I move through the woods hunting, I am constantly aware of my proximity to these chosen stopping places, and I move from one to another, settling into each one with the intention of staying until I am prompted to move on.

PAY ATTENTION TO AIR MOVEMENT

Before choosing a stand, check the wind direction. Then choose a stand that will be on the downwind side of the trails or feeding area you will be overlooking so that your scent will not be carried to the places from which you expect the deer to come. Even if there is no real wind, general air current patterns will affect the direction in which your scent will travel. In the morning, on windless days, air currents move uphill as the air temperature rises. This indicates that you should take a stand on the uphill side of the trails or feeding areas on windless mornings and expect deer to be moving in from below or from the sides.

Air currents are reversed in the late afternoon, flowing downhill as the air temperature drops on windless days. Thus, you should take a stand on the downhill side of the trails or feeding area on windless evenings and expect deer to come from uphill or from the sides where your scent will not be carried.

MY FAVORITE STAND

My favorite stand is a 20-minute walk from my hunting camp. That is where I head before dawn every morning and where I wind up for the last hour of daylight most evenings.

It is on an edge of a rise in the ground, overlooking a wide hardwood bench where deer feed regularly and a junction of trails that deer use to travel up and down the valley. Above the stand is another rise of ground overgrown with heavy brush where deer commonly go to bed down during daylight. Thus, I can expect deer to be moving both above me and below me and can face in either direction according to the direction of the air currents.

The stand itself is just a wooden seat built within the angle of the broad crotch of an ancient maple that fell to the ground many years ago. I can sit in that crotch and oversee a wide swath of country. The embracing arms of the fallen tree hide my body so only my head protrudes, and I have a solid rest for my rifle no matter which direction I face.

I have killed several good bucks from that stand over the years. It pays off just often enough to keep me going back.

I had an uncle whose favorite deer stand was a tall, hollow stump that overlooked a junction of trails in a large wood lot that stood between two enormous cornfields in a big river valley. He used a chainsaw to cut the stump down to chest height and built steps up the back side of the stump so he could climb in. As a seat inside the stump, used a 5-gallon bucket with a boat cushion on top of it.

He could sit comfortably inside that stump all day, and he often did. He was protected from wind and could move around without being seen. When a deer came along he could turn in any direction to face it.

He killed a good buck from that stump every year I can remember until he grew too old to hunt and turned the stump over to a younger member of his hunting group, who still takes good bucks there regularly.

7

What Is Still-Hunting, and How Do You Do It?

THE TERM "still-hunting" is misleading because a good still-hunter does not stand still but moves. But the still-hunter moves so slowly and so unnoticeably that you rarely see any motion.

You see a still-hunter in the shadows, leaning against a tree. A few moments later you see the hunter stopped beside another tree a few feet farther on, but you have to watch carefully to actually see the movement.

Still-hunting works anytime, but it is particularly effective when deer are not moving because of storm conditions or when hunting pressure has made them seek shelter. "You can stay on a good stand all day and not see a thing if the deer aren't moving," notes expert New Hampshire still-hunter Alfred Balch. "If the deer don't move and the hunter doesn't move, there's not goin' to be an encounter."

A good still-hunter relies on the ability to get within close range of a deer by using stealth and knowledge of deer behavior. The hunter expects to see deer before being seen and, consequently, moves in a state of suspended animation.

WIND DIRECTION

Still-hunters stay alert to wind direction and adjust their hunting course so they will be moving into the wind (with the breeze in their faces) or across the wind (with the breeze on their cheeks). If the wind is on their backs, their scent will be blown ahead of them, warning deer of their approach.

You can't move too slowly when you are still-hunting. If you are seeing deer tails bouncing away, you are moving too fast. Those are deer that saw you before you saw them.

Deer have extremely keen noses and can pick up the scent of a hunter at very long distances. When they smell a person approaching, they're gone.

YOU CAN'T MOVE TOO SLOWLY

You can't move too slowly when you're still-hunting. If you see deer tails bouncing away, you're moving too fast. Those are deer that saw you before you saw them. If you have to look down at the ground to place your feet when you move forward, you're walking too fast. Good still-hunters look at the ground and plan their next few steps before they leave a stopping place. Then they move forward a few steps with their eyes up, watching their surroundings for any changes while they are in motion.

Move in the shadows, and avoid bright spots. When you stop, stop on the shaded side of a tree or other large object.

Move in the Shadows

Effective still-hunters move in the shadows, avoiding bright, open places. When they stop, they stop on the shaded side of a tree or other obstruction that will break up their outlines. At each stop they pause for a long time, searching the surrounding woods until they are satisfied that no deer is watching them. Their eyes are alert for anything that doesn't quite fit with its surroundings—anything that might be a piece of a deer that is partially hidden. Then they check the ground, planning their next few steps, before they move again. They move with utmost stealth.

How to Walk Quietly

In order to move quietly, the still-hunter places the feet carefully with each step, keeping weight on the back foot while the front foot moves ahead. The hunter avoids branches that might catch the advancing foot and sets the foot down heel first. When the heel is secure, the still-hunter rolls forward slowly onto the front foot, crushing the twigs beneath the foot into the ground rather than breaking them and causing them to snap loudly.

The little crushing sounds your feet make at ground level don't carry far, but sounds made above ground level echo through the woods with loud reports that deer notice from long distances. Knowing this, the still-hunter is careful to avoid catching a foot on upright branches, thumping a boot on a log, or tipping over loose rocks and making them clunk. The hunter avoids low branches that could snag clothing and snap.

DON'T BUMP SAPLINGS

When passing through groves of saplings, still-hunters avoid bumping the slender trunks, which would cause the upper branches to thrash and rattle, alerting nearby deer to their approach.

KNOW WHERE DEER WANT TO BE

Advancing cautiously through the woods in this manner, still-hunters use their knowledge of deer behavior to steer their progress. They know from experience where deer are most likely to seek shelter, and they approach those places with extreme caution. They use the terrain, the shadows, tree trunks, boulders, and blowdowns to their advantage, always trying to make themselves unnoticeable.

STILL-HUNTING TECHNIQUES ARE ESSENTIAL

Using the still-hunting techniques described above will make you a more effective deer hunter in any situation. Most still-hunters combine still-hunting with hunting from stands. They use still-hunting techniques as they move to a stand, and then they settle in to wait and watch during periods when they expect deer to be moving on their own. When deer don't seem to be moving, still-hunters slowly move into an area where they expect to find bedded deer.

CHAPTER

When to Use Scents

THE USE of scents to attract deer is not new. In Paleolithic times, native hunters wrapped themselves in gamy-smelling skins and anointed themselves with scents made from animal extracts that were either attractive to game or served to mask human odors.

In recent years a huge industry has grown around the manufacturing of attractive deer scents and human scent eradicators, so today's hunters have a vast array of deer-hunting scents available to them.

There is no question that scents can be helpful when used properly. But be warned: The use of too much scent can be worse than no scent at all, and there is no scent that can be relied on to attract deer when careful hunting techniques are ignored.

HOW SCENTS WORK

Bucks in the rut are on constant alert to find does in breeding condition. They are constantly searching for the scent of does that are entering estrus.

Does in estrus mark trails and ground scrapes with their urine to signal bucks that they are in breeding condition. The urine of does in estrus, therefore, is a particularly powerful attractant during the rut.

Modern manufacturers collect and bottle urine from does raised in zoos and on farms that produce venison for the market. Then they use glandular extracts as well as urine actually collected from does in estrus to produce scents and lures advertised as being sexually attractive to bucks in the rut. Read the labels carefully and check with other hunters to find out which brands seem to work best.

How to Use Scents and Lures

Although some loud-smelling hunters apparently believe otherwise, it is not necessary to soak your clothes in doe urine to be an effective deer hunter. Instead, hunters can carry doe-in-estrus urine in a small bottle with either a spray cap or a cap that emits droplets. As they proceed through the woods to their stands, they stop occasionally to scatter a few drops or emit a small mist of spray at random spots. Some hunters attach scent-saturated pads to their boots in order to leave a trail of attractive scent.

When you come to an area that shows heavy signs of buck use in the form of ground scrapes, antler rubs, and tracks, squirt some doe-in-estrus urine into the ground scrapes and then pin a scented ball of cotton head high above the ground nearby. Then take a stand that overlooks the scrape from the downwind side.

Food Scents

Sexually attractive scents are most effective once the rut begins. Bucks, however, feed heavily prior to the rut and at that time may also be attracted to the scent of particularly appealing foods. Most popular is apple concentrate or a molasses-based scent applied in a feeding area upwind from a deer stand.

The use of actual apples or molasses would be equally effective, but using real foods to bait deer is prohibited in most states during hunting season.

Cover Scents

Cover scents are used to mask human odor. Most popular are skunk essence and the oils of pine, fir, and cedar, all of which emit lasting natural forest odors that may help overcome human scent. An artificial skunk cover scent recently came on the market that does not emit the noxious odor until two separate scentless ingredients are mixed, thus avoiding the problem of the powerful skunk scent leaking or spilling on clothing.

To use cover scents, put a few drops on cotton balls and pin them up around the location of your deer stand so that the scent travels out away from the stand with air currents from any direction.

Users must be careful to avoid applying too much cover scent. Heavy doses smell unnatural and may actually alarm deer.

SCENT-ERADICATING SOAPS

Scent-eradicating soaps, said to remove human odors from clothing and skin, are also available from a number of manufacturers. The makers recommend that deer-hunting clothes be washed in these soaps before the hunt and that hunters wash their hands and face with the soaps before going into the woods.

Many hunters who believe that tobacco, cooking odors, and wood smoke permeate clothing and make them more noticeable to deer hang their hunting coats and pants outside to dry rather than near the stove. Some hunters stuff cloth bags of pine or balsam needles in their clothes at night to gather a natural scent.

Used sparingly, scents, lures, cover scents, and soaps may help to attract deer and to eliminate or overcome human and other alarming scents. But scents and lures are unlikely to attract a deer to a place it does not want to be, and cover scents never make you totally unnoticeable to deer. No matter what scents or lures you use, you will be a more effective hunter if you put yourself in places where the signs indicate deer want to be and use air currents to your advantage by making sure your scent is not being blown into the area where you expect the deer to be.

CHAPTER

9

Deer Calls
and How to Use Them

EER are generally quiet creatures, but they do vocalize at certain times.

Anyone who has been around deer much recognizes the snort or "blow" that an alarmed deer emits to warn other deer of danger. Snorts are often repeated again and again as deer bound away from perceived dangers, and they may be heard from immobile deer that have spotted movement or heard a noise that warns them of something they have not yet identified. Snorts are more often made by antlerless deer than by mature bucks, which usually do not vocalize alarm but take evasive action silently.

Less often heard are the communications between does and fawns. Does sometimes use a low grunt to call their fawns when ready to offer a nursing opportunity, and fawns sometimes bleat to call their mothers when they're afraid or lonesome.

From the hunter's standpoint, the most important deer vocalizations are the loud grunts bucks commonly make when trailing does during the rut and the grunt-snort combination bucks sometimes make when confronting one another and threatening to do battle. Both calls can be used to attract bucks during the rut.

Many hunters learn to make loud and effective grunt calls and snorts with their mouths, using no manufactured calls whatsoever. Those who have mastered these calls have the advantages of being able to call instantly, without having to dig around in their pockets for a manufactured call at moments when a buck is seen passing in the distance, and to vary the call and the volume according to the situation.

Historically, not many hunters have been able to master voice-calling. Museums contain many examples of hand-held deer calls that were crafted by native hunters long before the manufacturing industry got into the act. Today, sporting goods stores and hunting catalogs are crammed with deer calls that can work well when used by practiced callers.

How to Use the Grunt Call

When a buck in the rut is following the trail of a doe, he often emits long, drawn-out grunts that can be compared to the sounds made by a rusty barn-door hinge. The call is commonly repeated two or three times over a period of about a minute.

The sound is attractive to other bucks because it suggests that there is a buck nearby trailing a doe in breeding condition. A buck that hears the sound may move in its direction, hoping to get on the doe's trail himself, even if it means he will have to drive the grunting buck off the trail.

If you are the "grunting buck," you're likely to get a shot. Bucks that respond to grunt calls are often large, mature, dominant bucks that are not afraid to rush into a situation that may result in a fight.

A grunt calls sends the signal that a buck is trailing a doe in breeding condition. When they hear that sound, other bucks may be drawn in its direction, hoping to get on the doe's trail themselves.

Grunt calls work best during the rut when it is not too windy and sounds travel farthest. Use the grunt call from your stand or whenever you see a distant deer passing that is not coming toward you. Make two or three long, drawn-out calls over the space of about a minute. Then stay silent for about 20 minutes before you repeat the series of two or three calls.

Success Can Happen Fast

I know an outfitter in Maine who built deer stands in excellent places, but his clients' success rate was low because the clients would get cold or lonesome and wander back to camp rather than stay on their stands. "I needed a way to make them stay in the woods," he recalls.

The outfitter bought a box of grunt calls off the shelf. The next season he presented a call to every client and told them, "blow it two or three times every 20 minutes and don't move—the bucks'll run right over you."

He was as surprised as the hunters when three clients bagged big bucks the first morning. Each one said the bucks just came running shortly after they had blown the calls. The next day a couple more big bucks were bagged by hunters who followed the outfitter's advice.

"When the word spread that the calls worked, everybody in camp started believing in them. That year our success rate soared, and it has stayed high ever since. To tell you the truth, I don't know if the difference is because the hunters are using calls or because they now have a reason to stay on their stands rather than wandering back to camp. Either way, using the calls sure helped us," he reports.

Stories abound regarding deer over-running hunters who use grunt calls. Hunters who have seen a buck come running after they have used a call are ardent believers in the call's effectiveness. The calls do not guarantee success, however. Most hunters who use grunt calls have never seen a buck come to them.

Grunt-Snort Combinations

The grunt-snort combination is made by bucks that are squaring off to fight. It is an excellent call to make in combination with antler rattling. (See Chapter 13 on rattling antlers.)

Bleat Calls

Hunters commonly use calls that imitate the bleat of a fawn during antlerless seasons to attract mature does to their stands. The bleat is given softly two or three times every 20 minutes from a stand or by a moving hunter who thinks a deer may be nearby.

During the rut the bleat call can sometimes attract a doe being followed by a buck. It can, therefore, be an effective way to bring in a preoccupied buck not likely to be attracted to a grunt call, scents, or rattling antlers.

Knocking on Wood

When a buck wants to call in nearby does, he sometimes does so by knocking his hoof repeatedly against the root of a tree where it enters the ground. The resonant knocking sound can be heard for a fair distance.

Once, when I was hunting in Quebec, we inadvertently jumped a bunch of deer that bounded off, snorting and flagging their tails in alarm. "Get down," whispered my French-Canadian guide. He knelt at the base of a big fir tree and unsheathed his hunting knife. Then he knocked the handle of the knife loudly five times against the root of the tree, just where it entered the frozen ground. Five minutes later he repeated the sounds; about 5 minutes after that, he repeated them again.

Then he raised his head above the undergrowth to peek. Suddenly he dropped down and motioned for me to get ready. He gestured that the deer were returning and put his spread fingers up by his head to indicate that one was a buck. A minute later four antlerless deer came into view, heads up, ears fanned, tails flicking in anticipation as they searched for the maker of the sounds. Then came the fifth deer. I could see his antlers before I could see his body. A moment later he stepped into view—a fine 8-pointer that dressed out just under 200 pounds.

CHAPTER 10

Rattling Antlers
for Big Bucks

JUST AS ABORIGINAL HUNTERS used scents and calls to attract deer, they also rattled antlers together to create the sounds of two bucks fighting as a means of luring bucks into bow-and-arrow range.

During the rut, bucks are attracted to the sounds of other bucks fighting because they expect the fight to be over a doe in estrus. Big bucks in particular can't resist checking out the sounds of a fight, hoping to drive off the combatants and take the doe they are fighting over for themselves.

Rattling is effective during three stages of the rut. Just before does begin coming into estrus and active breeding begins, bucks do a lot of fighting to settle dominance issues. When they hear the sounds of two bucks fighting, other bucks are drawn to the sounds. When a fight begins bucks run to watch, just as people do. During the peak of breeding season, the sounds of a fight indicate that the bucks are battling over a doe in estrus. After the peak of breeding activity passes, dominant bucks continue to search for does that have not yet conceived. Now the competition between bucks becomes even more intense. They respond to any sound or scent that indicates a doe in estrus may be near. I have had bucks respond to rattling antlers from late October through early January in the northern states and provinces where I hunt most frequently.

Some hunters believe that the size of the antlers used for rattling has a bearing on the size of the bucks that respond. They say that both medium-sized and large bucks are drawn to the sounds of medium-sized antlers clashing together, but that only large bucks are attracted to the sounds made by large antlers.

The sounds of a buck fight, made by rattling antlers, indicates that two bucks are fighting over a doe that is in breeding condition. Other bucks may be drawn to the sounds, hoping to claim the doe themselves.

That has not been my experience, however. I have used the same pair of relatively heavy antlers that I took from a large 8-point buck many years ago and have seen bucks of all sizes drawn to the sounds they make. I think *how* you use them is more important than how large the antlers are.

How to Use Rattling Antlers

To rattle antlers most effectively you should try to simulate as closely as possible the sounds of two bucks really fighting. Picture a buck fight in your mind as you clash, twist, and rattle your antlers in ways that make the sounds of the fight that you are mentally creating. Stamp your feet, crack brush, grunt, and snort. Make it a dramatic performance.

Start with light antler sounds, which can be heard by bucks that may be nearby. As you continue, increase the volume and the intensity

Clash the antlers together, then twist them back and forth under pressure. When you reach the end of a rattling sequence, continue to twist the antlers together as you pull them apart.

of the fighting sounds in order to be heard farther away. Make each rattling session last about 30 seconds, then put down your antlers, pick up your rifle, and watch for an approaching deer. If no buck appears after 3 minutes, repeat the rattling session for another 30 seconds, then put down the antlers and pick up your rifle once more. Continue to repeat 30 seconds of rattling and 3 minutes of rest until 15 minutes have passed. If a buck has not shown himself after 15 minutes, the chances are good that one will not appear. Then it's time to move to another spot.

HOW BUCK FIGHTS SOUND

When bucks fight, they begin by lightly sparring with their antler tips. This activity usually escalates into pushing and twisting contests that includes light antler sounds, followed by the thumping of hooves and the sounds of grinding antlers. The bucks continue pushing and twisting for a few seconds at a time, followed by periods of rest.

If pushing and twisting fail to prove which buck dominates, the action increases. Now the bucks clash their antlers together with greater force, then twist and shove, making heavier, grinding antler sounds as each buck attempts to get past the other's antlers and injure his opponent.

Hooves thump repeatedly as the two attempt to throw each other off balance. Sometimes one buck is thrown to the ground with a loud body slam. The bucks push each other into blown-down timber, causing cracking and crashing sounds. At pauses in the battle, they may emit loud grunt-snort combinations and stamp their hooves or paw the ground furiously as they work up their rage for the next clash of antlers.

Try to make all of these sounds. You can make hoof thumps by hitting the butt of an antler on the ground. Pawing sounds can be made by raking the tips of an antler on the ground forcefully. Smash some dry brush with your feet to imitate the sounds of bucks fighting amid underbrush and blown-down timber. Add grunt-snort calls, particularly during rest periods.

The most effective antler-rattling sounds are made by clashing the antlers together, then twisting them back and forth under pressure, just as bucks do. When you reach the end of each rattling session, continue to twist the antlers together forcefully as you pull them apart. This action adds a very realistic sound because bucks usually stop fighting when the eye of one is threatened by the antler tip of the other, and he backs away as the other buck continues to push and twist, thus pulling the antlers apart under force.

As long as you have a little underbrush around you, don't be afraid of having your movements seen by a buck drawn to the sounds. He expects to see the movement of two bucks fighting and will not usually be put off by the sight of your partially screened actions. In fact, he may be attracted by seeing a little movement. He is more likely to become wary if he does not see some movement coming from the source of such violent sounds.

WHERE TO RATTLE

Good locations for rattling sessions have these requirements: They are located in country that indicates lots of buck use; they offer some cover, so you are not right out in the open; they offer visibility, so you can see and shoot in all directions; and there are dry branches around for you to crack and smash as part of your fighting-sounds repertoire.

If you are following a buck track that crosses an opening and then leads into heavy cover, don't expose yourself by crossing the opening. Instead, crouch down in a semicovered location and put on a dramatic rattling performance. If the buck is in the thick cover, he is likely to come out to your sounds, and you will have a clear shot as he approaches through the opening.

Likewise, whenever signs indicate that you are in a heavy-use deer area, rattling may be effective in bringing a buck to you that you might not otherwise see. If you are hunting big country, mixing still-hunting and rattling can be very effective. Pause and rattle whenever you come to a good place. If nothing responds after 15 minutes or so, move on slowly to the next good location and rattle again.

If you are hunting from a stand, put on a 15-minute rattling session about once an hour. You may be heard by a buck that is traveling through the area, out of your range of vision.

When conditions are right, rattling antlers may attract bucks at any hour of the day. I have actually had more bucks come to rattling antlers between 11 A.M. and 1 P.M. than at any other times. Whenever the wind is still and the woods are quiet, rattling may work.

THE SECRET IS BEING HEARD

Rattling works only if it is heard. Unless you are in country with a high deer population, your rattling will *not* be heard by deer more times than it *is* heard. Don't expect frequent success.

Once, when hunting in an area that bragged 35 deer per square mile and a 50 to 50 buck to doe ratio, I rattled up three bucks in one day. That's the best I've ever done, and that was in an area in which I was probably being heard by a buck every time I put on a rattling performance.

WHY BUCKS SOMETIMES REFUSE TO RESPOND

To be effective, your rattling must not only be heard, it must be heard by a buck that is willing to respond.

Bucks that are traveling with does will usually not respond to rattling. They already have what they want, so why risk losing it by entering into a fight? In areas where hunting pressure is high, bucks that have been scared by seeing people in the woods are less apt to respond. If they have been duped before by a hunter rattling antlers, they may avoid the sounds. Rattling works only when hunting pressure is limited and where bucks feel safe and are following their sexual instincts, not running and hiding. Subdominant bucks that have already lost a few fights may remember their previous whippings and want to avoid further indignities. Old bucks may have passed breeding age and no longer respond to any sexual attractants. On top of all that, you have to be close enough to a responsive buck for your sounds to be heard.

Does respond to rattling almost as often as bucks do when conditions are right. If you see a doe approaching, don't be quick to move away. Does that respond to the sounds of a buck fight are often traveling with a buck. He may follow the doe toward the rattling sounds even though he may not be responsive to the sounds of a fight himself.

HOW BUCKS APPROACH

I usually expect almost immediate action if rattling is going to work. Most of the time I see the buck within the first 5 minutes after

When they respond to rattling, bucks keep hidden in cover as they approach. Suddenly, they just appear, staring straight at you.

I begin a rattling session. I may continue for 15 minutes without seeing one, but I know that most of the time, if I have been heard by a responsive buck, I'll see him right away.

Usually what you see does not look like a buck coming toward you. You'll see a slight deer-like movement in the distance, or a deer tail will flash far up ahead. Sometimes you'll see the whole deer, but he may appear to be moving away. The rule is this: If you see any deer movement when you are rattling, keep it up. You've been heard. Give the buck a chance to respond.

Some bucks come in as if they were being pulled on a rope. Others bound into view and run right up to you. Usually the approach is much less dramatic. You'll see an ear and the curl of an antler sticking out from behind a tree. You'll wonder how the buck got there without you having seen him before. The deer will keep trees and obstructions between you as he approaches, and you won't see him most of the time. Keep your rifle near at hand.

The buck will probably travel toward you on a course that will take him past you on one side or the other as he attempts to get downwind of your position. If he succeeds in reaching your downwind side, he will pick up your scent and drift off, so be prepared to shoot before he gets downwind.

Once in a while a buck will just appear right in front of you. His neck will be fully extended, his ears will be flared, his nose will be searching for your scent, and his eyes will be focused on the spot where you are making the sounds. Either way, when a buck comes to your rattling antlers, it will be one of the high points of your deer-hunting career, and you will become a confirmed believer in rattling antlers.

How to Make Rattling Antlers

Plastic rattling antlers are available, and some people make antler sounds by using hard wooden rods, but real antlers make the most realistic sounds. Antlers sawn off freshly killed deer make the best sounds, but shed antlers that you find in the woods can also be used if they are still hard.

Antlers of medium thickness are choice. They should have three long tines and a curve that makes them comfortable to handle. If they have a short brow tine near the base, cut it off and file the base of the tine flat so it will not stab you in the hand when you are performing a violent rattling scene. Use a wood file to smooth the shafts of the antlers into comfortable hand grips. Drill holes in the butts of the antlers so you can connect the antlers with a short line if you wish. To keep the antlers resonant, coat them with linseed oil at the end of each hunting season and hang them up. Next season, wipe off any excess oil.

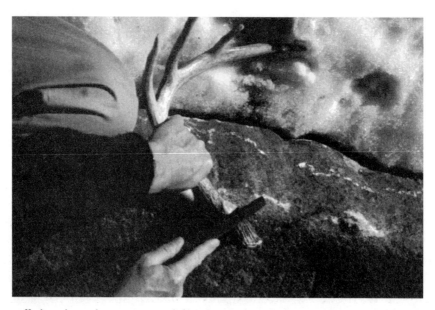

Cut off the short brow tine and file the antler shafts smooth to make a comfortable hand grip. Give the antlers an annual coat of linseed oil to keep them resonant.

Firearms and Cartridge Choices

T
HE CHOICE of a deer rifle is entirely personal. Any rifle or caliber that is legal in the states in which you plan to hunt is capable of killing deer cleanly when aimed accurately at a target that is within its killing range.

In the brushy, timbered country where whitetails spend most of their daylight hours, the need to make a shot beyond 200 yards is rare; most whitetails are shot at ranges of less than 100 yards. However, there are occasions when long-range, open shots present themselves, and you may find yourself needing a rifle capable of long-range accuracy and extended killing range.

CHOOSING AN ACTION

You must first choose the type of action that suits you best.

Lever-action rifles can be less expensive than other types and are light and fast handling. They are the choice of many hunters who believe them to be more convenient for carrying in thick cover. Most popular in 30/30, .300 Savage, and .35 Remington calibers, and usually considered to be "100-yard rifles," they usually lack long-range accuracy and "knockdown power." Another disadvantage is that lever-action rifles must be unloaded by jacking cartridges through the chamber with the hammer cocked. This requirement presents a safety concern that does not exist with bolt-action, pump, and semi-automatic rifles, which are loaded and unloaded through a separate magazine rather than through the chamber.

Pump-action and semiautomatic rifles are fastest to use and may be operated without taking the rifle from the shoulder. Their devotees want a gun that offers the quickest follow-up shots. Pumps and semiautos come in a wide variety of high-speed calibers that offer relatively flat trajectory and extended killing range.

Bolt-action rifles are slower to operate, but they can seat a cartridge in the chamber tighter, which can result in superior long-range accuracy. Bolt-action rifles are offered in the widest choice of calibers and are the most popular type of action overall.

"Brush Busters"

A persistent myth is that big, slow bullets "bust brush" without losing accuracy and that bullets traveling at higher speeds are deflected when they hit twigs. Don't be misled. The truth is that all bullets are deflected when they hit brush, and the deflection becomes more severe as range increases.

Ideally, you want to be able to deliver your bullet on target by shooting through holes in the timber where no interference will be encountered. In order to do that, you'll need a rifle that allows you to get your sights on your target quickly and a cartridge that will deliver a bullet to your target before it gets past such an opening.

"Flat-Shooting" Calibers

There is no such thing as a "flat-shooting" rifle, caliber, or bullet. All bullets from all rifles drop at the same rate from the instant they leave the barrel. The difference is that faster-traveling bullets cover more distance in a given time than do slower bullets. Therefore, in the time it takes for all bullets to drop an inch, the faster bullets will have gone farther than the slower bullets. Thus, a bullet that covers 200 yards in the time it takes all bullets to drop an inch is termed "flatter-shooting" than a bullet that travels only 100 yards in the time it takes all bullets to drop an inch.

Bullet Trajectories

The table on page 482 gives a comparison of the trajectories of bullets in the 11 most popular deer-rifle calibers. As you can see, the

It takes more than 800 pounds of energy per square inch for a bullet to achieve the shocking power and penetration necessary to consistently kill deer under most circumstances. The maximum distance at which a bullet maintains 800 pounds of energy per square inch should be considered the deer-killing range of that cartridge.

faster the bullet travels, the less it drops at normal deer-hunting distances. Slower bullets drop farther at the same distances.

Most hunters agree that the best calibers for general-purpose big-game hunting in North America fire 150-grain bullets at speeds in excess of 2,000 feet per second at 200 yards range and drop less than 8 inches at 300 yards.

"Knockdown Power"

It takes more than 800 pounds of energy per square inch for a bullet to achieve the degree of shocking power and penetration necessary to kill a deer under most circumstances. The maximum distance at which a bullet maintains 800 pounds of energy per square inch should, therefore, be considered the deer-killing range of that cartridge. To be on the safe side, you really ought to shoot a deer rifle that delivers 1,000 pounds of energy per square inch to your target at whatever range is required.

The table on page 482 compares the "knockdown power" of the

same list of popular cartridges in terms of the number of pounds of energy per square inch they deliver downrange.

You can see from the tables that bullets from .250 Savage-, Winchester 30/30-, Winchester .32 Special-, and Remington .35-caliber rifles drop fast and push the limits of knockdown power when the range reaches 200 yards, whereas the other cartridges drop less and still carry plenty of knockdown power all the way out to 300 yards and beyond.

Trajectory Table

CARTRIDGE	BULLET WEIGHT	VELOCITY 100 YDS.	VELOCITY 200 YDS.	DROPS 100 YDS.	DROPS 200 YDS.	DROPS 300 YDS.
.243 Win.	100	2,790	2,540	0.5	2.2	4.7
.250 Sav.	100	2,410	2,070	0.6	3.0	6.4
.257 Rob.	100	2,540	2,210	0.6	2.7	7.7
.264 Win. Mag	100	3,260	2,880	0.4	1.6	4.2
.270 Win.	150	2,400	2,040	0.7	3.0	7.8
.280 Rem.	150	2,580	2,360	0.6	2.6	6.5
30/30 Win.	150	2,020	1,700	0.9	4.2	11.0
30–06 Spr.	150	2,670	2,400	0.6	2.4	6.1
.300 Sav.	150	2,390	2,130	0.7	3.0	7.6
.308 Win.	150	2,570	2,300	0.6	2.6	6.5
.32 Win. Sp.	170	1,870	1,560	1.0	4.8	13.0
.35 Rem.	150	1,960	1,580	0.9	4.6	13.0

Energy Table

CARTRIDGE	BULLET WEIGHT	ENERGY AT 100 YDS.	ENERGY AT 200 YDS.	ENERGY AT 300 YDS.
.243 Win.	100	1,730	1,430	1,190
.250 Sav.	100	1,290	950	695
.264 Win. Mag.	100	2,360	1,840	1,440
.270 Win.	150	1,920	1,380	1,020
.280 Rem.	150	2,220	1,850	1,510
30/30 Win.	150	1,360	960	680
30–06 Spr.	150	2,370	1,920	1,510
.300 Sav.	150	1,900	1,510	1,190
.308 Win.	150	2,200	1,760	1,400
.32 Win. Sp.	170	1,320	920	665
.35 Rem.	150	1,280	835	545

CHAPTER

Rifle Sights

Y OU HAVE A CHOICE of open, peep, or telescopic sights.

Open sights are at their best when you are shooting at a running target at close range in heavy cover because you can keep both eyes open and see your target as well as your surroundings as you aim. This enables you to anticipate when a running target is going to come into an opening and give you a clear shot.

Open sights, however, are very limiting when you want to take a shot at longer range. At 100 yards a deer looks so small that a broad front sight covers its entire chest when you are using an open sight. At longer ranges, open sights don't really tell you just exactly where you are aiming on the deer because they block out so much. Furthermore, people with "older eyes"—who have difficulty focusing on the sight and the target at the same time—find open sights give them a blurry sight picture, even at close range.

Open sights are fast to aim, but you must remember to get your face down tight on the gunstock and to pull the front bead all the way down into the bottom of the rear sight notch or you will shoot high or to the side no matter how well you have sighted-in the rifle.

Better open sights can be adjusted up, down, and sideways by use of a slide-and-locking screw arrangement. Less-expensive open sights must be driven to make sideways adjustments, and their elevation adjustments can be crude and may require filing.

Open

Open sights are fast to aim but block the view of your target at longer ranges.

483

Peep

Peep sights are very accurate because your eye automatically puts any object you focus on in the center of the space in which you see it.

PEEP SIGHTS

A peep sight is a small hole in a disk through which you view both your target and your front sight. The disk is mounted on an adjustable base attached to the rifle's receiver. Click-stop adjusting screws permit the shooter to move the disk up, down, and sideways for precise sighting-in.

Peep sights work because your eye automatically puts any object you focus on in the center of the space in which you see it. Your eye will automatically place your target in the center of the peep hole and line it up with the front sight. Once you have adjusted the sights to line up at the exact spot where your rifle delivers its bullets, you can expect to shoot very accurately with a peep sight.

The disadvantages of a peep sight are that the aperture hole sometimes gets clogged with snow or debris, and, like the open sight, the front bead may cover so much of the target at longer distances that it becomes difficult to know exactly where you are aiming.

TELESCOPIC SIGHTS

That leaves us with telescopic sights as the best answer for most hunters, most of the time.

No other sight gives you the ability to be as precise in your bullet placement. Furthermore, once you have adjusted the crosshairs to center on the exact point to which your rifle delivers its bullets at a certain range, you can be sure that at that range every bullet will go to the spot where the crosshairs cross, regardless of how you hold your head or the rifle itself.

Telescopic sights give you almost surgical precision when it comes to bullet placement. A telescopic sight magnifies the target according to its power, allowing you to center the crosshairs exactly where you want the bullet to strike. They also magnify light, as well as objects, making such sights extra helpful in dim light.

As magnification power increases, however, the width of the field of view you can see through the scope decreases. Too much power reduces the field of view to an unacceptable degree and may make your viewing picture too narrow for you to keep a running buck in view as he bounds in and out of cover.

For that reason, most manufacturers recommend no more than a 2½-power scope on rifles intended for use at short range and a 4-power scope for guns expected to be used on targets out to 200 yards.

VARIABLE SCOPES

The ideal scope, in my view, is the variable scope. A variable scope has a ring-type dial that you turn to increase or decrease the magnification. Changing the magnification does not affect the range at which the scope has been sighted-in. My personal favorite is the Leupold 2½-to-8× variable scope (× = power). I have one on every big-game rifle I own.

I carry my scope set on $2^1/_2$× when I'm walking in order to have the widest possible sight picture should I jump a deer up close. When I stop to watch or wait on a stand, I adjust the scope to 4× so I can magnify my target when I see a deer approaching. Just before I shoot I can adjust the scope to an even higher power, which gives me a large picture of the deer and allows me to place the bullet exactly where I want it to go.

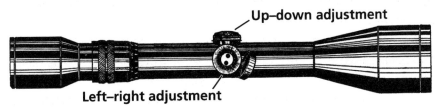

Telescopic sights give you almost surgical precision when it comes to bullet placement. A telescopic sight magnifies your target according to its power, allowing you to center the crosshairs exactly where you want the bullet to strike.

When I have a walking or standing target, I often screw the scope all the way up to 8× when I'm ready to shoot. This gives me the ability to place my bullet precisely and make a killing shot without damaging any more meat than necessary.

CHOICE OF RETICLES

When you buy a telescopic sight, you have a choice of reticles, which give different sight pictures depending on your requirements. A heavy post-and-crosshair reticle is quick to get on target and easier than others to see in dim light, but it may be too coarse for fine bullet placement at longer ranges. Thick crosshairs are also helpful in dim light, but may block out part of your target at long range. Thin crosshairs allow the most refinement in bullet placement, but may be difficult to see in dim light.

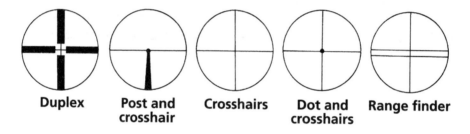

Duplex   **Post and**   **Crosshairs**   **Dot and**   **Range finder**
        crosshair   **crosshairs**

The reticle I like best is called a duplex. It has dual-thickness crosshairs, which are medium thick in the outer segments so I can get on my target in a hurry. The center segments of the crosshairs are of very thin wire, which allows me to refine my bullet placement.

Telescopic lenses vary in price according to how well they are made and the quality of the glass. Buy the best scope you can afford.

CHAPTER 13

Sighting-in Your Rifle

SIGHTING-IN MEANS adjusting your rifle's sights so they line up at exactly the point where your rifle delivers its bullets at whatever distance you choose. Remember, you are not changing the point at which the bullets strike; you are changing the point at which the sights line up. Your rifle will deliver its bullets on the same trajectory regardless of how the sights are adjusted. When you have adjusted the sights to line up at the point where your rifle delivers its bullets at your desired range, your rifle is sighted-in, or "zeroed," for that particular distance.

BULLETS DO NOT RISE

Bullets begin to drop the instant they leave the muzzle. Despite what you may have heard, bullets do not rise for a while and then begin to drop. They just drop.

To make the sights line up at the point a dropping bullet will impact at a range of 200 yards, we have to tip the rifle barrel up at an angle slightly above our actual line of sight to compensate for the drop that will occur as the bullet travels 200 yards. When you look at a diagram showing the bullet traveling above the line of sight, you could get the impression that the bullet rises after it leaves the muzzle. It doesn't. We have merely fired the bullet at a slightly upward angle, and that angle keeps the constantly falling bullet above our line of sight as it travels to its target.

Sight-Height Factor

The height at which the sight is mounted above the bore is another factor. The bullet actually begins its flight from below our line of sight because the sights are mounted considerably above the bore of the rifle. Thus, when we fire a bullet from a barrel that has been tipped up to compensate for bullet drop, the bullet coming from below our straight-to-the-target line of sight will cross that line at two places.

The upward-fired bullet will first intersect our line of sight a short distance beyond the muzzle. It remains above our line of sight throughout its downward-curving trajectory and eventually drops to intersect our line of sight again.

Sight-In at Short Range

Using trajectory tables published by ammunition manufacturers, we can accurately predict how high above our line of sight a bullet must be at 50 yards in order for it to drop back to our line of sight at any target distance. This gives us the ability to do our actual sight-in shooting at a convenient short range even though we actually want our bullets to drop to our line of sight and be on target at much longer ranges.

From the table on page 88, you can see that a .280 Remington

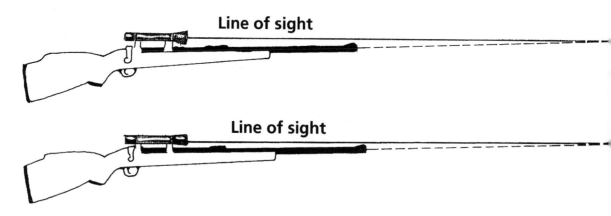

All bullets begin to drop as soon as they leave the muzzle. In order to compensate for the drop, we tip the barrel up slightly and then adjust the sights to line up at the spot when the bullet will drop to our target elevation.

150-grain bullet that hits 0.6 inches above the line of sight at 50 yards will be 0.9 inches above the line of sight at 100 yards, right on target at 150 yards and 2.3 inches below the line of sight at 200 yards. Knowing this, I need only sight-in my .280 so that its bullets hit 0.6 inches high at 50 yards and I know that it is sighted-in (zeroed) for 150 yards. If I need to make a 200-yard shot, I know that I must aim a little more than 2-inches high.

MOUNTING THE SCOPE

A telescopic sight should be mounted so that you see a full sight picture when you bring the rifle to your shoulder. Using a screwdriver that perfectly fits the screw slots, loosen the mounting rings and slide the scope forward or back to increase or decrease the distance between the scope and your eye until you find the point at which all dark obscurity vanishes and you see the full sight picture.

Next, while the mounting rings are still loose, twist the scope tube in the mount until the crosshairs are perfectly vertical and horizontal. Once these adjustments are made, the scope will be adjusted to suit the manner in which you hold your rifle. Tighten the mounting screws again.

Now, mount the rifle to your shoulder and aim at the sky. Are the crosshairs sharp and black, or do they appear somewhat fuzzy? If they are fuzzy, you need to focus the eyepiece. The eyepiece is

Actual bullet trajectory

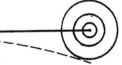

Actual bullet trajectory

focused by loosening the eyepiece lock ring, then turning the eyepiece clockwise or counterclockwise until the crosshairs are sharp and black. When the adjustment is made to your satisfaction, tighten the eyepiece lock ring and you're ready to start sighting-in.

SIGHTING-IN PROCEDURE

1. Before shooting your rifle, clean it well to remove any dirt or grease that may be in the bore, and check that the sight mounts are very tight.
2. Always sight-in using the same cartridges you will use for hunting. Sighting-in is not the time to get rid of odd lots of cartridges.
3. Set up a target either 25 or 50 yards from the muzzle. (A bullet from a high-powered rifle drops so little between those initial distances that for deer-hunting purposes you are unlikely to notice any difference in long-range accuracy, and a target at 25 yards is more convenient to use.)
4. Use a bench rest with a sandbag or a log with a folded blanket or coat for support. Rest your hand on the support, not on the rifle barrel; then rest the rifle on your hand. Never rest the rifle barrel on a hard surface because the recoil will cause the barrel to jump, spoiling your shot.
5. Aiming at the center of the bull's-eye each time, fire three shots. This should give you a close group that shows where the bullets are hitting.
6. Measuring from the center of the group, determine how many inches high or low and how many inches to the right or left the bullets are hitting from the center of the bull's-eye.
7. Adjust the sights to compensate for the difference.

Telescopic and receiver/peep sights have click-stop adjustment screws that usually move the sight picture by one-quarter minute of angle per click. A minute of angle (four clicks) equals one inch at 100 yards.

Adjust the sight in the direction you want the bullets to go. If the bullets are hitting to the right of your point of aim, adjust the sight to the left. If you are hitting high, adjust toward low.

If you are using a receiver/peep sight, adjust in the same manner.

If you are using open sights, move the rear sight in the direction you want the bullet to go. However, if you need to adjust the front sight, move it in the opposite direction. If your open sights do not have windage adjustments, they must be driven right or left with a hammer and a brass or wooden drift pin. Rear-sight elevation is usually adjusted up or down by moving a graduated steel insert beneath the sight tang. The front sight can be filed down if it is too high.

9. Adjust the point of aim until your bullets are grouping where you want them. Remember that you are sighting-in at short range, so use the bullet path table to determine how high above your point of aim bullets must impact at 25 or 50 yards in order to be right on target at the longer range you want to be "zeroed" at.

10. Once you have the rifle shooting the correct degree high at 25 or 50 yards, go out and shoot it at your designated zero range of 100, 150, or 200 yards and make any necessary final sight adjustments.

**Bullet path above or below line of sight (inches)
on rifles with low-mounted scopes or metallic sights**

CARTRIDGE	WEIGHT	50 YDS.	100 YDS.	150 YDS.	200 YDS.
.243 Win.	100 gr.	+0.5	+0.9	Zero	-2.2
.250 Sav.	100 gr.	+0.2	Zero	-1.6	-4.7
.257 Rob.	100 gr.	+0.1	Zero	-1.3	-4.0
.264 Win. Mag.	140 gr.	+0.5	+0.8	Zero	-2.0
.270 Win.	150 gr.	+0.6	1.0	Zero	-2.4
.280 Rem.	150 gr.	+0.6	+0.9	Zero	-2.3
.30/30 Win.	150 gr.	+0.5	Zero	-2.6	-7.7
.300 Sav.	150 gr.	+0.3	Zero	-1.8	-5.4
.308 Win.	150 gr.	+0.2	Zero	-1.6	-4.8
.30-06 Win.	150 gr.	+0.6	+0.9	Zero	-2.2
.32 Win. Sp.	170 gr.	+0.6	Zero	-3.1	-9.2
.35 Rem.	200 gr.	+0.8	Zero	-3.8	-11.3

Picking Your Target:
Where to Shoot a Deer

I HAVE NO RESPECT for hunters who want to knock a deer down any way they can. My goal (and I hope yours, too) is always a one-shot kill. Ideally, I want a clear shot at a walking or standing deer. I want to be able to place my bullet precisely, so that even if the deer runs off, I know that it will fall dead within a short distance.

This is not to say that you should never shoot at a running deer. I have killed a number of deer that were moving fast, but they were at close range when I fired, I had a clear view of my target, and I was able to place the bullet where I wanted it. When given an opportunity to take a chance shot at a deer that I don't have "dead to rights," I always pass up the shot and wait for a better opportunity. I want to kill the deer, not wound it, and I don't want to ruin any more meat than necessary.

I believe the ideal way to kill a deer is to shoot it through the lungs. A lung-shot deer often runs off a short distance, but it nearly always drops dead within 100 yards or so. During the time it takes the animal to run that 100 yards, its heart continues to pump blood from its body tissues into the destroyed lung area, which bleeds out the carcass efficiently and makes the flesh much better tasting.

WHERE TO AIM

If the deer is passing broadside to me, my target is the "engine room" right behind the shoulder, halfway between the top and bottom of the deer's body. It's a big area that contains the deer's most vital organs. If my bullet flies true, it will destroy the lungs. If it hits a bit high, it will strike the spine with instant paralyzing effect. If my aim is low, the bullet will hit the heart, just below the lungs. To the rear of the lungs is the liver. A liver shot will also cause an immediate bleed out and quick death.

If a deer is coming toward me, my target is the center of the chest, just where the neck joins. A bullet striking there will destroy lungs and liver. If a bit high it will strike the neck vertebrae; if low, it gets the heart.

When a deer approaches at an angle that does not offer a straight-on or perfect broadside shot, the "engine room" may be blocked by a shoulder. When this is the best shot I can get, I aim directly at the point of the shoulder. This shot will sacrifice about two pounds of stew meat, but the bullet will pass through the shoulder directly into the vital area.

If the deer is moving away from me, I try for an angle shot behind the ribs into the "engine room." If that is not possible, I aim just above the shoulders at the base of the neck. If the shot is a little high, it will hit higher on the neck, which is also deadly. If the bullet hits low, it will hit the spine and paralyze the deer.

Neck and spine shots do not produce the beneficial bleed out that a lung shot provides, but they are deadly and usually drop the deer in its tracks. A heart shot is also deadly, of course, but it also fails to cause a complete bleed out since it destroys the pump that pulls the blood from the tissues when an animal's lungs are destroyed. Also, the heart is a small target; if your aim is low, you will shoot under the deer.

Speed Means Lead

If a deer is moving fast but offers a clear shot at the vital area, you can hit your mark only if you compensate for the deer's speed and lead your target, just as you must when shooting a shotgun at flying game.

When you shoot a high-powered rifle at a running deer at a range of 100 yards or less, you must fire when your sights are some distance ahead of the shoulder, depending on the range and the animal's speed. When shooting a slower cartridge, the lead must be even greater.

The table below explains why so many hunters miss running deer.

From any angle, your target should be the heart-lung area. For a broadside shot, aim just behind the front shoulder, halfway between the top and bottom of the deer's body. From head-on, aim at the base of the neck in the center of the chest. If the deer is angling away, aim just behind the ribs. If it is running straight away from you, aim above the back at the base of the neck.

How accurately can you place a bullet fired at a running deer when leads such as this are required? These figures are for a 30/30 rifle shooting a 170-grain bullet at a deer moving at typical slow-running and fast-running speeds.

Unless you are a crack shot and have practiced shooting at fast-moving targets at a variety of distances, you will be a much more effective and humane deer hunter if you limit your shots at running deer to only those that can be taken at close range where the required lead is minimal.

The greatest challenge of deer hunting is to hunt in such a way that you are in a position to take close shots at deer that are standing still or walking slowly. This may require more hunting skill, but developing the ability to get within close range of unsuspecting deer is what deer hunting should be about.

RANGE (YDS.)	DEER'S FORWARD SPEED (MPH)	REQUIRED LEAD (INCHES)
50	10	12
50	20	25
75	10	20
75	20	38
100	10	28
100	20	52

15

Trailing Wounded Deer

I DO NOT SUBSCRIBE to the often-stated recommendation to sit down and wait a half hour before trailing a deer that was hit and ran off after the shot. Although it is true that waiting before you trail the deer will give the animal time to die or become immobilized before you approach it, waiting also provides time for another hunter to find your deer and claim it before you do. This is especially true if you are hunting on heavily pressured public land.

Don't be discouraged if you don't find your deer right away. Keep going in the direction the deer was headed when you last saw it, and check all thick places carefully. When hit, deer head for heavy cover.

When you shoot, watch the deer as far as you can and mentally mark the spot where it disappeared. Now, mark the spot you shot from with a strip of surveyor's tape. Next, reload your rifle, put it on safety, and walk to the spot where you last saw the deer. If you can't see the downed deer, mark that spot by tying a strip of surveyor's tape to an overhead branch and search the ground for blood, hair or tracks. Continue in the direction in which the deer was traveling, moving slowly and scanning ahead for a sight of the deer while searching the ground for signs.

A deer shot through the lungs, heart, or liver may drop in its tracks or run at full speed until the blood supply to its brain decreases and the animal piles up wherever it is. Usually, the deer tumbles into a hollow in the ground and is found stretched out in the open. But on several occasions I have had a hard time finding bucks that fell dead within 100 yards of where I shot them because they fell into holes or leaped into heavy cover in their mad rush to escape.

I well remember a 10-pointer that I shot when he came to my rattling horns. When I fired, he was standing broadside no more than 40 yards away, and my crosshairs were settled tight behind his shoulder, halfway between the top of his back and the bottom of his chest. "Dead!" I said to myself, as he hunched up and bounded off after the shot.

I walked to where the buck had been standing and looked in the direction in which he ran. Nothing. I checked the ground for hair and blood and found neither. Moving off in the direction he had taken, I found the ground was frozen hard and his tracks indistinguishable. I expected to find him within 100 yards or so, but did not. Nor could I find any trace of blood or hair along my route. Ahead lay a thicket of young firs and spruces with interlacing branches. Only by lying on my stomach was I able to view the ground beneath them.

After nearly an hour of pacing methodically back and forth through the thick woods, I still had not found my deer. Still, I was positive my shot had been good and that he must be lying dead somewhere close by.

After another fruitless half hour I was completely frustrated. I was tempted to think that I had missed. Only the fact that I had experienced this sort of frustration before, yet finally found my deer, made me persist.

USE YOUR NOSE

Suddenly, I smelled him. The musky smell of a buck in the rut is unmistakable. You smell it instantly when you walk up to a dead deer, and I smelled it then. Turning to face the soft breeze that bore the scent to me, I crawled forward into the densest part of the thicket and within a few yards came to a deep depression that was totally obscured by overlapping fir branches that drooped close to the ground. My buck lay dead in the depression, with not even the wide curve of his big rack showing above the ground. He had run that far, leaped into the thicket, and fallen dead in the one spot where he could not be seen.

That is not the only time I have found dead deer by smelling them, and I recommend using your nose as well as your eyes when searching for a deer you know was hit.

MODERN BULLETS MAY NOT EXIT

Modern bullets are designed to lose all of their force inside a big-game animal, so they often do not exit. The lack of a large exit wound considerably reduces the amount of blood a deer spills and makes trailing a wounded deer that much more difficult. Bullet manufacturers say that modern bullets deliver such a high degree of shocking power that more deer are killed in their tracks with no trailing necessary, but the fact is that when you do hit a deer that runs off but does not spill blood, trailing it can be a real challenge.

Even deer that may be suffering enormous internal bleeding sometimes spill little blood. Fat layers often plug the small bullet entry wound and prevent much blood from being lost. Deer that are shot through the lungs lose blood through their mouth and nose, but deer shot in the heart, liver, or spinal column may lose very little blood before they fall.

CHECK THE THICK SPOTS

A deer that is mortally wounded may run uphill or downhill or stay on the level. It may go anywhere, but if it is hit badly enough to have to stop, it will head for the thickest cover it can find. Knowing this, pay close attention to any heavy cover that may hide it, and search those places closely if you do not have a blood trail leading you to its location.

Carry your rifle with the safety on, but in a position from which you can mount it quickly for a close shot. If your rifle is equipped with a variable-power telescopic sight, set it on the lowest magnification in order to have the widest possible field of view if the deer should suddenly jump up close to you and begin to run.

You should find a clump of hair at the spot where the deer was hit. There may or may not be blood at that place, depending on whether or not the bullet passed through the deer's body. The blood trail usually begins a few yards down the deer's escape route. Skidding tracks indicate that the deer was hit hard and is disoriented. If the deer falls, it leaves torn earth and scattered leaves. Bright, frothy blood implies a lung shot; you can expect to find the deer dead not far down the trail. Dark, blackish blood suggests that the deer was hit in the paunch. It will die, but not for a while. Right now, it will head for heavy cover. Bits of bone may be from the lower leg. A deer hit there can go a long way.

As you move along the trail, be careful not to step on the deer's tracks or spots where blood or hair is found. Walk beside the signs, not on them. You may have to go back over a portion of the trail if you lose it, and it may prove impossible to do so if you have disturbed the signs.

Mark the Trail

If you have only a sparse blood trail to follow, mark the trail with bits of surveyor's tape as you go so that you can always return to the last blood spot when you have difficulty finding the next one. If you fail to find the deer by the end of the day, you will have an easier time finding the trail again the next morning if you have marked it well. (After you either find your deer or are forced to abandon the trail, go back and remove the surveyor's tape marks because they may create confusion for others who find them later.)

Follow Up Every Shot

Don't be discouraged if you don't find your deer right away. If you feel the shot was good, you probably have a deer down, and it is up to you to find it. If there is snow on the ground or if the deer is bleeding heavily, you won't have any trouble following its trail. It is when the ground is bare and frozen hard and the deer has stopped bleeding that the trail becomes hard to read.

All you can do in those situations is to keep going in the direction in which the deer was headed and search hardest in the thickest places. If you are hunting with one or more partners, call them for assistance. Separate yourselves at a distance that allows you to see the ground clearly between you, and then move through the woods abreast.

If the deer travels a long distance and you have not caught up with it by day's end, mark the spot clearly and return the next morning to follow the trail again. It is very likely that you will find the deer wherever it bedded for the night. If the ground is cold, the meat of a dead deer that has lain out overnight will not be spoiled.

If in the end you are forced to abandon the trail without finding the deer, ask yourself what went wrong, and try to avoid making that mistake in the future. Most deer that are wounded but get away are the result of hunters taking long shots at running targets. Close shots at standing or walking deer usually result in dead deer where you can find them within a few minutes.

CHAPTER 16

Field Dressing
Your Deer

DEER RARELY FALL in a place that is suitable for field dressing the carcass. They tumble into hollows in the ground or fall in thick cover where you will be too confined to field dress the deer properly. To make field dressing easier, you want your deer out in the open on raised ground where you can stretch out the carcass. So, before you get out your knife, drag the deer to an open place on level or gently sloping ground. Place it so the deer's head is either on the level or slightly uphill. If possible, place large rocks or logs beside the deer's shoulders to prevent the carcass from rolling.

YOU DON'T NEED A BIG KNIFE

A large knife is not necessary. Knives with 3½-inch blades are ample. If you are using a folding knife, choose one with a locking blade that will not fold up on your fingers while you are using it.

Some hunters begin by removing the deer's tarsal scent glands from the inside of the hind legs in order to prevent the spread of the strong, musky scent to the meat. I do not recommend doing this, however, because removing the glands gets the scent on your hands, so that the scent is transmitted to every part of the deer you touch. I prefer to leave the scent glands in place and avoid touching them. The scent will not spread from the glands if they do not come into contact with the deer's flesh. They will come off cleanly with the hide when the deer is skinned at home.

Once you have the deer firmly positioned on its back, cut around the scrotum, detach the testicles and penis, and throw them away from the carcass. If the deer is a female, remove the udder and throw it away.

Next, find the soft spot at the base of the chest, just below the ribs, and make a small 2-inch cut through the skin and into the cavity. Straddle the carcass, facing the animal's tail. If you hold the knife in your right hand, put the first two fingers of your left hand into the incision you have made. Turn your knife so that the cutting edge is up. Slip the point of your knife blade between the two fingers that are inside the carcass. Don't let the blade tip extend into the body cavity and nick the organs. With the tip of the blade protected between your fingers, push both hands forward, with your left-hand fingertips advancing just ahead of the blade. This action will cause the blade to cut through the skin and belly lining from the inside while your fingers prevent the blade from touching the organs. Cut all the way to the pelvis in this manner.

Now, turn and straddle the carcass, facing the head, and get ready to open the chest cavity.

Splitting the breastbone, or sternum, is not necessary. This 2-inch wide, 10-inch long piece of cartilage can be completely removed a lot easier than it can be split; once it is out of the way, you will have a wide opening into which you can reach with both hands to free the lungs, heart, windpipe, and esophagus.

To remove the sternum, split the skin that covers it all the way up to the base of the throat. Next, peel the skin and the thin layer of flesh under it back about an inch from each side of the sternum to expose the points where the ribs join the sternum. These joints are soft "buttons" that you can easily cut with your knife.

Once you have exposed the sternum, cut through the "buttons" on each side of it. Then grasp the base of the sternum with one hand and pull up. The sternum will break off at the throat end. Cut it off and toss it away. You now have a broad opening from the pelvis all the way to the throat. Reach into the throat and cut through the windpipe and esophagus and pull them out of the carcass.

Now roll the carcass on its side and scoop out the intestines and stomach onto the ground. Next, use your knife to free the lungs and heart, and cut through the diaphragm membrane that separates the chest cavity from the body cavity. Pull these organs out onto the ground as well. The carcass is now empty, but the large intestine is still attached through the pelvic opening to the rectum. Turn the carcass on its belly to let the blood drain out of the open cavity. Once it is drained, turn it on its back again.

Use the point of your knife to make a circular cut through the

With the knife held in your right hand and the tip of the blade protected between the fingers of your left hand, you can cut through the skin and belly lining from the inside without having the blade touch the organs.

To remove the sternum (or breastbone), peel the skin back to expose the points where the ribs join the sternum. Then cut through these "buttons" with your knife while pulling up on the sternum with your free hand. When the "buttons" are cut, the sternum will break loose and can be thrown away, exposing a wide opening to the interior of the chest.

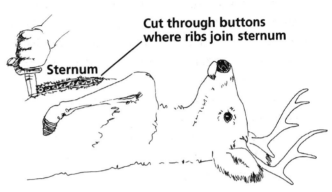

Cut through buttons where ribs join sternum

Sternum

Turn the carcass on its side and scoop out the intestines and stomach on to the ground, leaving the large intestine attached through the pelvic opening to the rectum. Use your knife to cut through the diaphragm and free all remaining organs.

Make a circular cut through the skin around the rectum to free it from the carcass without cutting the intestine. Tie off the exposed section of intestine with a short piece of string. Next, use your knife to free the intestine from the pelvic wall. Gently pull the intestine and rectum through the pelvis from the belly side.

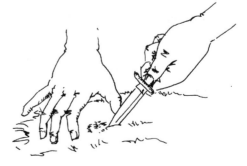

skin around the rectum to free it from the carcass without cutting the intestine. When the rectum is free, hold it with your left hand and push your knife blade full length into the pelvic opening outside the intestine to free the intestine from the pelvic walls. Then pull the rectum and a few inches of the attached intestine outside the carcass and tie it off with a short piece of string. This precaution will prevent excrement from emerging from the intestine later. Now, push your knife into the pelvic opening from the belly side, and gently probe the outside of the intestine within the pelvic wall as you pull gently on the intestine from the point where it enters the pelvis. The freed intestine, with the intact bladder attached, will pull through. Try not to spill the bladder's urine contents on the carcass. If it does spill, wash the urine away as soon as possible.

Pull the carcass a few feet away from the gut pile, turn it on its belly, and let it drain while you wash your hands with water or snow. Now drag the carcass to the nearest water and rinse out the body cavity as thoroughly as possible. A well-washed carcass will be much more happily received at home.

You've completed your hunt, you have your deer, and it's dressed and ready to drag out of the woods. Now the work begins!

CHAPTER

17

Dragging
Your Deer Home

BEFORE YOU BEGIN dragging your deer home, make sure you know where you are. Take a break. Locate yourself on your map and plan a route out of the woods. The best route is not always a straight shot back to your vehicle or camp. Study the terrain and choose a route that will be downhill as much as possible. Avoid swamps.

Dragging a deer out of the woods is never easy, but there is one way that is less taxing than all others. You'll need a six-foot piece of rope. Make the drag rope a permanent part of your deer-hunting outfit and carry it with you every time you go out.

Tie one end of the rope around the base of the deer's antlers, or around its neck, just behind the ears, if it is antlerless. Then wrap the rope once around the muzzle in a half hitch so that you will be pulling the deer directly from that point rather than from the antlers. This will help to keep the deer's head from tangling in brush as you go.

Now, search around and find a 2-foot-long stick about 2 inches thick. The wood should be cured, not rotten. Tie the free end of the rope in the center of the piece of wood. This is your draw bar. The wooden draw bar will be much more comfortable to pull on than the rough deer's antlers, and you will not have to lift the deer's forequarters when you pull.

Grip the wooden draw bar at both ends with your hands held behind you and throw your weight into the effort as you begin to pull. Lean forward as you progress so that your weight does the pulling, not just your arms.

A wooden draw bar is much more comfortable to pull on than the rough edges of a deer's antlers, and you will not have to lift the deer's forequarters when you pull.

From time to time the carcass will become snagged on something—a log, saplings, a blowdown, whatever gets in the way. Try to avoid these kinds of obstacles, although the deer will probably snag anyway.

When the deer gets caught, turn around to face it and pull backwards, using your arms to lift the deer's head when necessary. It may help to shorten the rope by wrapping it around the wooden draw bar a few times and tying it with a half hitch when lifting is required.

If you have a helper, you may want to use a somewhat longer draw bar—say 3 feet. Each person grasps a side with one hand and you pull together shoulder to shoulder. Having a helper makes the job more than twice as easy, so don't hesitate to call for help if you can.